004

攻殻機動隊

STAND ALONE COMPLEX

衣 谷 遊

EPISODE 4 : ¥€$

004

攻殻機動隊

STAND ALONE COMPLEX

本谷

土郎正宗・「ProductionI.G」原作 ·（ 攻殻機動隊製作委員会

SHIROW MASAMUNE
PRODUCTION I.G
KODANSHA

#025: Hideout Assault

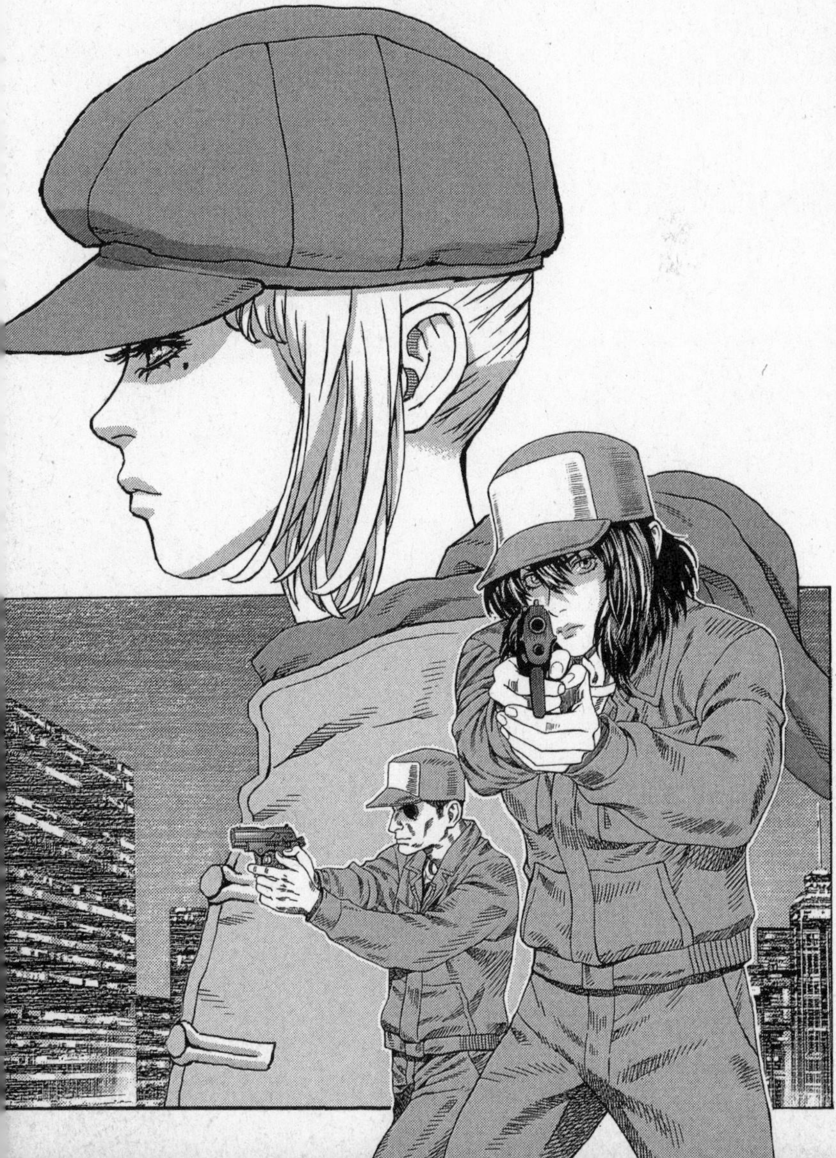

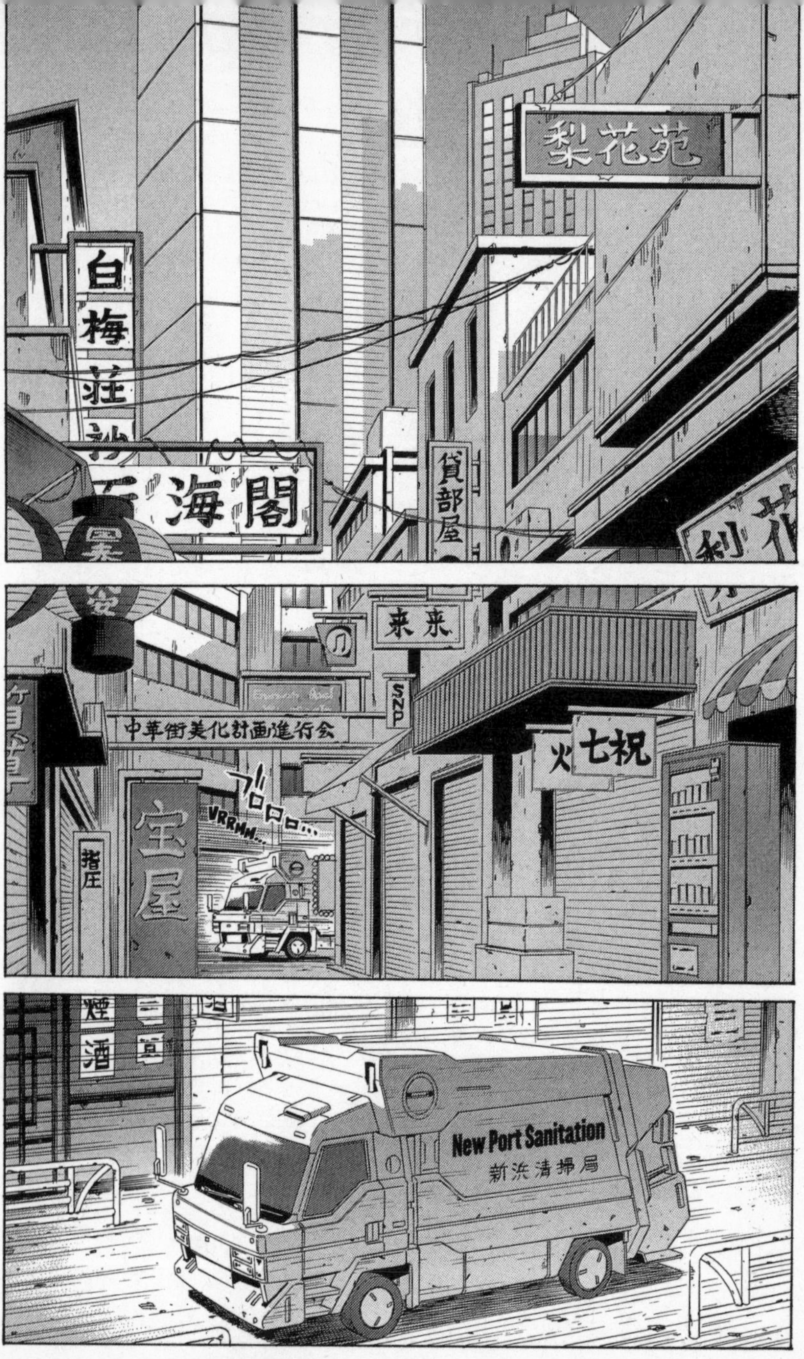
梨花苑
貸部屋
海閣
白梅荘
来来
SNP
七祝
中華街美化計画進行会
ブロロロ…
VRRMM...
宝屋
指圧
New Port Sanitation
新浜清掃局
煙
酒

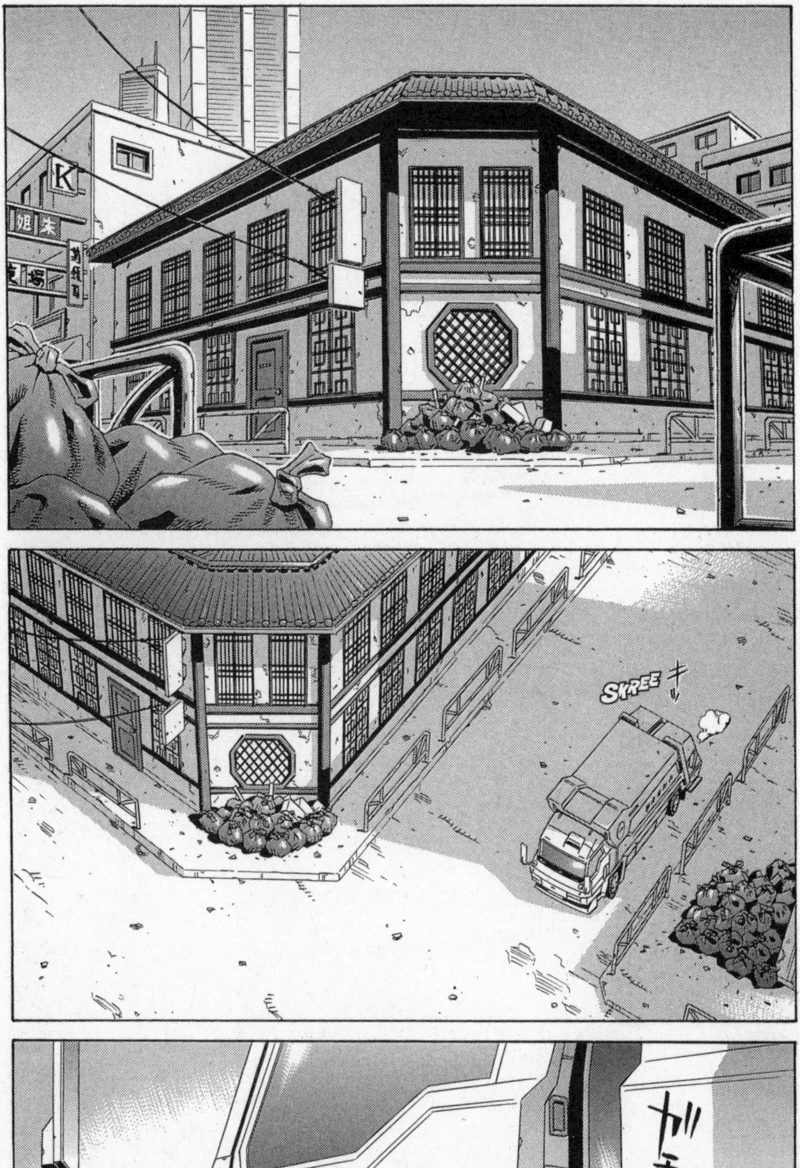
K
SKREE
キ
ガチャ
click

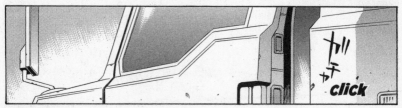

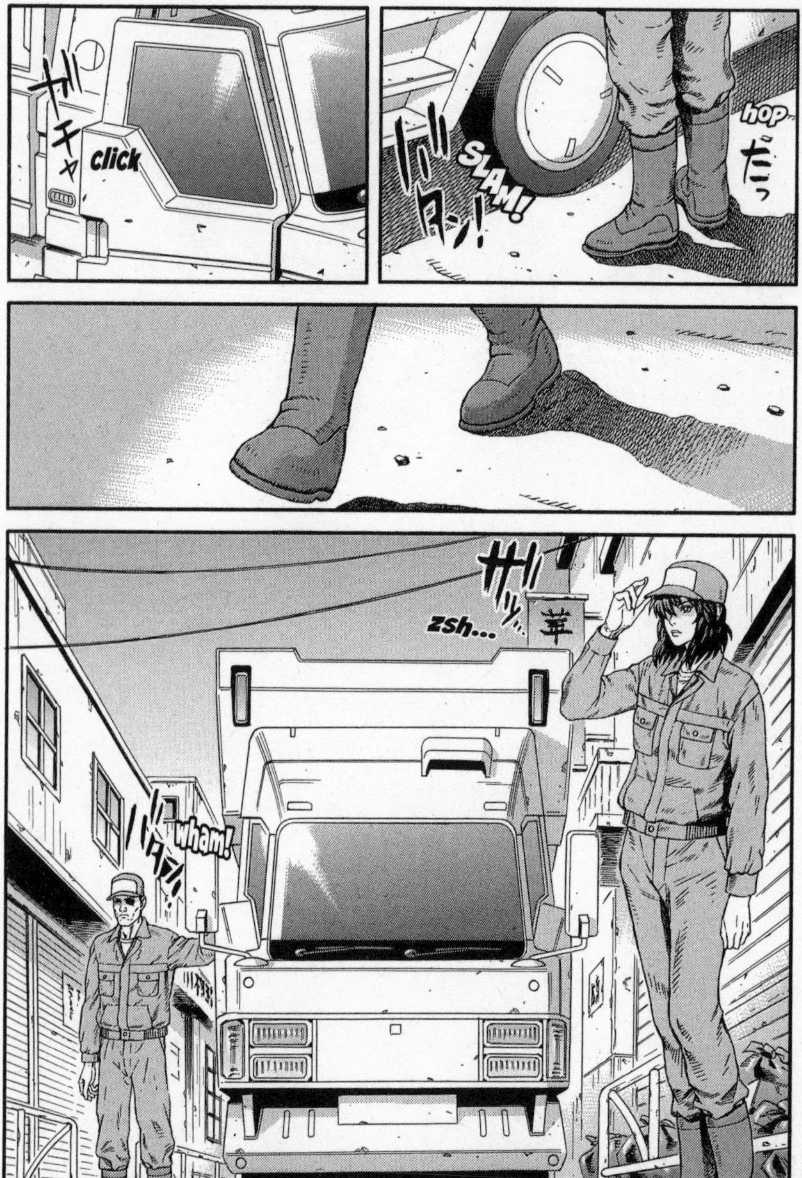

hop
だっ
バタン!
SLAM!
ガチャ
click
ザッ
zsh...
華
バタン!
wham!

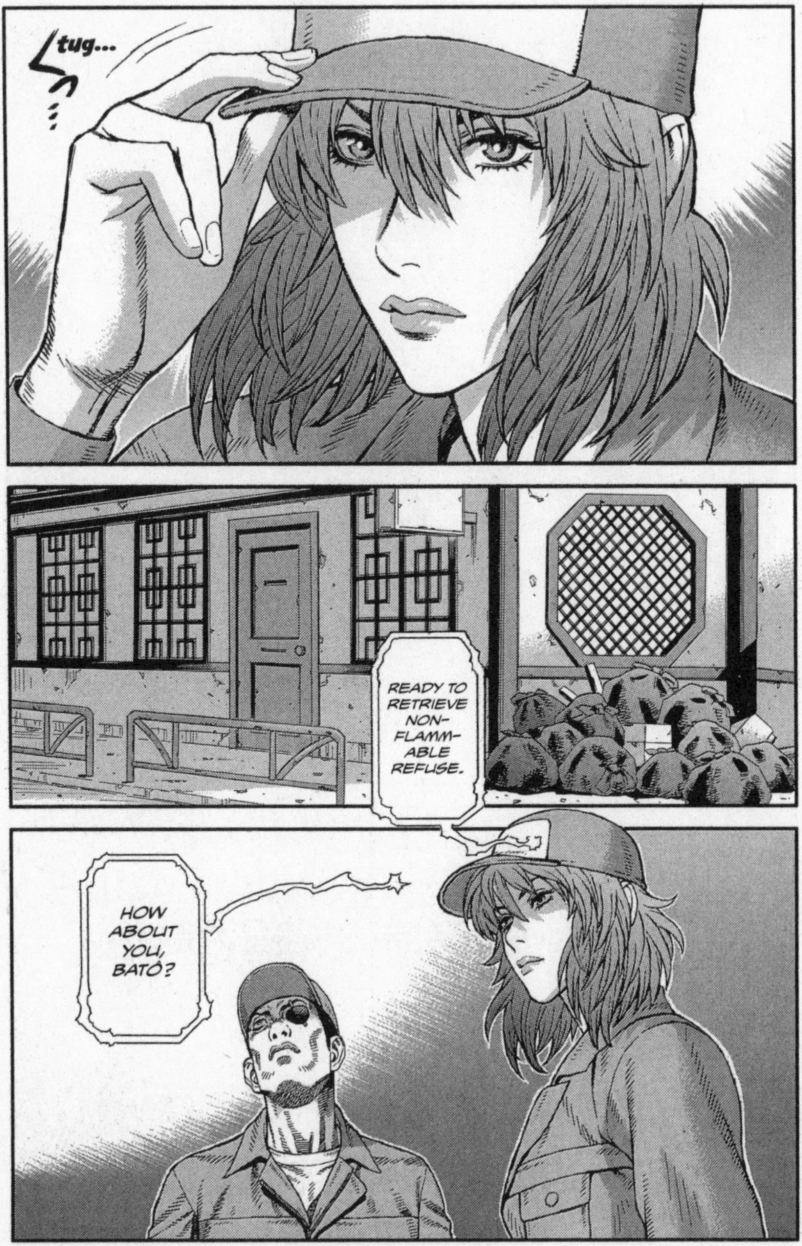
tug...
READY TO RETRIEVE NON-FLAMMABLE REFUSE.
HOW ABOUT YOU, BATÓ?

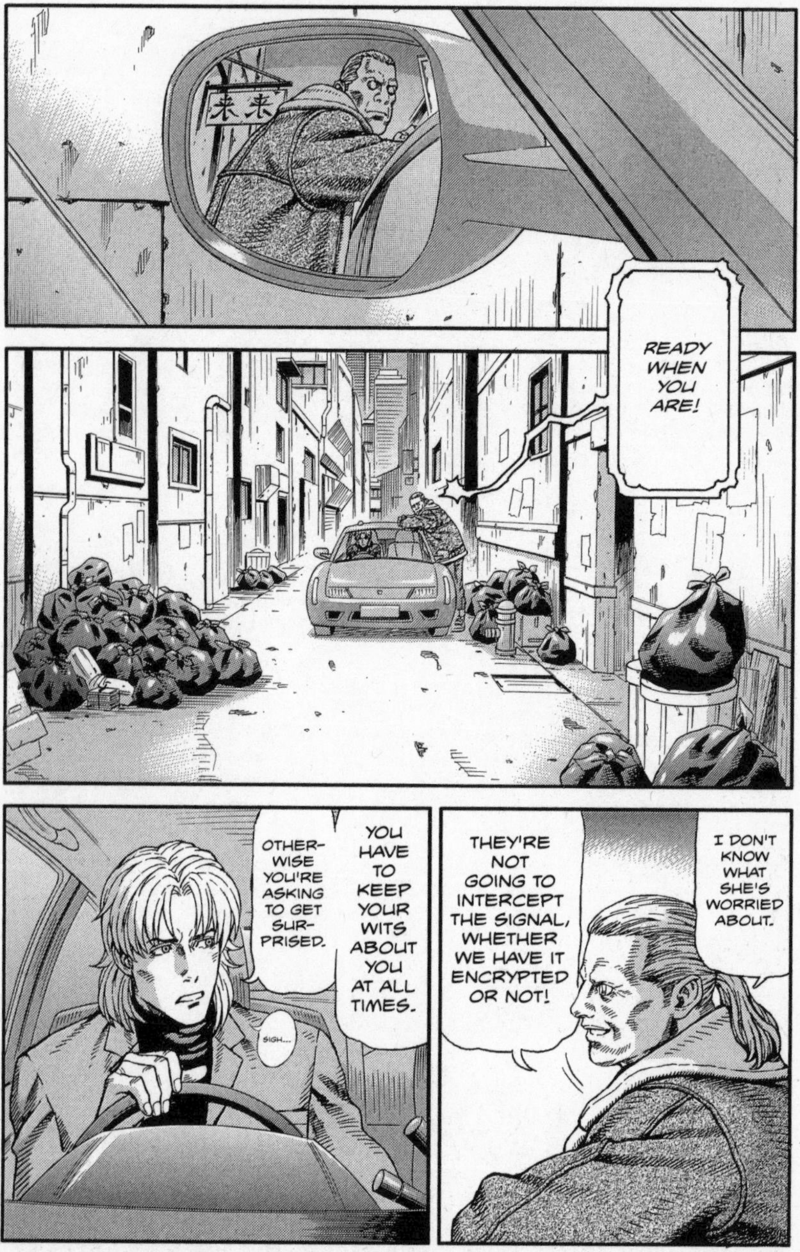
来来
READY WHEN YOU ARE!
I DON'T KNOW WHAT SHE'S WORRIED ABOUT.
THEY'RE NOT GOING TO INTERCEPT THE SIGNAL, WHETHER WE HAVE IT ENCRYPTED OR NOT!
YOU HAVE TO KEEP YOUR WITS ABOUT YOU AT ALL TIMES.
OTHER-WISE YOU'RE ASKING TO GET SUR-PRISED.
SIGH...

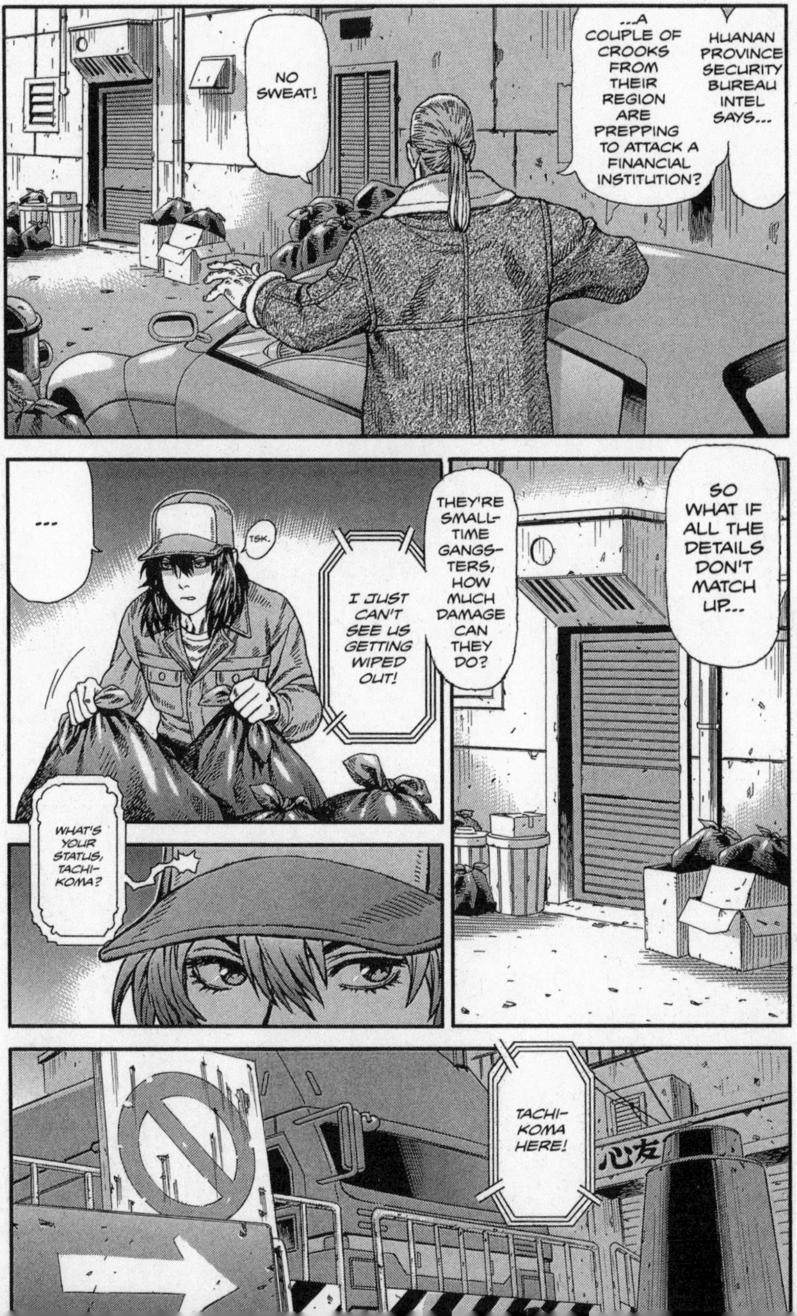
HUANAN PROVINCE SECURITY BUREAU INTEL SAYS...
...A COUPLE OF CROOKS FROM THEIR REGION ARE PREPPING TO ATTACK A FINANCIAL INSTITUTION?
NO SWEAT!
SO WHAT IF ALL THE DETAILS DON'T MATCH UP...
THEY'RE SMALL-TIME GANGSTERS, HOW MUCH DAMAGE CAN THEY DO?
I JUST CAN'T SEE US GETTING WIPED OUT!
TSK.
...
WHAT'S YOUR STATUS, TACHIKOMA?
TACHIKOMA HERE!
心友

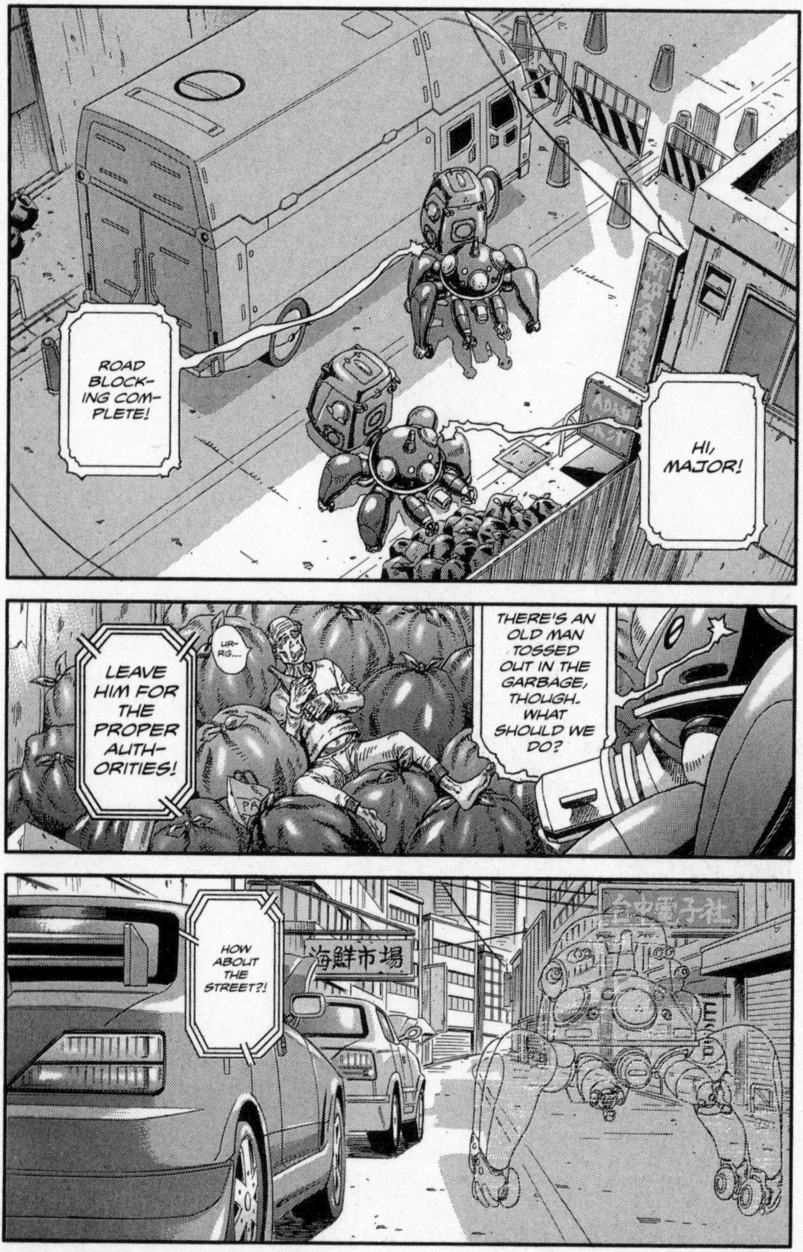
HI, MAJOR!
ROAD BLOCKING COMPLETE!
THERE'S AN OLD MAN TOSSED OUT IN THE GARBAGE, THOUGH. WHAT SHOULD WE DO?
URRG...
LEAVE HIM FOR THE PROPER AUTHORITIES!
HOW ABOUT THE STREET?!
海鮮市場

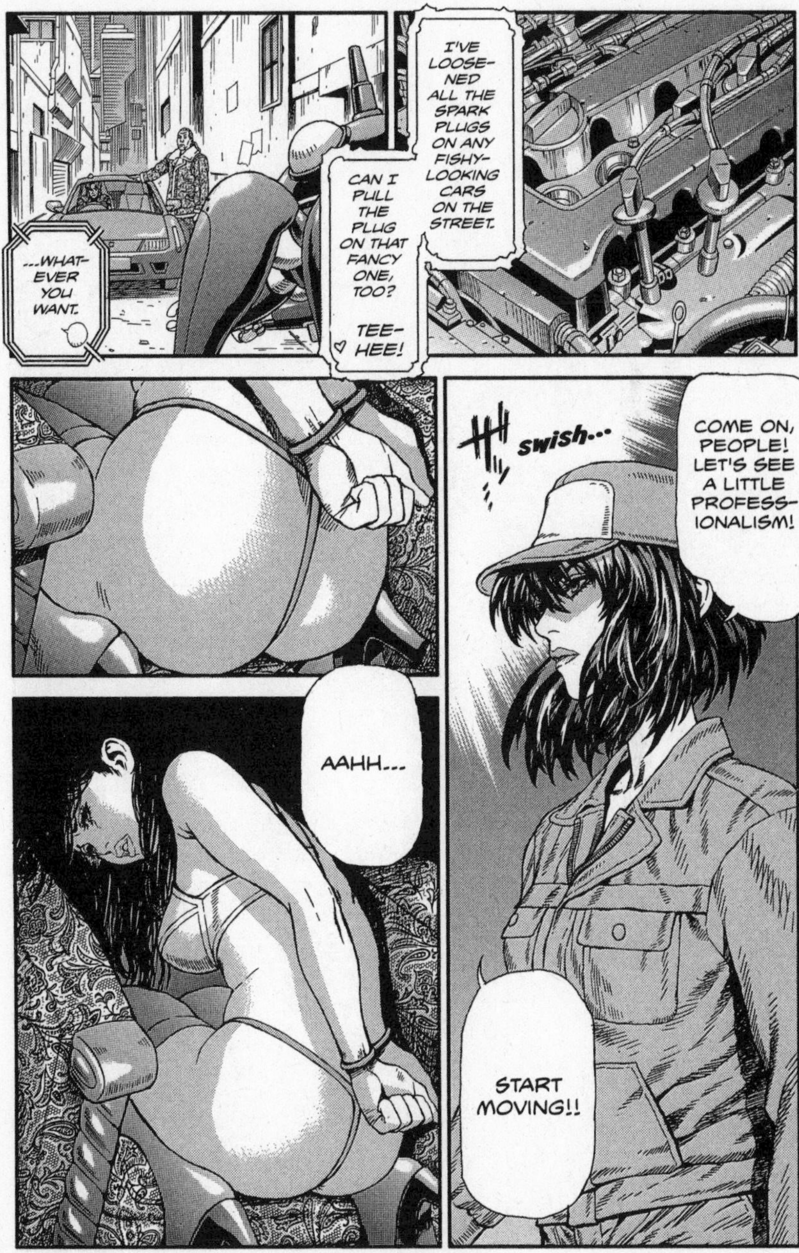
I'VE LOOSENED ALL THE SPARK PLUGS ON ANY FISHY-LOOKING CARS ON THE STREET.
CAN I PULL THE PLUG ON THAT FANCY ONE, TOO?
TEE-HEE!
...WHATEVER YOU WANT.
swish...
COME ON, PEOPLE! LET'S SEE A LITTLE PROFESSIONALISM!
START MOVING!!
AAHH...

AHH...
捍卫第三★★★
在线
在线
MM-M...
HEH HEH HEH...

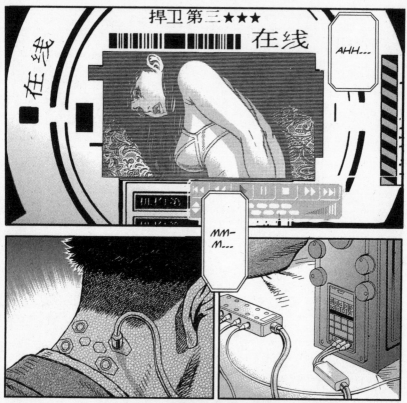

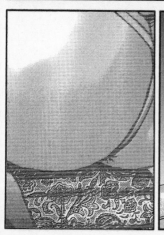

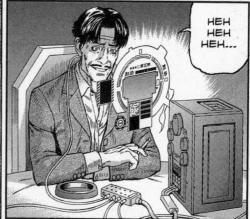

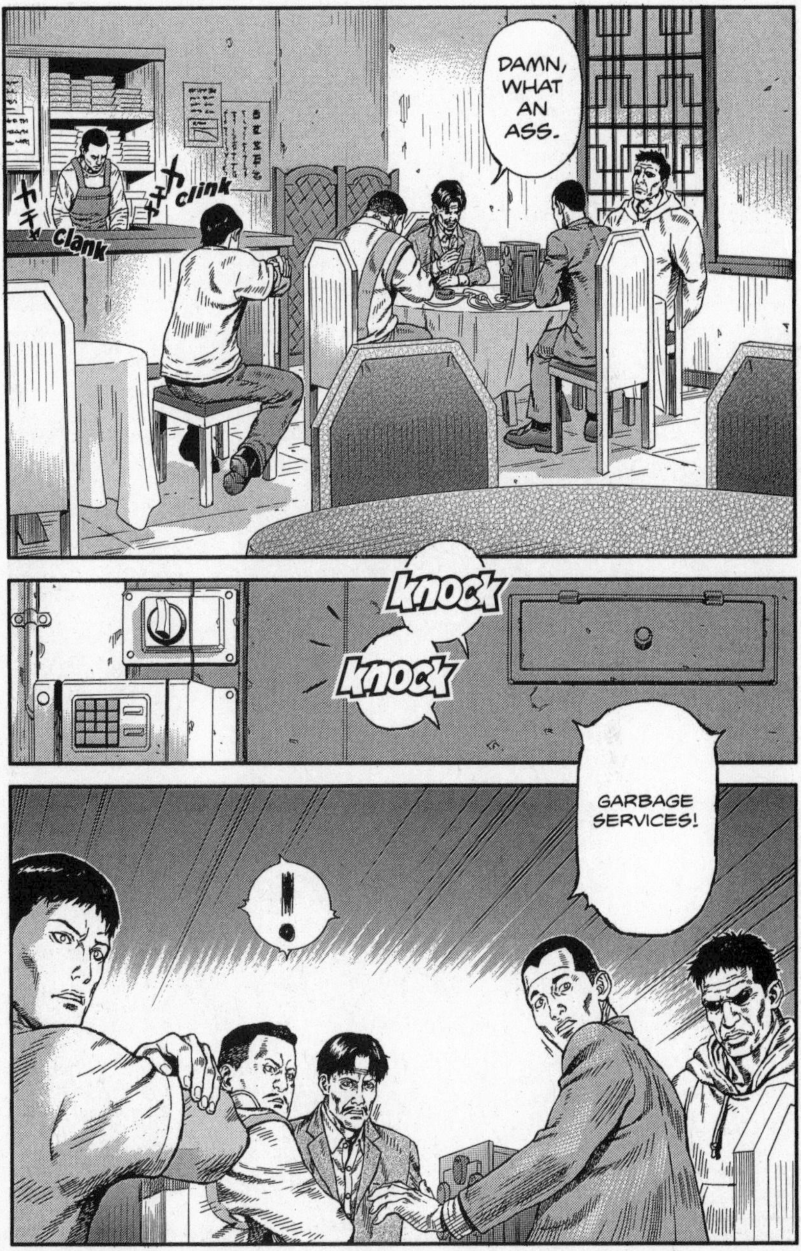
DAMN, WHAT AN ASS.
clink
clank
knock
knock
GARBAGE SERVICES!
!

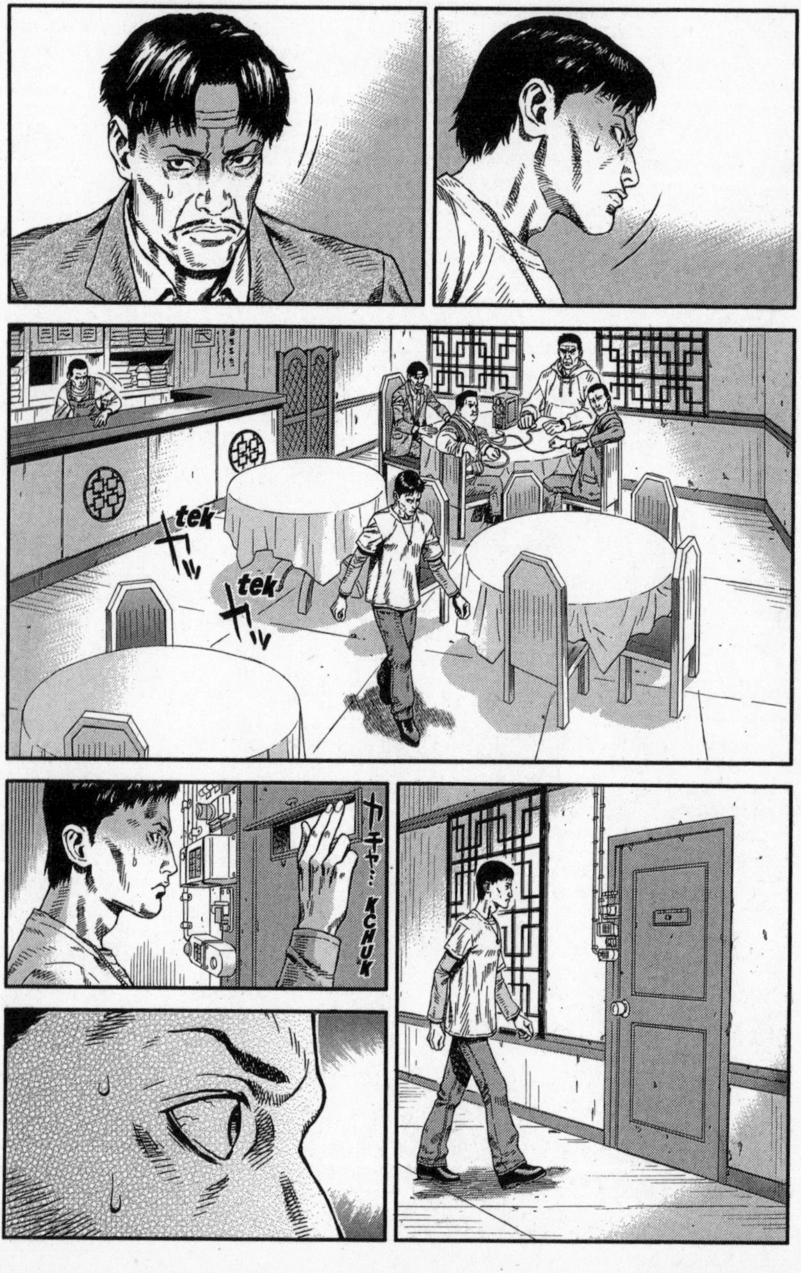
tek
tek
カチャ…
KCHUK

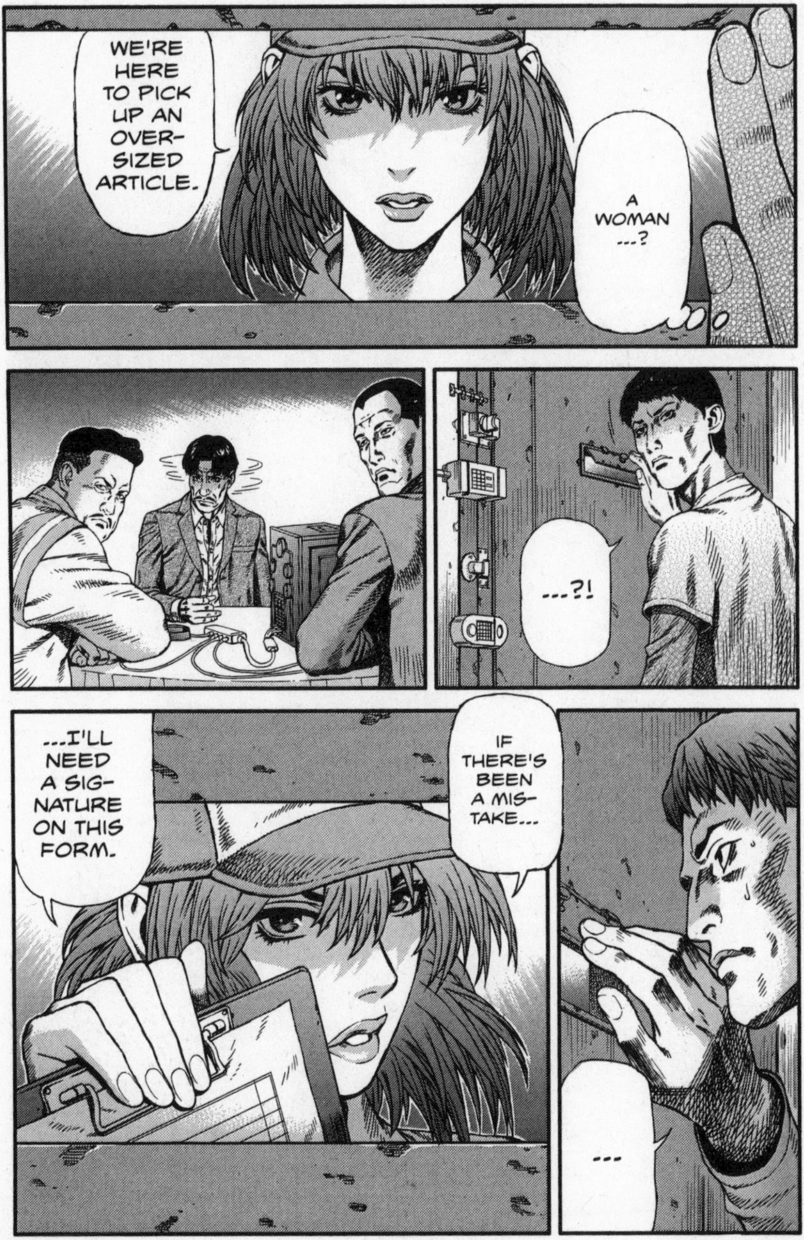
WE'RE HERE TO PICK UP AN OVER-SIZED ARTICLE.
A WOMAN ---?
---?!

IF THERE'S BEEN A MIS-TAKE...
...I'LL NEED A SIG-NATURE ON THIS FORM.

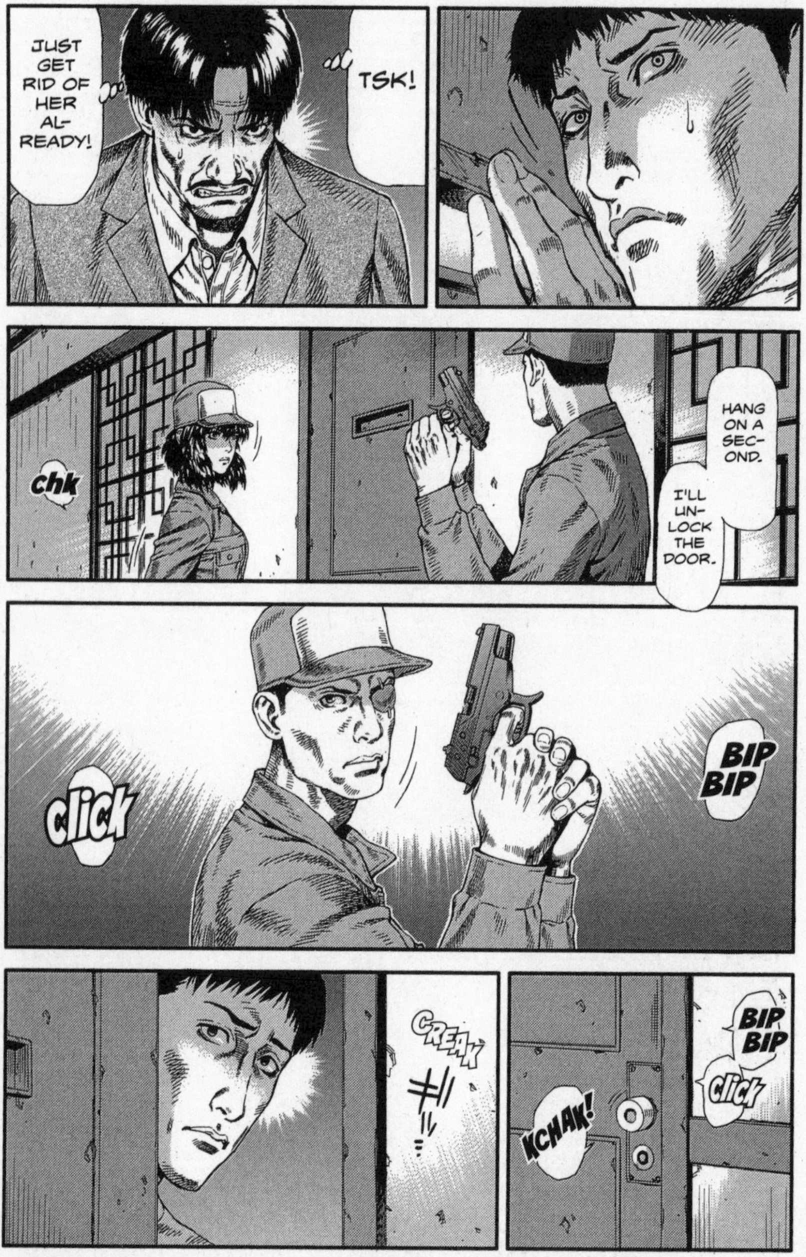
TSK!
JUST GET RID OF HER AL-READY!
HANG ON A SEC-OND.
I'LL UN-LOCK THE DOOR.
chk
BIP BIP
click
BIP BIP
click
KCHAK!
CREAK

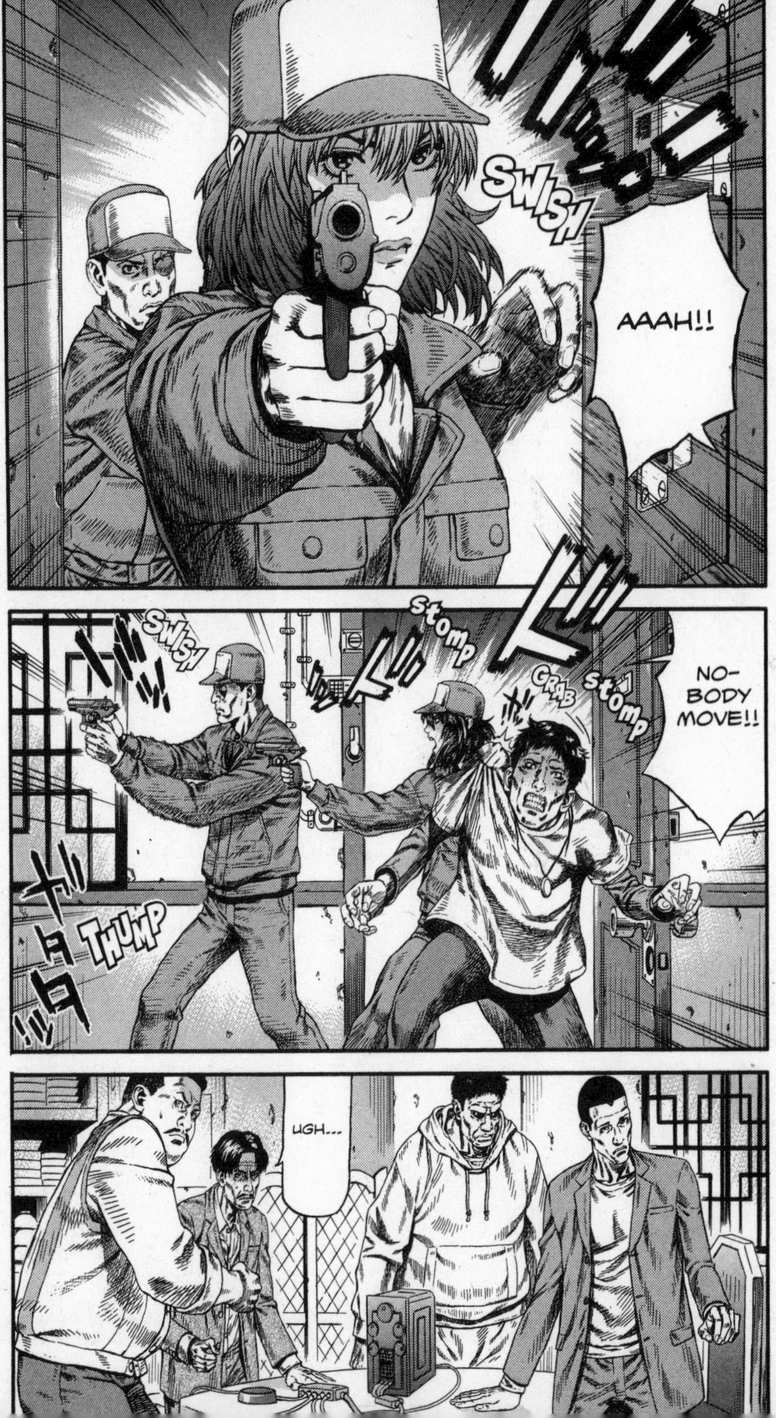
SWISH
AAAH!!
NO-BODY MOVE!!
stomp
stomp
GRAB
SWISH
THUMP
UGH...

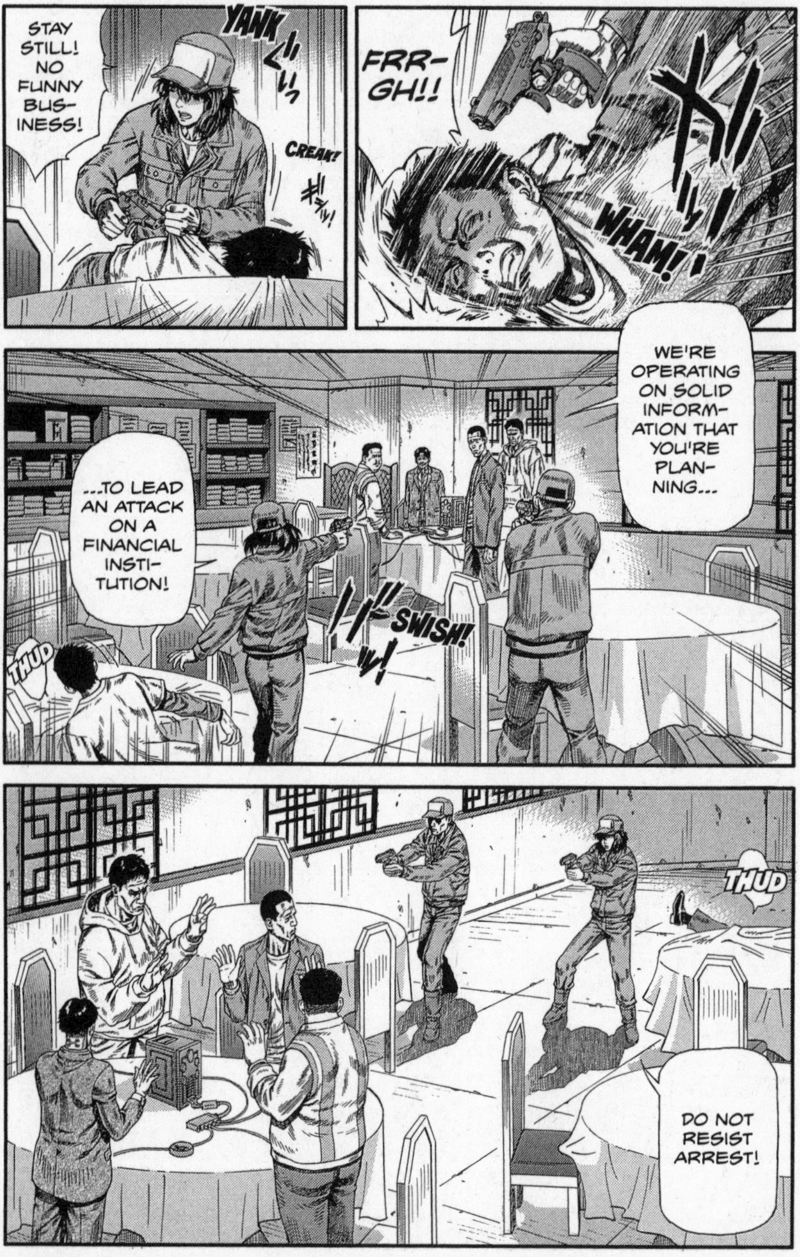
FRR-GH!!
WHAM!
STAY STILL! NO FUNNY BUS-INESS!
YANK
CREAK!
WE'RE OPERATING ON SOLID INFORM-ATION THAT YOU'RE PLAN-NING...
...TO LEAD AN ATTACK ON A FINANCIAL INSTI-TUTION!
SWISH!
THUD
THUD
DO NOT RESIST ARREST!

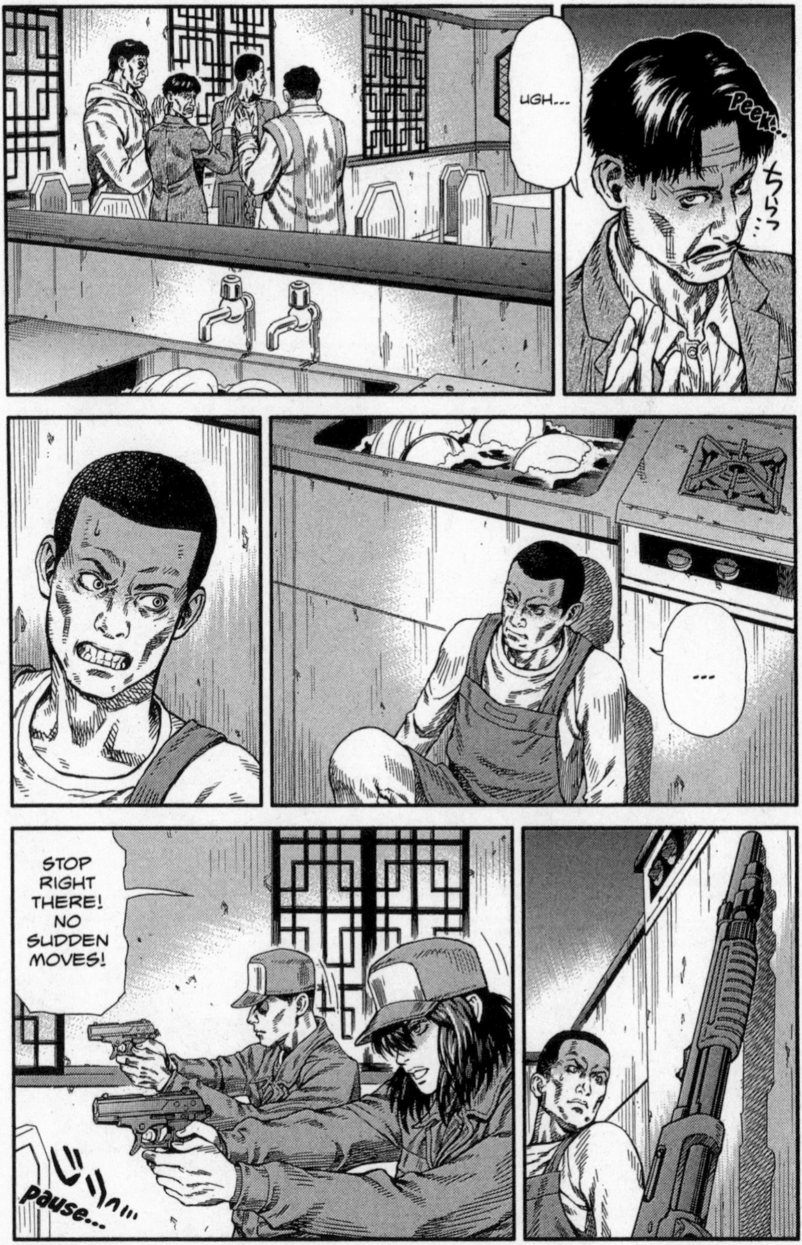

Peek...
ちらっ...
UGH...
...
STOP RIGHT THERE! NO SUDDEN MOVES!
じりっ...
Pause...

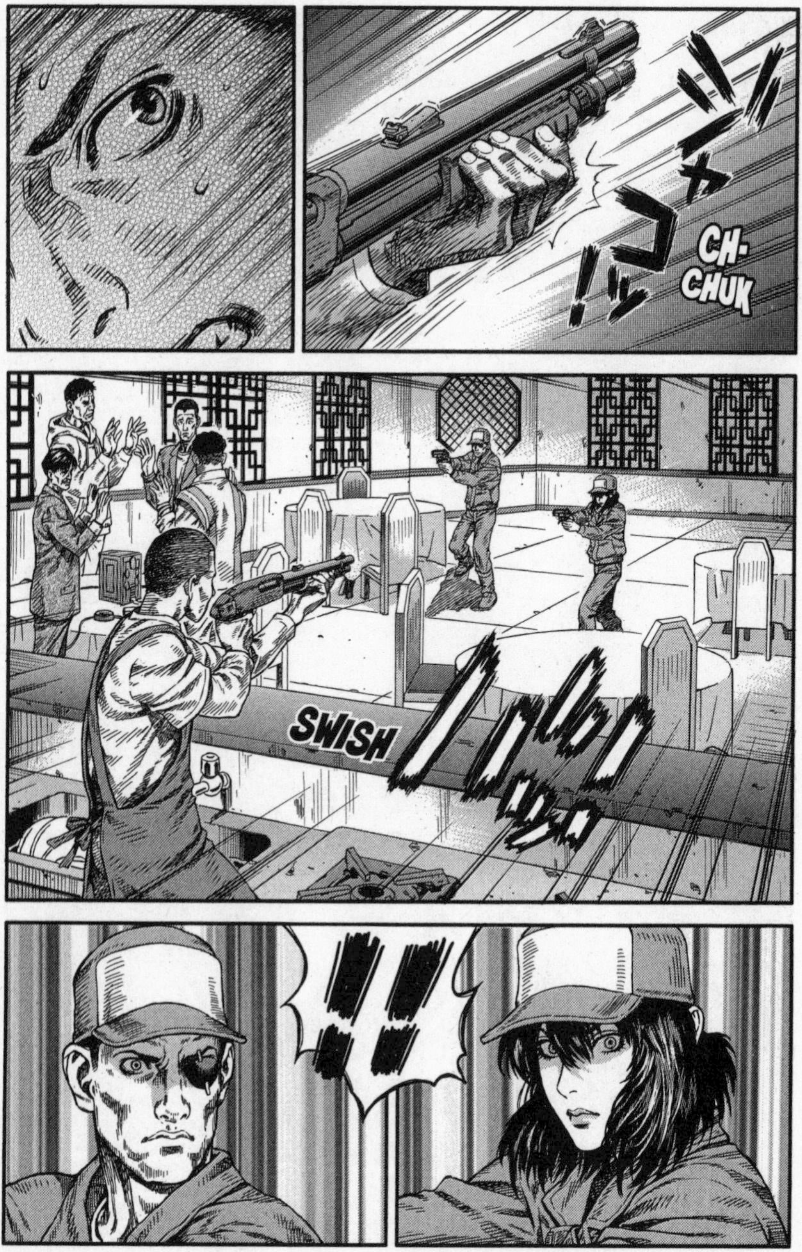
CH-
CHUK
SWISH

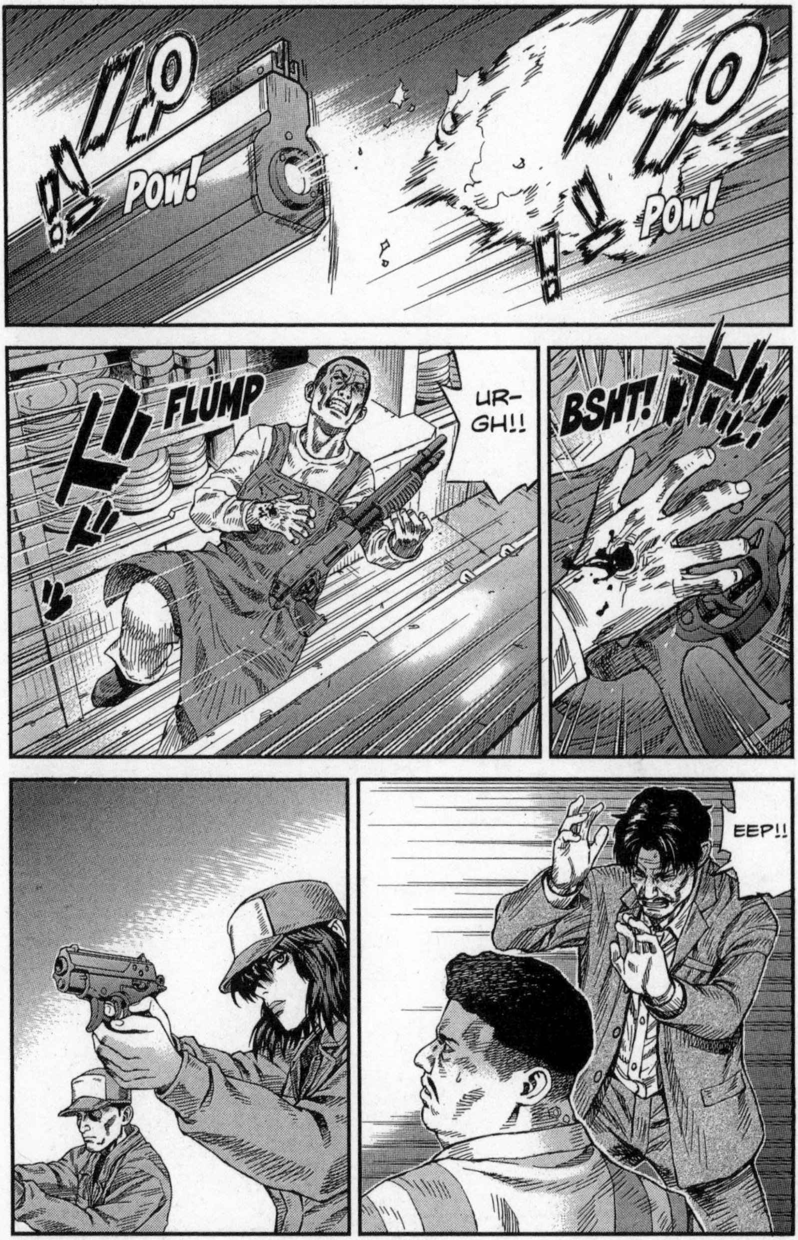
POW!
POW!
BSHT!
UR-GH!!
FLUMP
EEP!!

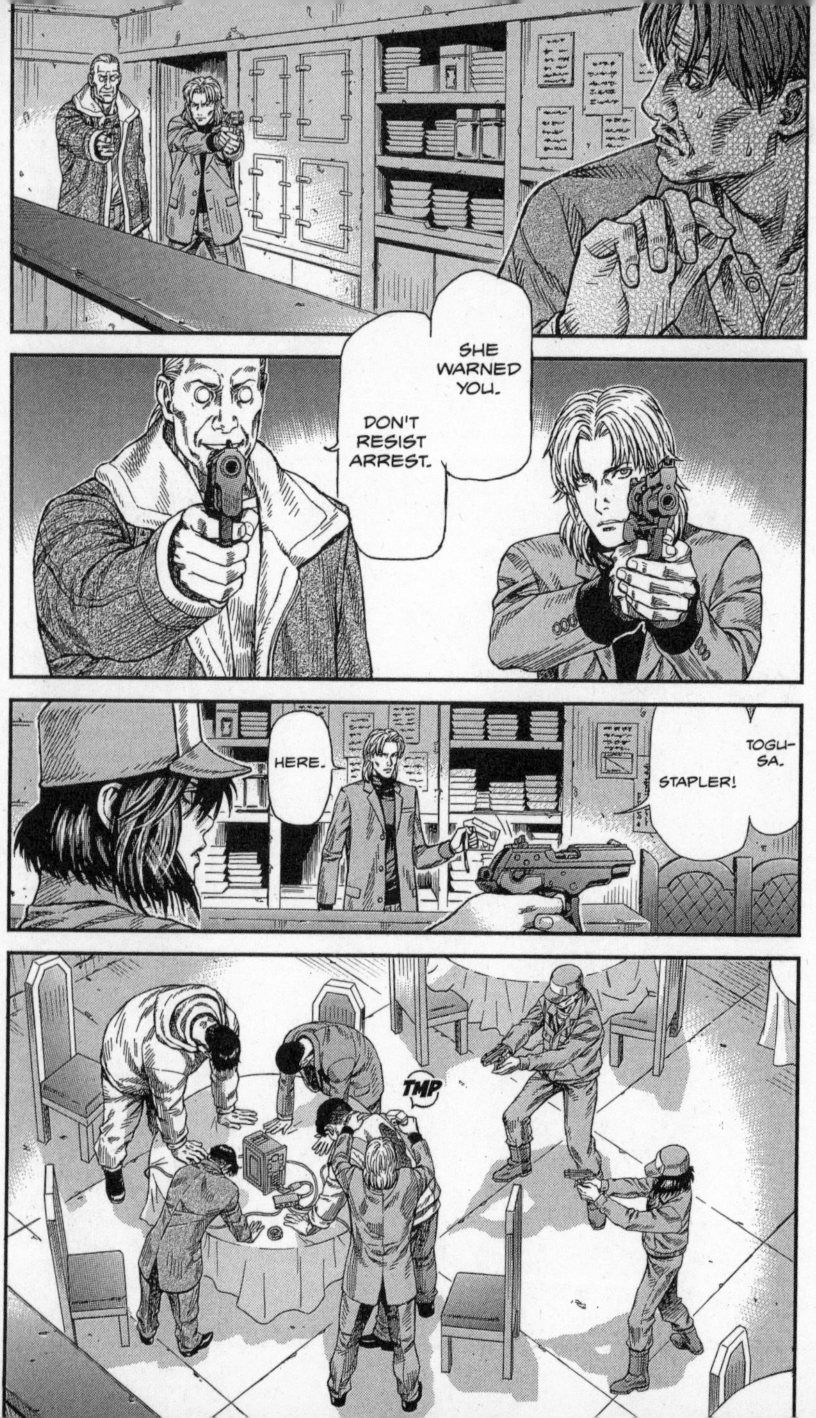
SHE WARNED YOU.
DON'T RESIST ARREST.
TOGU-SA.
STAPLER!
HERE.
TMP

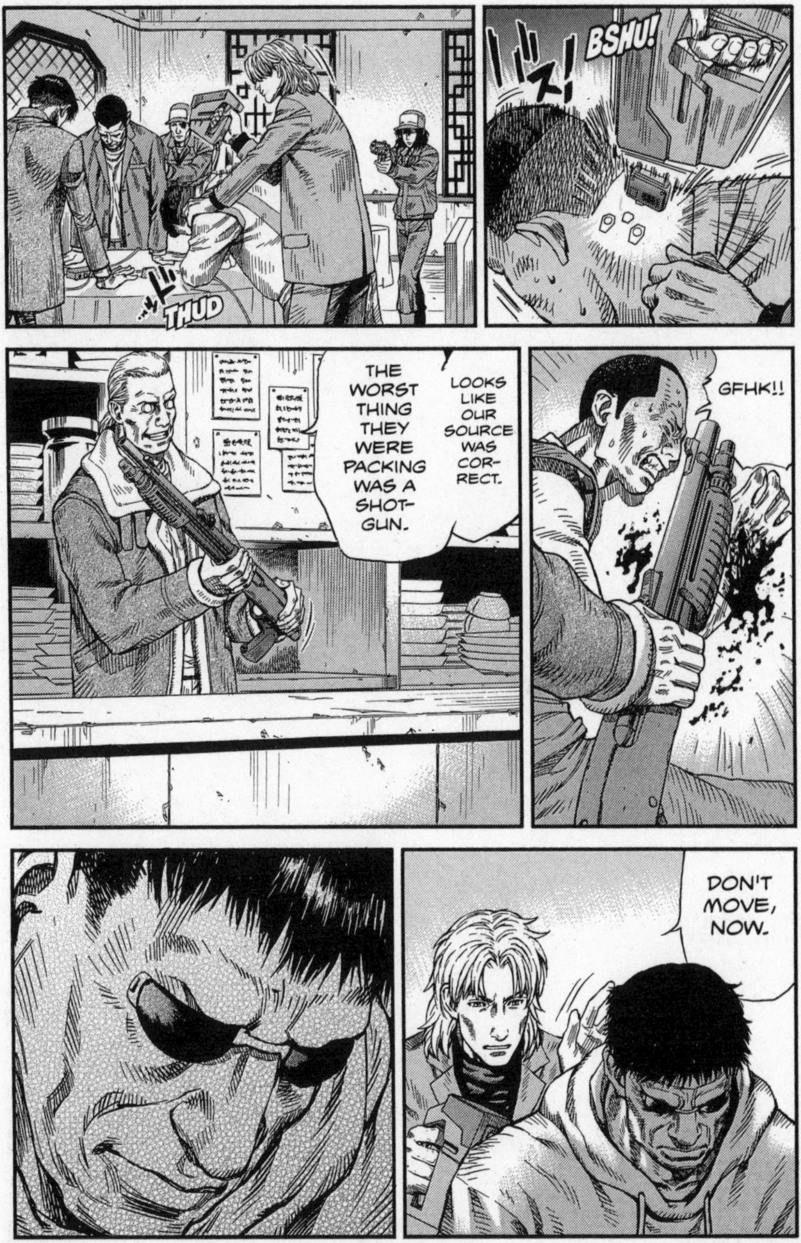

BSHU!
THUD
GFHK!!
LOOKS LIKE OUR SOURCE WAS COR-RECT.
THE WORST THING THEY WERE PACKING WAS A SHOT-GUN.
DON'T MOVE, NOW.

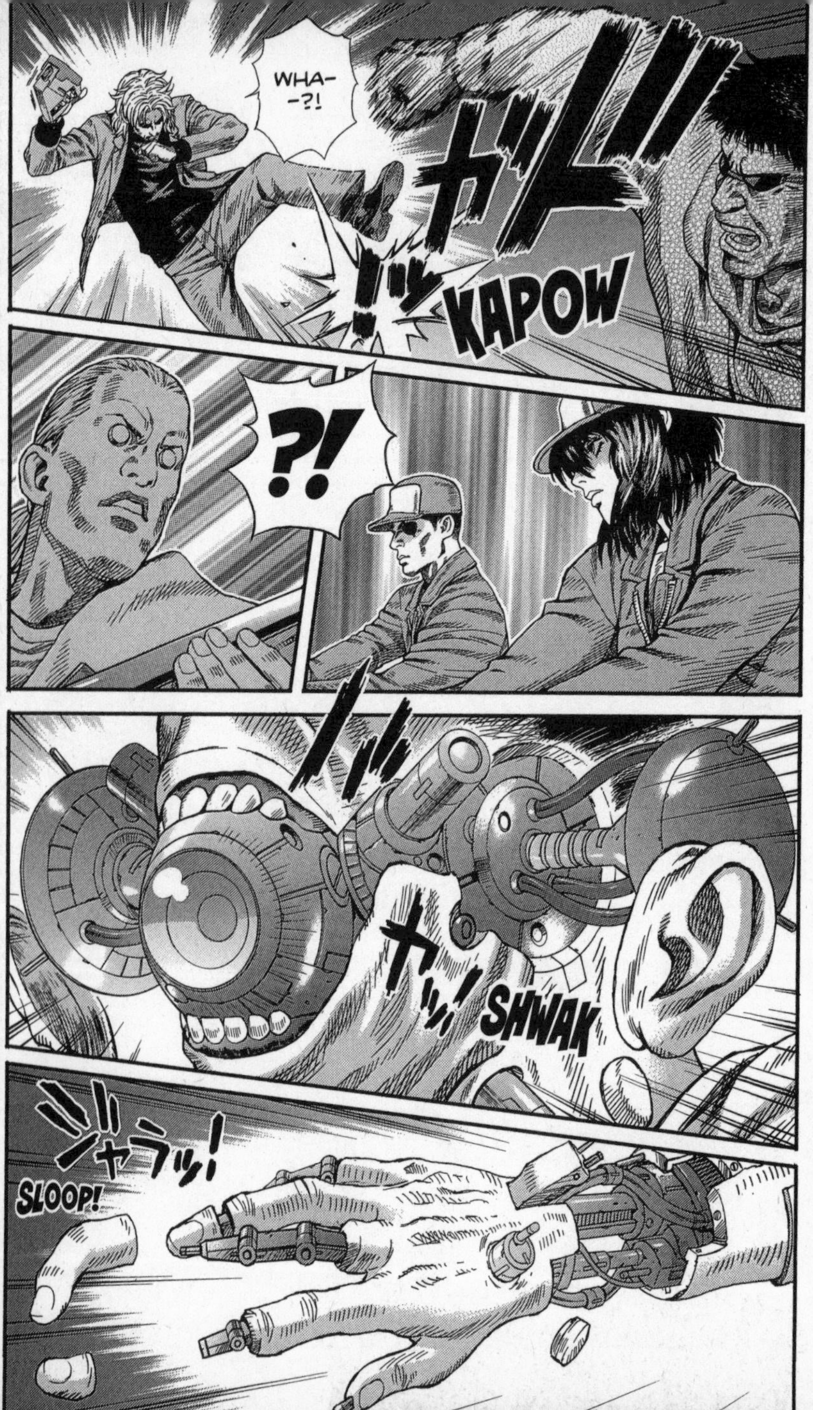
KAPOW
WHA— —?!
?!
SHWAK
ジャラッ!
SLOOP!

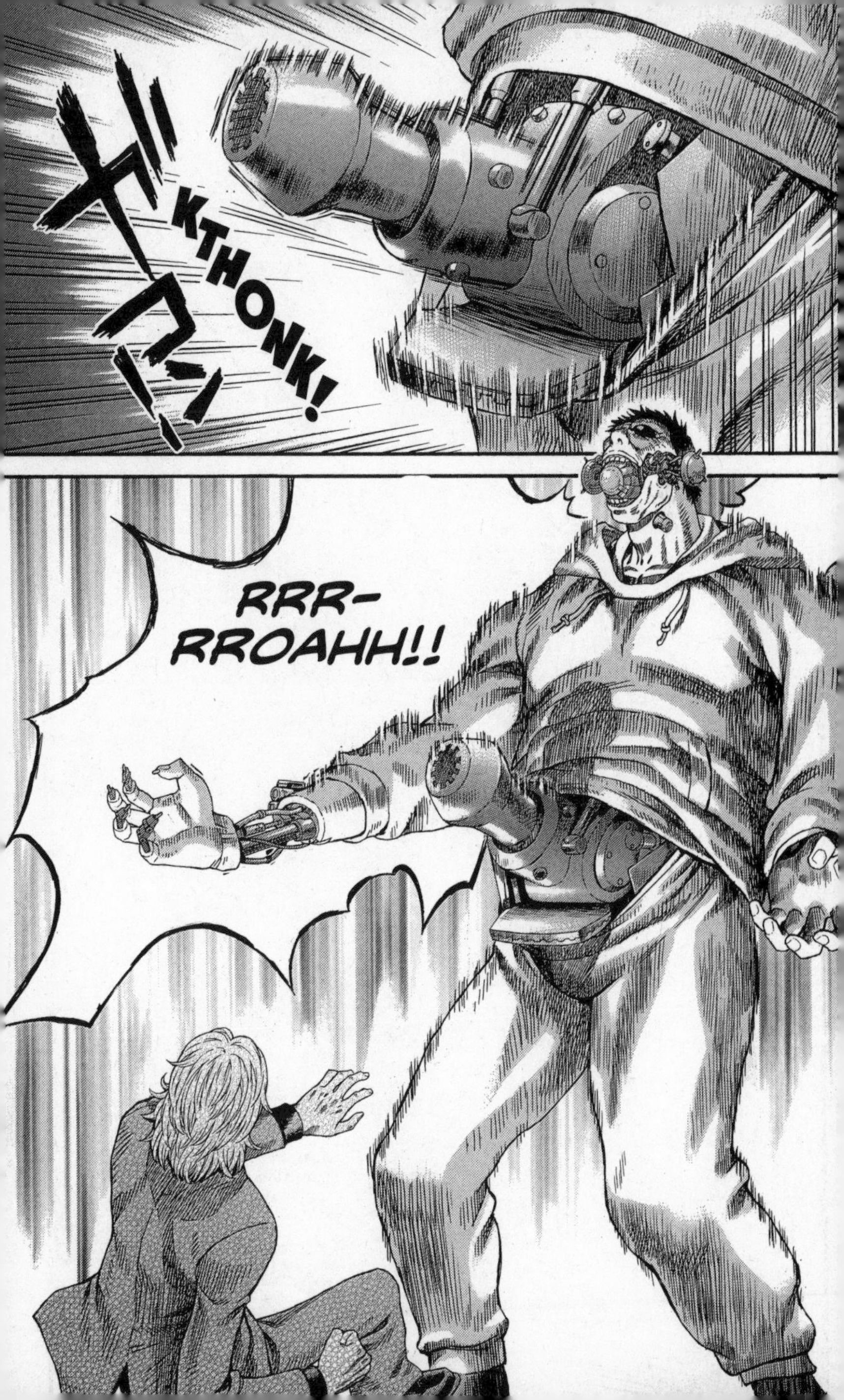
KTHONK!
RRR-
RROAHH!!

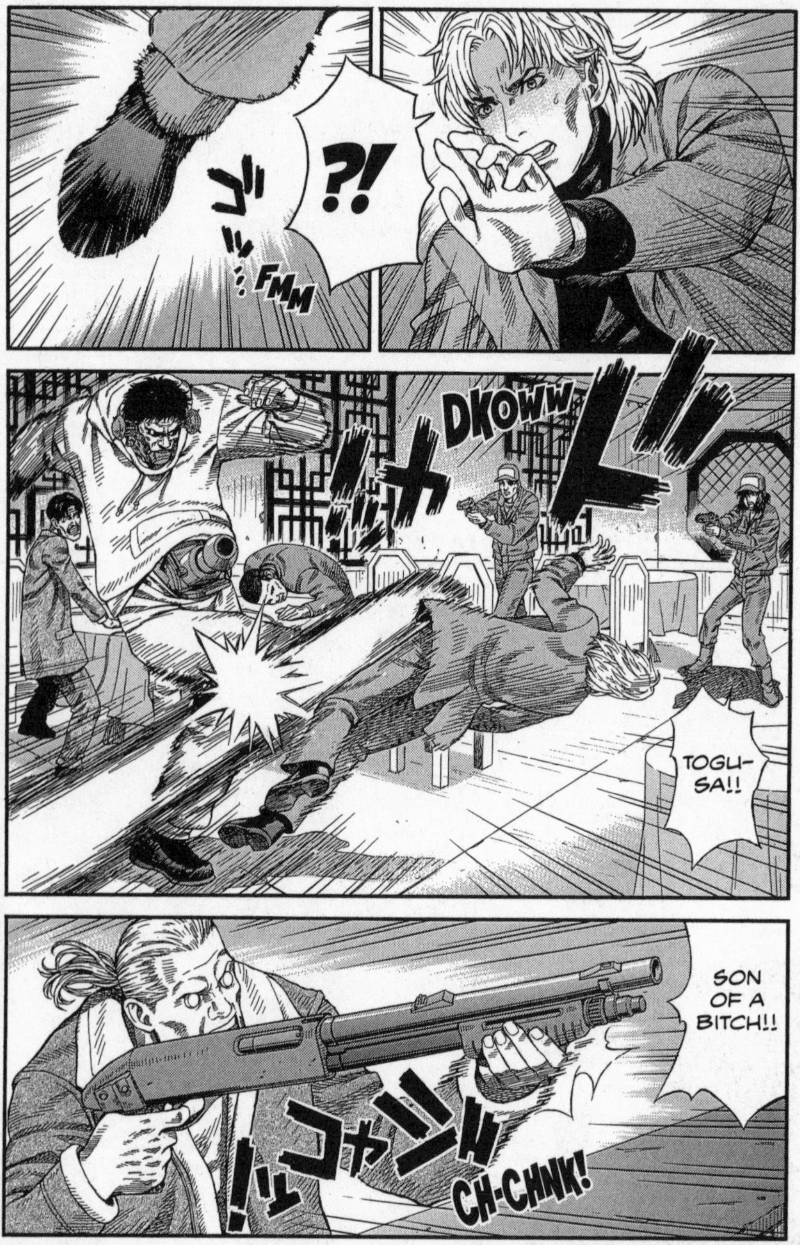
?!
FMM
DKOWW
TOGUSA!!
SON OF A BITCH!!
CH-CHNK!

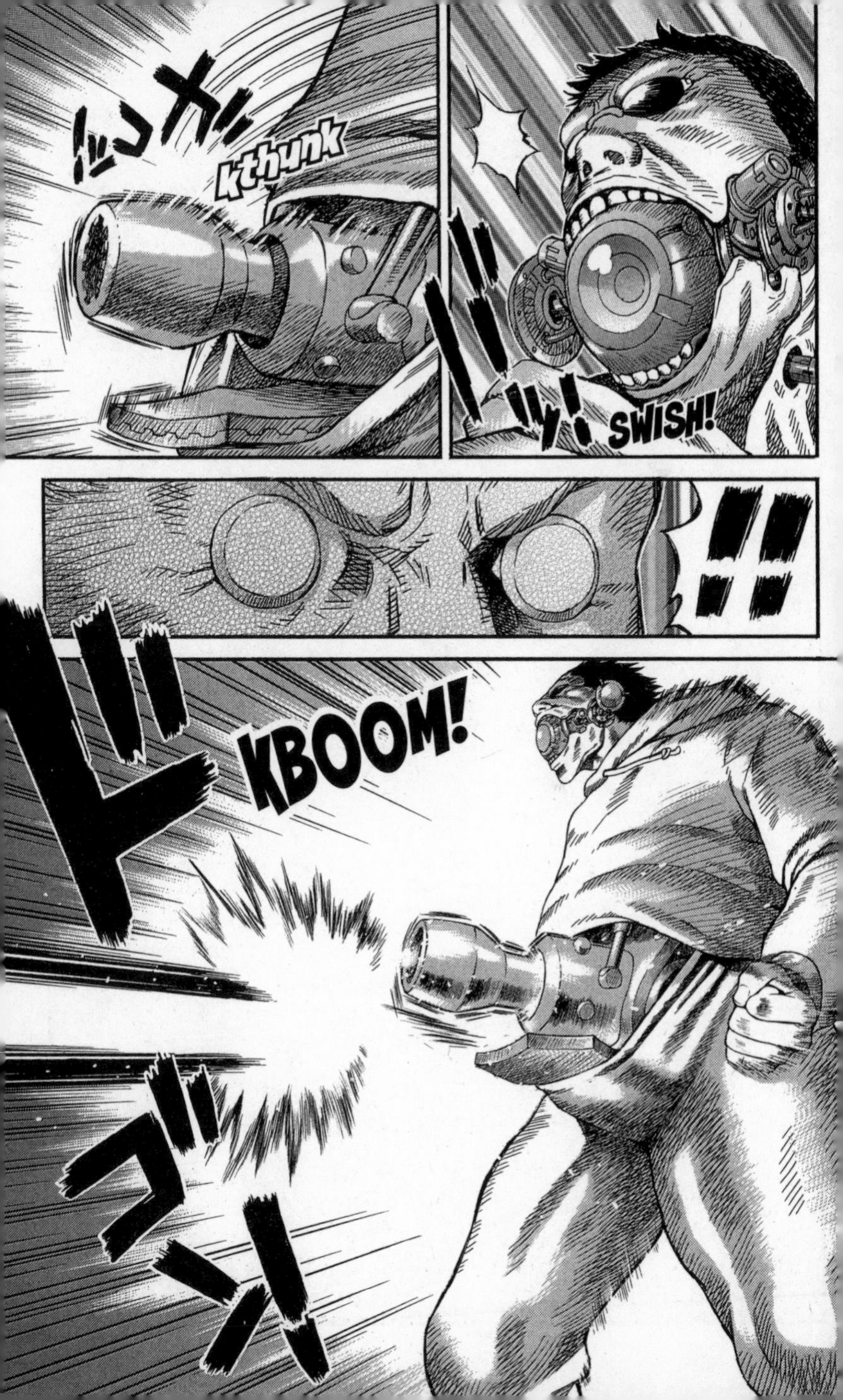
SWISH!
kthunk
!!
KBOOM!

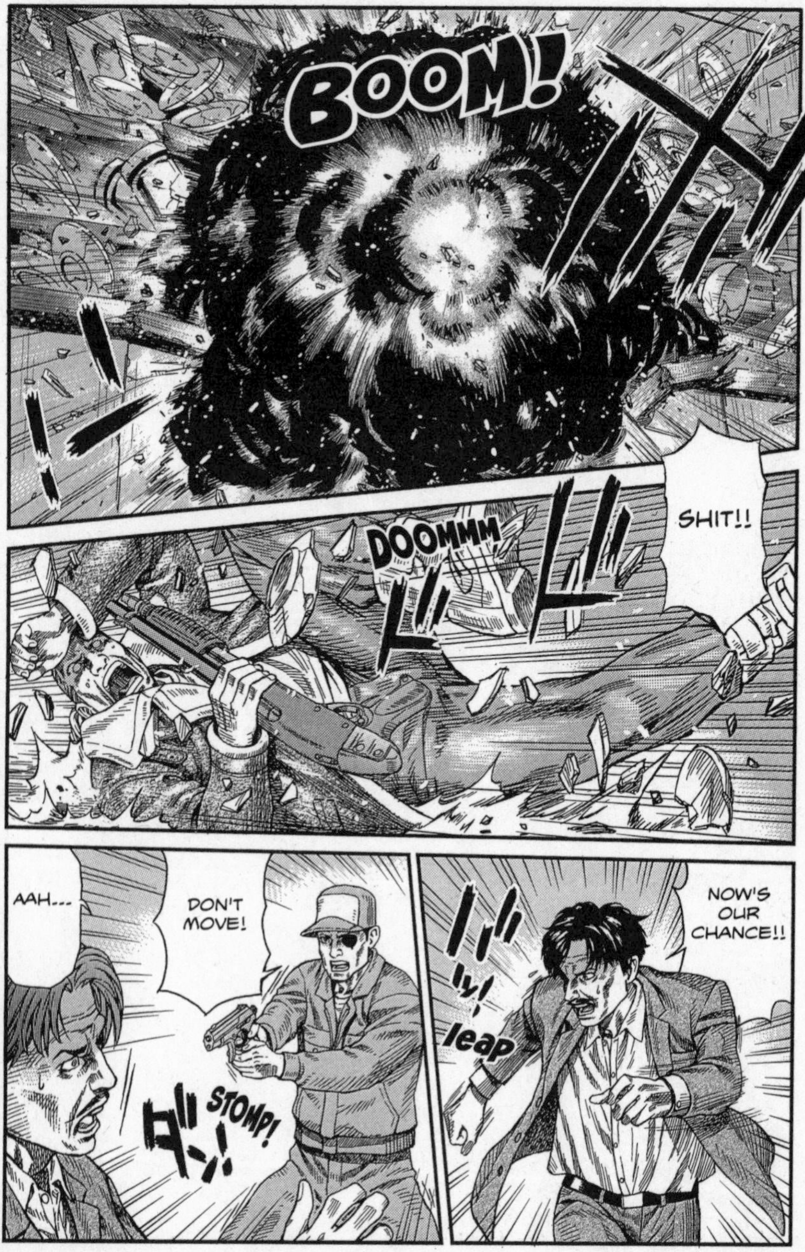
BOOM!
SHIT!!
DOOMMM
NOW'S OUR CHANCE!!
leap
DON'T MOVE!
AAH...
STOMP!

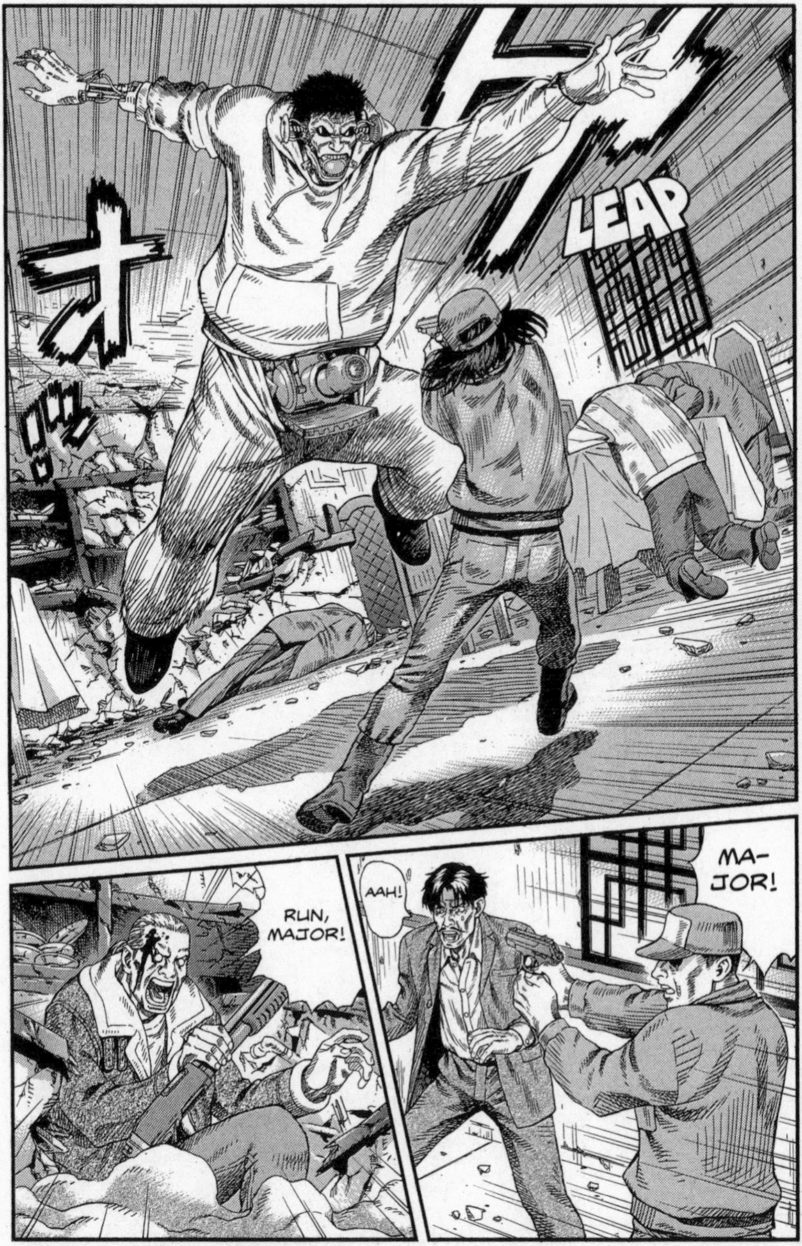
LEAP
MA-
JOR!
AAH!
RUN,
MAJOR!

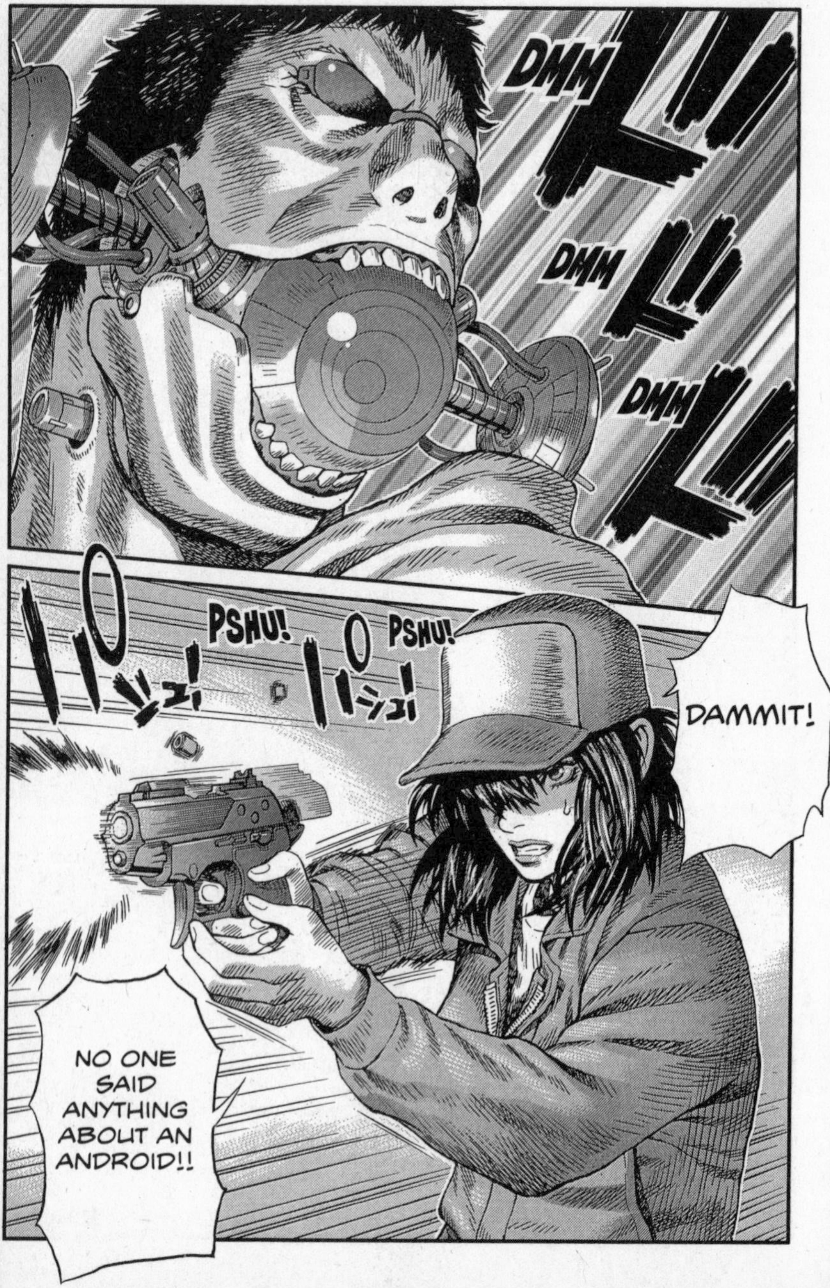
DMM
DMM
DMM
DAMMIT!
PSHU!
PSHU!
NO ONE SAID ANYTHING ABOUT AN ANDROID!!

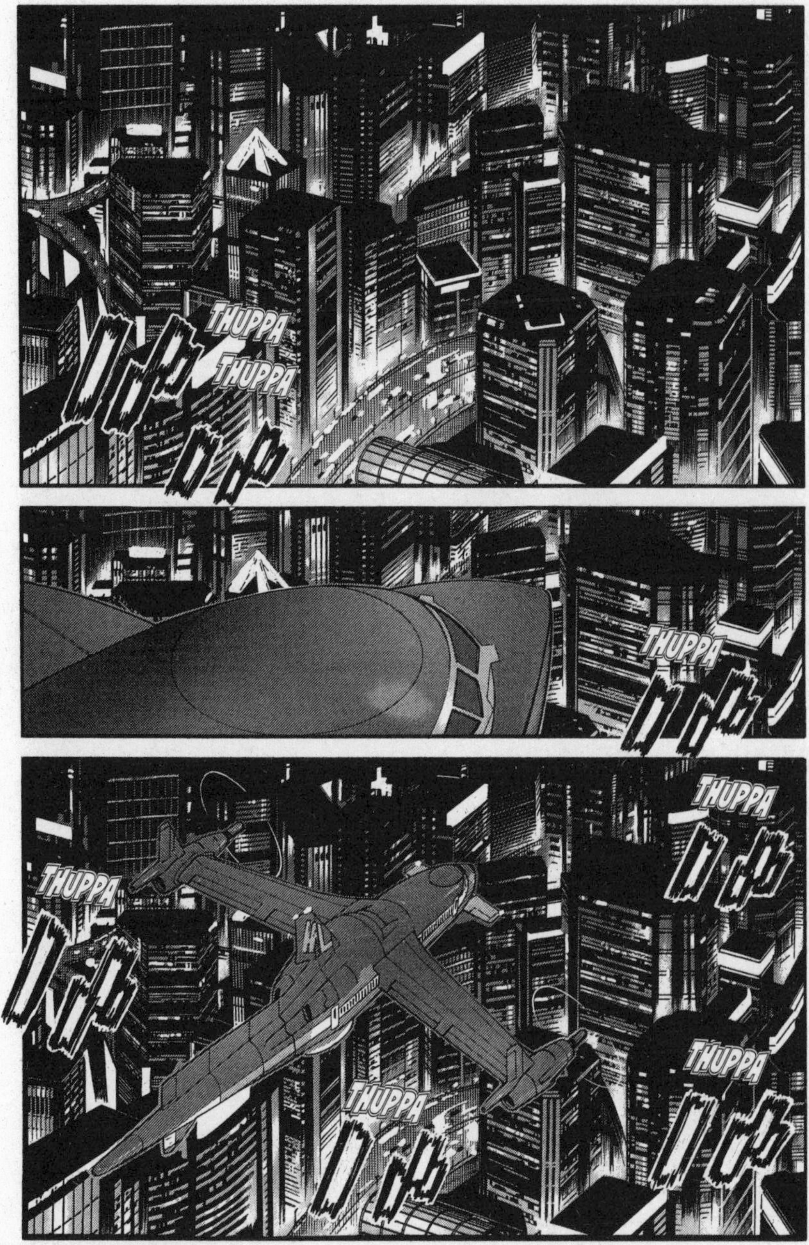
THUPPA
THUPPA
THUPPA
THUPPA
THUPPA
THUPPA
THUPPA

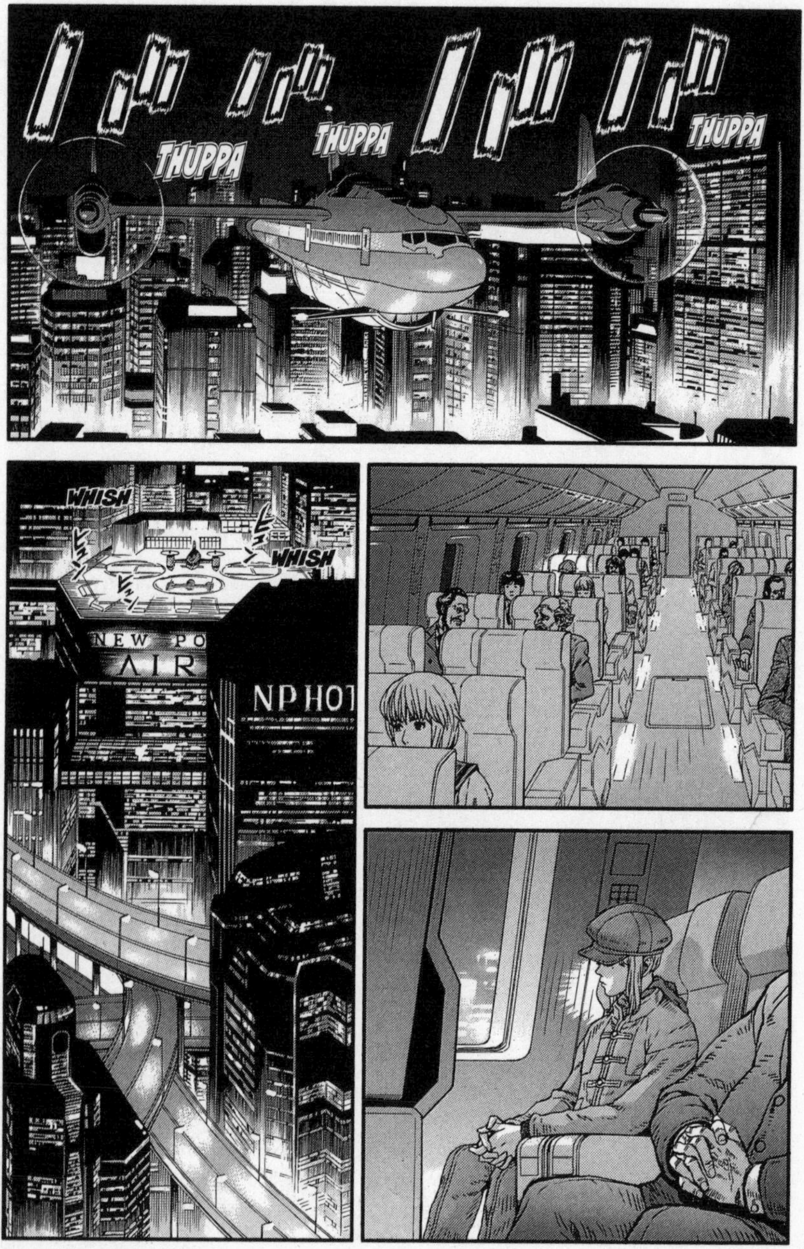
THUPPA
THUPPA
THUPPA
WHISH
WHISH
NEW PO
AIR
NP HOT

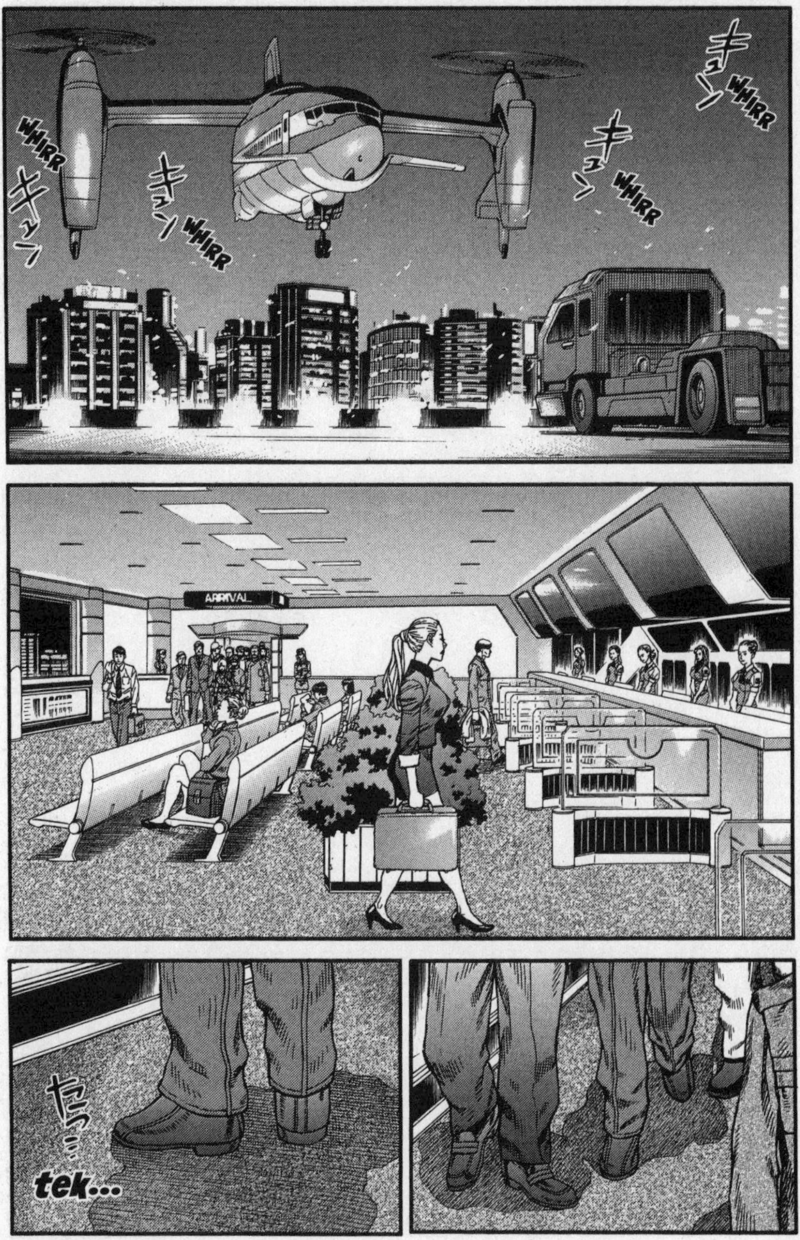
キュン
WHIRR
キュン
WHIRR
キュン
WHIRR
WHIRR
キュン
ARRIVAL
たっ…
tek...

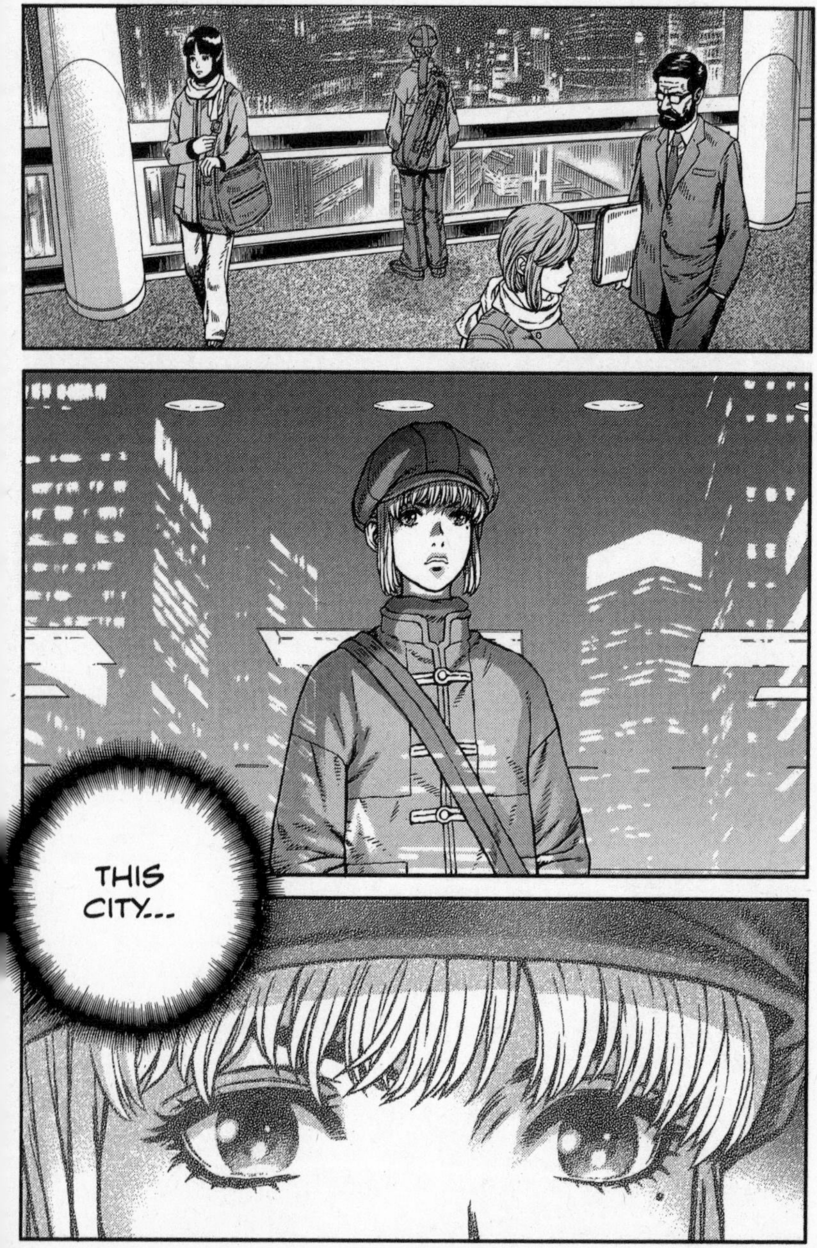
THIS CITY...

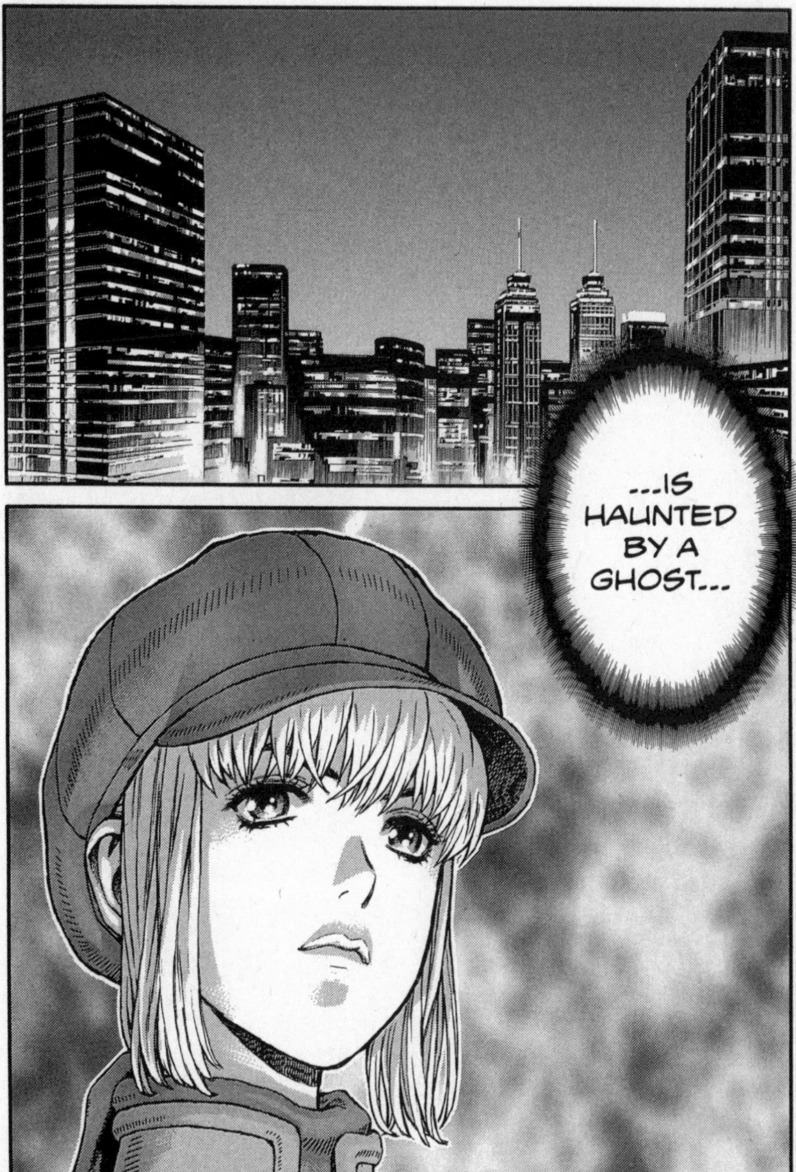
...IS HAUNTED BY A GHOST...

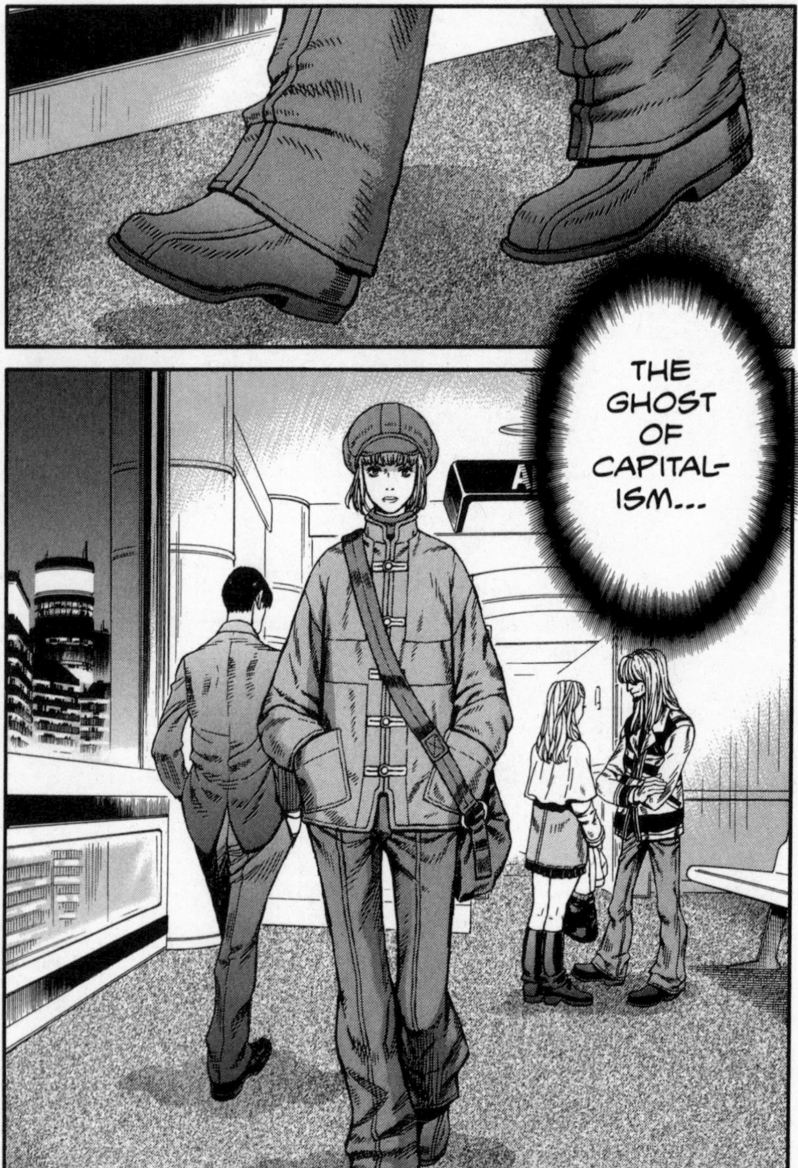
THE GHOST OF CAPITAL-ISM...

#025: END

#026: True Aim

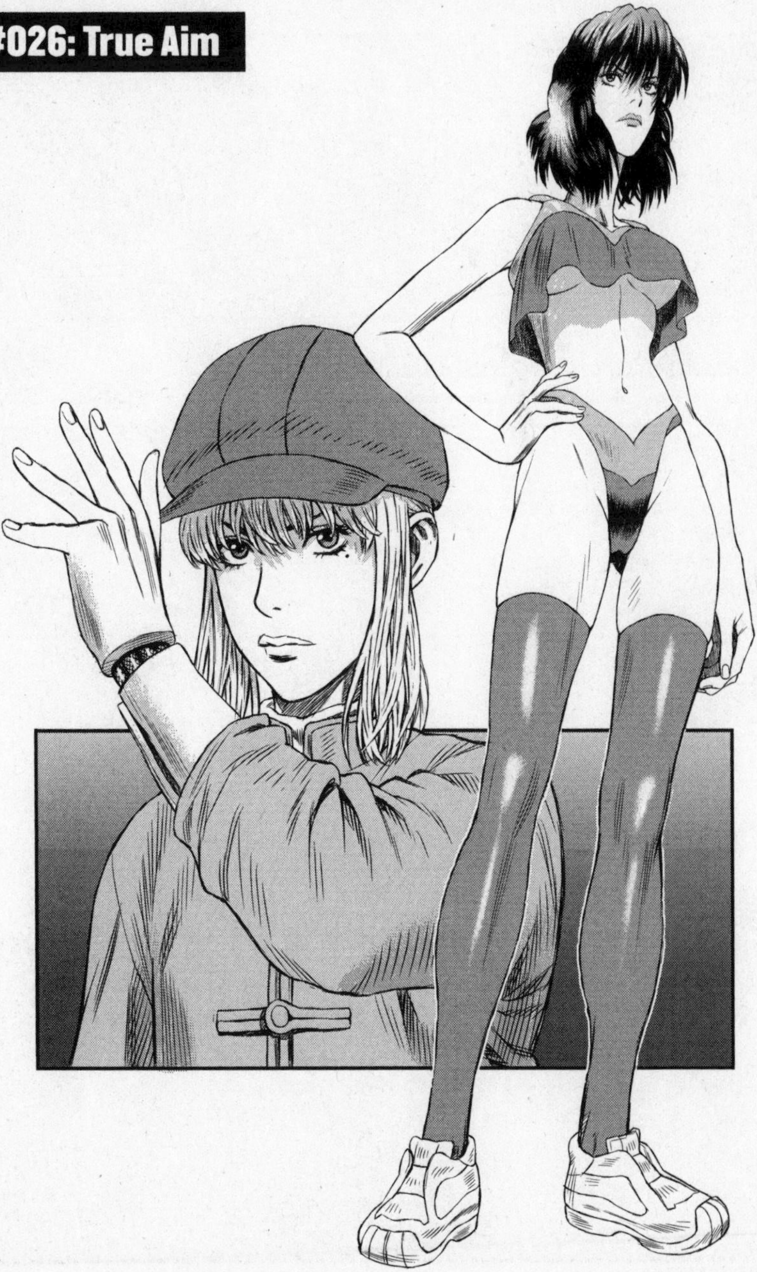

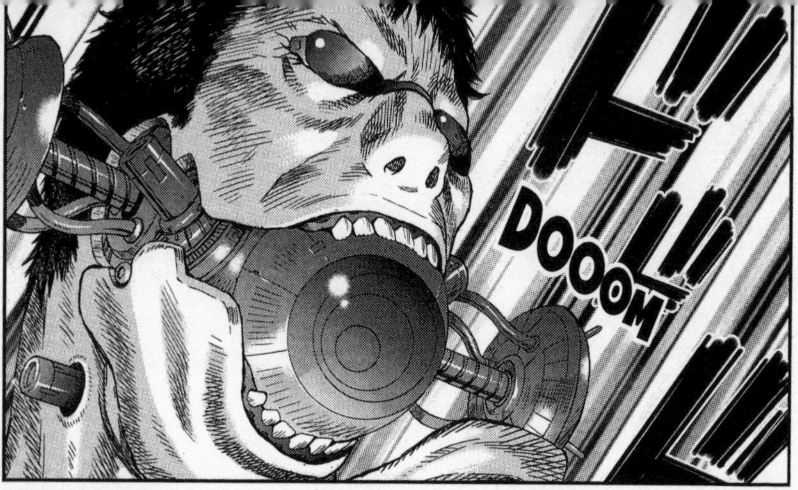
DOOOM

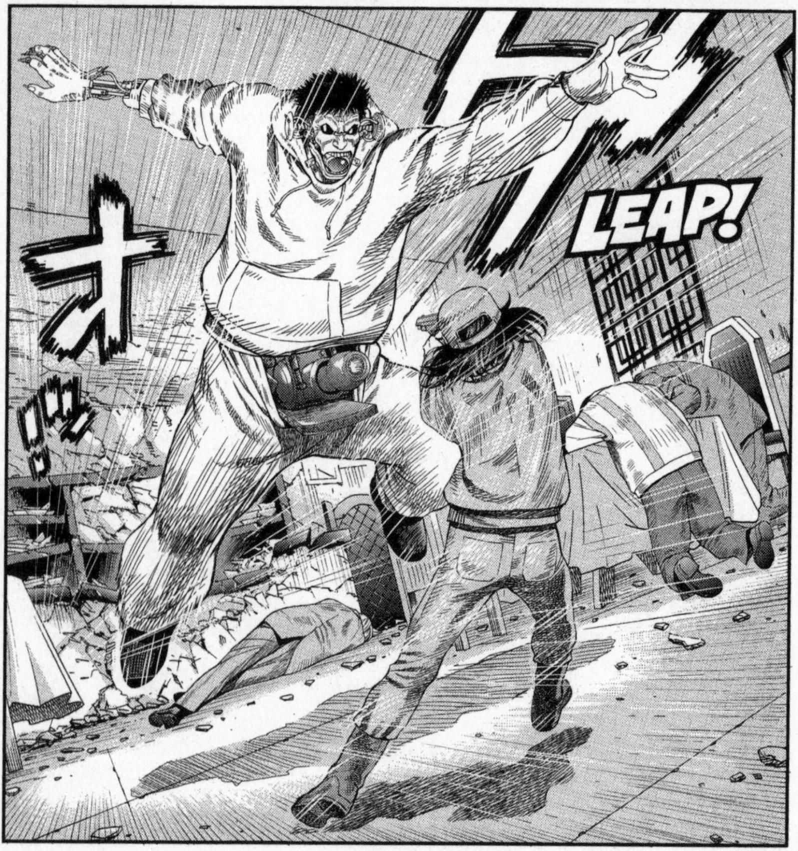
LEAP!

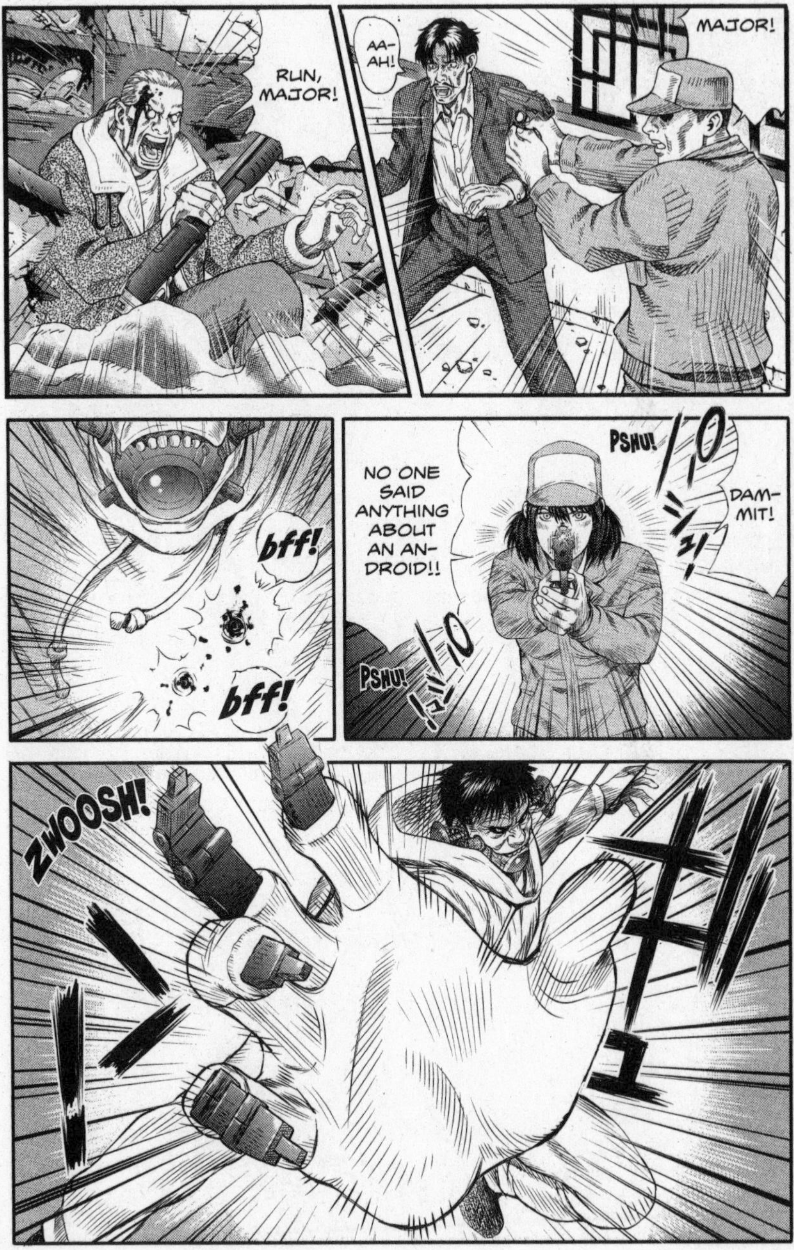
MAJOR!
AA-AH!
RUN, MAJOR!
PSHU!
DAM-MIT!
NO ONE SAID ANYTHING ABOUT AN AN-DROID!!
PSHU!
bff!
bff!
ZWOOSH!

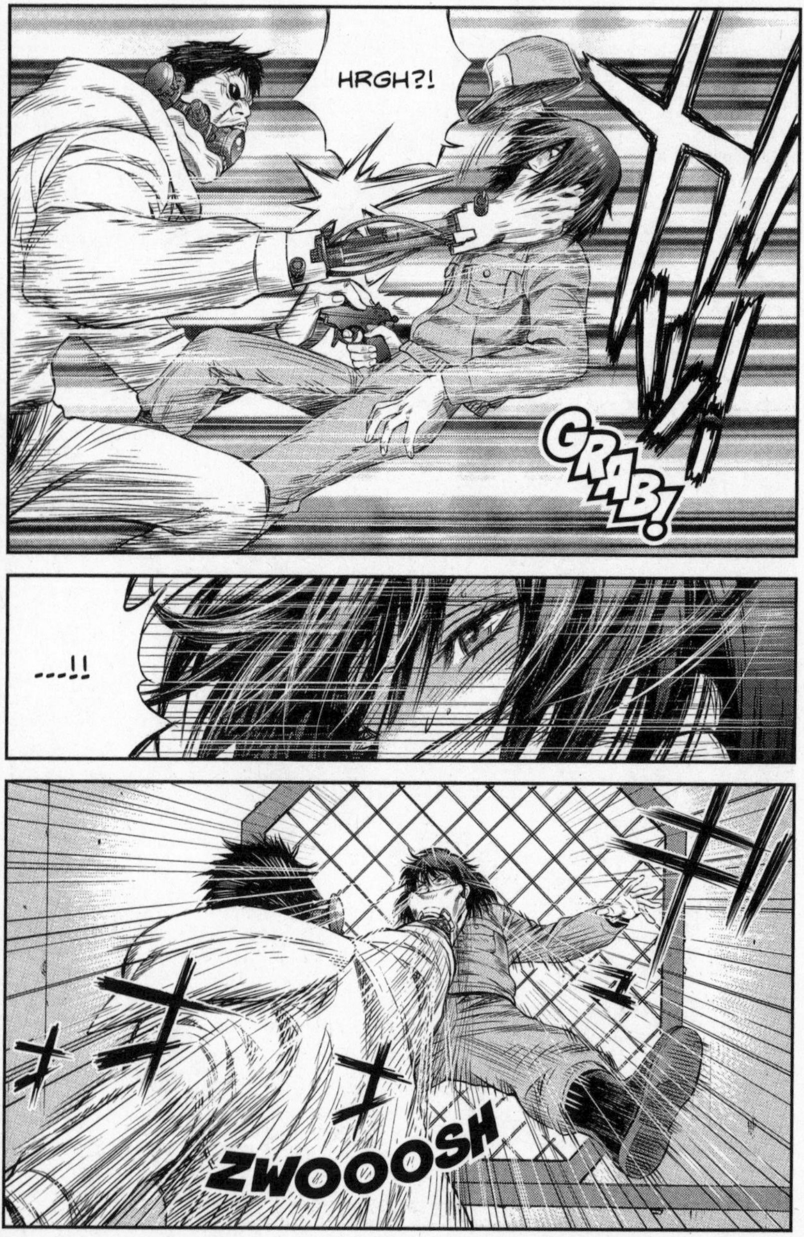
HRGH?!
GRAB!
---!!
ZWOOOSH

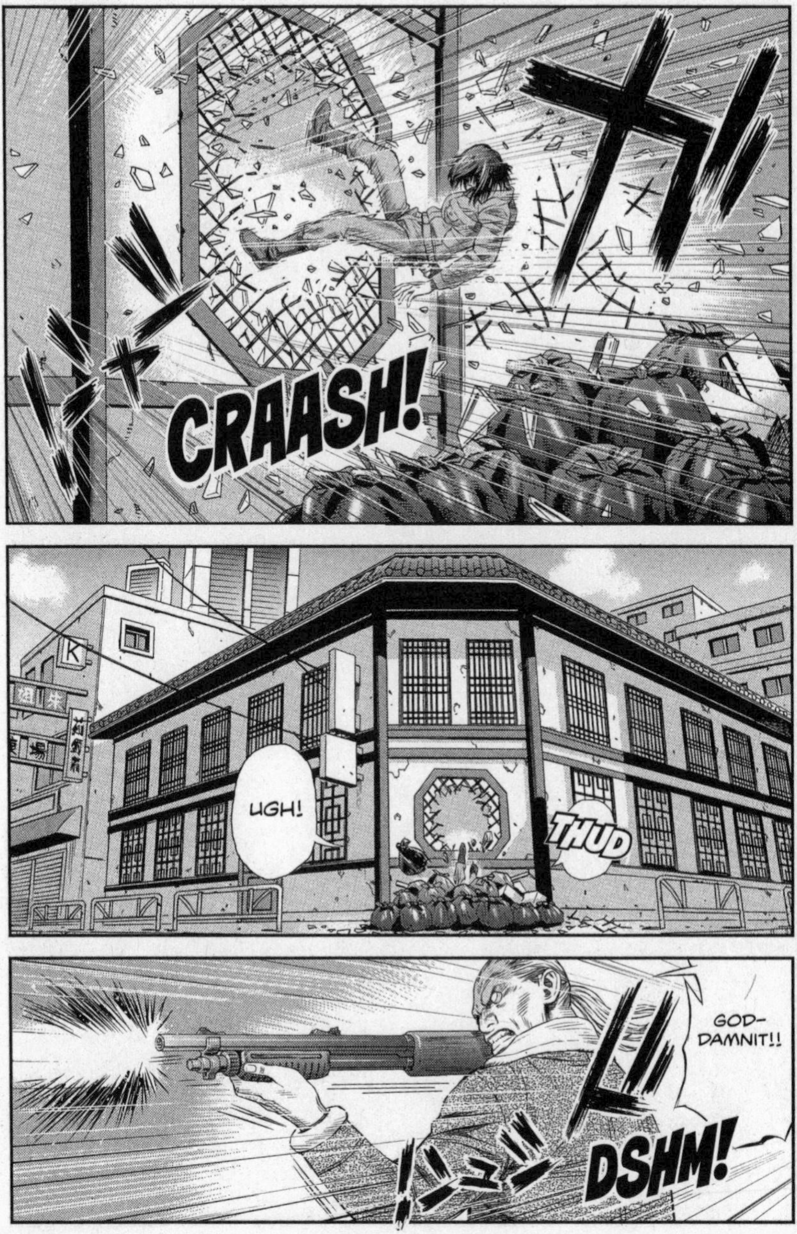
CRAASH!
THUD
UGH!
GOD-DAMNIT!!
DSHM!

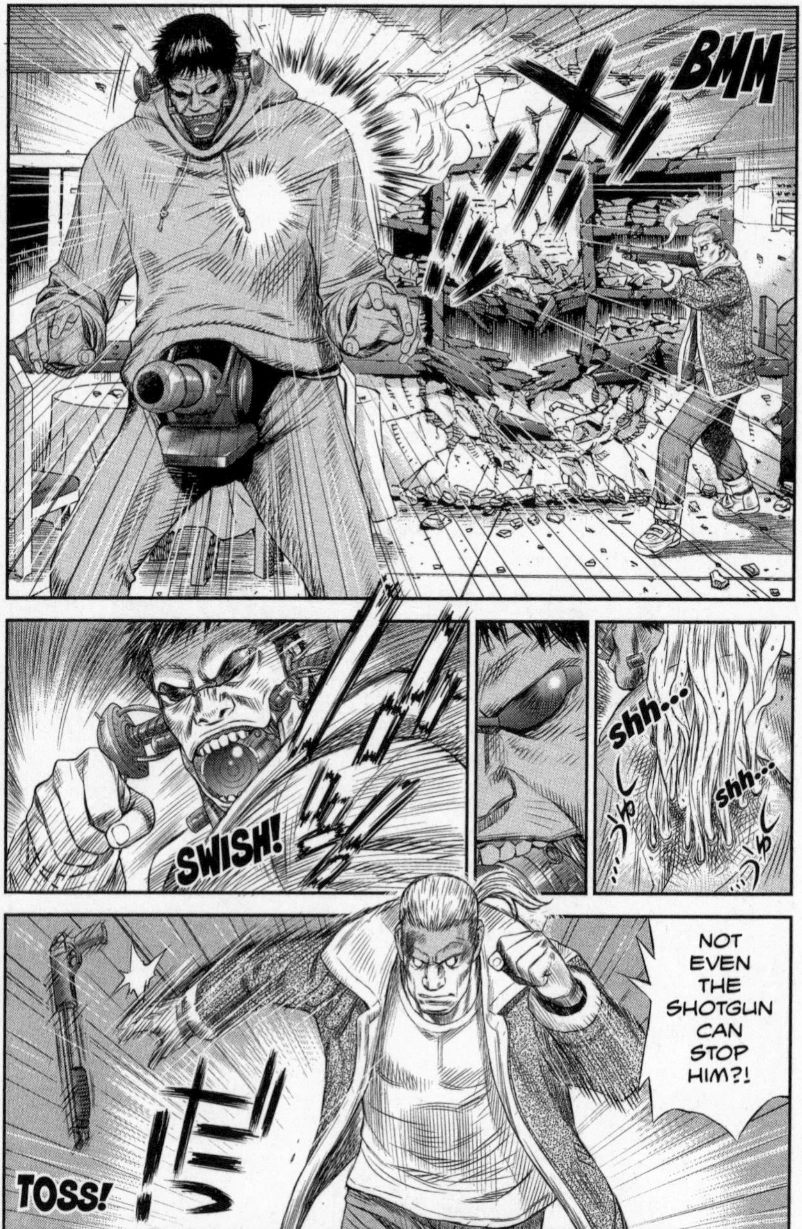
BMM
shh...
shh...
SWISH!
NOT EVEN THE SHOTGUN CAN STOP HIM?!
TOSS!

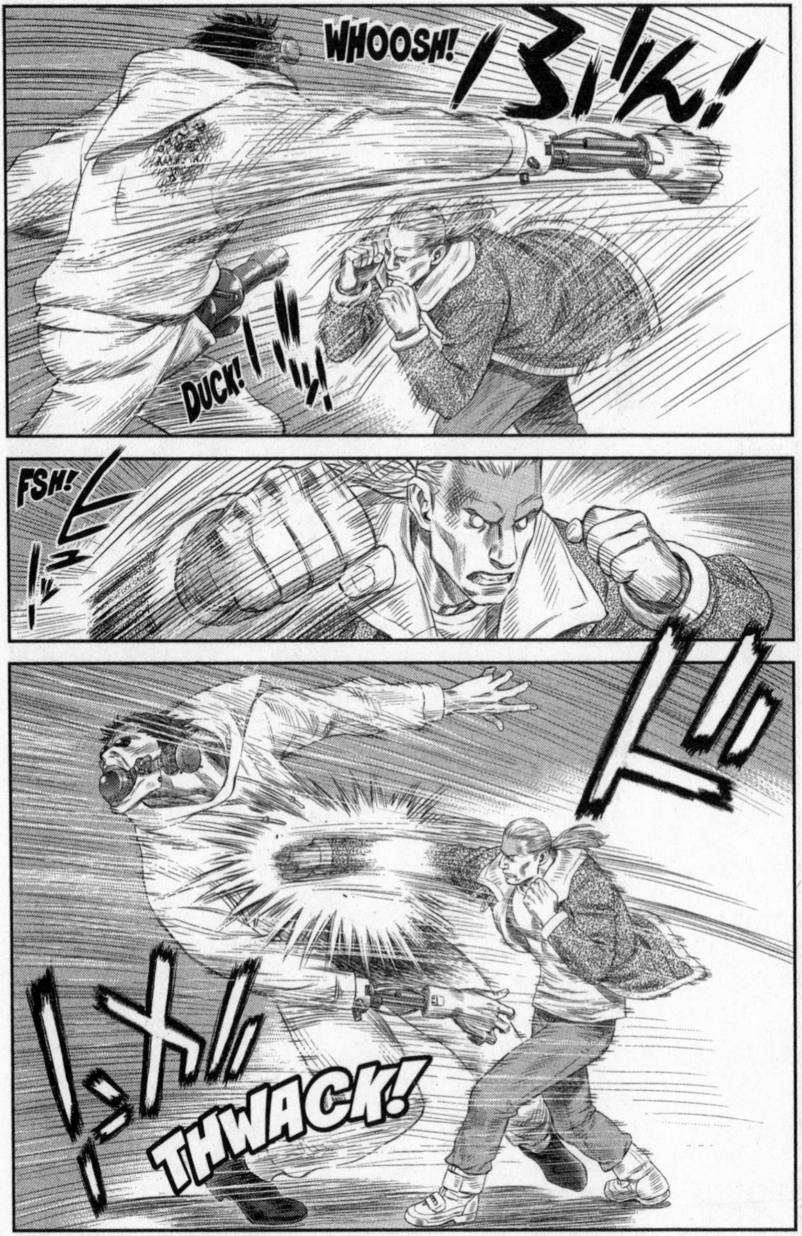
WHOOSH!
DUCK!
FSH!
THWACK!

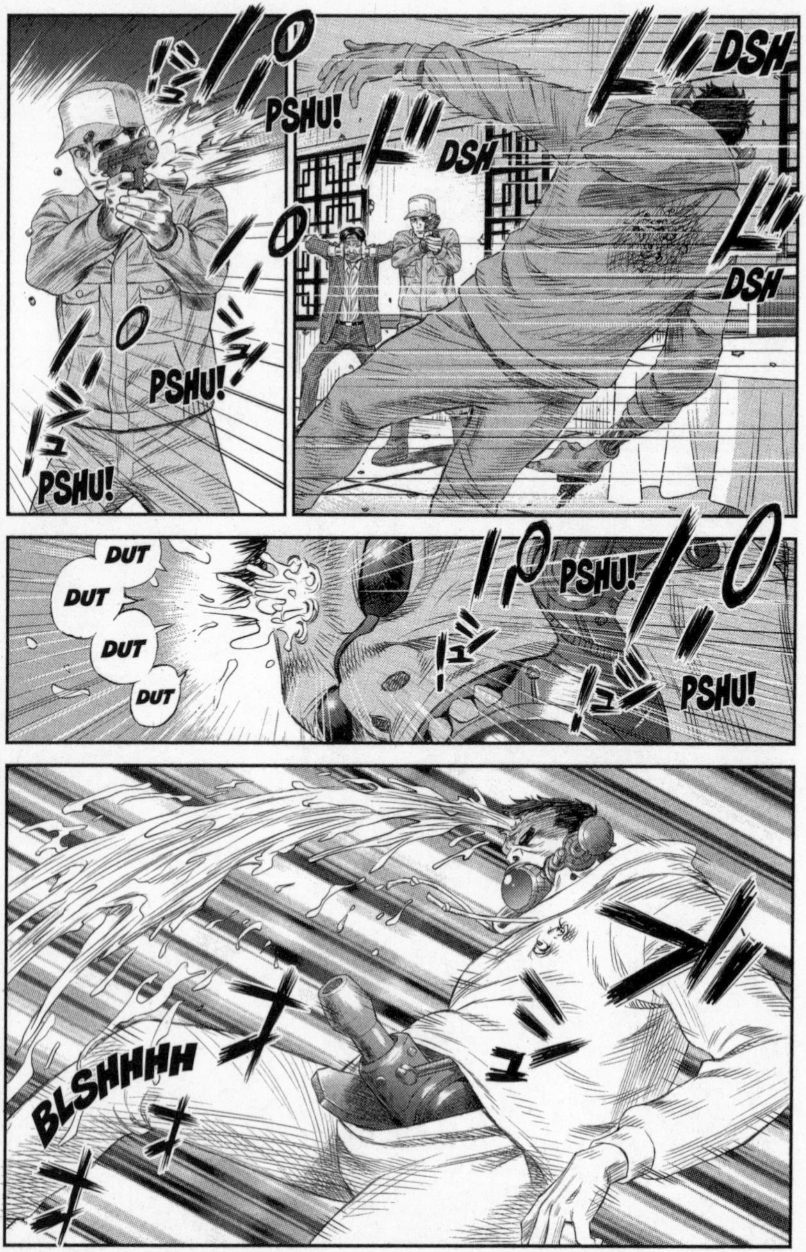
DSH
DSH
DSH
PSHU!
PSHU!
PSHU!
PSHU!
PSHU!
DUT
DUT
DUT
DUT
BLSHHHH

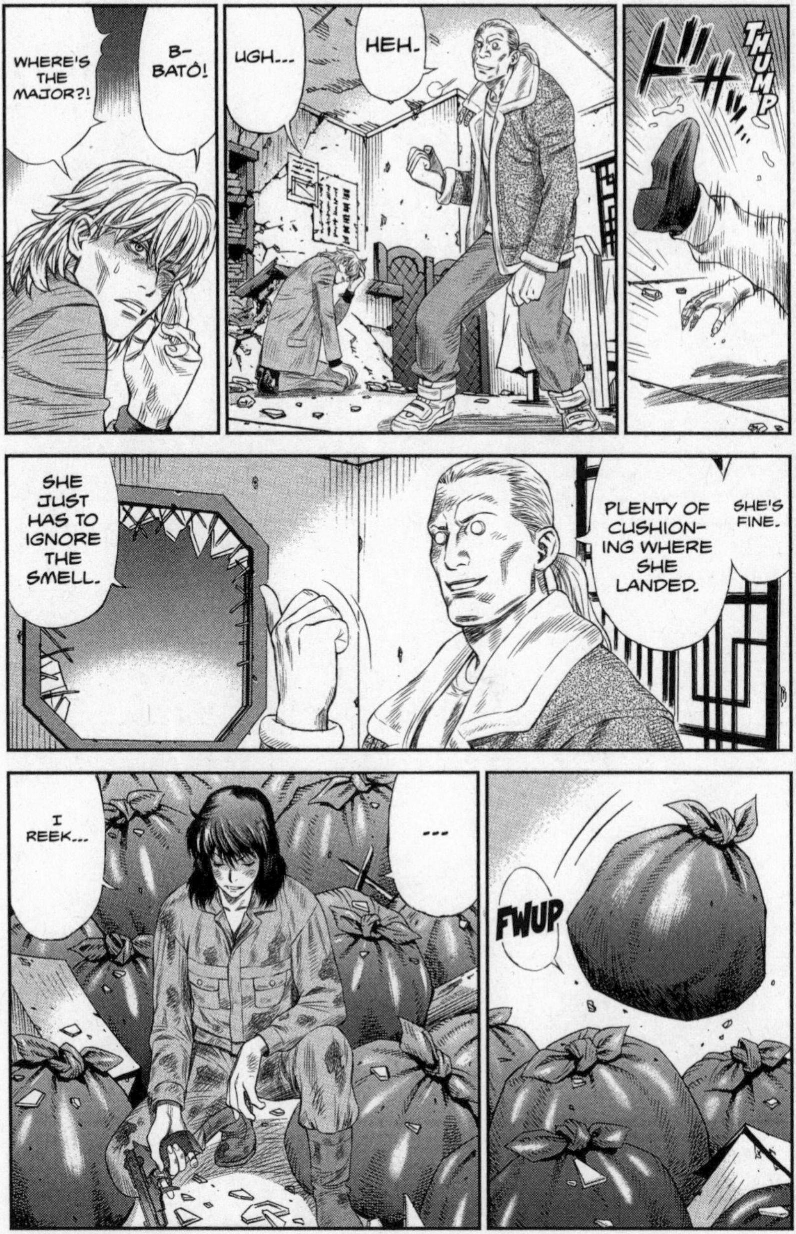
THUMP
HEH.
UGH...
B-BATÔ!
WHERE'S THE MAJOR?!
SHE'S FINE.
PLENTY OF CUSHIONING WHERE SHE LANDED.
SHE JUST HAS TO IGNORE THE SMELL.
FWUP
...
I REEK...

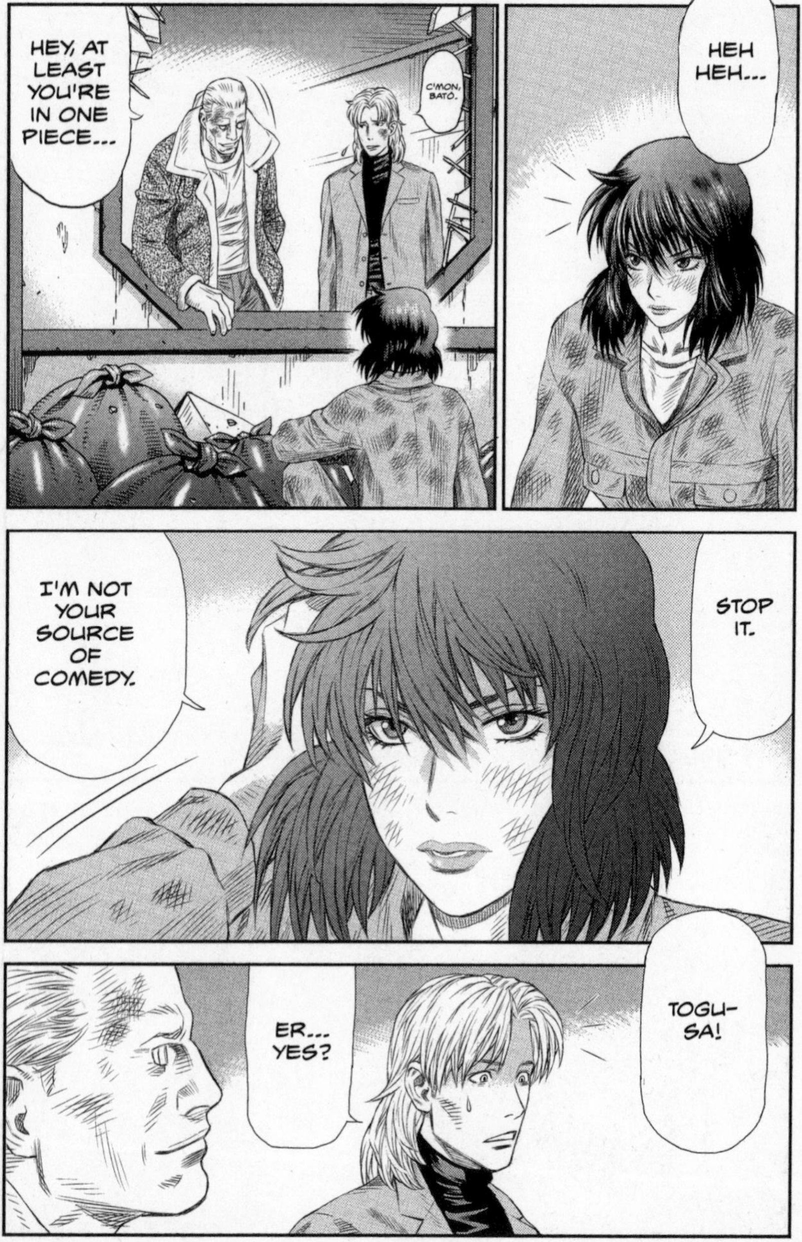
HEH HEH...
HEY, AT LEAST YOU'RE IN ONE PIECE...
C'MON, BATÓ.
STOP IT.
I'M NOT YOUR SOURCE OF COMEDY.
TOGU-SA!
ER... YES?

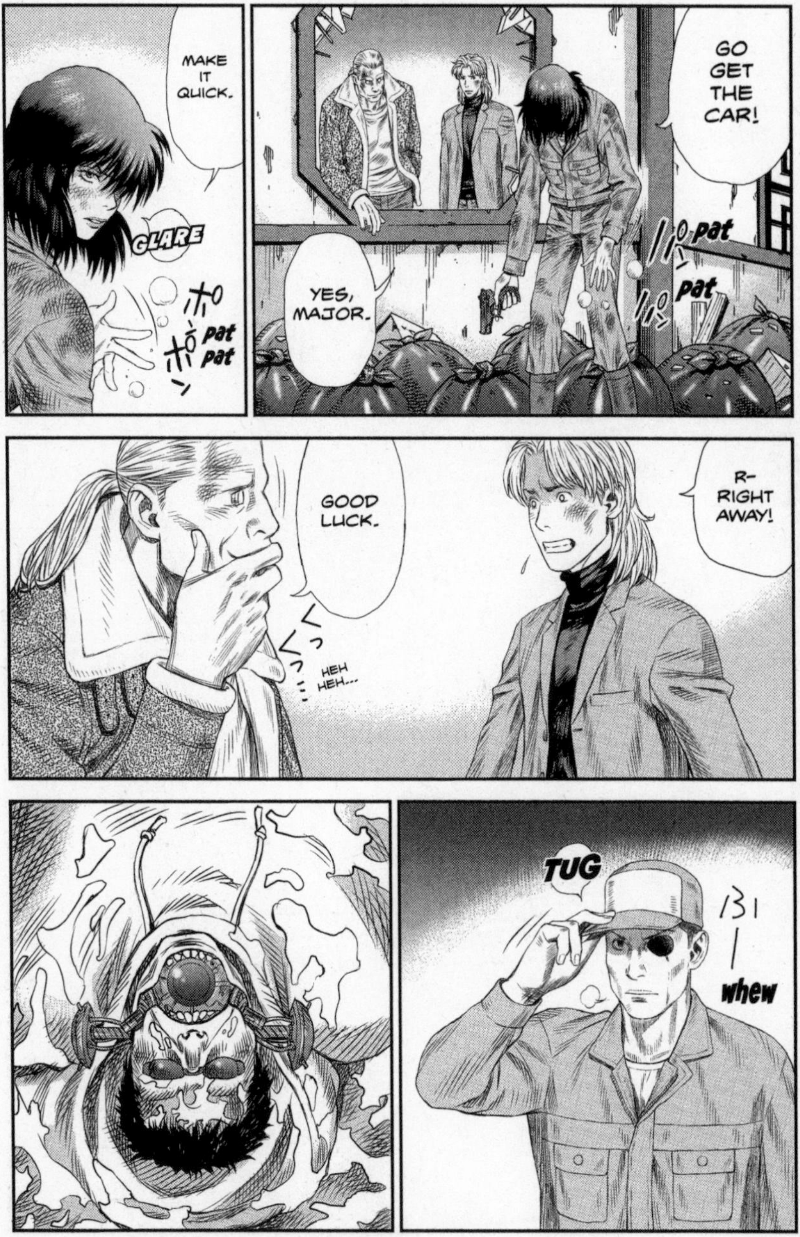
GO GET THE CAR!
YES, MAJOR.
pat
pat
MAKE IT QUICK.
GLARE
pat pat
R- RIGHT AWAY!
GOOD LUCK.
HEH HEH...
TUG
whew

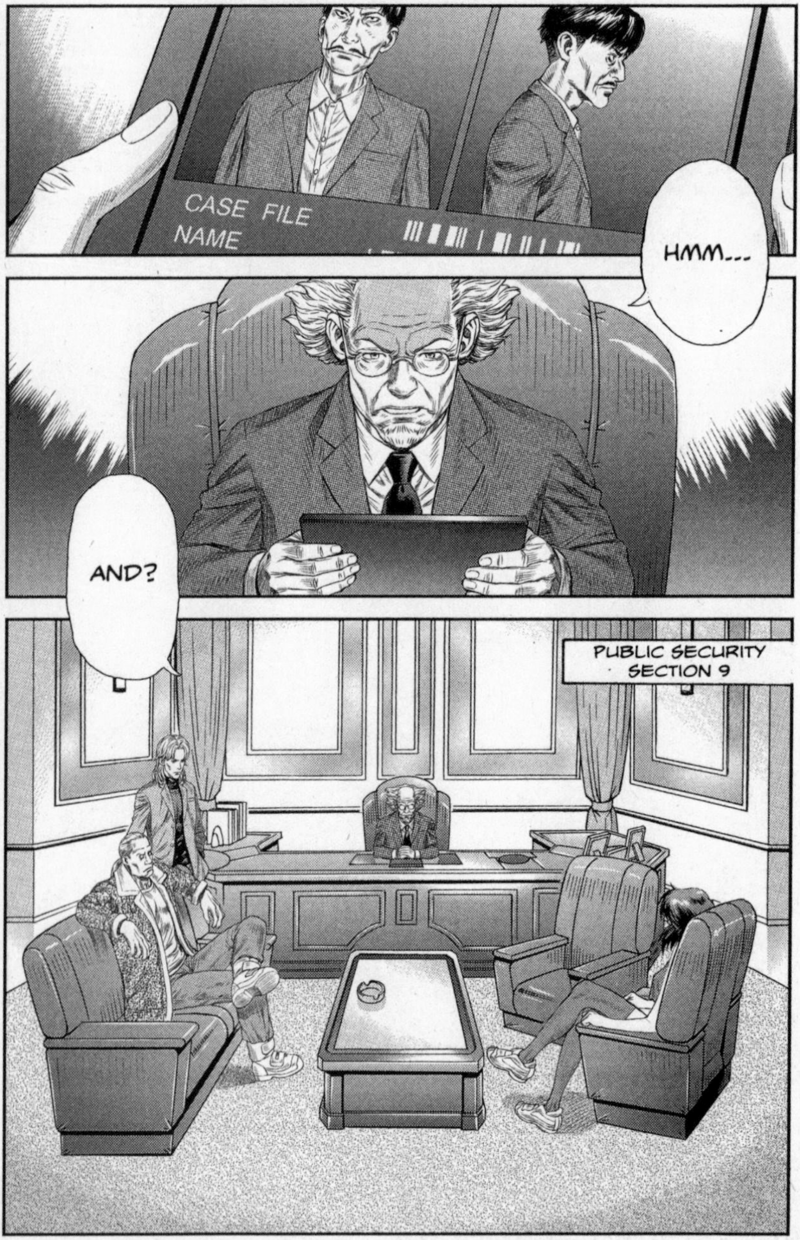
CASE FILE
NAME
HMM...
AND?
PUBLIC SECURITY
SECTION 9

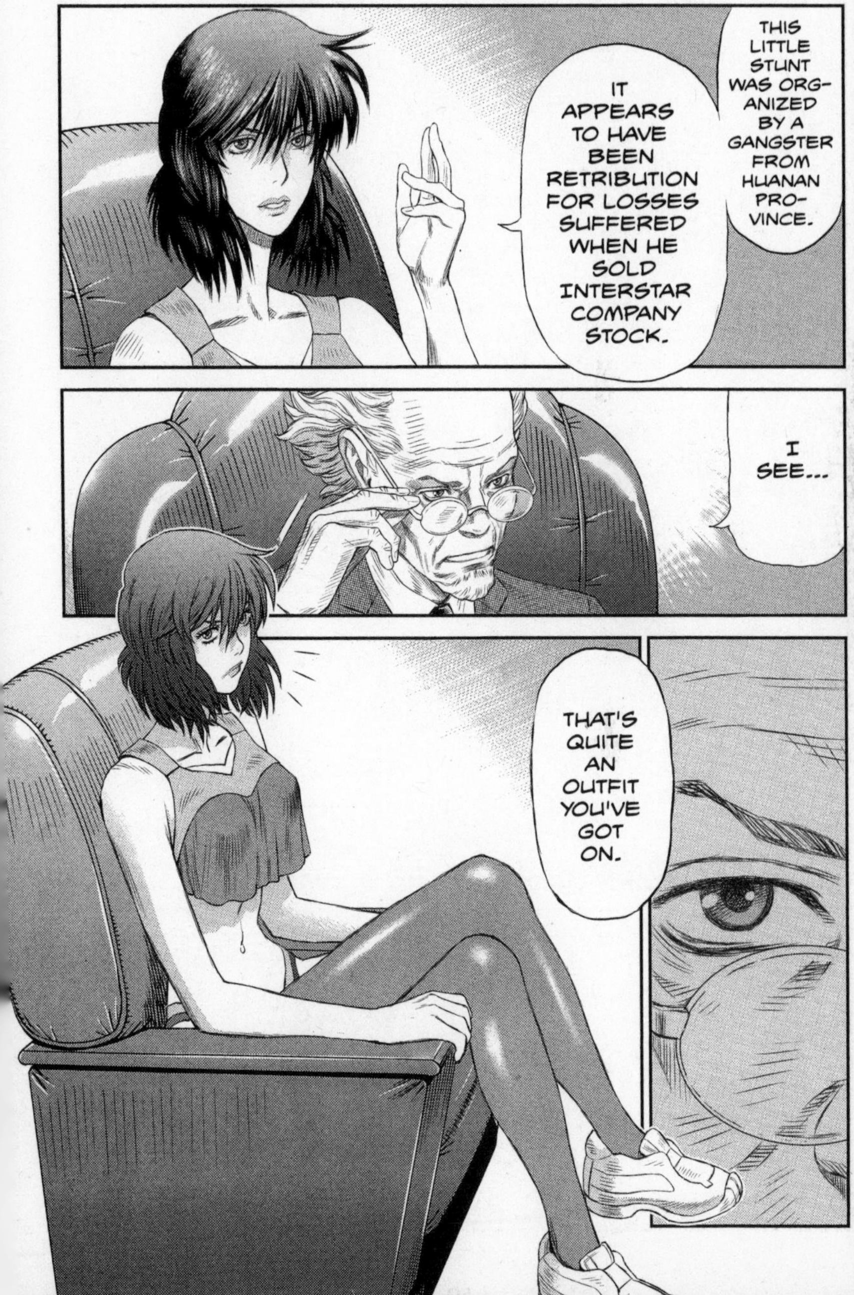
THIS LITTLE STUNT WAS ORGANIZED BY A GANGSTER FROM HUANAN PROVINCE.
IT APPEARS TO HAVE BEEN RETRIBUTION FOR LOSSES SUFFERED WHEN HE SOLD INTERSTAR COMPANY STOCK.
I SEE...
THAT'S QUITE AN OUTFIT YOU'VE GOT ON.

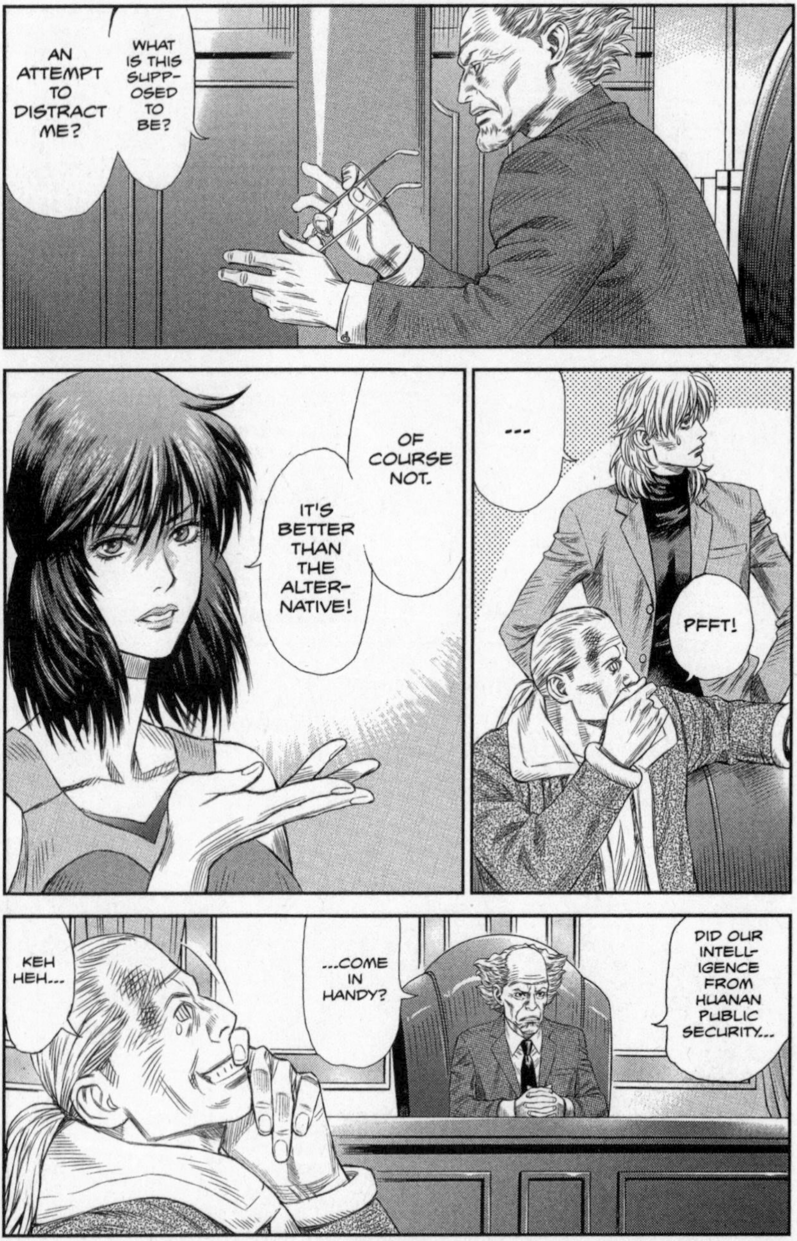
WHAT IS THIS SUPP-OSED TO BE?
AN ATTEMPT TO DISTRACT ME?
...
PFFT!
OF COURSE NOT.
IT'S BETTER THAN THE ALTER-NATIVE!
DID OUR INTELL-IGENCE FROM HUANAN PUBLIC SECURITY...
...COME IN HANDY?
KEH HEH...

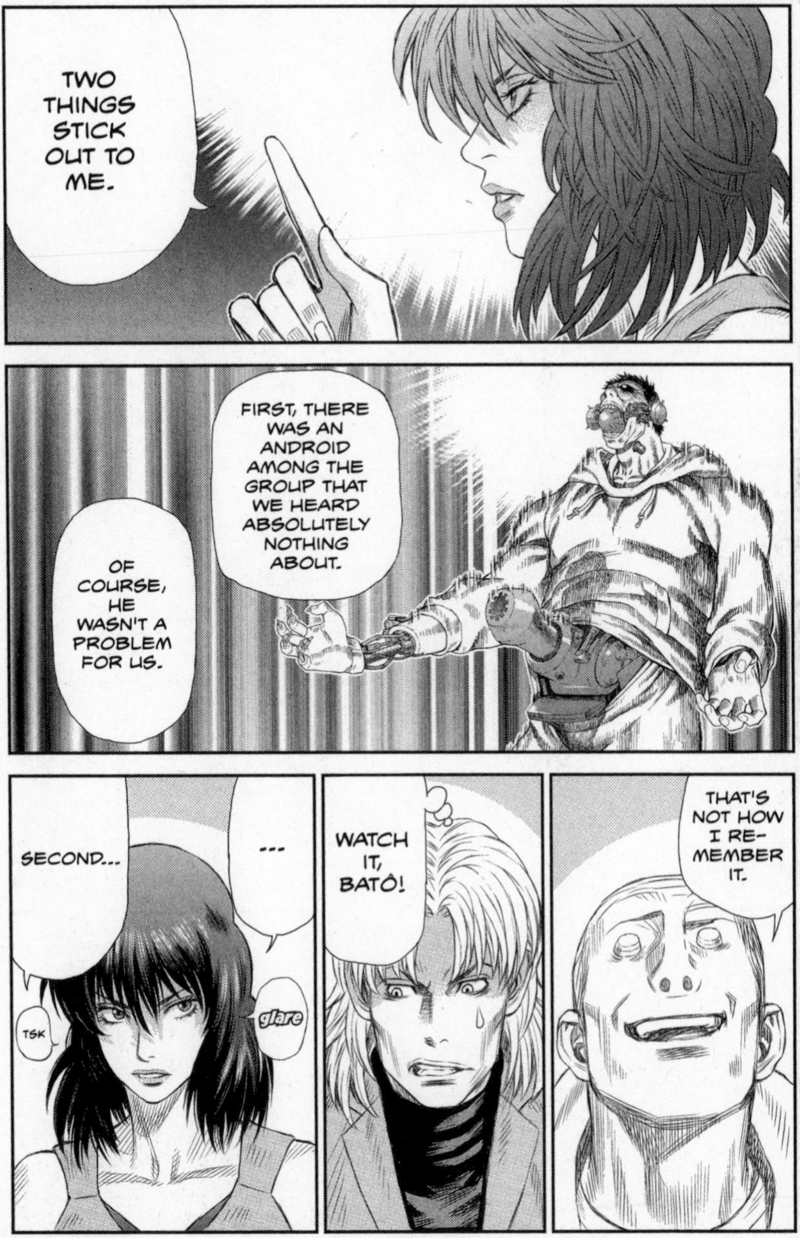
TWO THINGS STICK OUT TO ME.
FIRST, THERE WAS AN ANDROID AMONG THE GROUP THAT WE HEARD ABSOLUTELY NOTHING ABOUT.
OF COURSE, HE WASN'T A PROBLEM FOR US.
THAT'S NOT HOW I RE-MEMBER IT.
WATCH IT, BATÔ!
...
SECOND...
glare
TSK

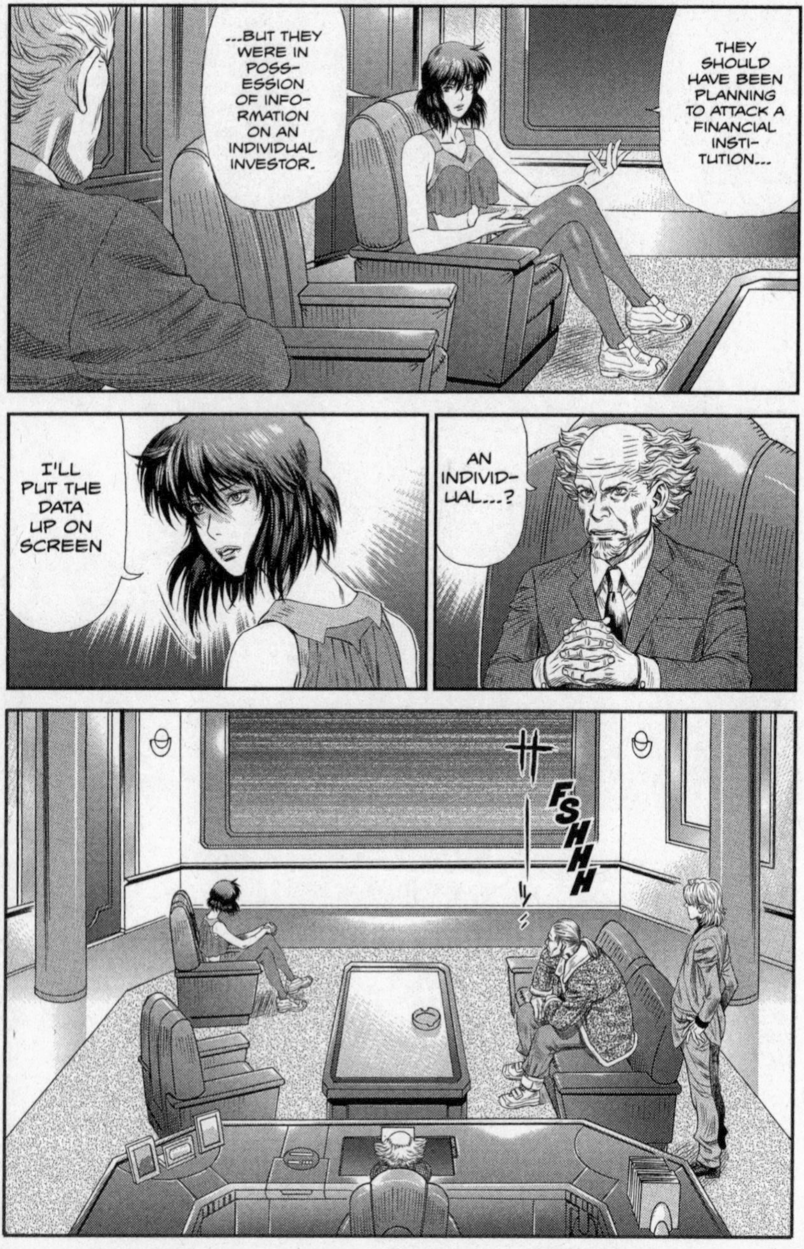
THEY SHOULD HAVE BEEN PLANNING TO ATTACK A FINANCIAL INSTITUTION...
...BUT THEY WERE IN POSSESSION OF INFORMATION ON AN INDIVIDUAL INVESTOR.
AN INDIVIDUAL...?
I'LL PUT THE DATA UP ON SCREEN
FSHHH

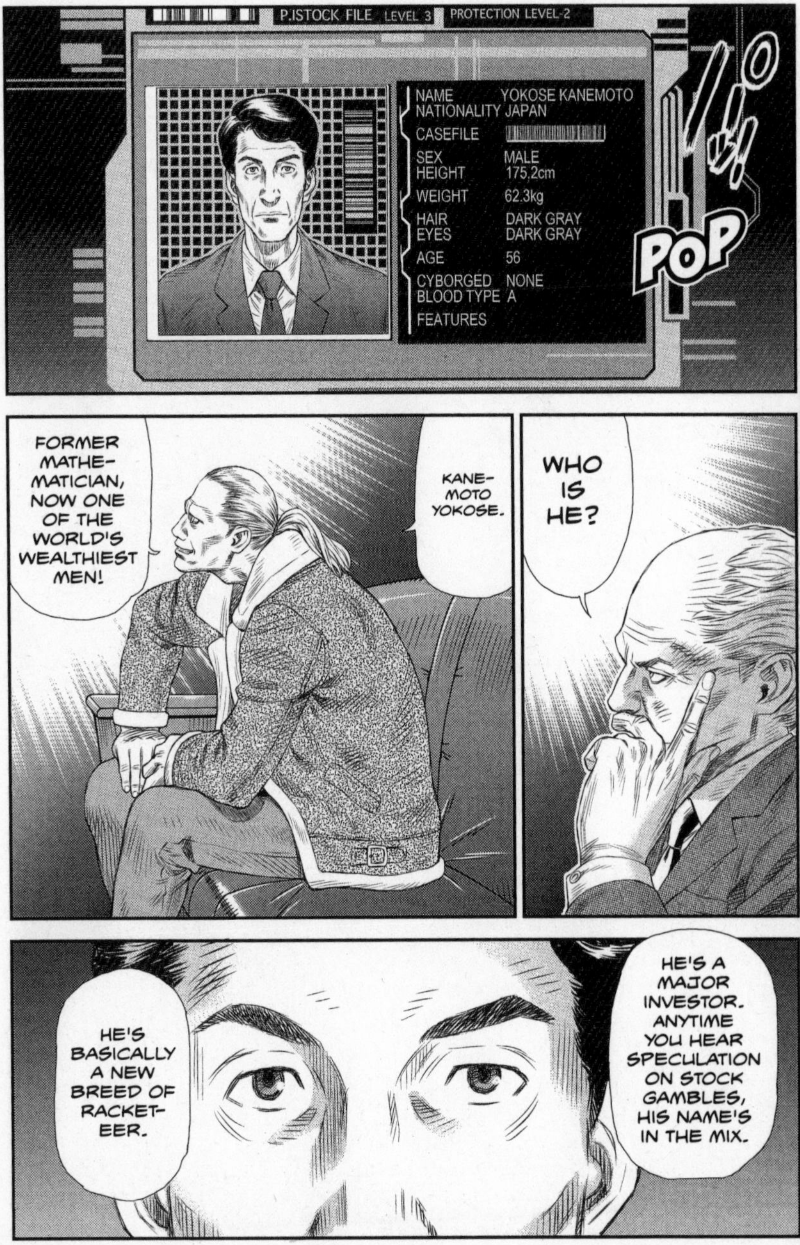
P.ISTOCK FILE LEVEL 3
PROTECTION LEVEL-2
NAME YOKOSE KANEMOTO
NATIONALITY JAPAN
CASEFILE
SEX MALE
HEIGHT 175,2cm
WEIGHT 62.3kg
HAIR DARK GRAY
EYES DARK GRAY
AGE 56
CYBORGED NONE
BLOOD TYPE A
FEATURES
POP
WHO IS HE?
KANE-MOTO YOKOSE.
FORMER MATHE-MATICIAN, NOW ONE OF THE WORLD'S WEALTHIEST MEN!
HE'S A MAJOR INVESTOR. ANYTIME YOU HEAR SPECULATION ON STOCK GAMBLES, HIS NAME'S IN THE MIX.
HE'S BASICALLY A NEW BREED OF RACKET-EER.

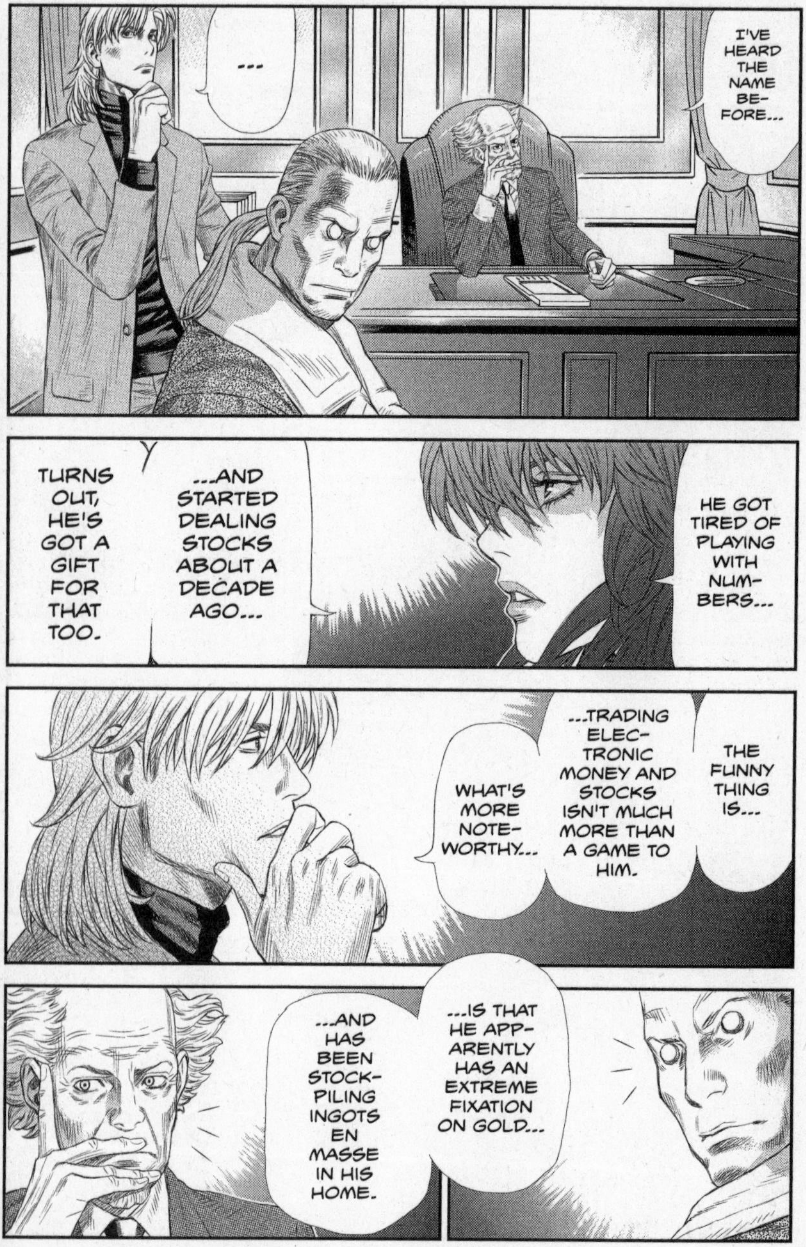
I'VE HEARD THE NAME BEFORE...
...
HE GOT TIRED OF PLAYING WITH NUMBERS...
...AND STARTED DEALING STOCKS ABOUT A DECADE AGO...
TURNS OUT, HE'S GOT A GIFT FOR THAT TOO.
THE FUNNY THING IS...
...TRADING ELECTRONIC MONEY AND STOCKS ISN'T MUCH MORE THAN A GAME TO HIM.
WHAT'S MORE NOTEWORTHY...
...IS THAT HE APPARENTLY HAS AN EXTREME FIXATION ON GOLD...
...AND HAS BEEN STOCKPILING INGOTS EN MASSE IN HIS HOME.

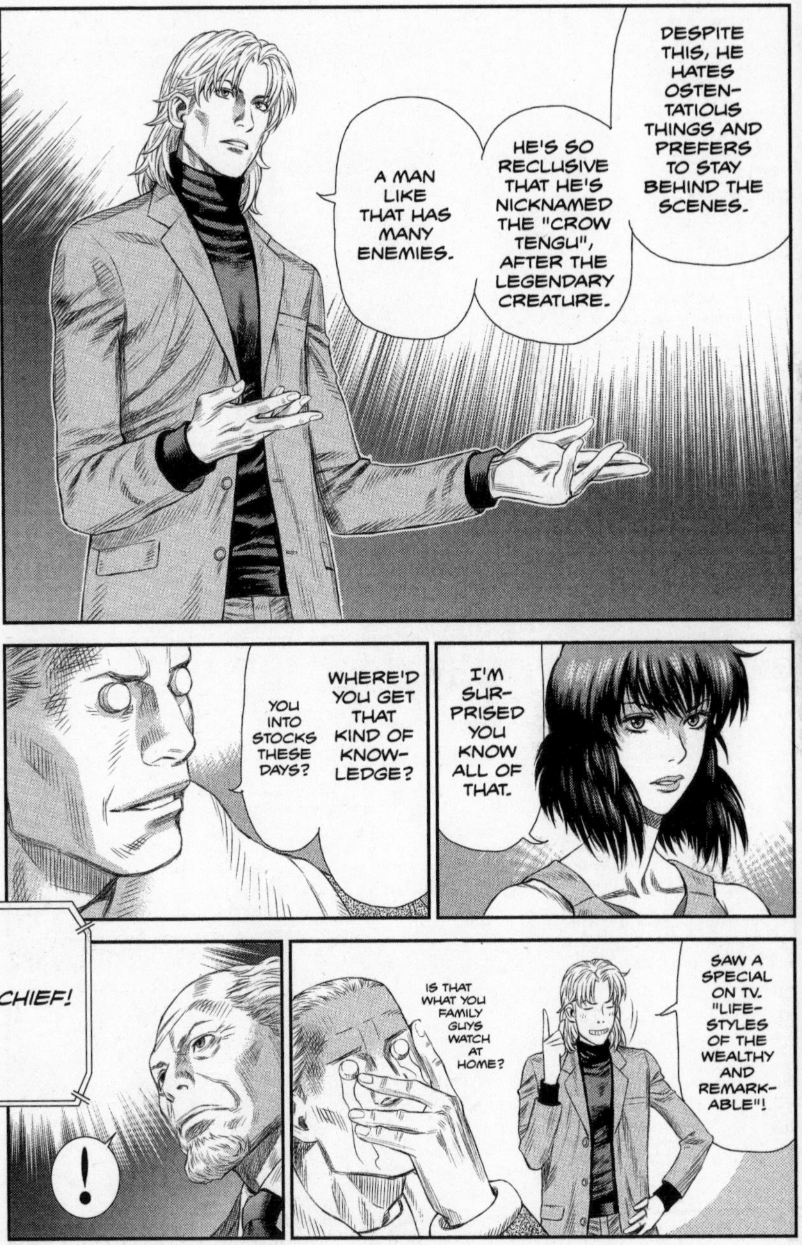
DESPITE THIS, HE HATES OSTENTATIOUS THINGS AND PREFERS TO STAY BEHIND THE SCENES.
HE'S SO RECLUSIVE THAT HE'S NICKNAMED THE "CROW TENGU", AFTER THE LEGENDARY CREATURE.
A MAN LIKE THAT HAS MANY ENEMIES.
I'M SURPRISED YOU KNOW ALL OF THAT.
WHERE'D YOU GET THAT KIND OF KNOWLEDGE?
YOU INTO STOCKS THESE DAYS?
SAW A SPECIAL ON TV. "LIFESTYLES OF THE WEALTHY AND REMARKABLE"!
IS THAT WHAT YOU FAMILY GUYS WATCH AT HOME?
CHIEF!
!

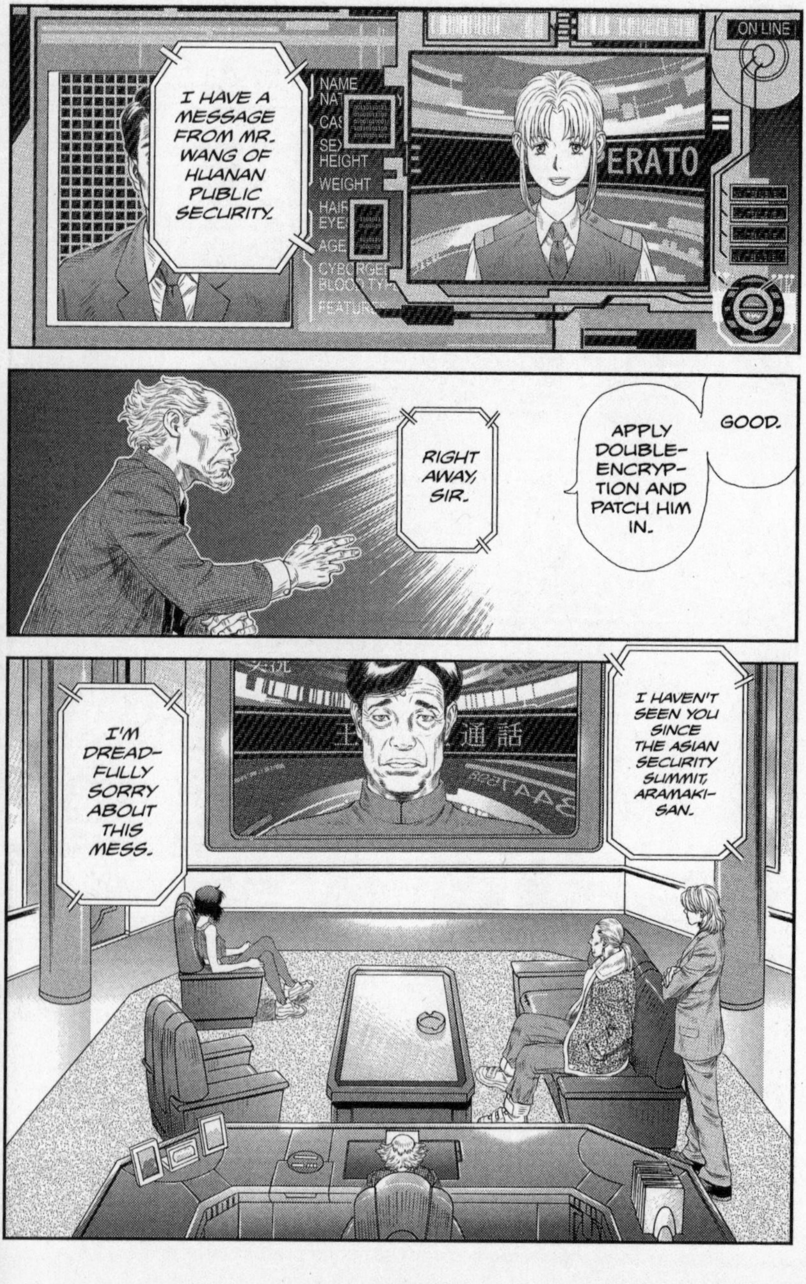
ON LINE
NAME
HEIGHT
WEIGHT
I HAVE A MESSAGE FROM MR. WANG OF HUANAN PUBLIC SECURITY.
GOOD.
APPLY DOUBLE-ENCRYPTION AND PATCH HIM IN.
RIGHT AWAY, SIR.
I HAVEN'T SEEN YOU SINCE THE ASIAN SECURITY SUMMIT, ARAMAKI-SAN.
I'M DREADFULLY SORRY ABOUT THIS MESS.

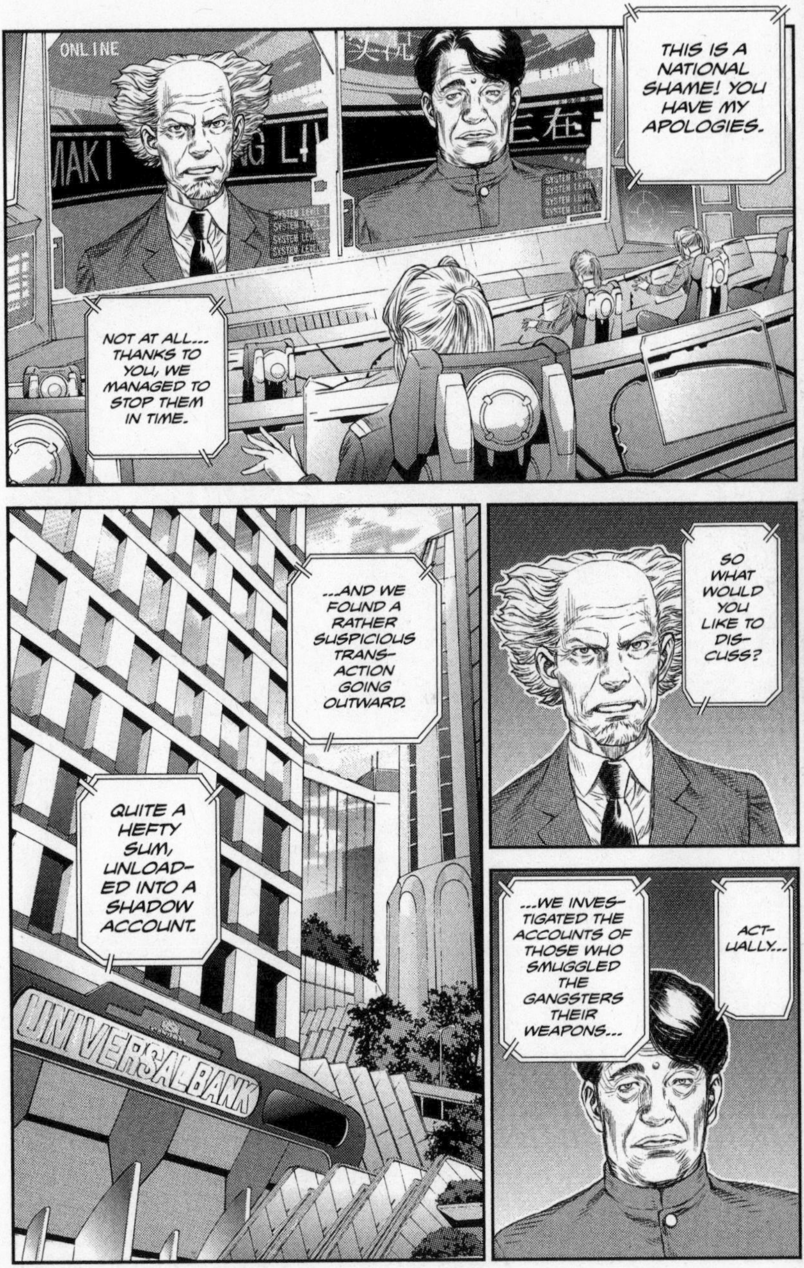
THIS IS A NATIONAL SHAME! YOU HAVE MY APOLOGIES.
ONLINE
NOT AT ALL... THANKS TO YOU, WE MANAGED TO STOP THEM IN TIME.
SO WHAT WOULD YOU LIKE TO DIS-CUSS?
ACT-UALLY...
...WE INVES-TIGATED THE ACCOUNTS OF THOSE WHO SMUGGLED THE GANGSTERS THEIR WEAPONS...
...AND WE FOUND A RATHER SUSPICIOUS TRANS-ACTION GOING OUTWARD.
QUITE A HEFTY SUM, UNLOAD-ED INTO A SHADOW ACCOUNT.
UNIVERSAL BANK

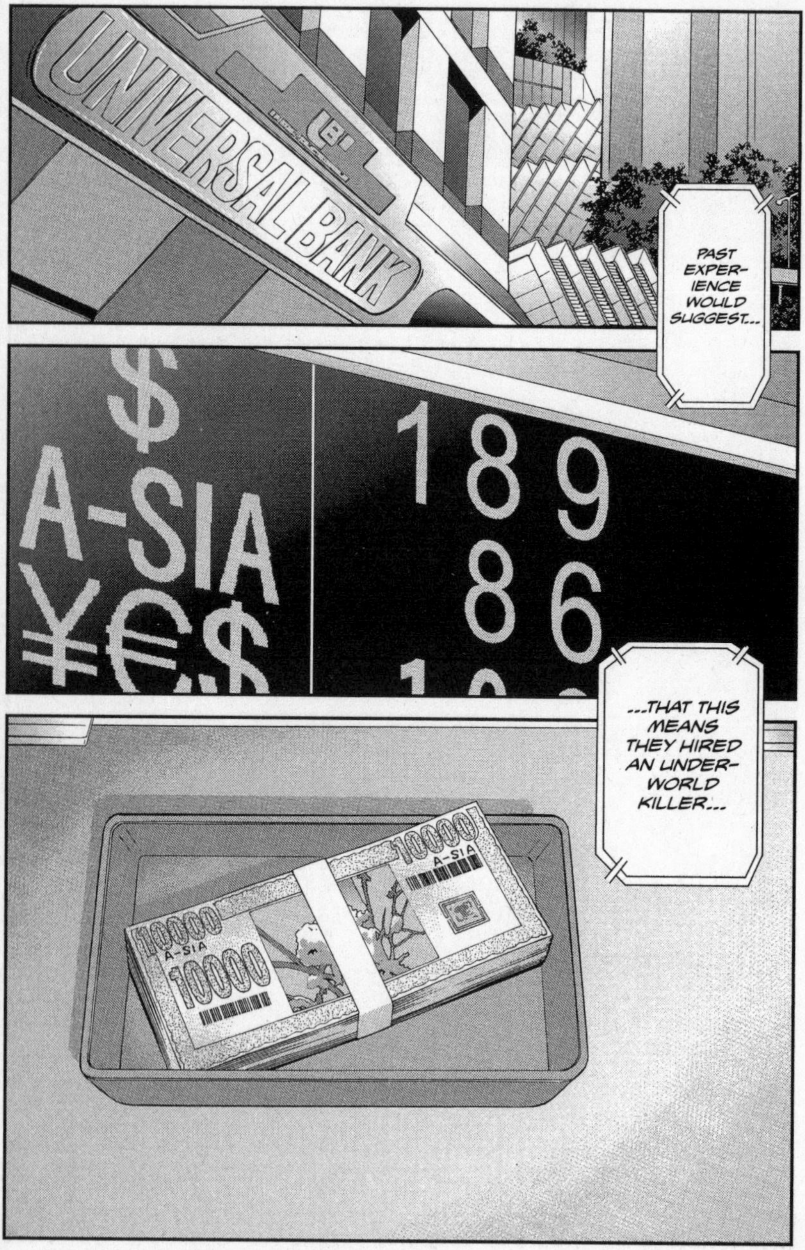
UNIVERSAL BANK
PAST EXPERIENCE WOULD SUGGEST...
$
A-SIA
¥€$
189
86
...THAT THIS MEANS THEY HIRED AN UNDER-WORLD KILLER...
10000
A-SIA
10000
A-SIA
10000

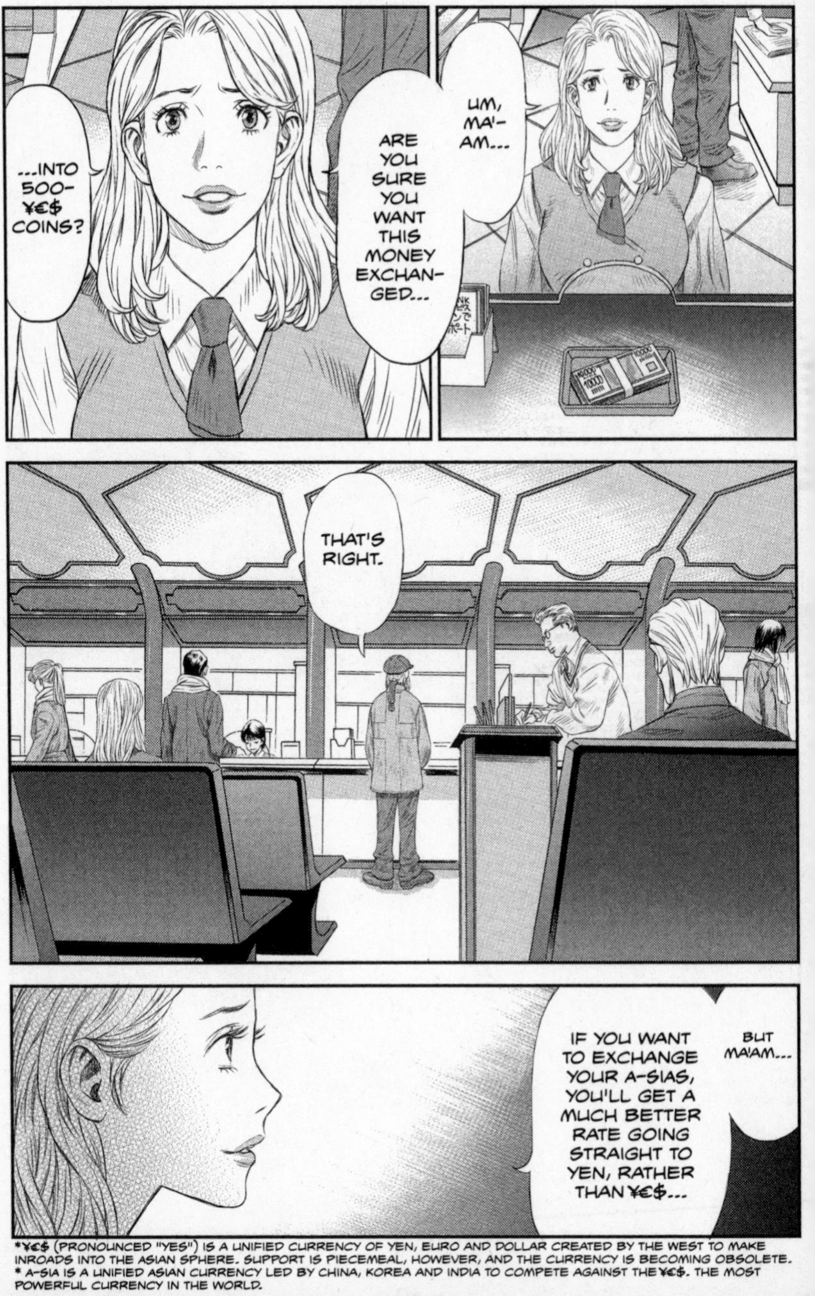
UM, MA'AM...
ARE YOU SURE YOU WANT THIS MONEY EXCHANGED...
...INTO 500-¥€$ COINS?
THAT'S RIGHT.
BUT MA'AM...
IF YOU WANT TO EXCHANGE YOUR A-SIAS, YOU'LL GET A MUCH BETTER RATE GOING STRAIGHT TO YEN, RATHER THAN ¥€$...

*¥€$ (PRONOUNCED "YES") IS A UNIFIED CURRENCY OF YEN, EURO AND DOLLAR CREATED BY THE WEST TO MAKE INROADS INTO THE ASIAN SPHERE. SUPPORT IS PIECEMEAL, HOWEVER, AND THE CURRENCY IS BECOMING OBSOLETE.

* A-SIA IS A UNIFIED ASIAN CURRENCY LED BY CHINA, KOREA AND INDIA TO COMPETE AGAINST THE ¥€$. THE MOST POWERFUL CURRENCY IN THE WORLD.

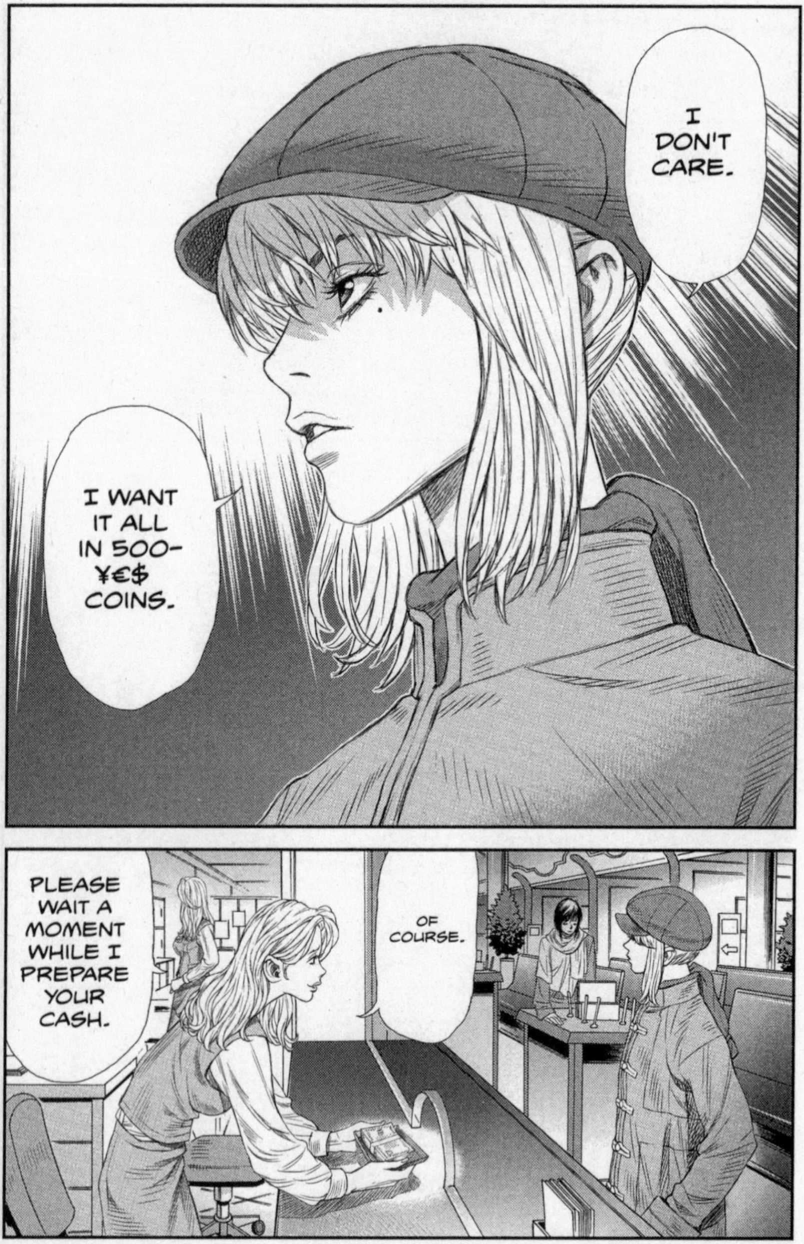
I DON'T CARE.
I WANT IT ALL IN 500-¥€$ COINS.
OF COURSE.
PLEASE WAIT A MOMENT WHILE I PREPARE YOUR CASH.

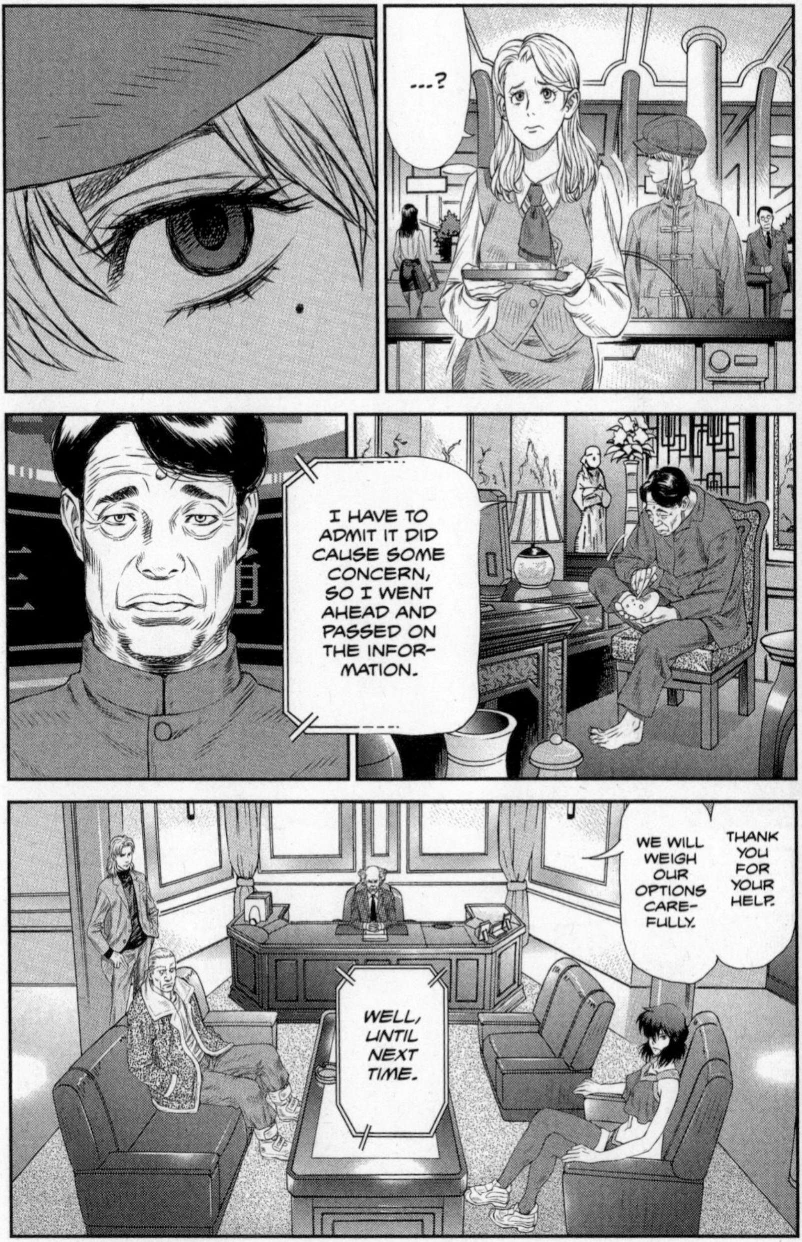
...?
I HAVE TO ADMIT IT DID CAUSE SOME CONCERN, SO I WENT AHEAD AND PASSED ON THE INFORMATION.
THANK YOU FOR YOUR HELP.
WE WILL WEIGH OUR OPTIONS CAREFULLY.
WELL, UNTIL NEXT TIME.

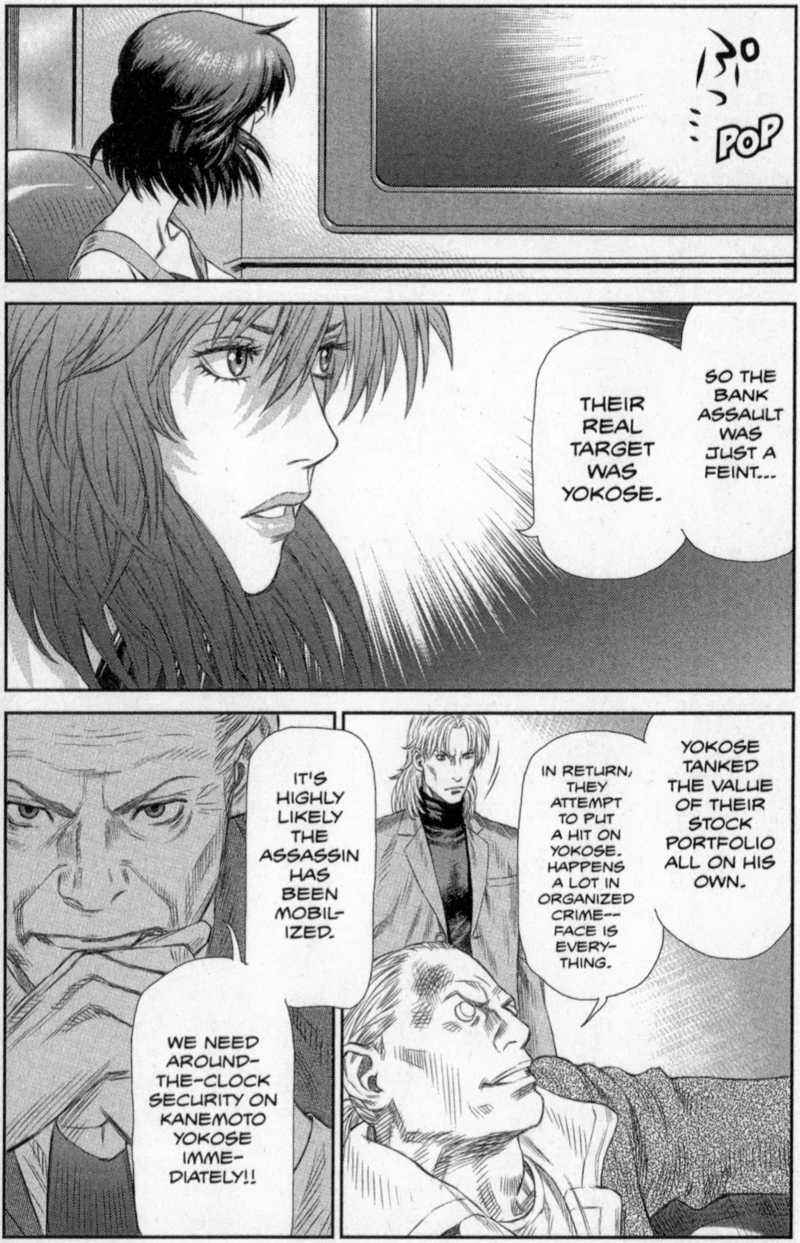
POP
SO THE BANK ASSAULT WAS JUST A FEINT...
THEIR REAL TARGET WAS YOKOSE.
YOKOSE TANKED THE VALUE OF THEIR STOCK PORTFOLIO ALL ON HIS OWN.
IN RETURN, THEY ATTEMPT TO PUT A HIT ON YOKOSE. HAPPENS A LOT IN ORGANIZED CRIME--FACE IS EVERY-THING.
IT'S HIGHLY LIKELY THE ASSASSIN HAS BEEN MOBIL-IZED.
WE NEED AROUND-THE-CLOCK SECURITY ON KANEMOTO YOKOSE IMME-DIATELY!!

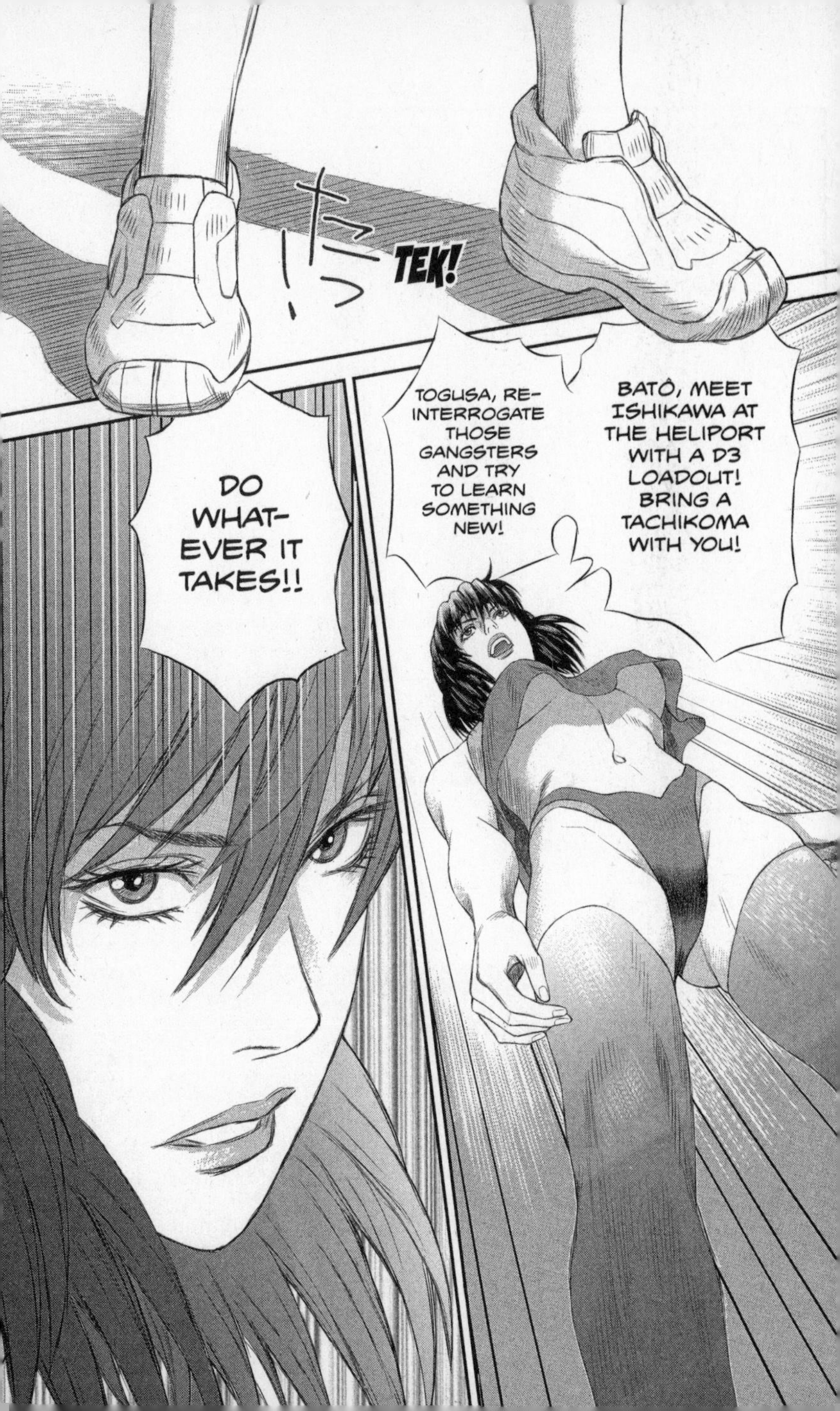
TEK!
BATÔ, MEET ISHIKAWA AT THE HELIPORT WITH A D3 LOADOUT! BRING A TACHIKOMA WITH YOU!
TOGUSA, RE-INTERROGATE THOSE GANGSTERS AND TRY TO LEARN SOMETHING NEW!
DO WHAT-EVER IT TAKES!!

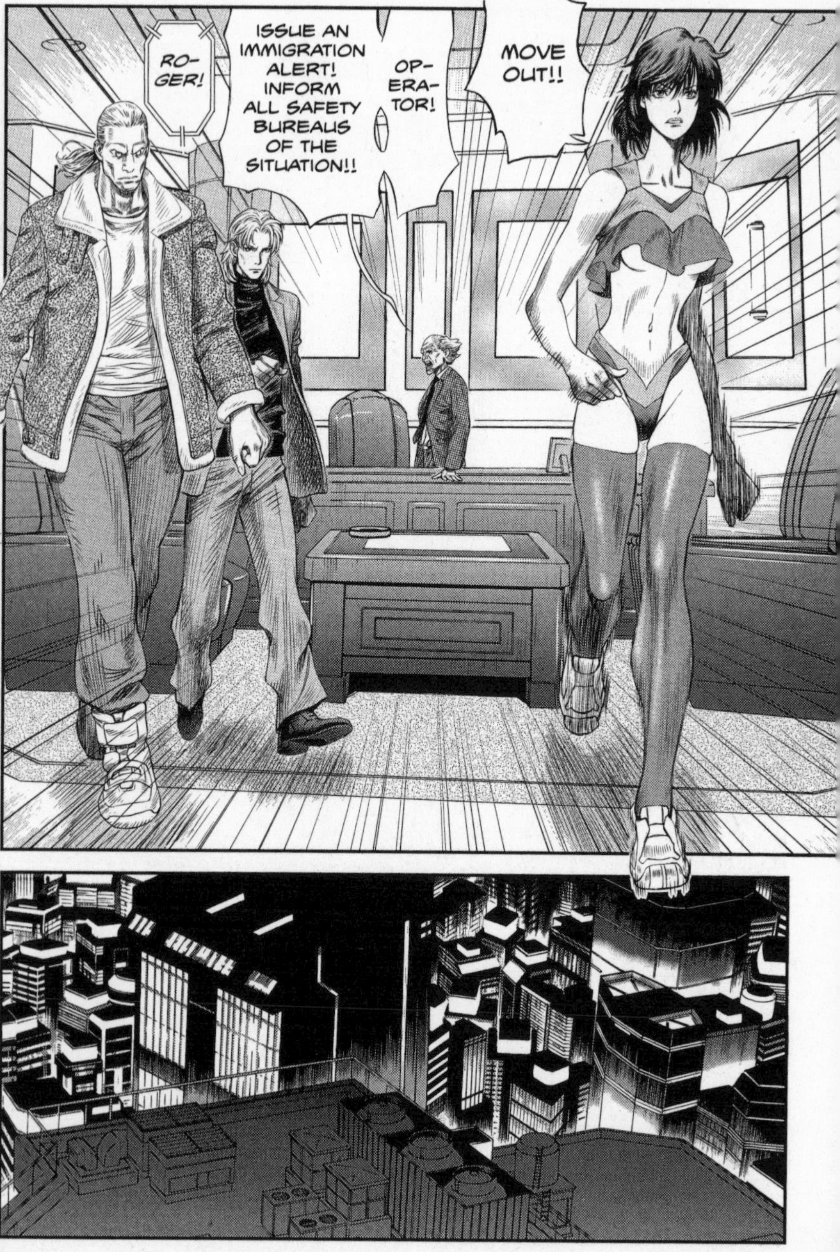
MOVE OUT!!
OP-ERA-TOR!
ISSUE AN IMMIGRATION ALERT! INFORM ALL SAFETY BUREAUS OF THE SITUATION!!
RO-GER!

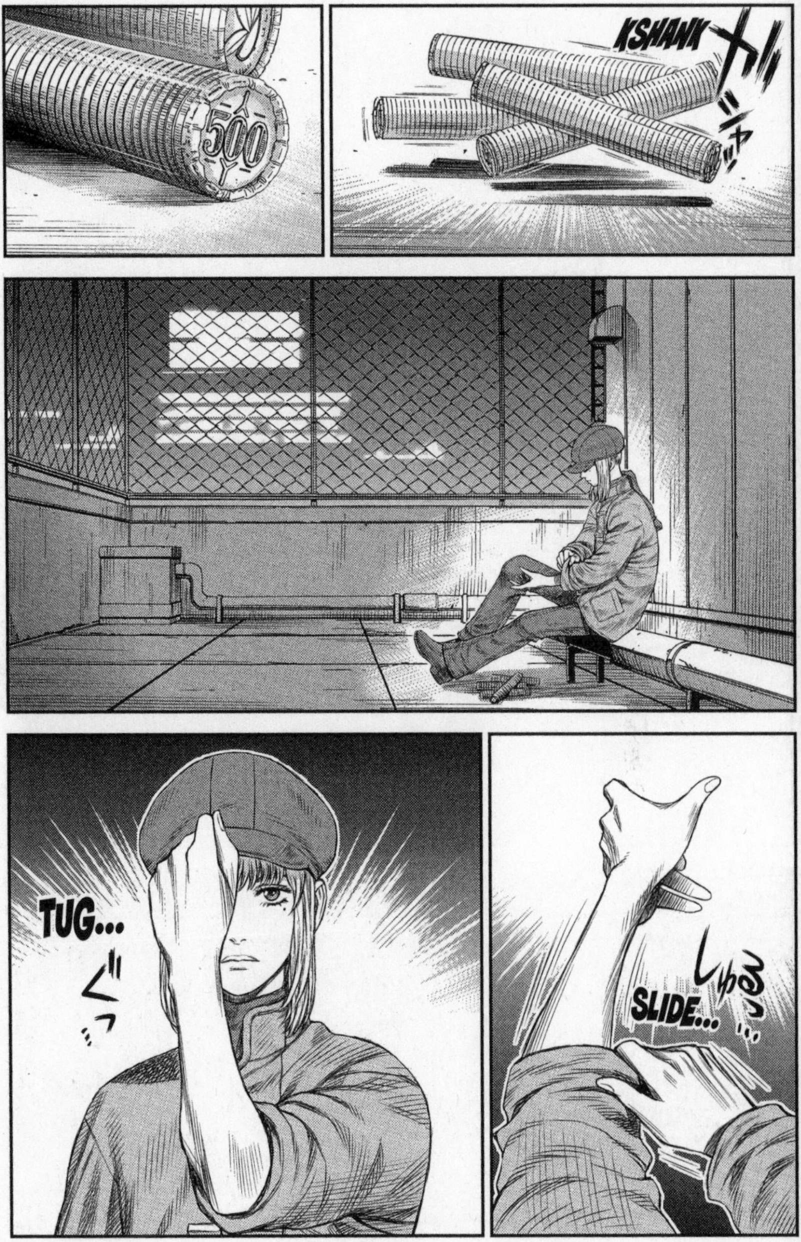
KSHANK
ジャッ
SLIDE...
しゅるっ...
TUG...
ぐっ...

BA-CHUNK!

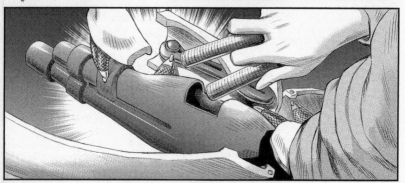

K-CHAK...

click...

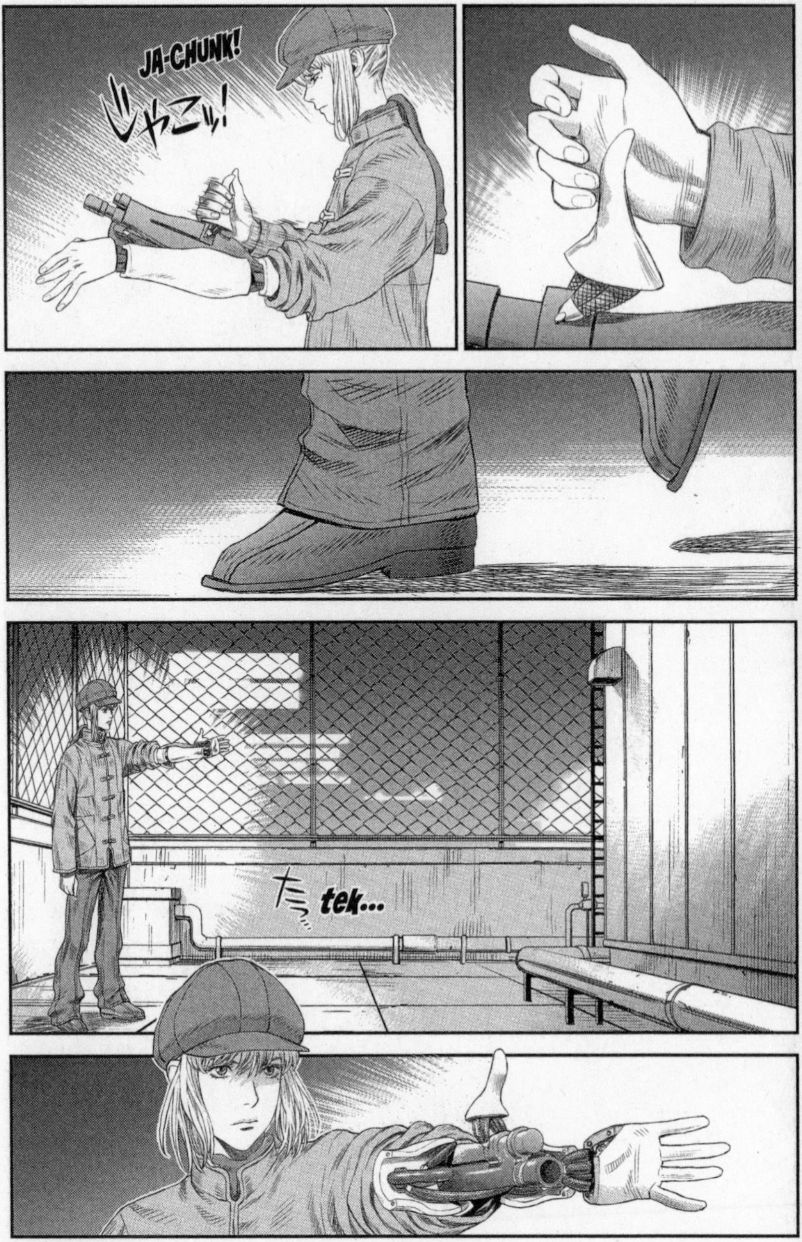
JA-CHUNK!
じゃこッ!
たっ
tek...

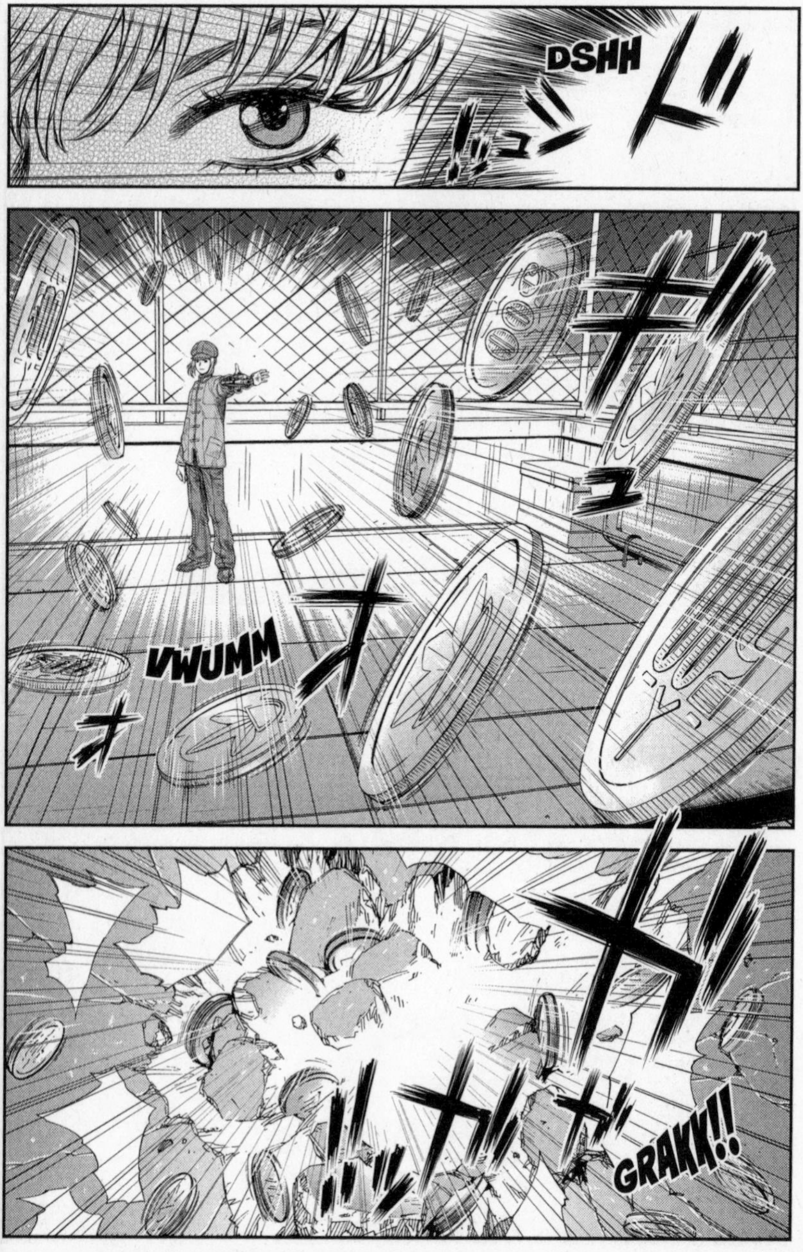
DSHH
VWUMM
GRAKK!!

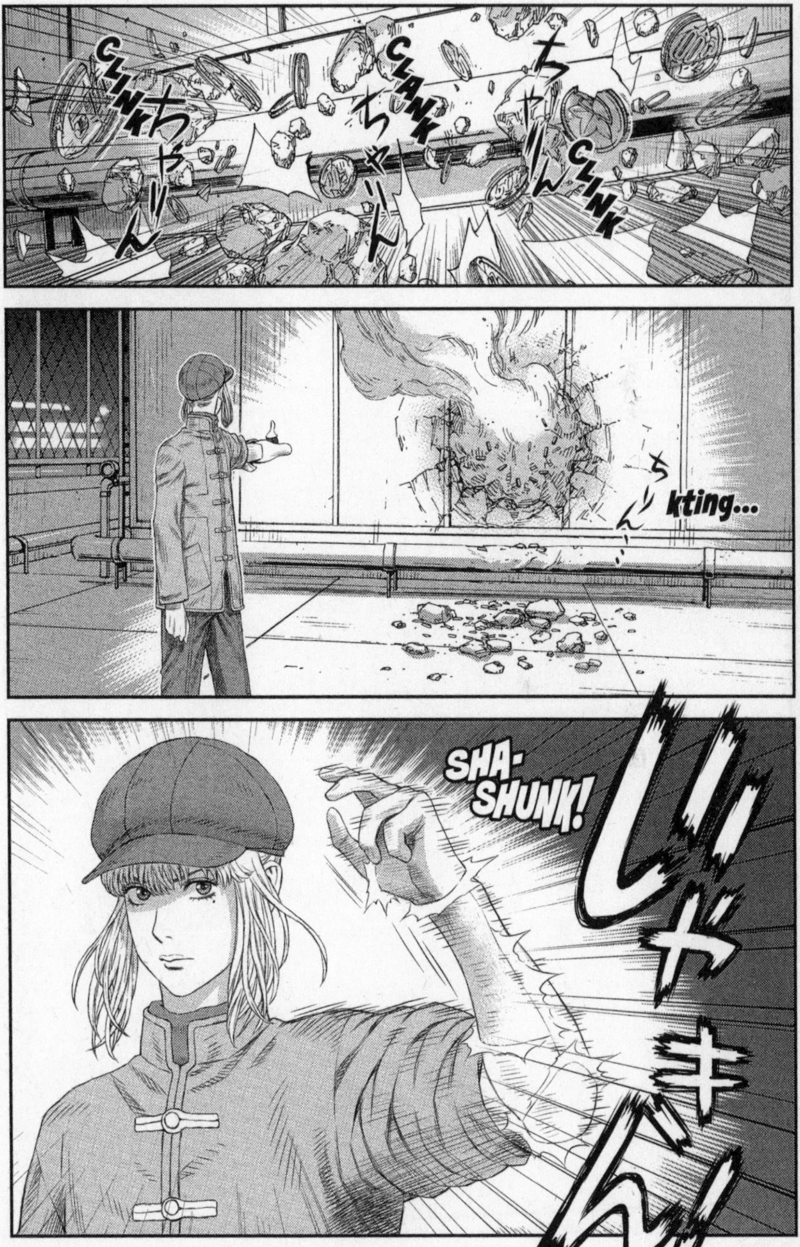
ちゃりーん
CLINK
ちゃりーん
CLANK
ちゃりーん
CLINK
ちりん…
kting...
じゃきん!
SHA-SHUNK!

heh ふっ

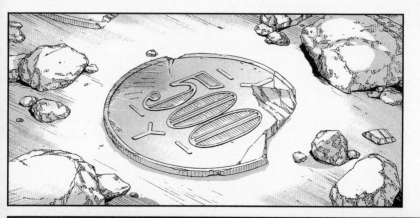

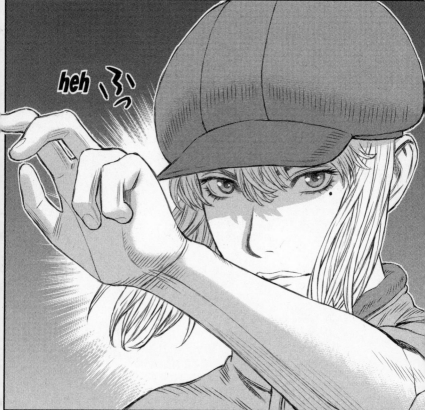

#026: END

#027: Palatial Mansion

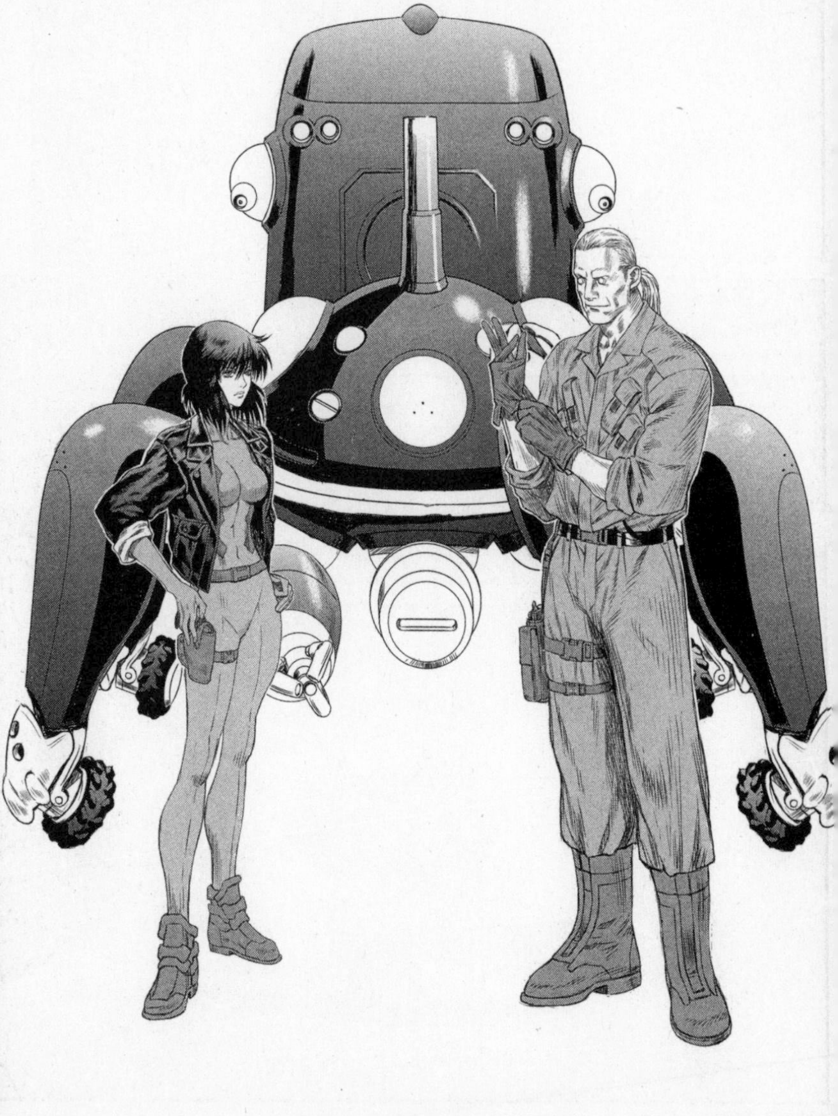

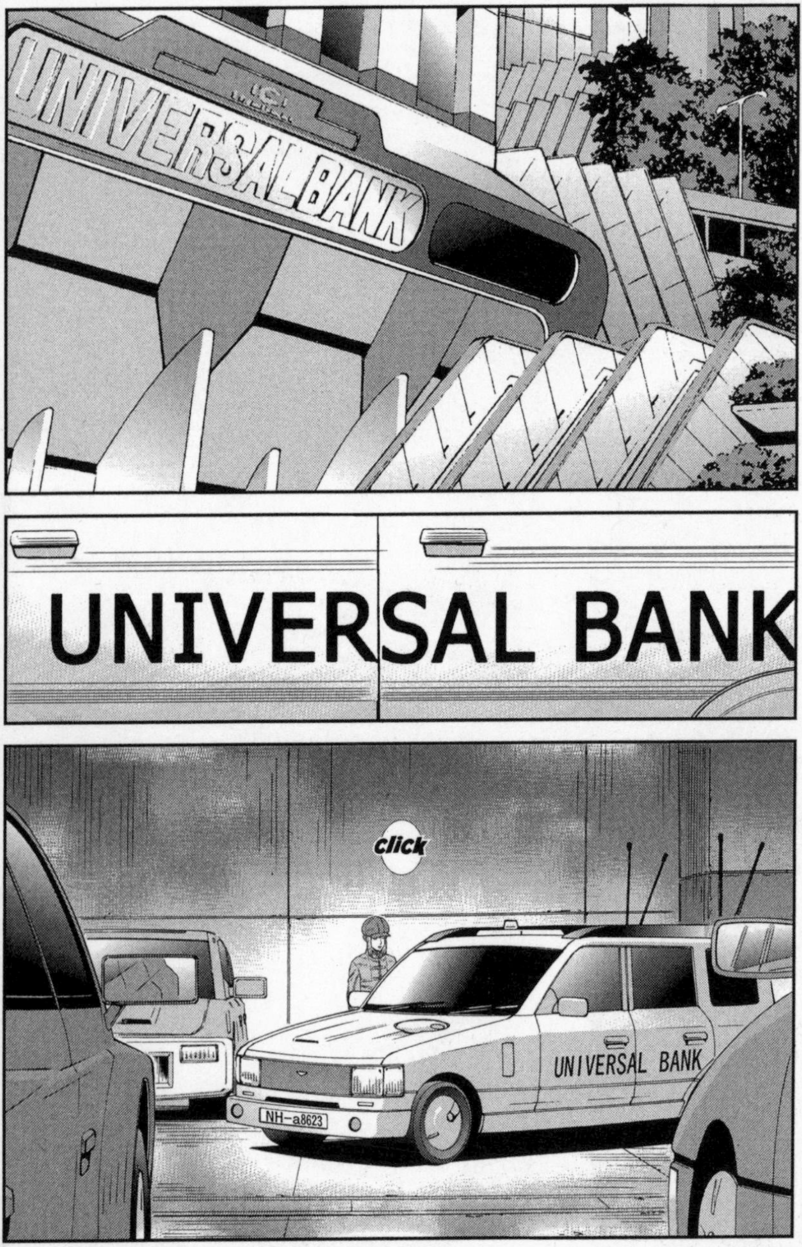
UNIVERSAL BANK
UNIVERSAL BANK
click
UNIVERSAL BANK
NH-a8623

THUMP!

BCHUNK!

PIP   SLIDE...

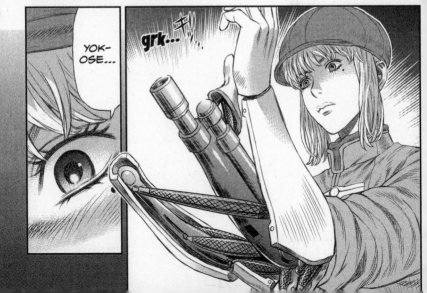

YOK-
OSE...

grk...

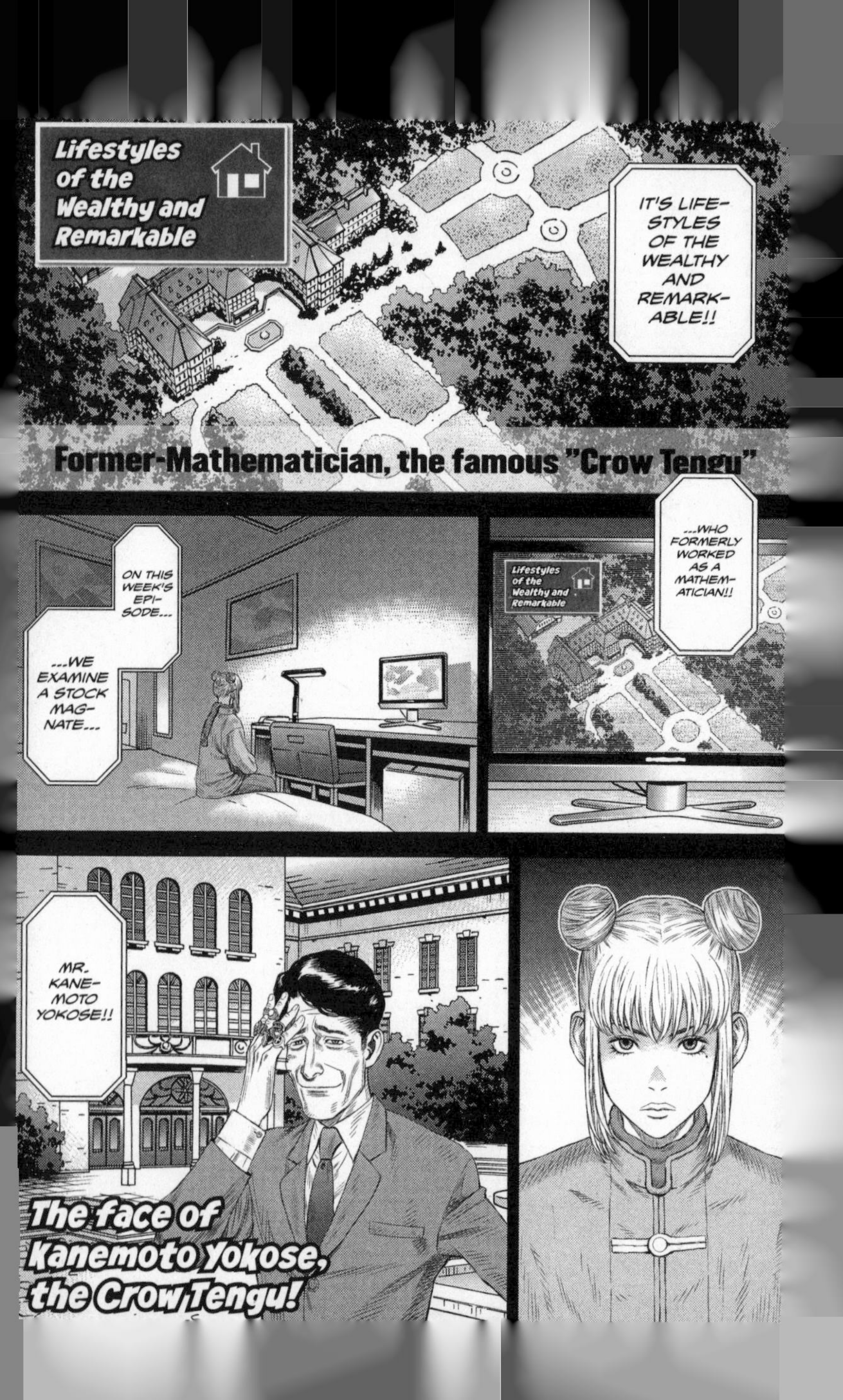
Lifestyles of the Wealthy and Remarkable
IT'S LIFE-STYLES OF THE WEALTHY AND REMARK-ABLE!!
Former-Mathematician, the famous "Crow Tengu"
ON THIS WEEK'S EPI-SODE...
...WE EXAMINE A STOCK MAG-NATE...
Lifestyles of the Wealthy and Remarkable
...WHO FORMERLY WORKED AS A MATHEM-ATICIAN!!
MR. KANE-MOTO YOKOSE!!
The face of Kanemoto Yokose, the Crow Tengu!

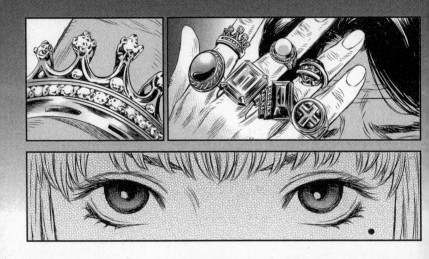

TUG!

GHOST OF CAPITAL-ISM!

YOU WILL DIE FOR YOUR CRIMES!!

SHWIP!

SCREE! SCREE!

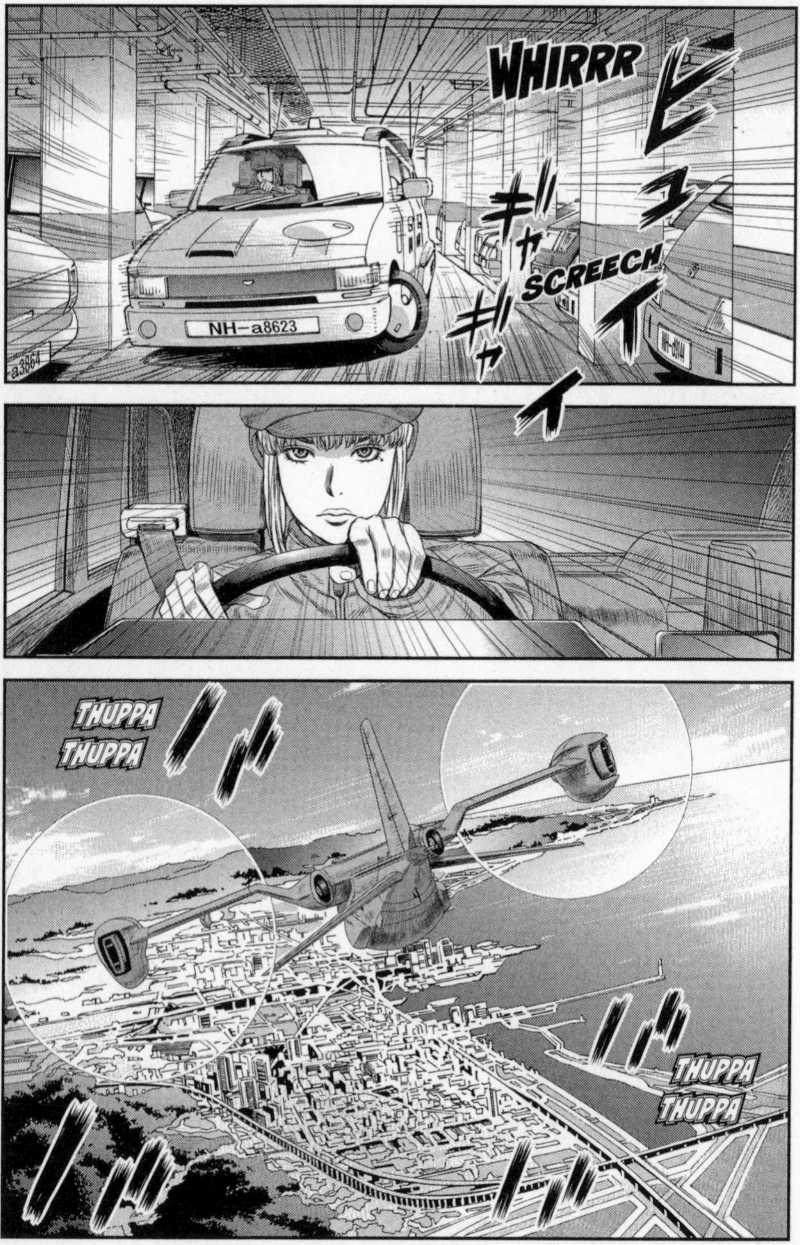
WHIRRR
ヒュイイイ
ギャギャ
SCREECH
NH-a8623
THUPPA THUPPA
THUPPA THUPPA

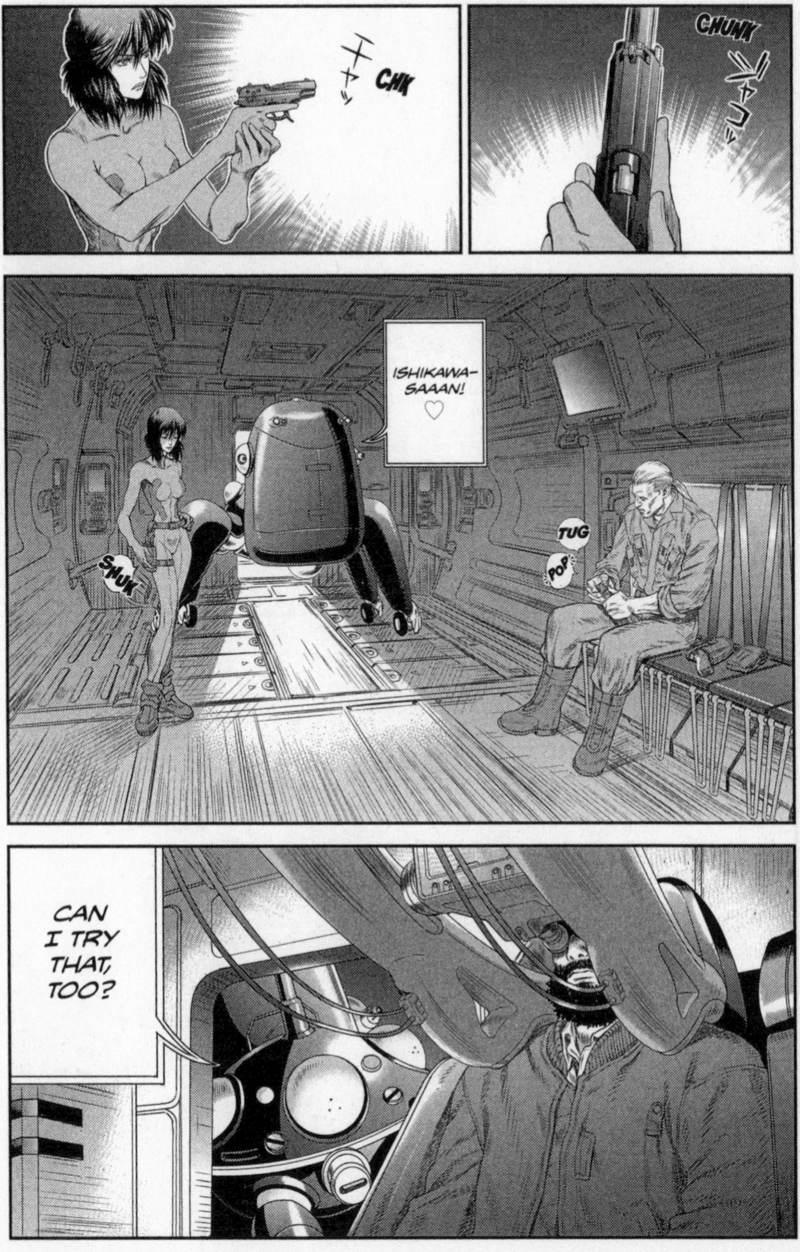
CHUNK
CHK
ISHIKAWA-SAAAN! ♡
TUG
POP
SHUK
CAN I TRY THAT, TOO?

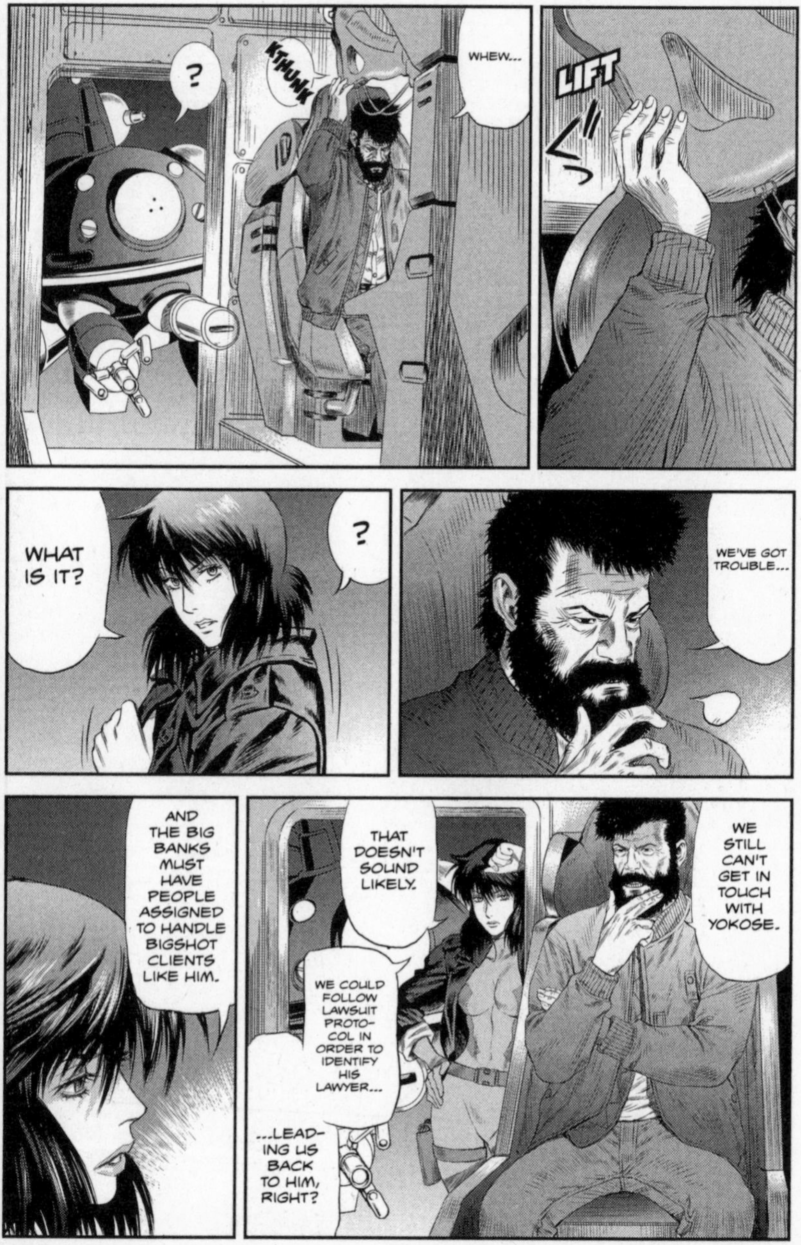
LIFT
WHEW...
KTHUNK
?
WE'VE GOT TROUBLE...
?
WHAT IS IT?
WE STILL CAN'T GET IN TOUCH WITH YOKOSE.
THAT DOESN'T SOUND LIKELY.
WE COULD FOLLOW LAWSUIT PROTOCOL IN ORDER TO IDENTIFY HIS LAWYER...
...LEADING US BACK TO HIM, RIGHT?
AND THE BIG BANKS MUST HAVE PEOPLE ASSIGNED TO HANDLE BIGSHOT CLIENTS LIKE HIM.

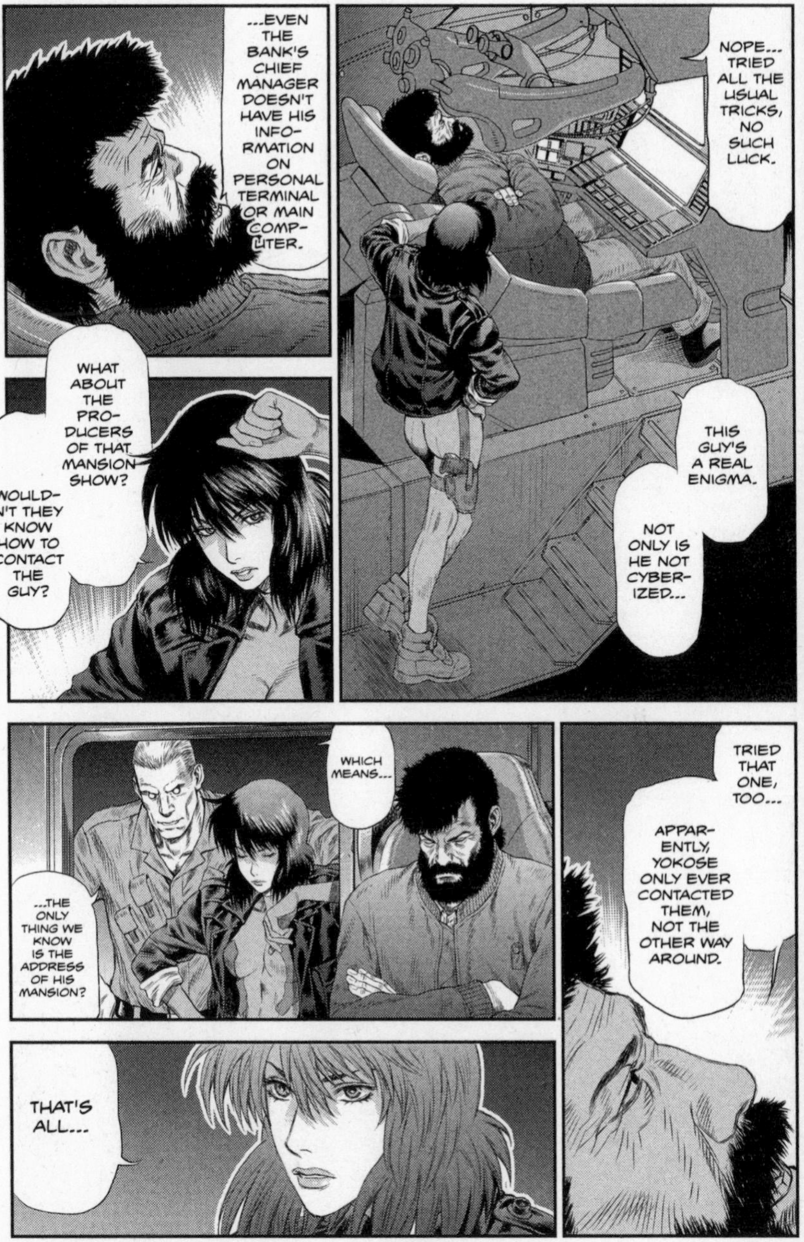
NOPE... TRIED ALL THE USUAL TRICKS, NO SUCH LUCK.
THIS GUY'S A REAL ENIGMA.
NOT ONLY IS HE NOT CYBERIZED...
...EVEN THE BANK'S CHIEF MANAGER DOESN'T HAVE HIS INFORMATION ON PERSONAL TERMINAL OR MAIN COMPUTER.
WHAT ABOUT THE PRODUCERS OF THAT MANSION SHOW?
WOULDN'T THEY KNOW HOW TO CONTACT THE GUY?
TRIED THAT ONE, TOO...
APPARENTLY, YOKOSE ONLY EVER CONTACTED THEM, NOT THE OTHER WAY AROUND.
WHICH MEANS...
...THE ONLY THING WE KNOW IS THE ADDRESS OF HIS MANSION?
THAT'S ALL...

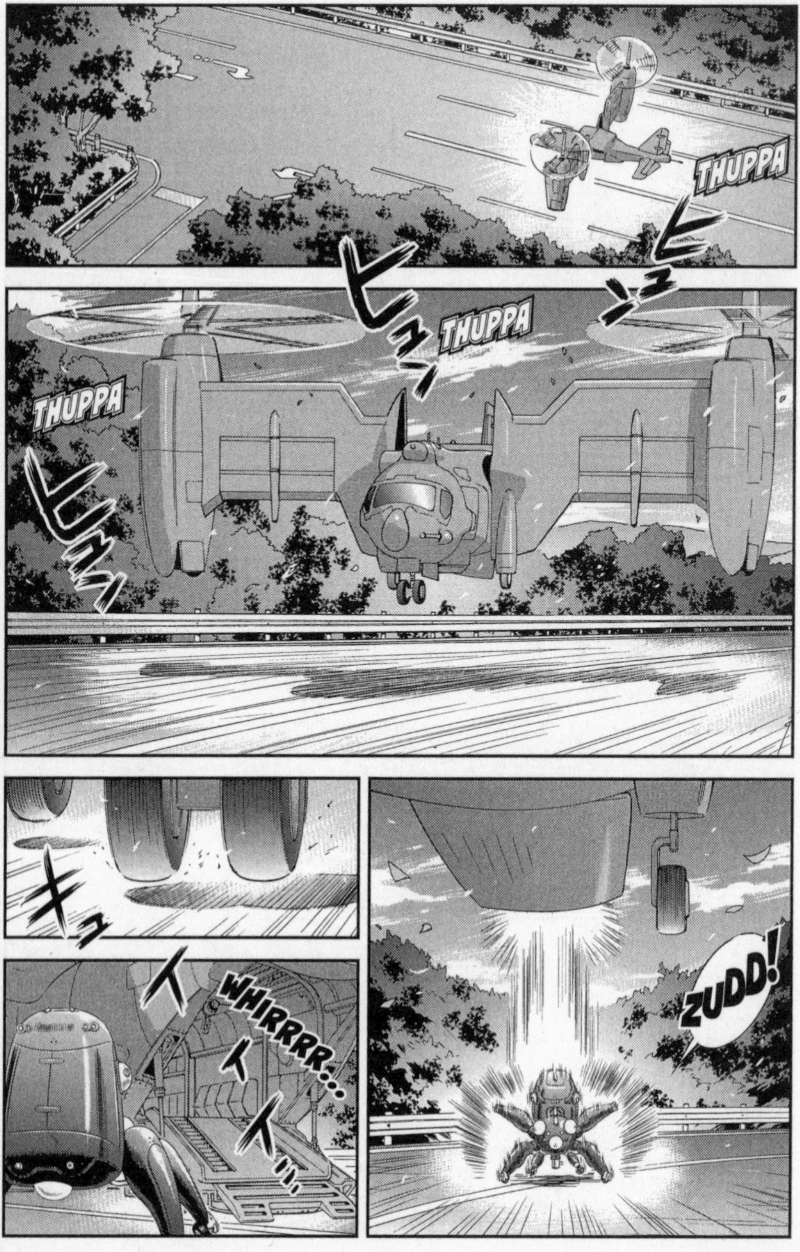
THUPPA
ヒュン
ヒュン
THUPPA
THUPPA
ヒュン
ZUDD!
キュイイイ
WHIRRRR...

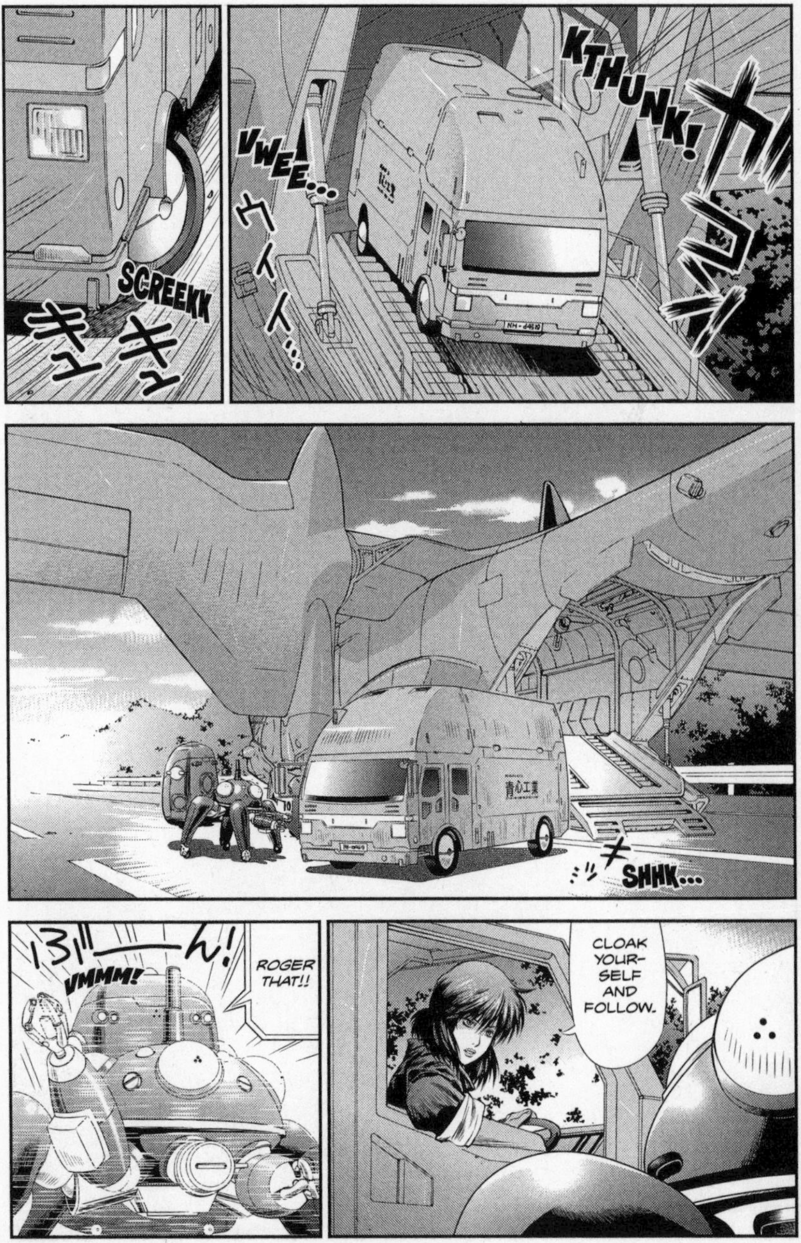
KTHUNK!
VWEE...
SCREEKK
キュキュ
SHHK...
CLOAK YOURSELF AND FOLLOW.
ROGER THAT!!
VMMM!

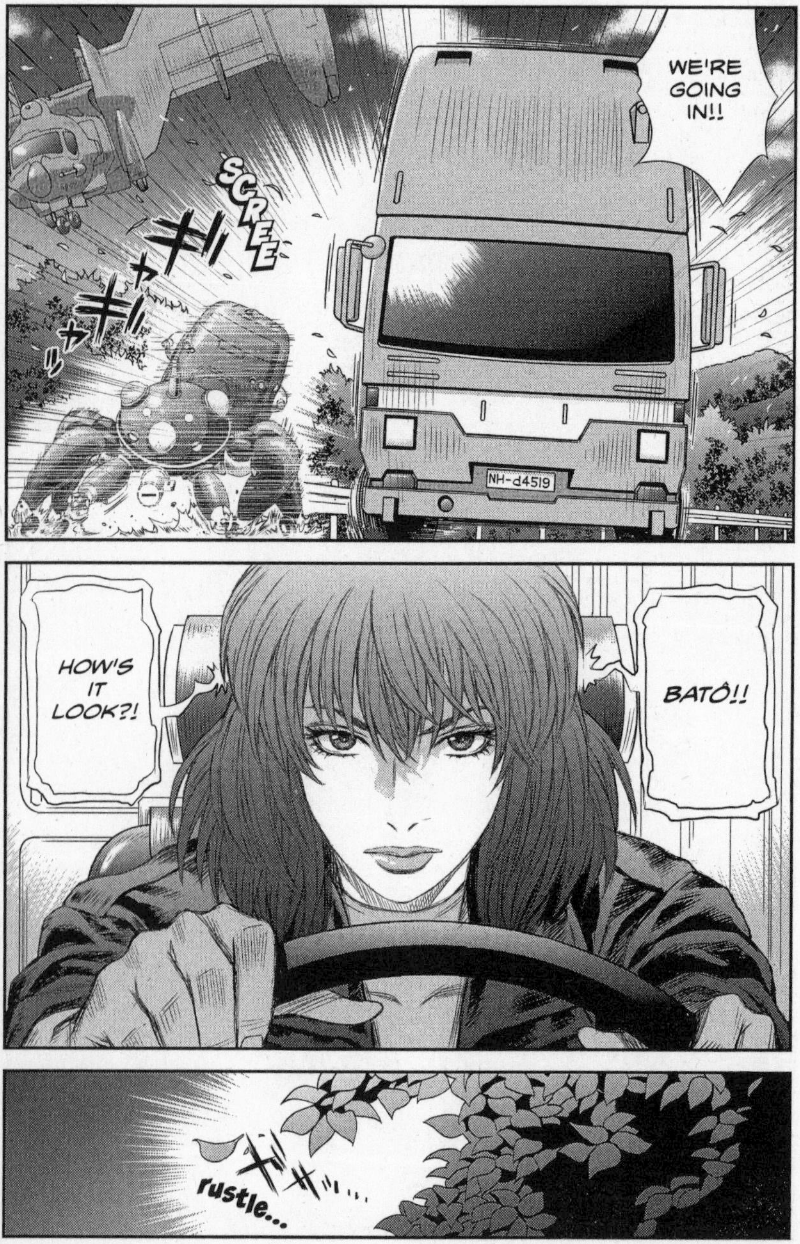
WE'RE GOING IN!!
SCREE
BATÔ!!
HOW'S IT LOOK?!
rustle...

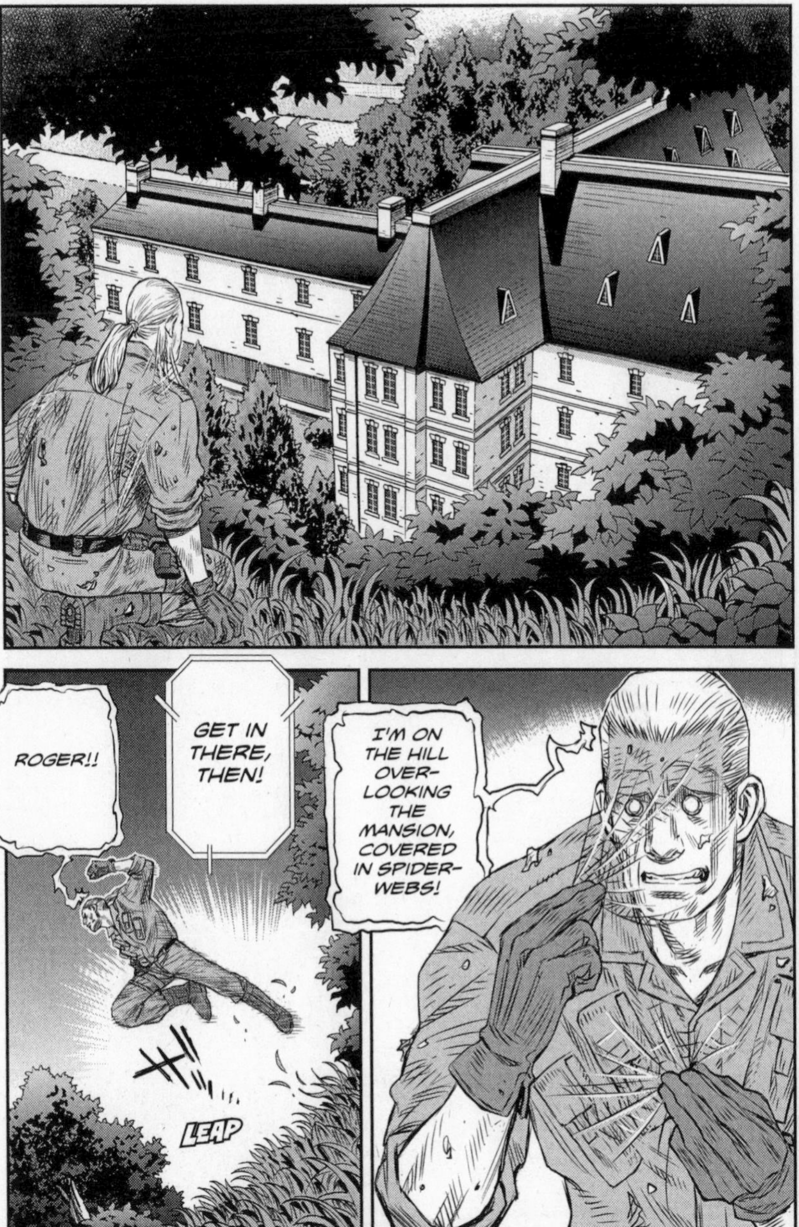
I'M ON THE HILL OVER-LOOKING THE MANSION, COVERED IN SPIDER-WEBS!
GET IN THERE, THEN!
ROGER!!
LEAP

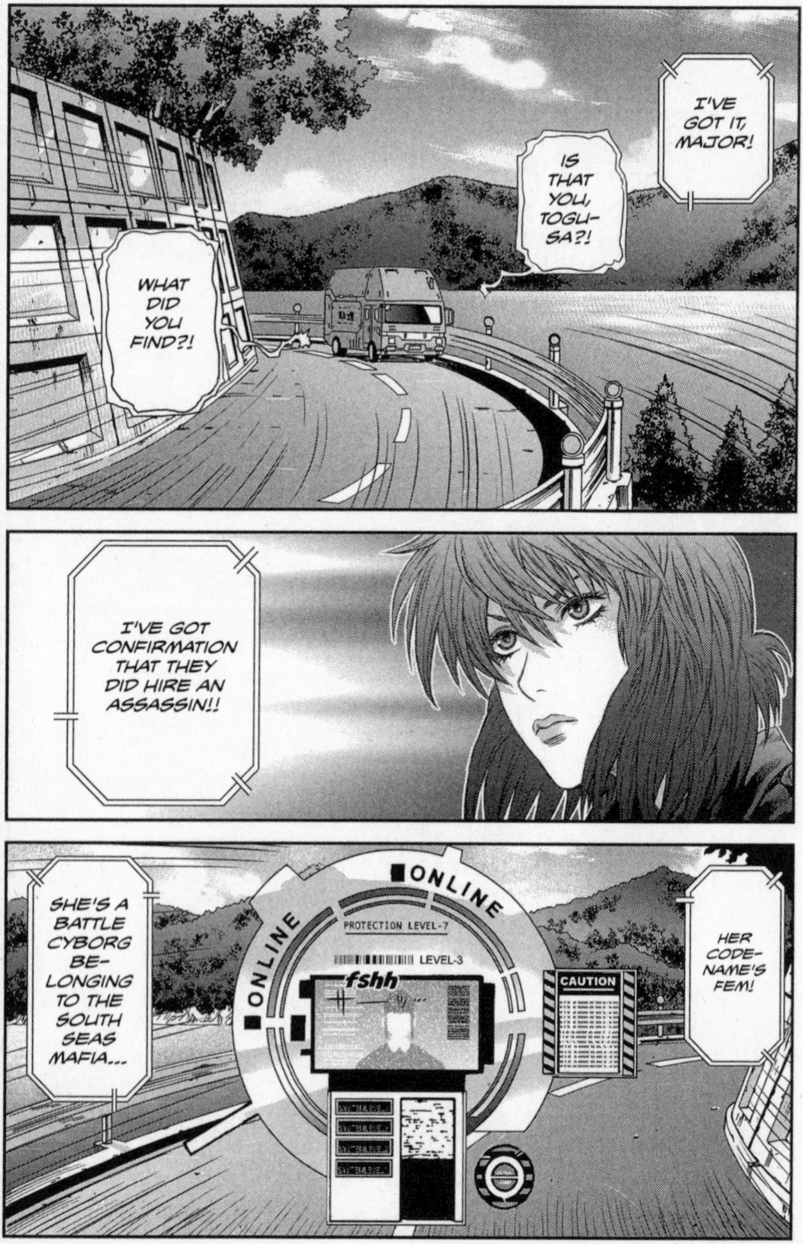
I'VE GOT IT, MAJOR!
IS THAT YOU, TOGU-SA?!
WHAT DID YOU FIND?!
I'VE GOT CONFIRMATION THAT THEY DID HIRE AN ASSASSIN!!
HER CODE-NAME'S FEM!
ONLINE
ONLINE
PROTECTION LEVEL-7
LEVEL-3
fshh
CAUTION
SHE'S A BATTLE CYBORG BE-LONGING TO THE SOUTH SEAS MAFIA...

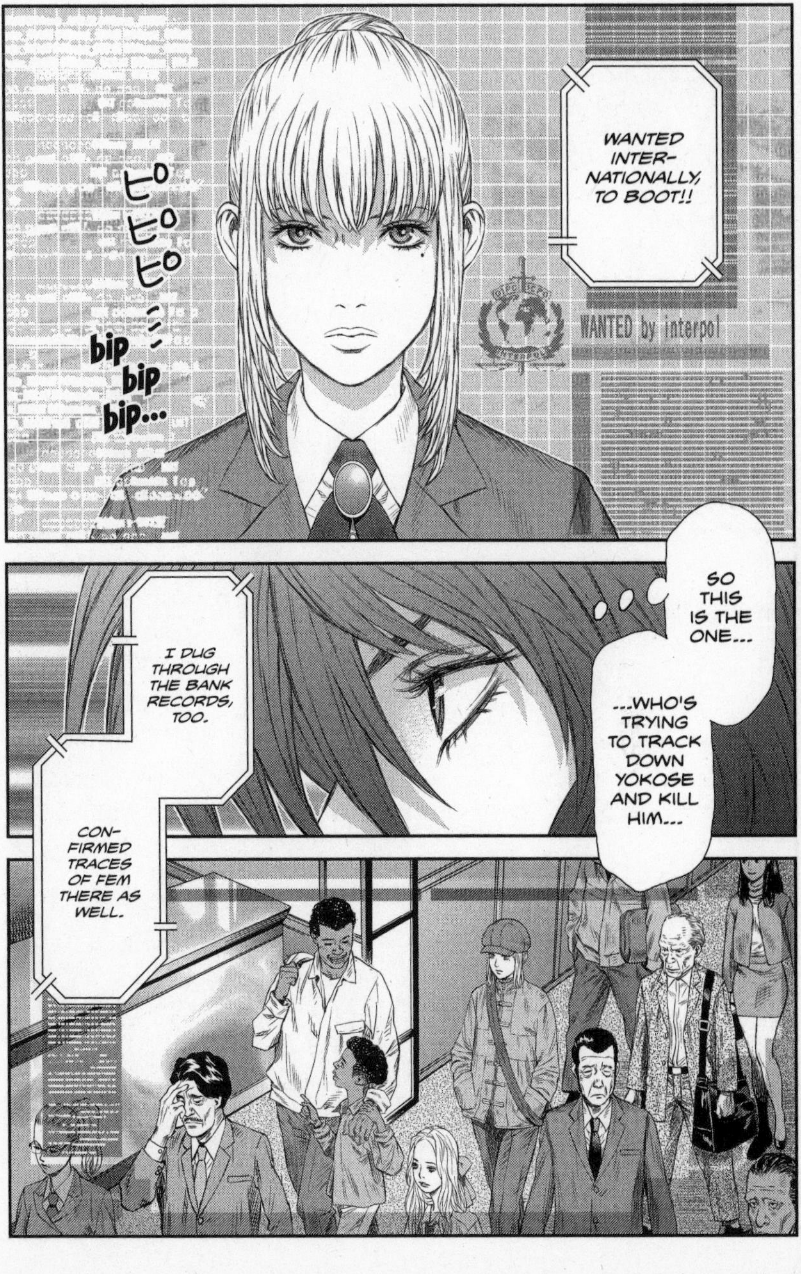
WANTED INTER-NATIONALLY, TO BOOT!!
WANTED by interpol
ピピピ……
bip bip bip...
SO THIS IS THE ONE...
...WHO'S TRYING TO TRACK DOWN YOKOSE AND KILL HIM...
I DUG THROUGH THE BANK RECORDS, TOO.
CON-FIRMED TRACES OF FEM THERE AS WELL.

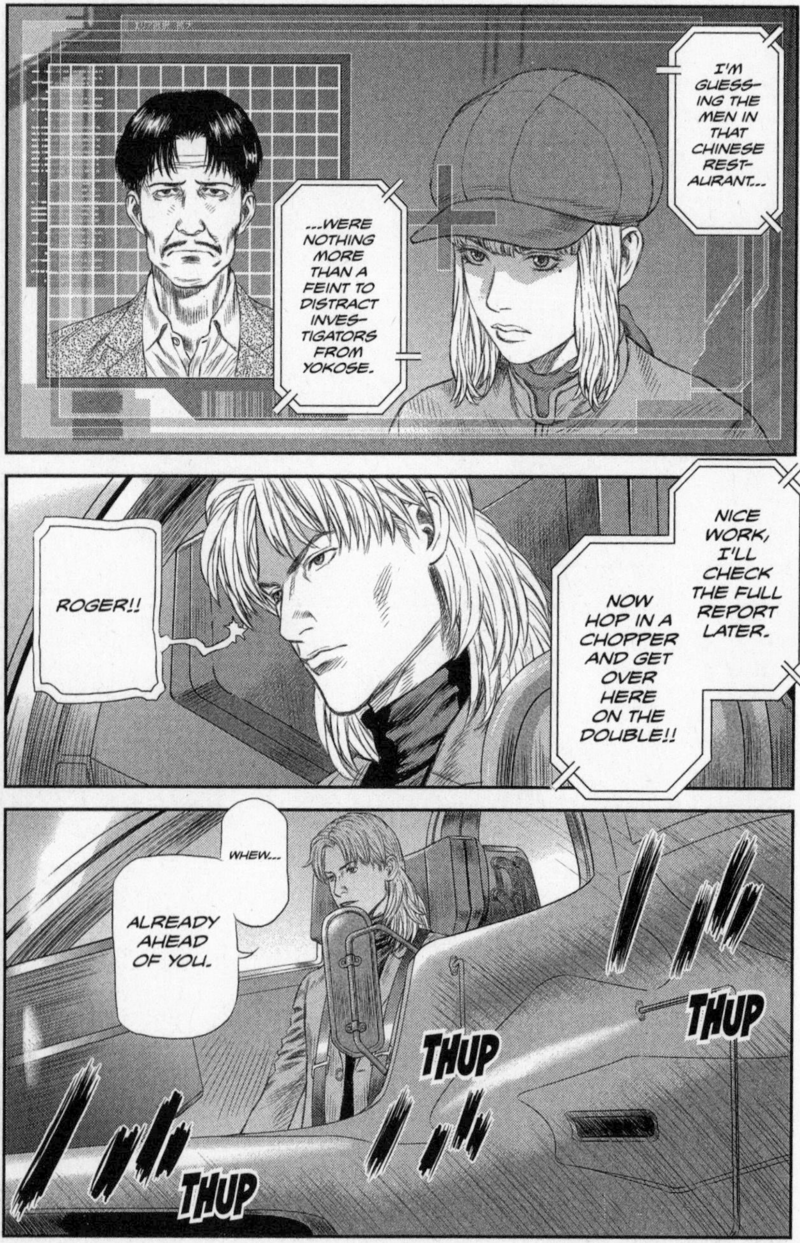
I'M GUESSING THE MEN IN THAT CHINESE RESTAURANT...
...WERE NOTHING MORE THAN A FEINT TO DISTRACT INVESTIGATORS FROM YOKOSE.
NICE WORK, I'LL CHECK THE FULL REPORT LATER.
NOW HOP IN A CHOPPER AND GET OVER HERE ON THE DOUBLE!!
ROGER!!
WHEW...
ALREADY AHEAD OF YOU.
THUP
THUP
THUP

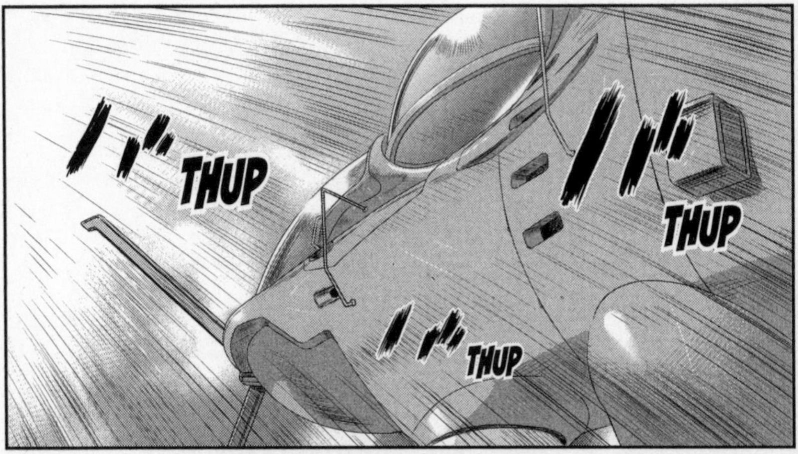
THUP
THUP
THUP

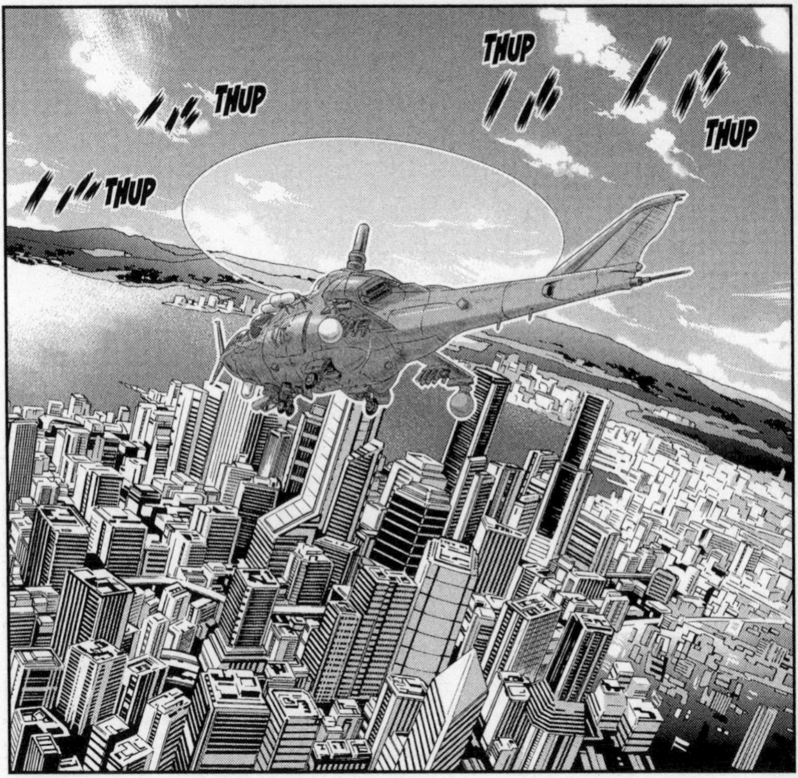
THUP
THUP
THUP
THUP

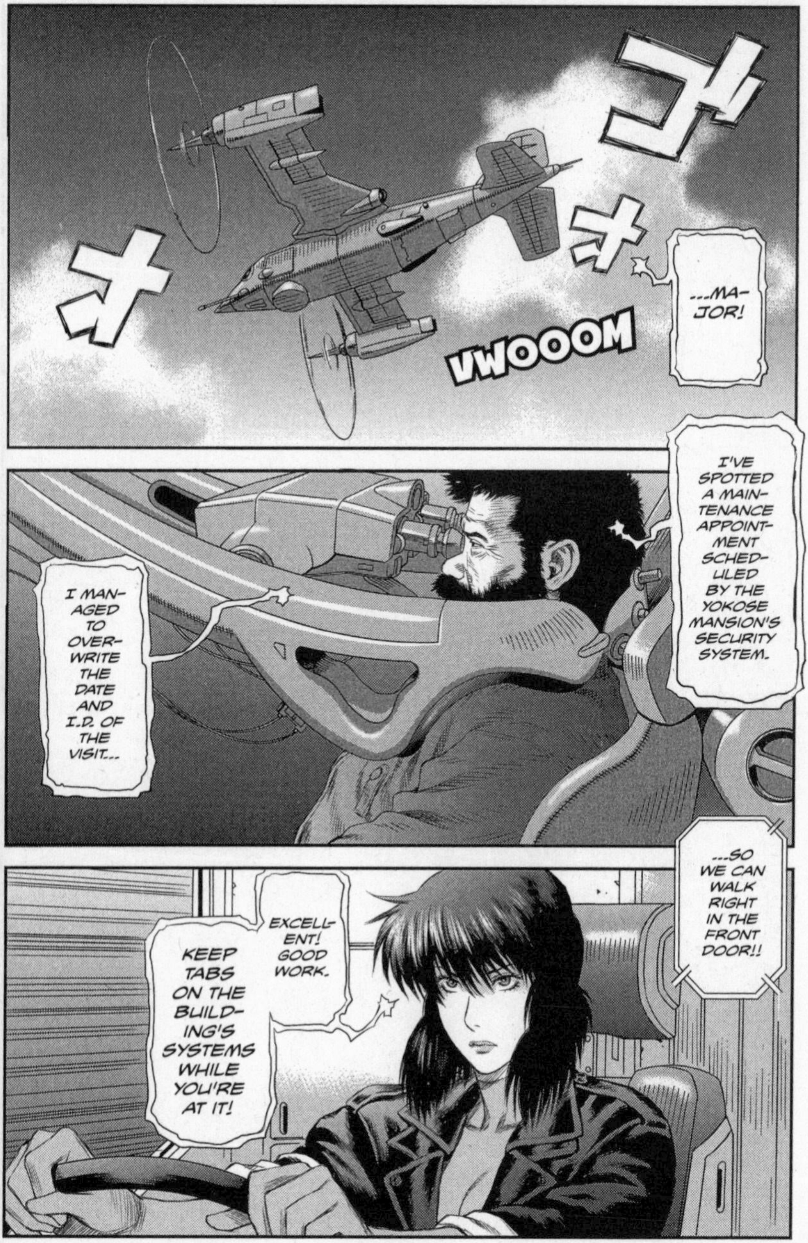
...MA-JOR!
VWOOOM
I'VE SPOTTED A MAINTENANCE APPOINTMENT SCHEDULED BY THE YOKOSE MANSION'S SECURITY SYSTEM.
I MANAGED TO OVERWRITE THE DATE AND I.D. OF THE VISIT...
...SO WE CAN WALK RIGHT IN THE FRONT DOOR!!
EXCELLENT! GOOD WORK.
KEEP TABS ON THE BUILDING'S SYSTEMS WHILE YOU'RE AT IT!

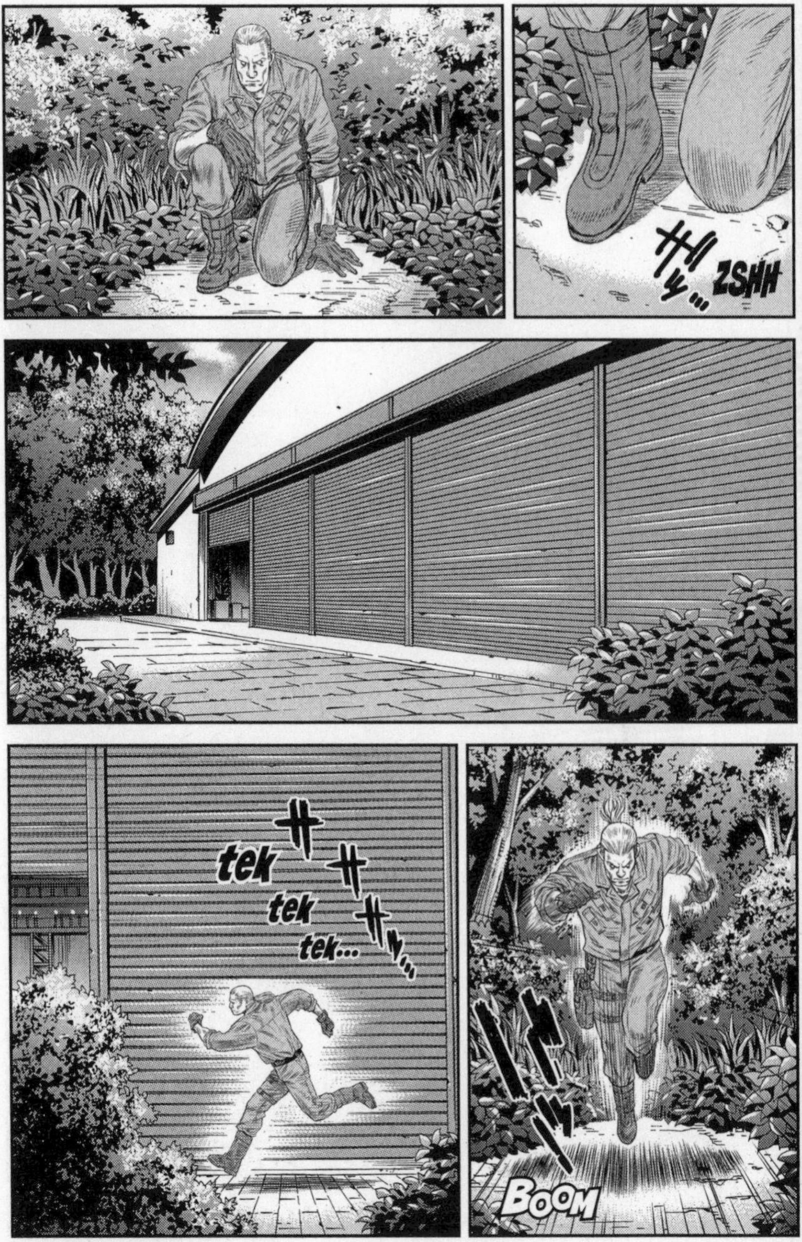
ZSHH
tek
tek
tek...
BOOM

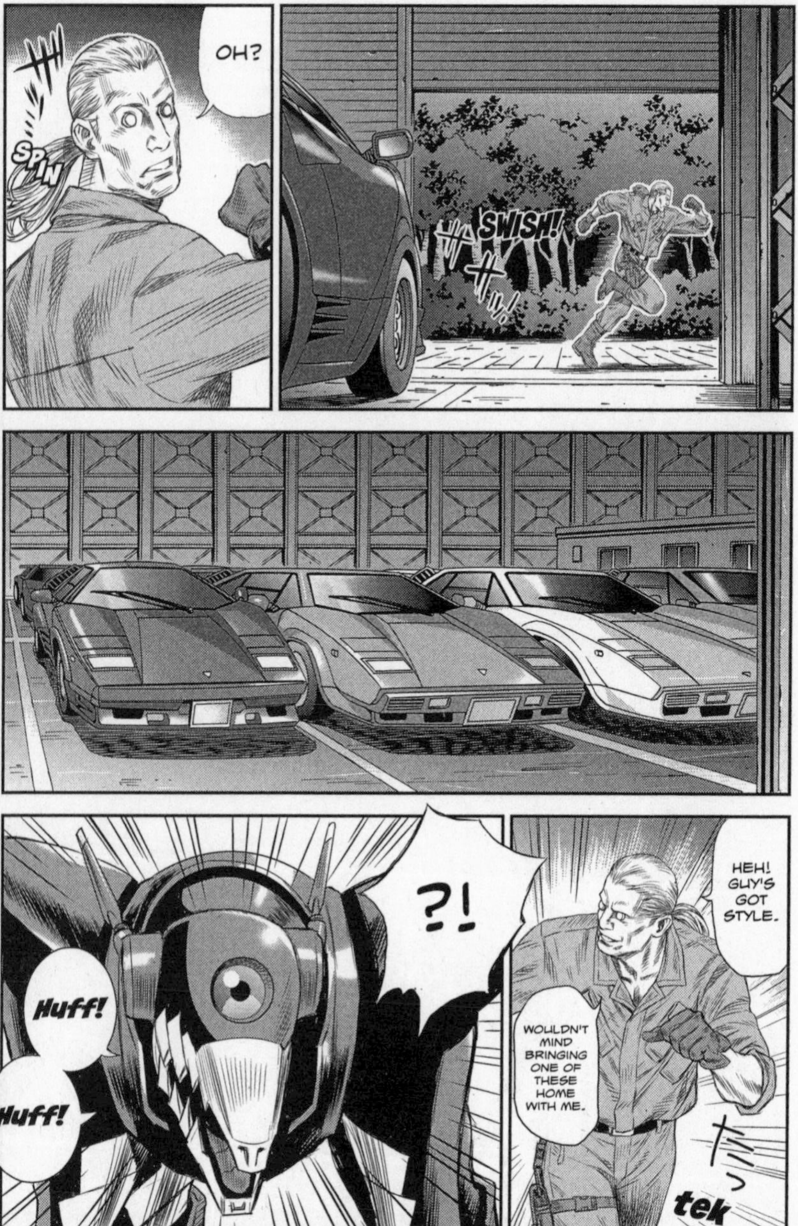
SWISH!
SPIN
OH?
HEH! GUY'S GOT STYLE.
WOULDN'T MIND BRINGING ONE OF THESE HOME WITH ME.
tek
?!
Huff!
Huff!

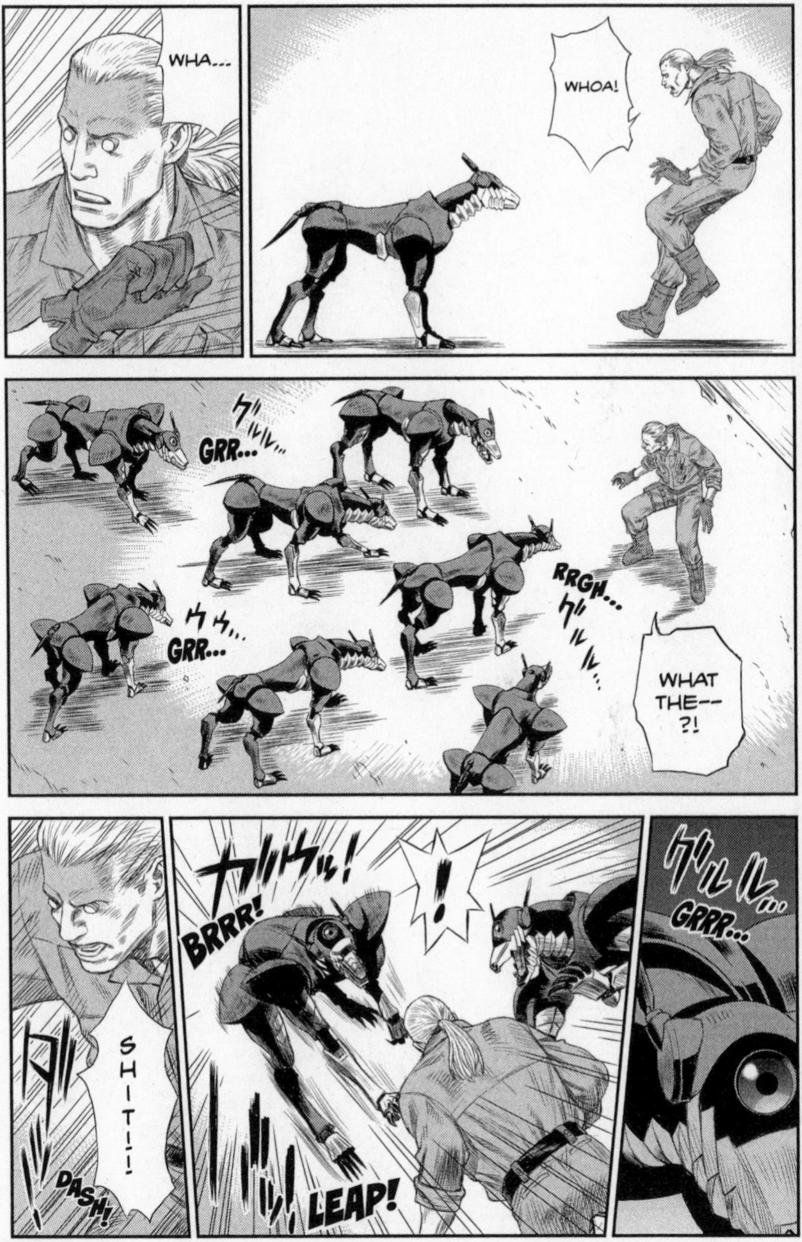
WHOA!
WHA...
RRGH...
WHAT THE--?!
GRR...
GRR...
GRRR...
!
BRRR!
LEAP!
SHIT--!
DASH!

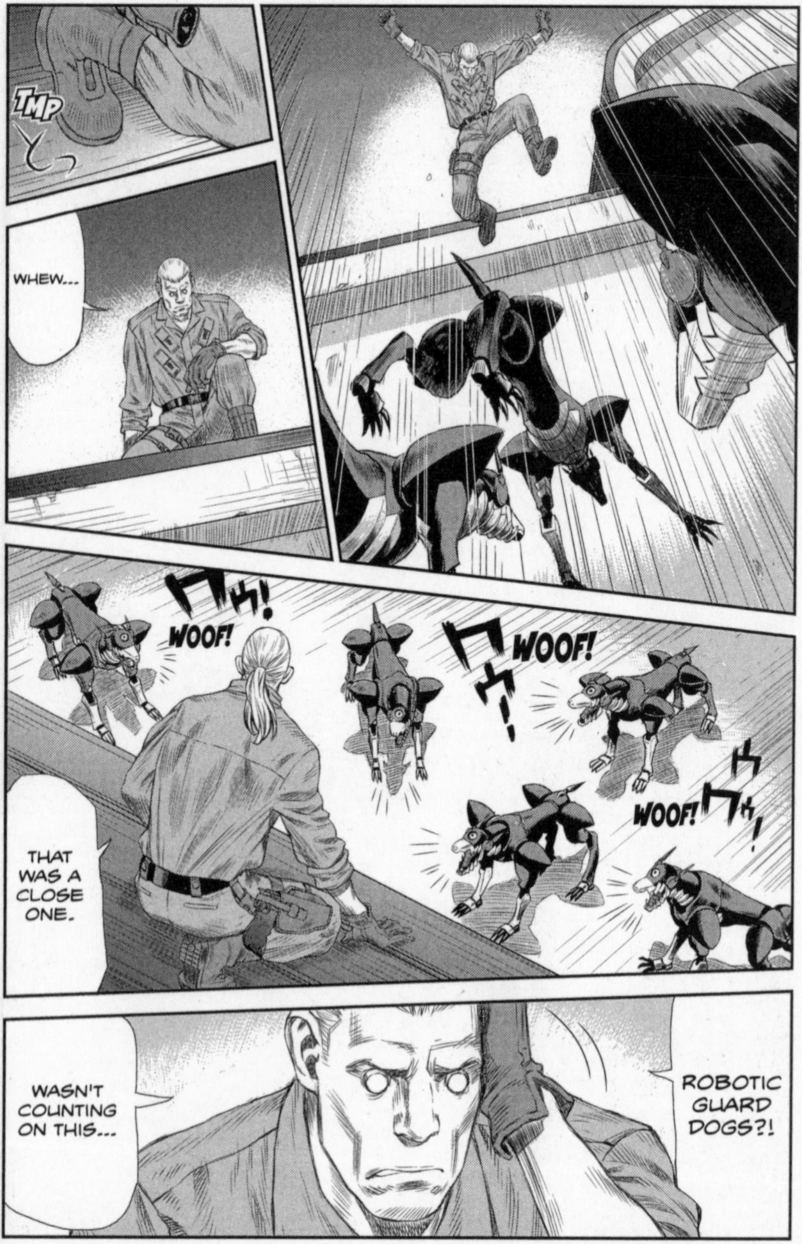
TMP
WHEW...
WOOF!
WOOF!
WOOF!
THAT WAS A CLOSE ONE.
ROBOTIC GUARD DOGS?!
WASN'T COUNTING ON THIS...

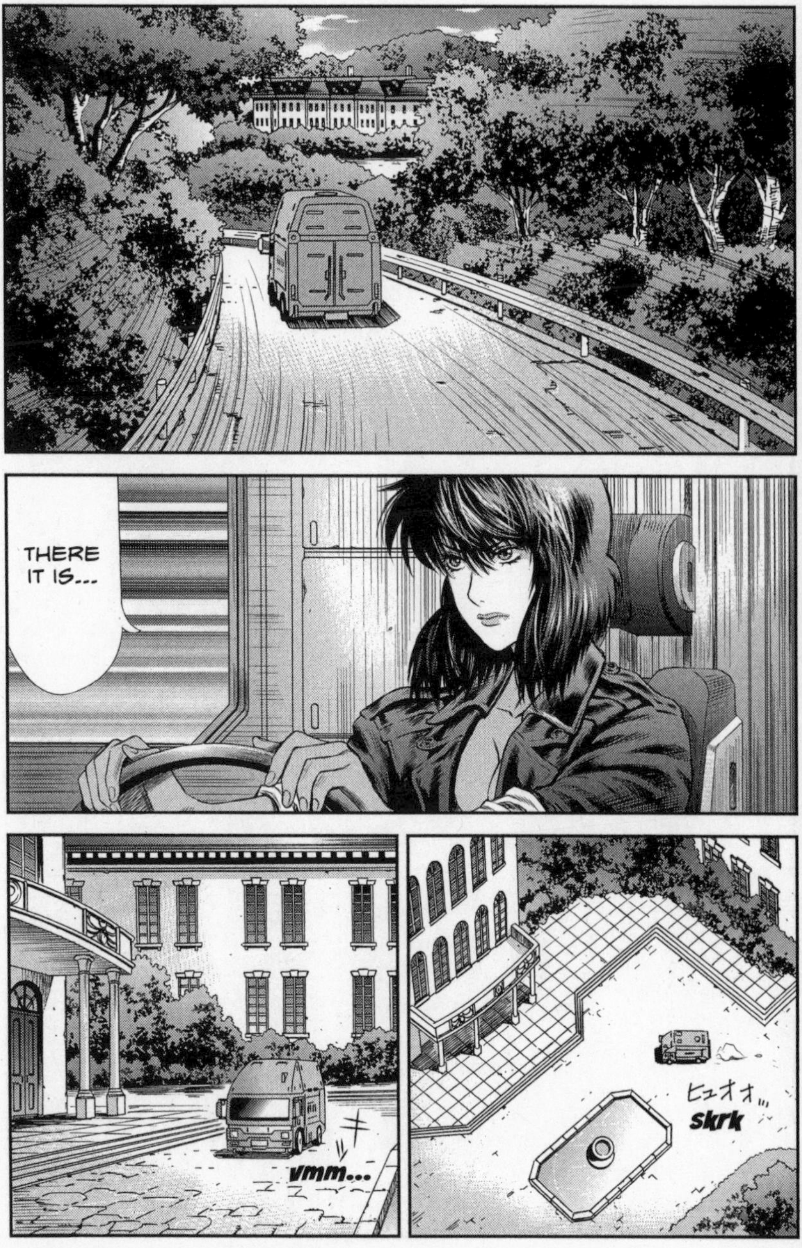
THERE IT IS...
skrk
vmm...

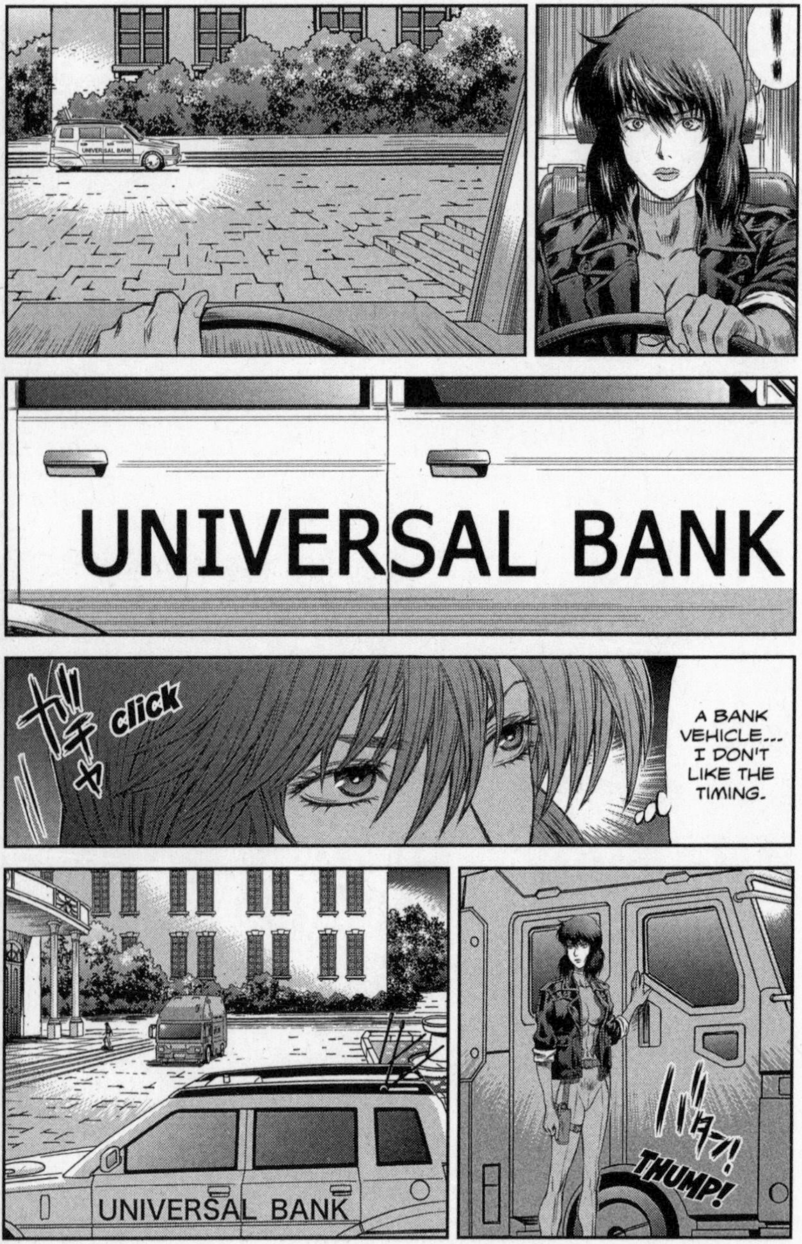
!!
UNIVERSAL BANK
A BANK VEHICLE... I DON'T LIKE THE TIMING.
click
THUMP!
UNIVERSAL BANK

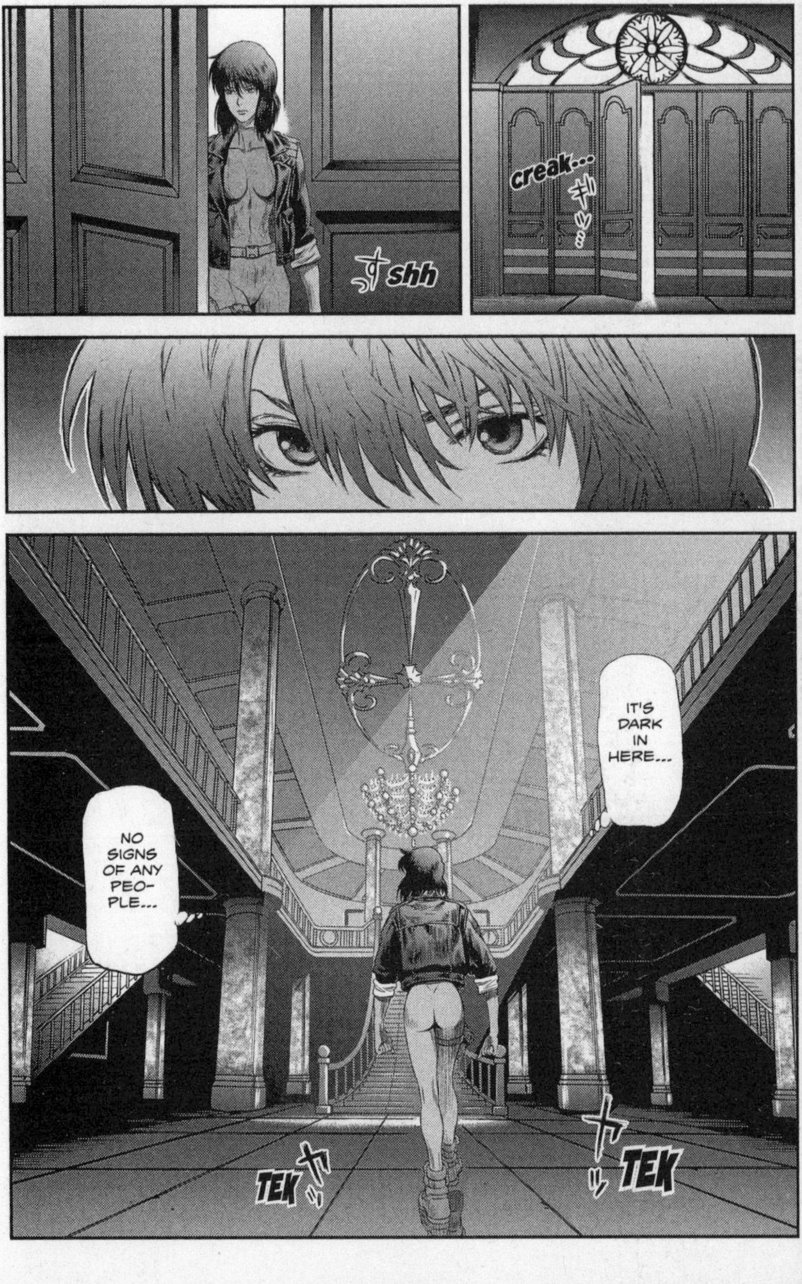
creak...
shh
IT'S DARK IN HERE...
NO SIGNS OF ANY PEO-PLE...
TEK
TEK

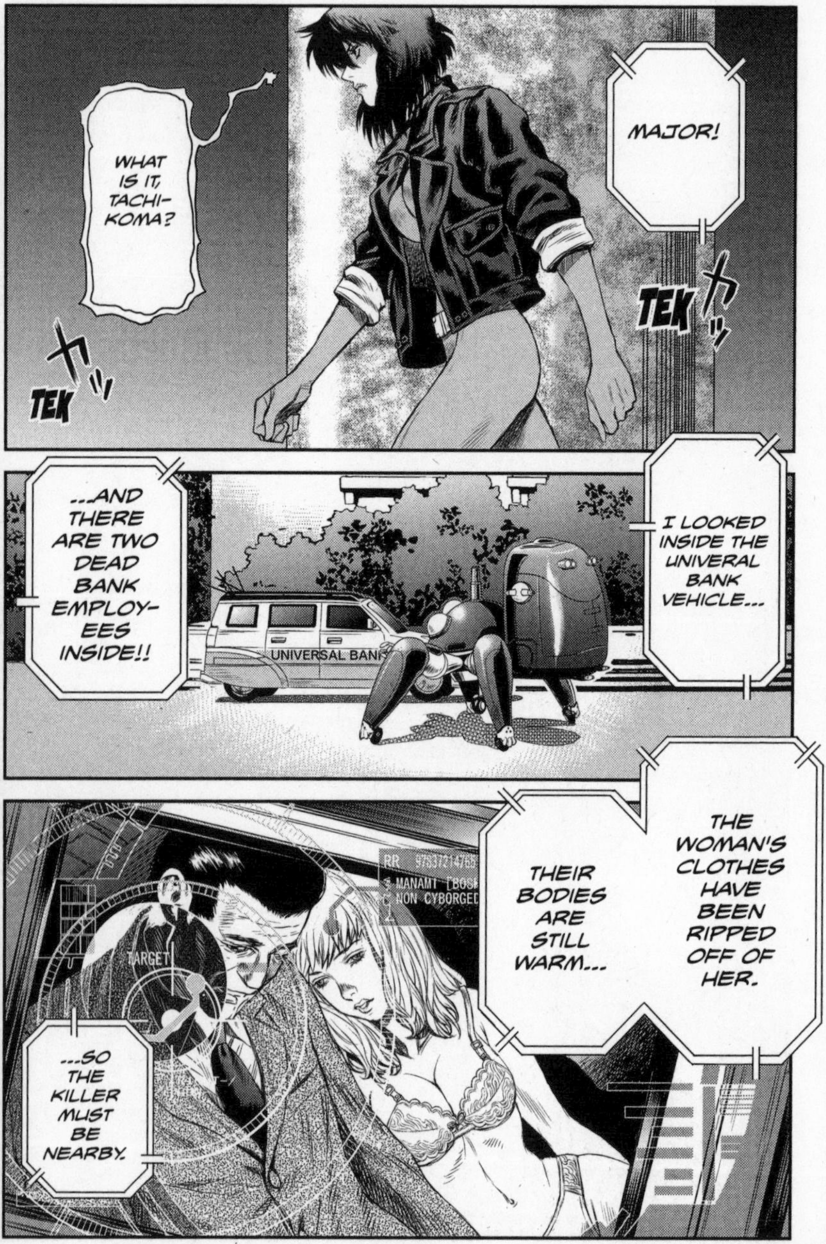
MAJOR!
TEK
ヤッ
WHAT IS IT, TACHIKOMA?
TEK
ヤッ
I LOOKED INSIDE THE UNIVERAL BANK VEHICLE...
...AND THERE ARE TWO DEAD BANK EMPLOYEES INSIDE!!
NON CYBORGED
TARGET
THE WOMAN'S CLOTHES HAVE BEEN RIPPED OFF OF HER.
THEIR BODIES ARE STILL WARM...
...SO THE KILLER MUST BE NEARBY.

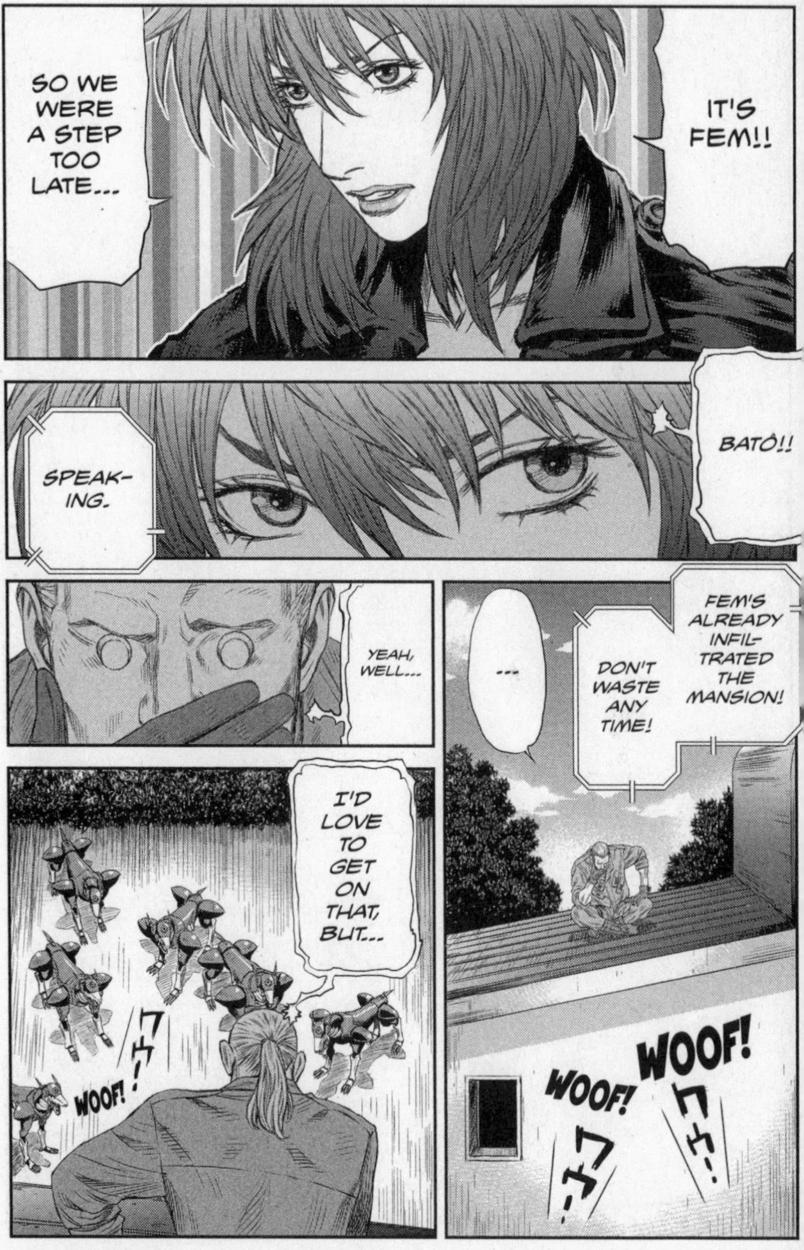
IT'S FEM!!
SO WE WERE A STEP TOO LATE...
BATÔ!!
SPEAKING.
FEM'S ALREADY INFILTRATED THE MANSION!
DON'T WASTE ANY TIME!
...
WOOF!
WOOF!
YEAH, WELL...
I'D LOVE TO GET ON THAT, BUT...
WOOF!

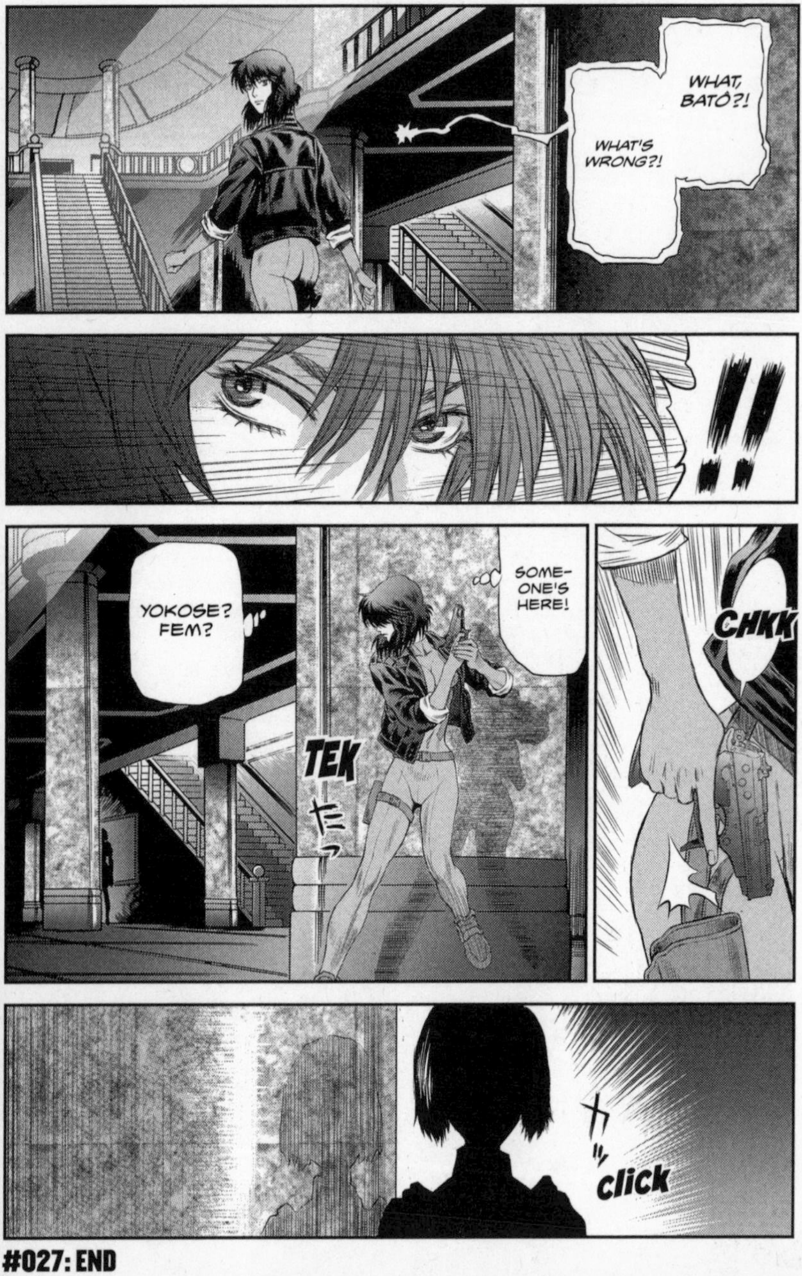
WHAT, BATÔ?!
WHAT'S WRONG?!
!!
CHKK
SOME-ONE'S HERE!
TEK
YOKOSE? FEM?
click

#027: END

#028: Suspicious Figures

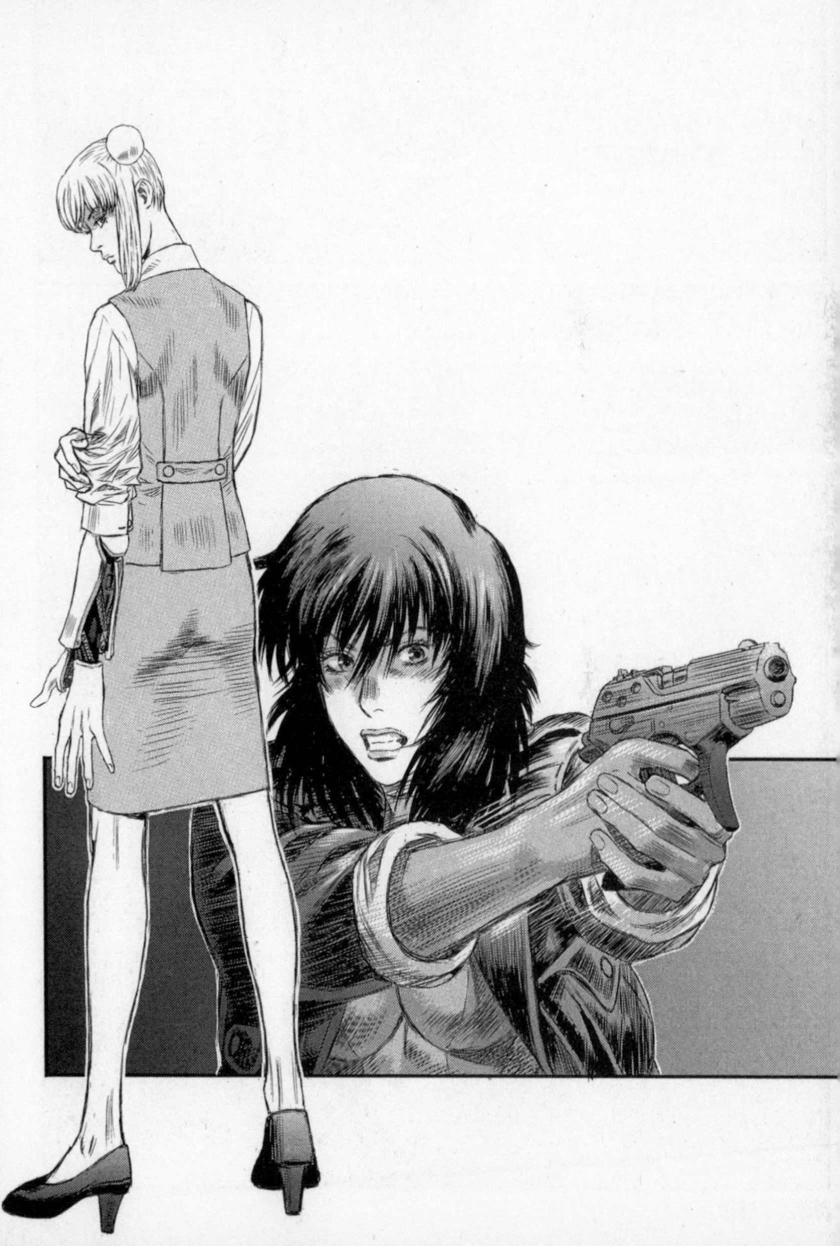

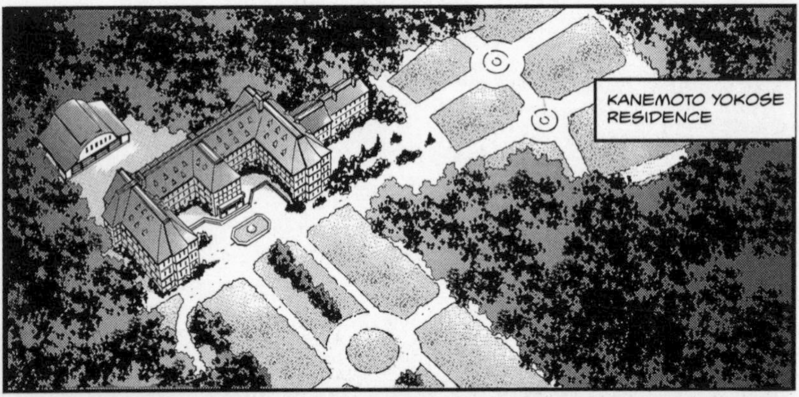
KANEMOTO YOKOSE
RESIDENCE

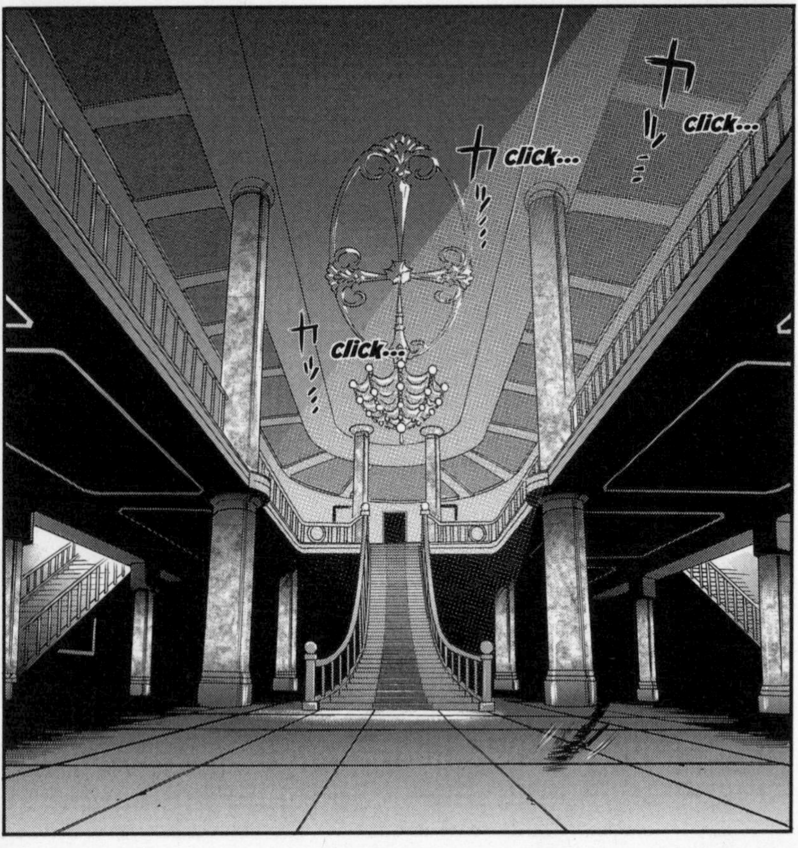
カッ…
click...
カッ…
click...
カッ…
click...

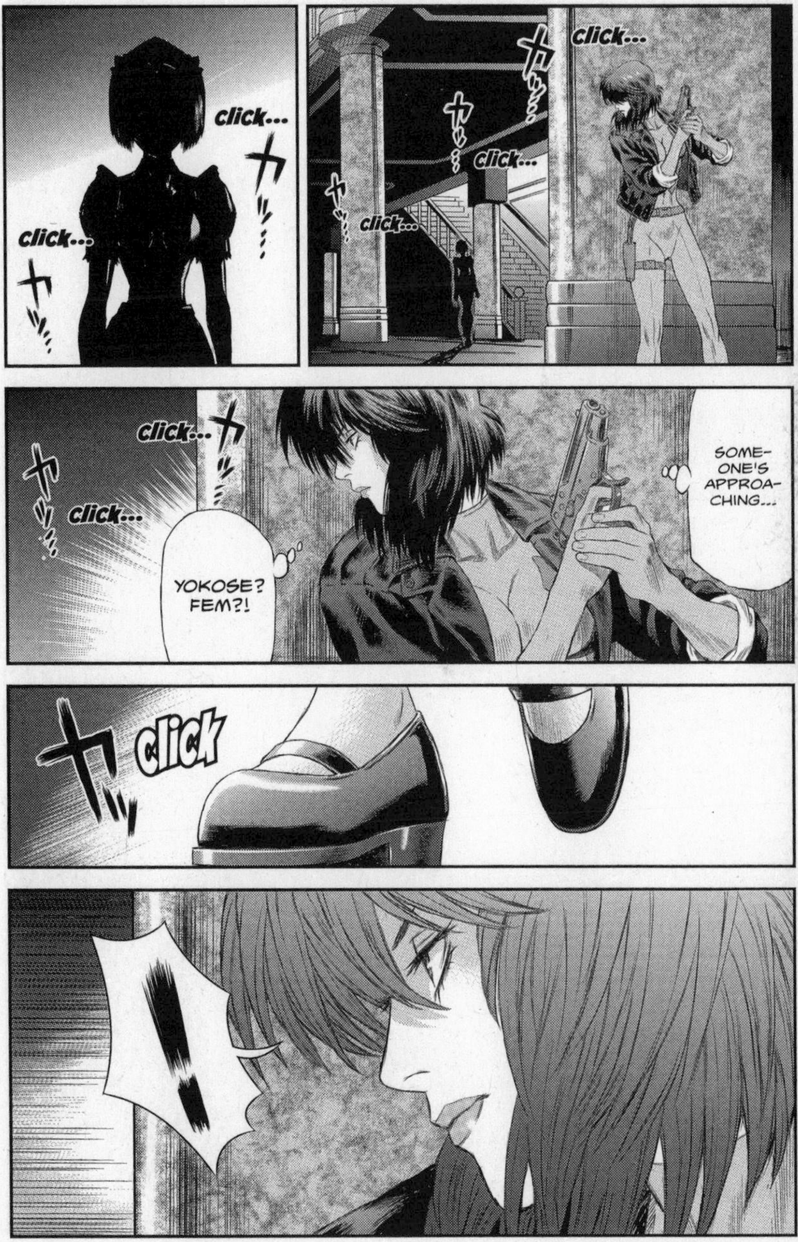
click...
click...
click...
click...
click...
SOME-ONE'S APPROACHING...
click...
click...
YOKOSE? FEM?!
click
!

TEK

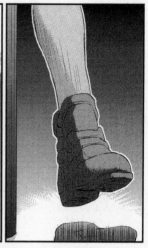

MAY I HAVE YOUR NAME?

WEL-COME.

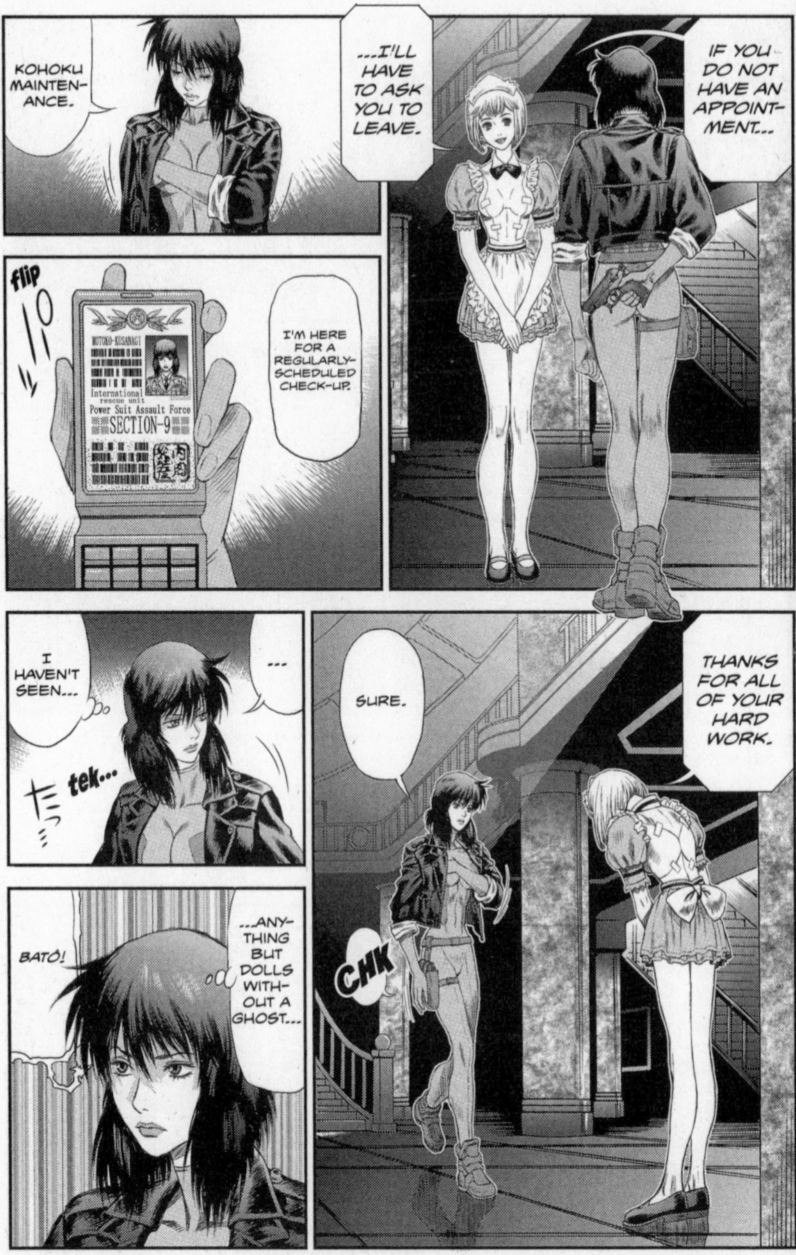
IF YOU DO NOT HAVE AN APPOINT-MENT...
...I'LL HAVE TO ASK YOU TO LEAVE.
KOHOKU MAINTEN-ANCE.
flip
MOTOKO-KUSANAGI
International rescue unit
Power Suit Assault Force
SECTION-9
I'M HERE FOR A REGULARLY-SCHEDULED CHECK-UP.
THANKS FOR ALL OF YOUR HARD WORK.
SURE.
CHK
...
I HAVEN'T SEEN...
tek...
...ANY-THING BUT DOLLS WITH-OUT A GHOST...
BATŌ!

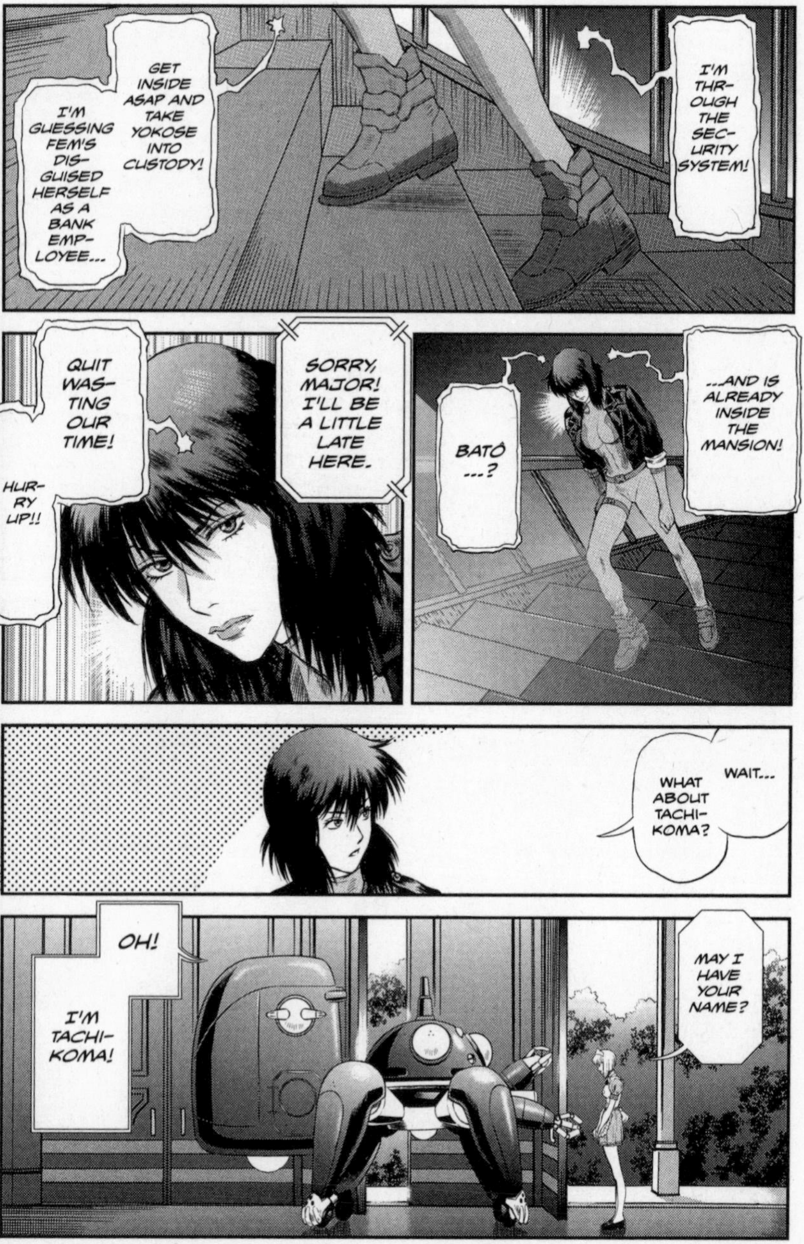
I'M THROUGH THE SECURITY SYSTEM!
GET INSIDE ASAP AND TAKE YOKOSE INTO CUSTODY!
I'M GUESSING FEM'S DISGUISED HERSELF AS A BANK EMPLOYEE...
...AND IS ALREADY INSIDE THE MANSION!
BATÔ...?
SORRY, MAJOR! I'LL BE A LITTLE LATE HERE.
QUIT WASTING OUR TIME!
HURRY UP!!
WAIT...
WHAT ABOUT TACHIKOMA?
MAY I HAVE YOUR NAME?
OH!
I'M TACHIKOMA!

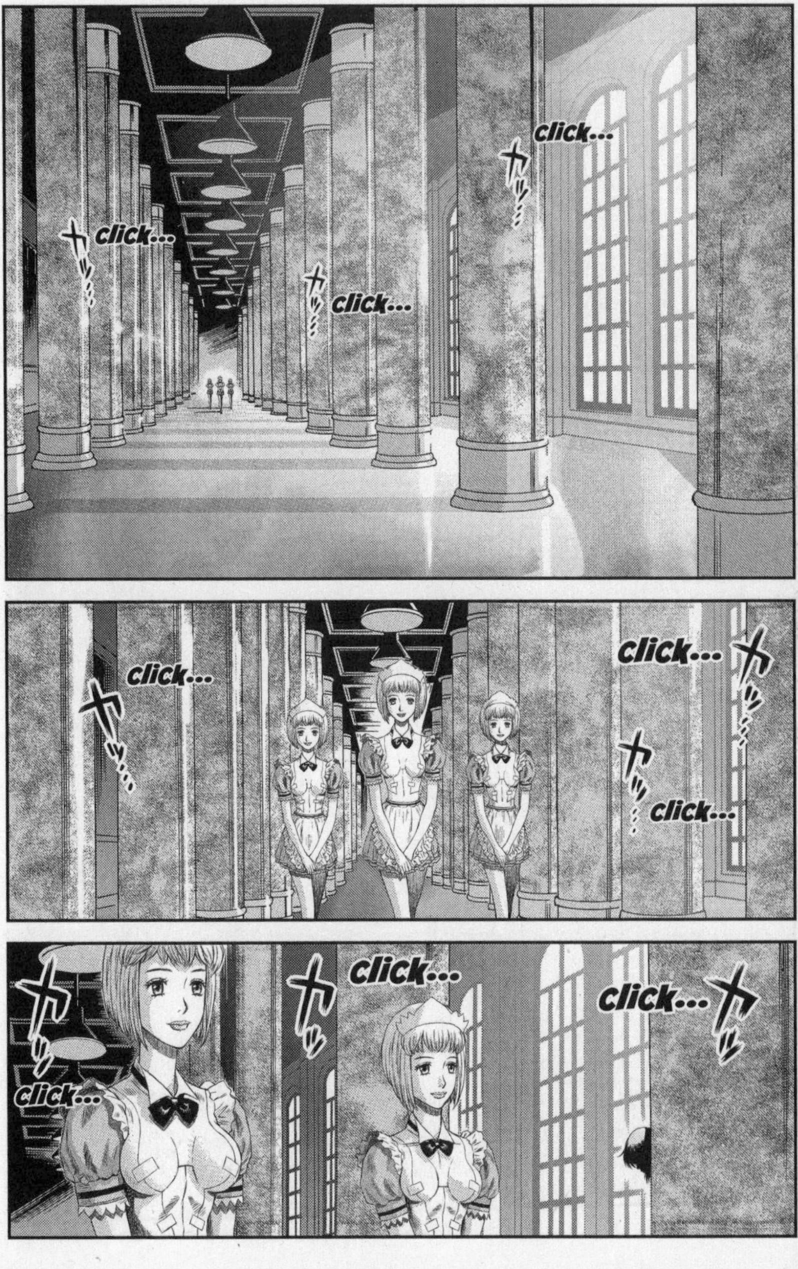
click...
click...
click...
click...
click...
click...
click...
click...
click...

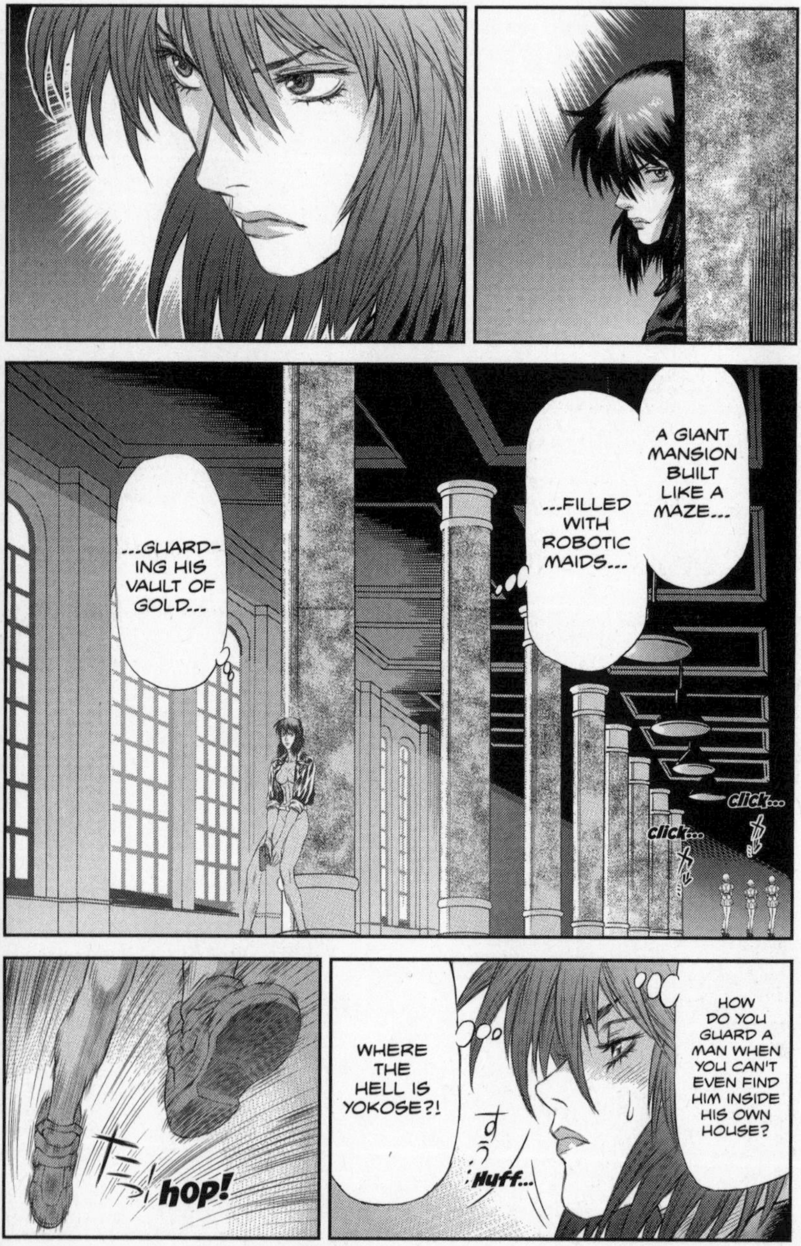
A GIANT MANSION BUILT LIKE A MAZE...
...FILLED WITH ROBOTIC MAIDS...
...GUARD-ING HIS VAULT OF GOLD...
click...
click...
HOW DO YOU GUARD A MAN WHEN YOU CAN'T EVEN FIND HIM INSIDE HIS OWN HOUSE?
WHERE THE HELL IS YOKOSE?!
Huff...
hop!

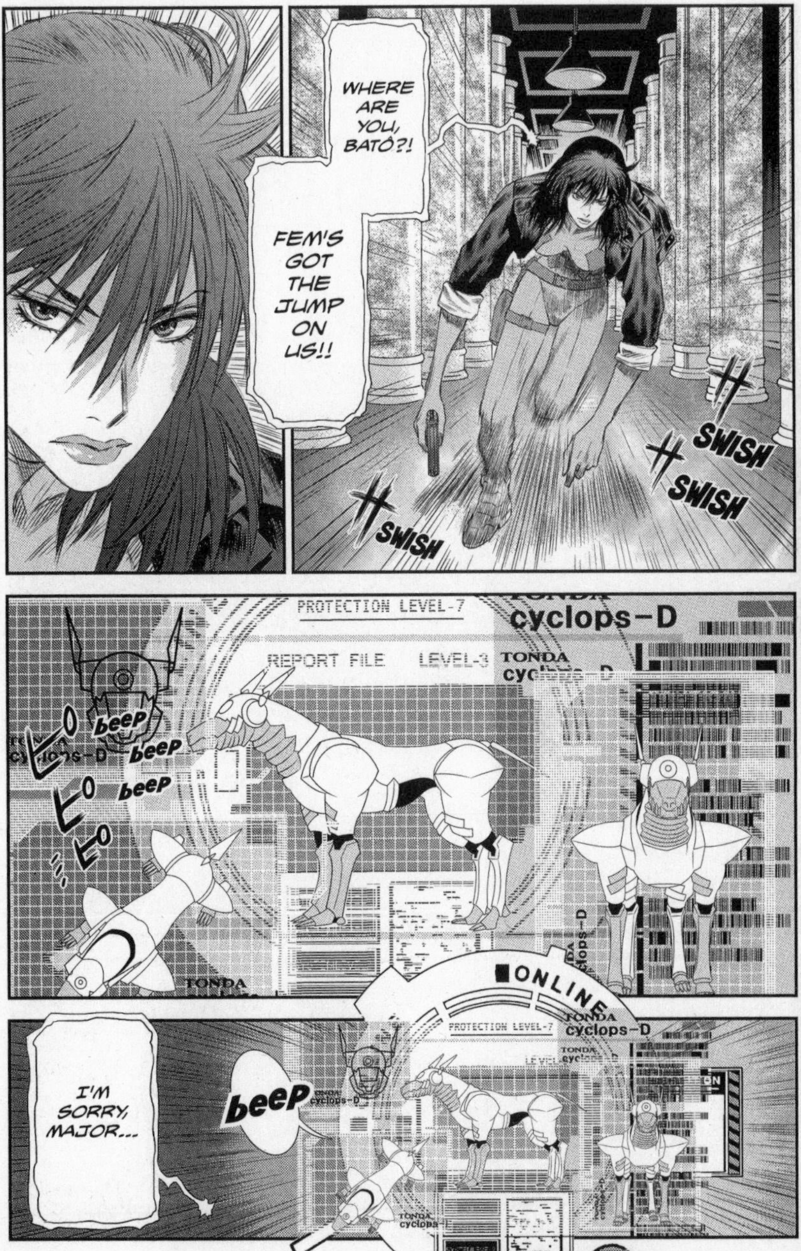
WHERE ARE YOU, BATÔ?!
FEM'S GOT THE JUMP ON US!!
SWISH
SWISH
SWISH
PROTECTION LEVEL-7
TONDA cyclops-D
REPORT FILE LEVEL-3
TONDA cyclops-D
beep
beep
beep
TONDA cyclops-D
TONDA
■ONLINE
PROTECTION LEVEL-7
TONDA cyclops-D
I'M SORRY, MAJOR...
beep

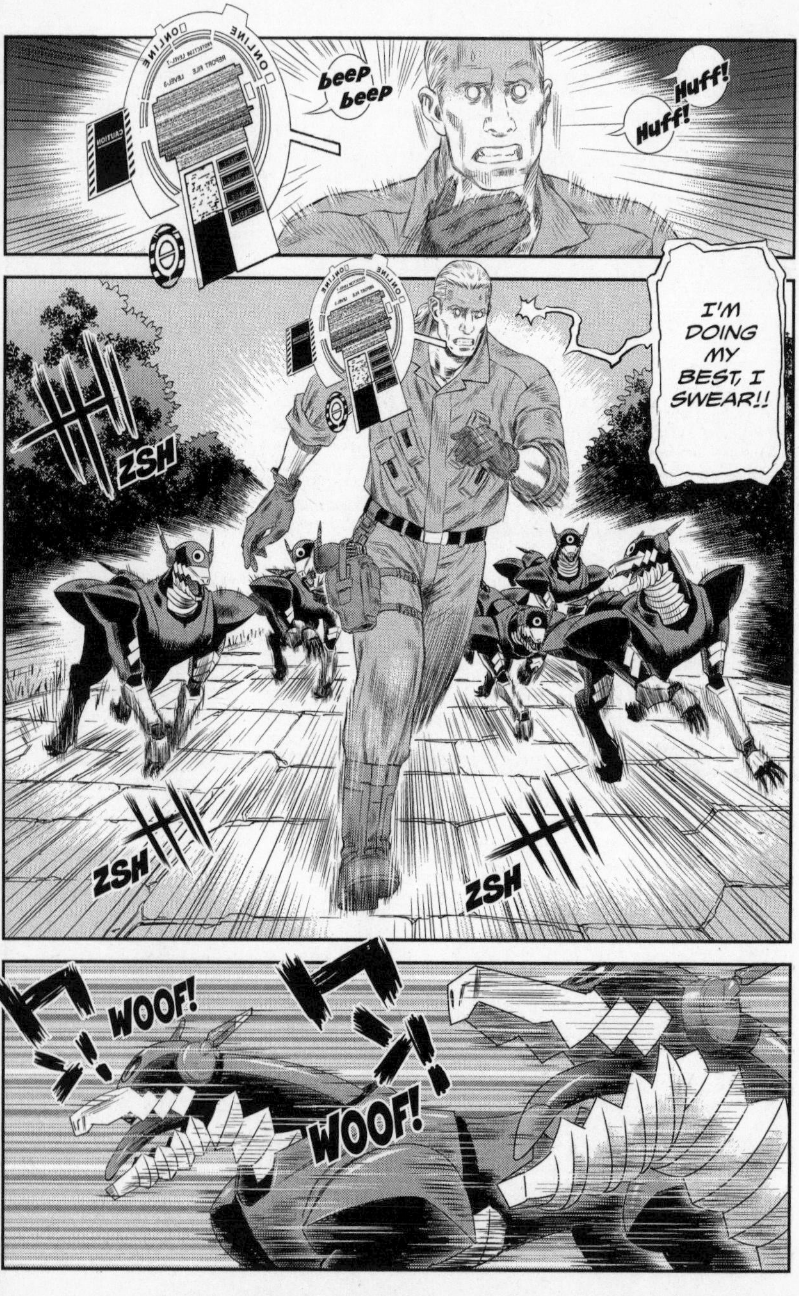
Huff!
Huff!
beep
beep
I'M DOING MY BEST, I SWEAR!!
ZSH
ZSH
ZSH
WOOF!
WOOF!

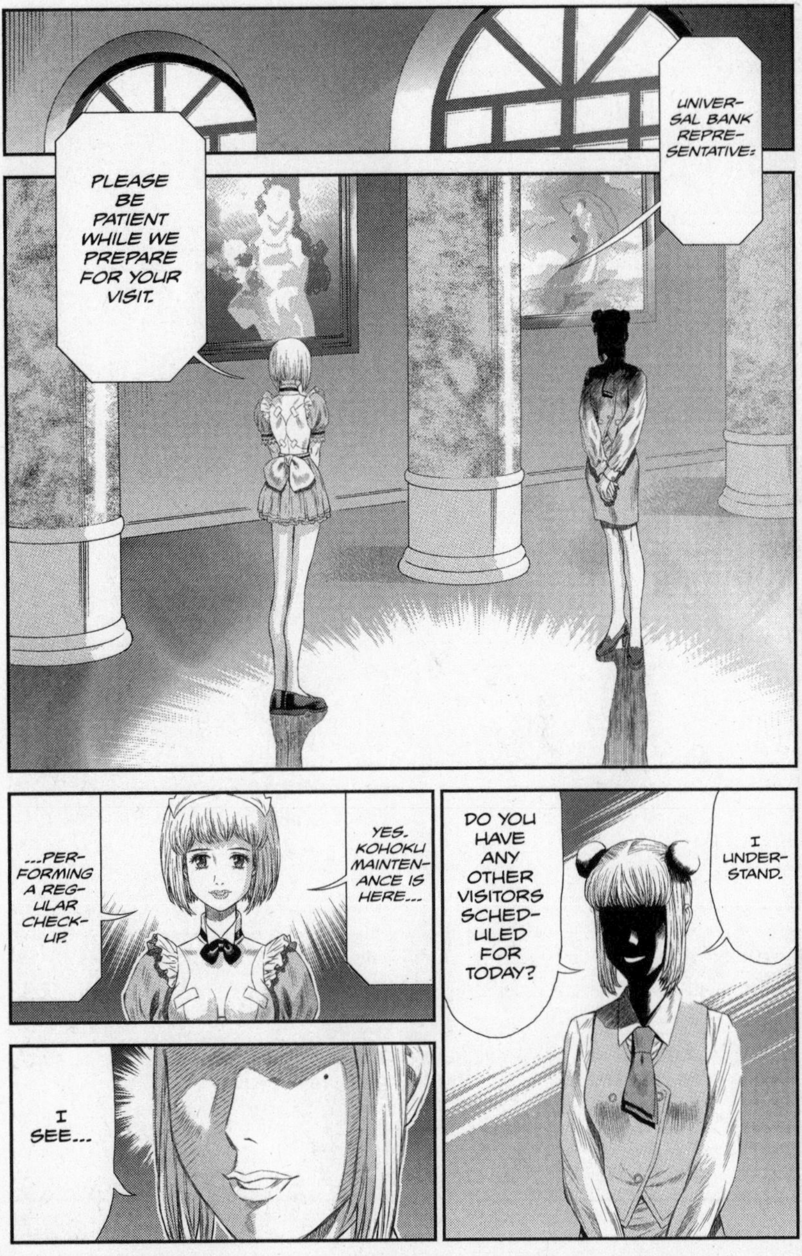
UNIVER-SAL BANK REPRE-SENTATIVE:
PLEASE BE PATIENT WHILE WE PREPARE FOR YOUR VISIT.
I UNDER-STAND.
DO YOU HAVE ANY OTHER VISITORS SCHED-ULED FOR TODAY?
YES. KOHOKU MAINTEN-ANCE IS HERE...
...PER-FORMING A REG-ULAR CHECK-UP.
I SEE...

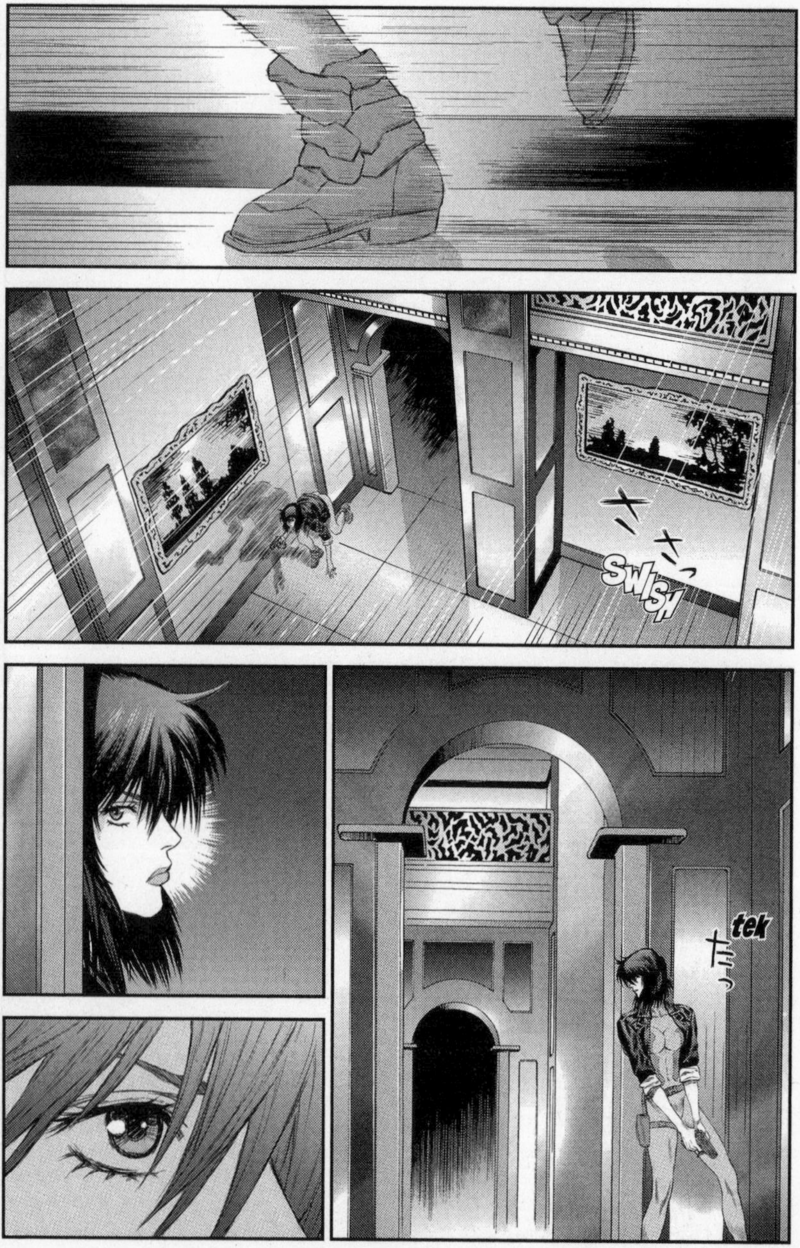
さっ さっ
SWISH
tek
たっ

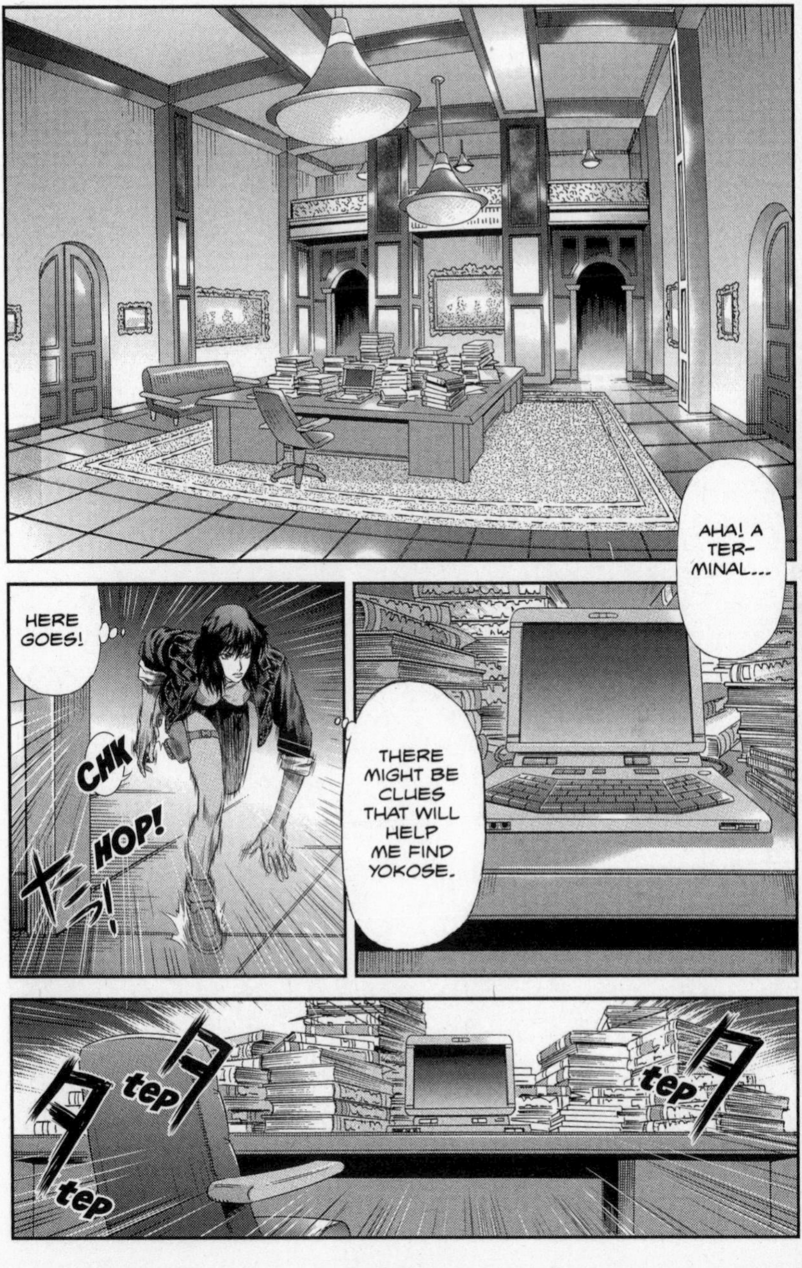
AHA! A TER-MINAL...
THERE MIGHT BE CLUES THAT WILL HELP ME FIND YOKOSE.
HERE GOES!
CHK
HOP!
tep
tep
tep

PLUG

TEP!

SWISH

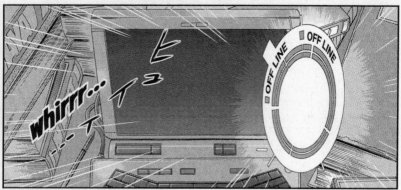

whirrr...

OFF LINE   OFF LINE

OFF LINE

SHK

COME ON!

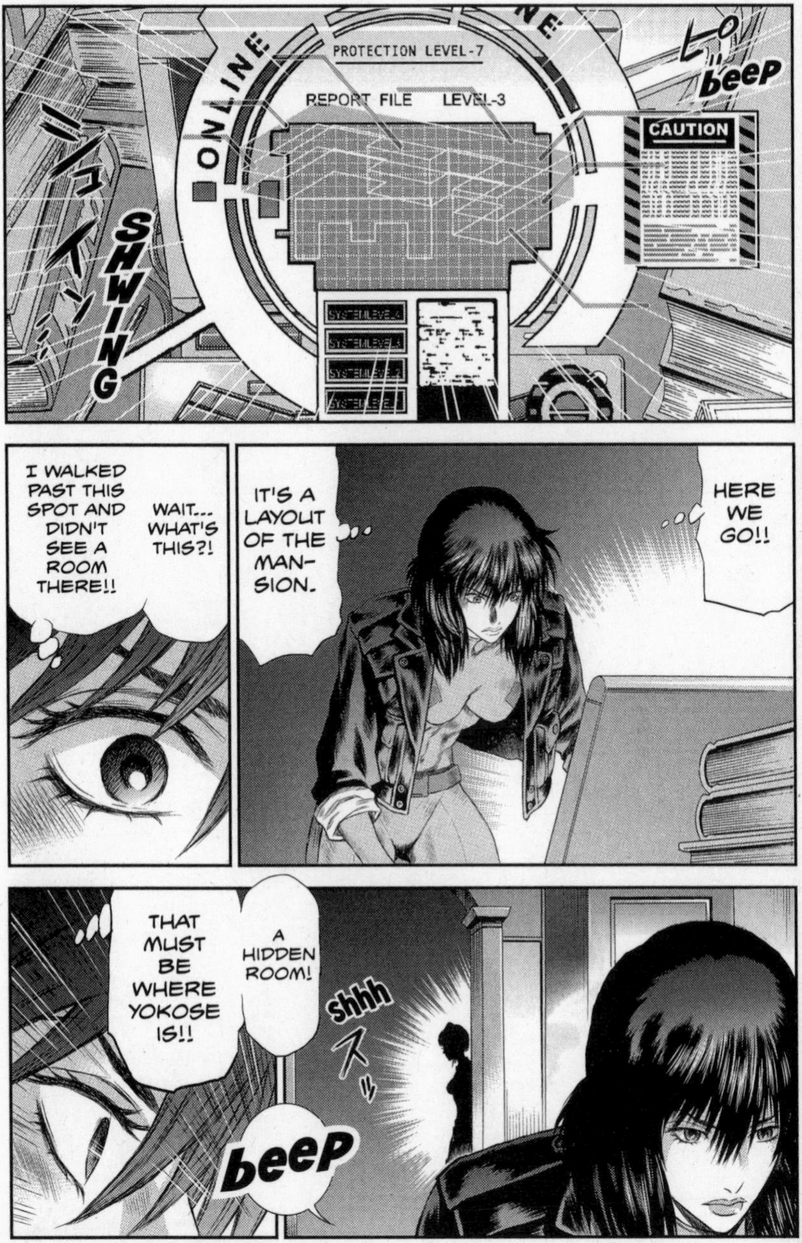
beep
CAUTION
PROTECTION LEVEL-7
REPORT FILE LEVEL-3
ONLINE
SHWING
HERE WE GO!!
IT'S A LAYOUT OF THE MANSION.
WAIT... WHAT'S THIS?!
I WALKED PAST THIS SPOT AND DIDN'T SEE A ROOM THERE!!
shhh
A HIDDEN ROOM!
THAT MUST BE WHERE YOKOSE IS!!
beep

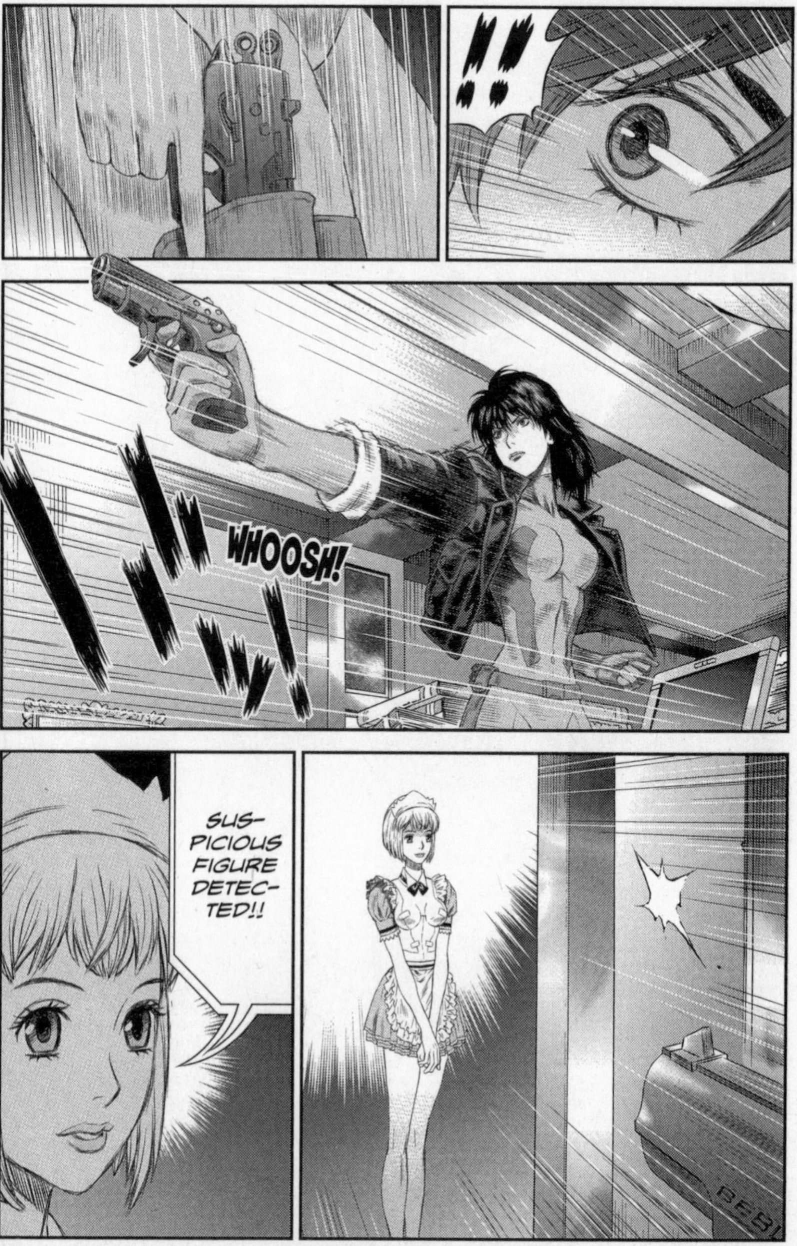
!!
WHOOSH!
SUS-PICIOUS FIGURE DETEC-TED!!

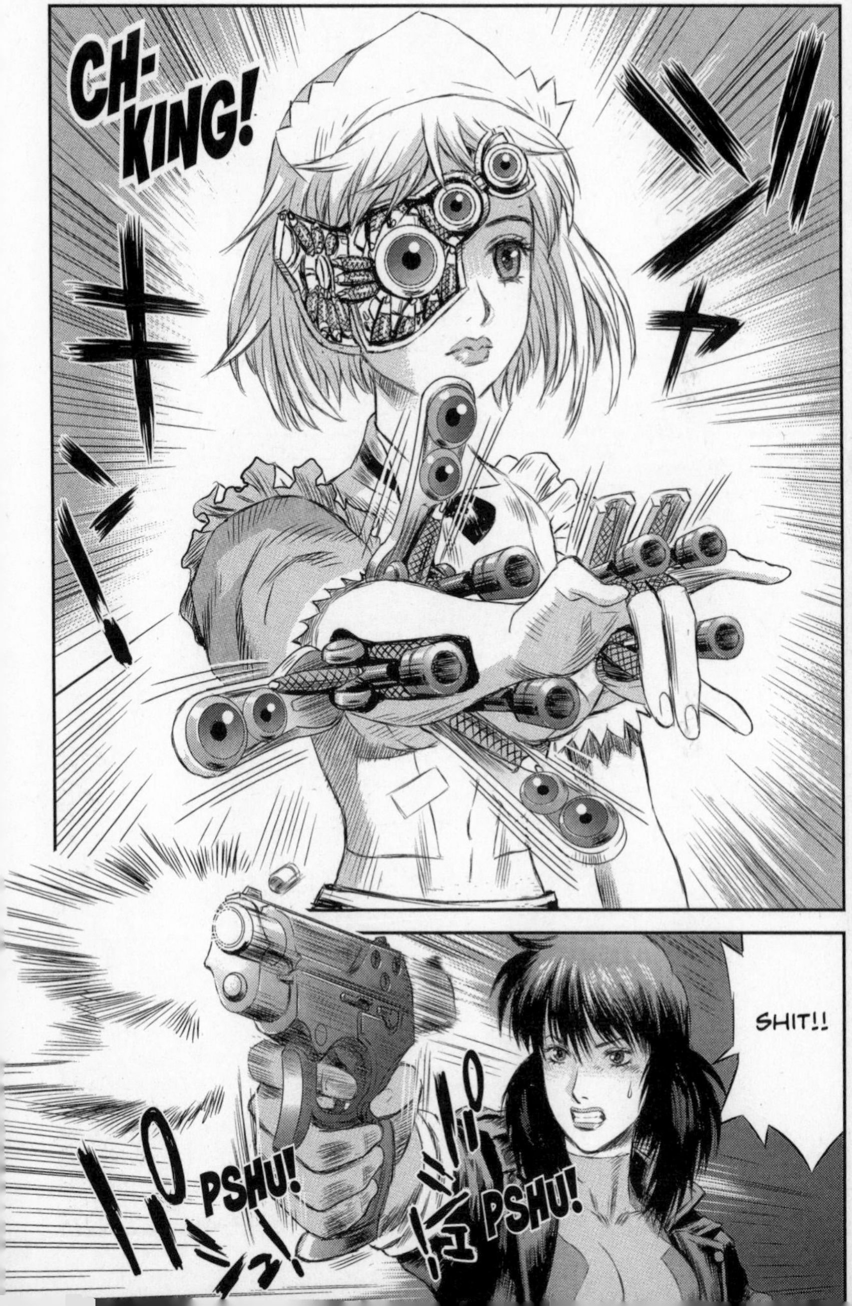
CH-KING!
SHIT!!
PSHU!
PSHU!

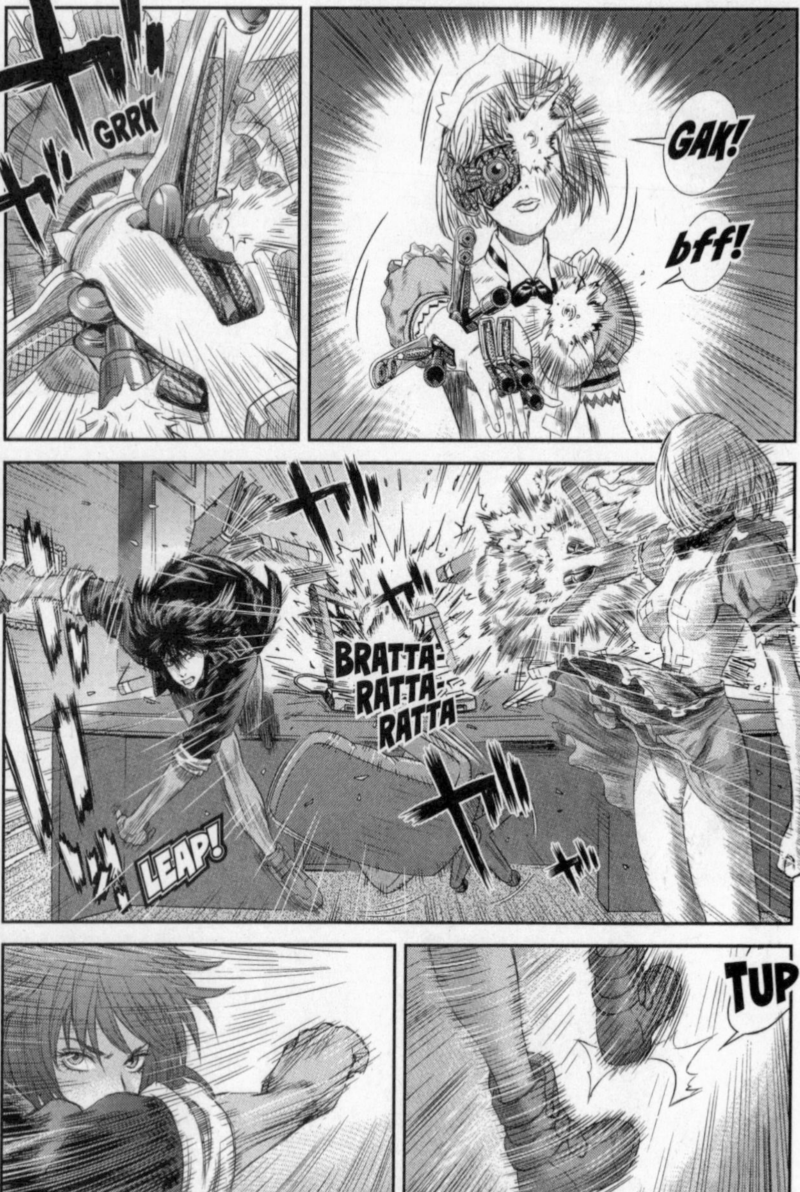
GAK!
bff!
GRRK
BRATTA-RATTA-RATTA
LEAP!
TUP

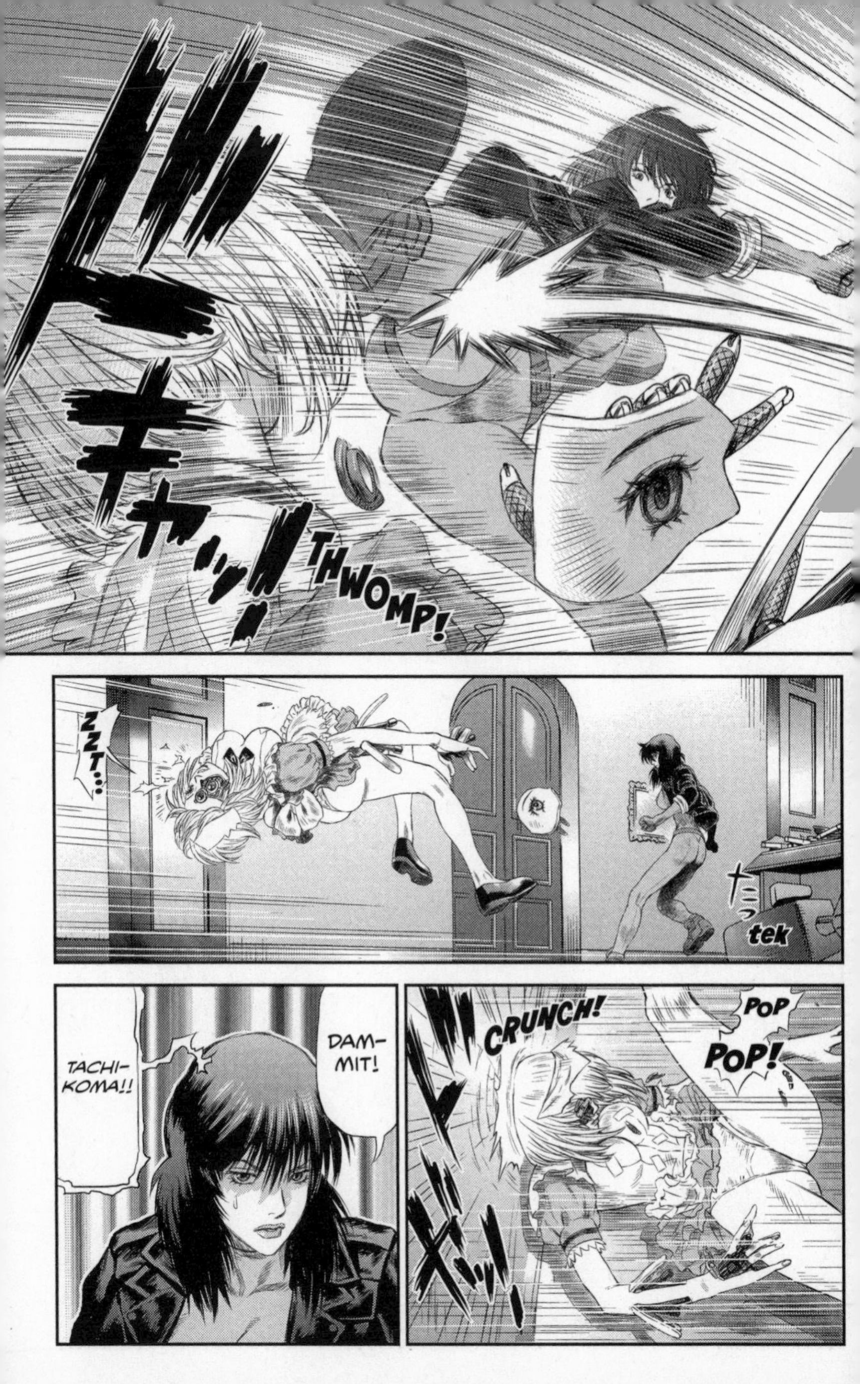
ドギャッ!!
THWOMP!
ZZT...
tek
CRUNCH!
POP
POP!
DAM-MIT!
TACHI-KOMA!!

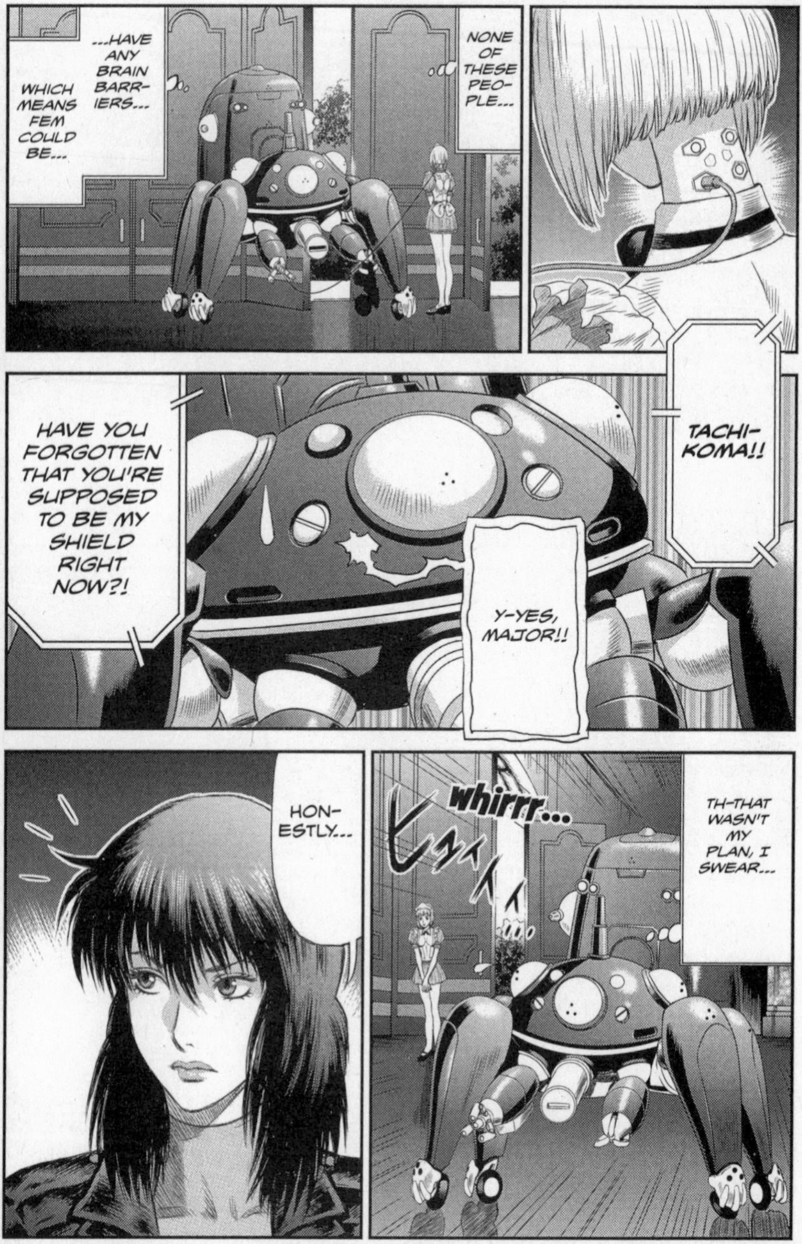

NONE OF THESE PEOPLE...
...HAVE ANY BRAIN BARRIERS...
WHICH MEANS FEM COULD BE...
TACHIKOMA!!
HAVE YOU FORGOTTEN THAT YOU'RE SUPPOSED TO BE MY SHIELD RIGHT NOW?!
Y-YES, MAJOR!!
TH-THAT WASN'T MY PLAN, I SWEAR...
whirrr...
HONESTLY...

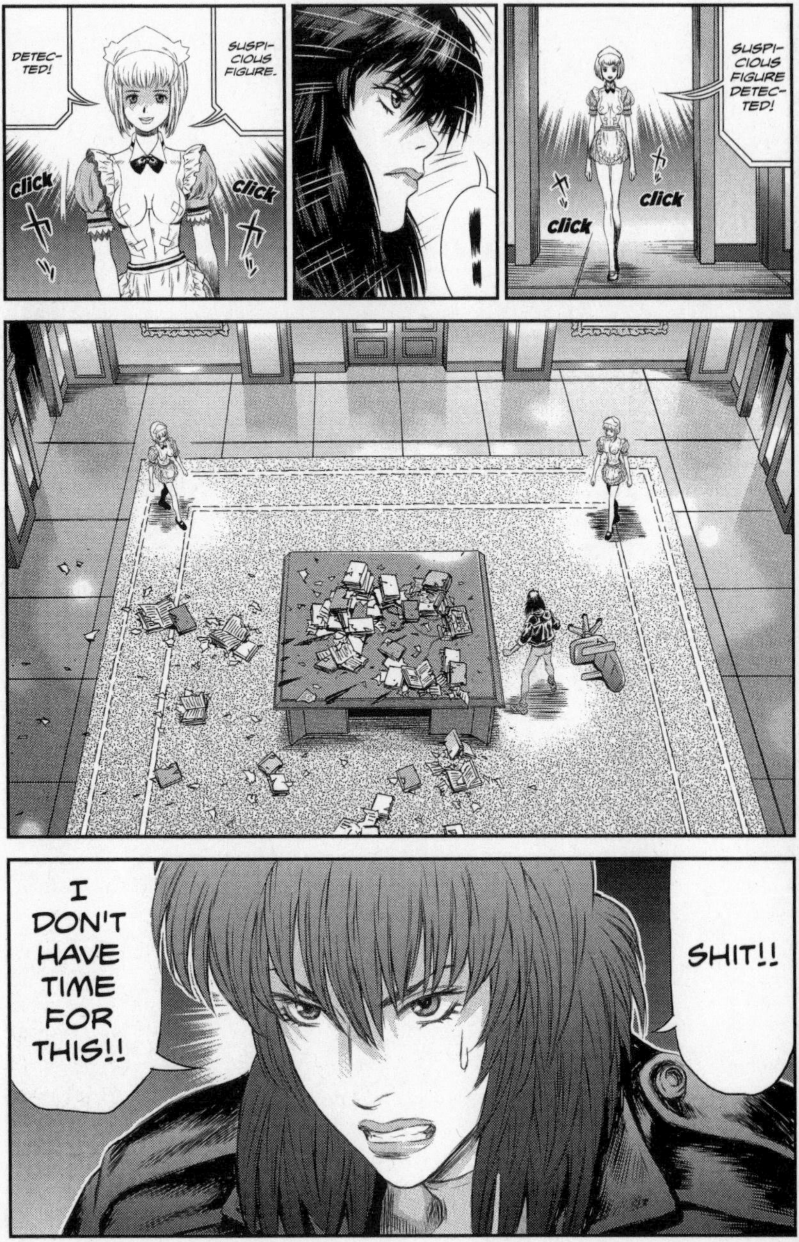
SUSPICIOUS FIGURE DETECTED!
click
click
!!
SUSPICIOUS FIGURE...
DETECTED!
click
click
SHIT!!
I DON'T HAVE TIME FOR THIS!!

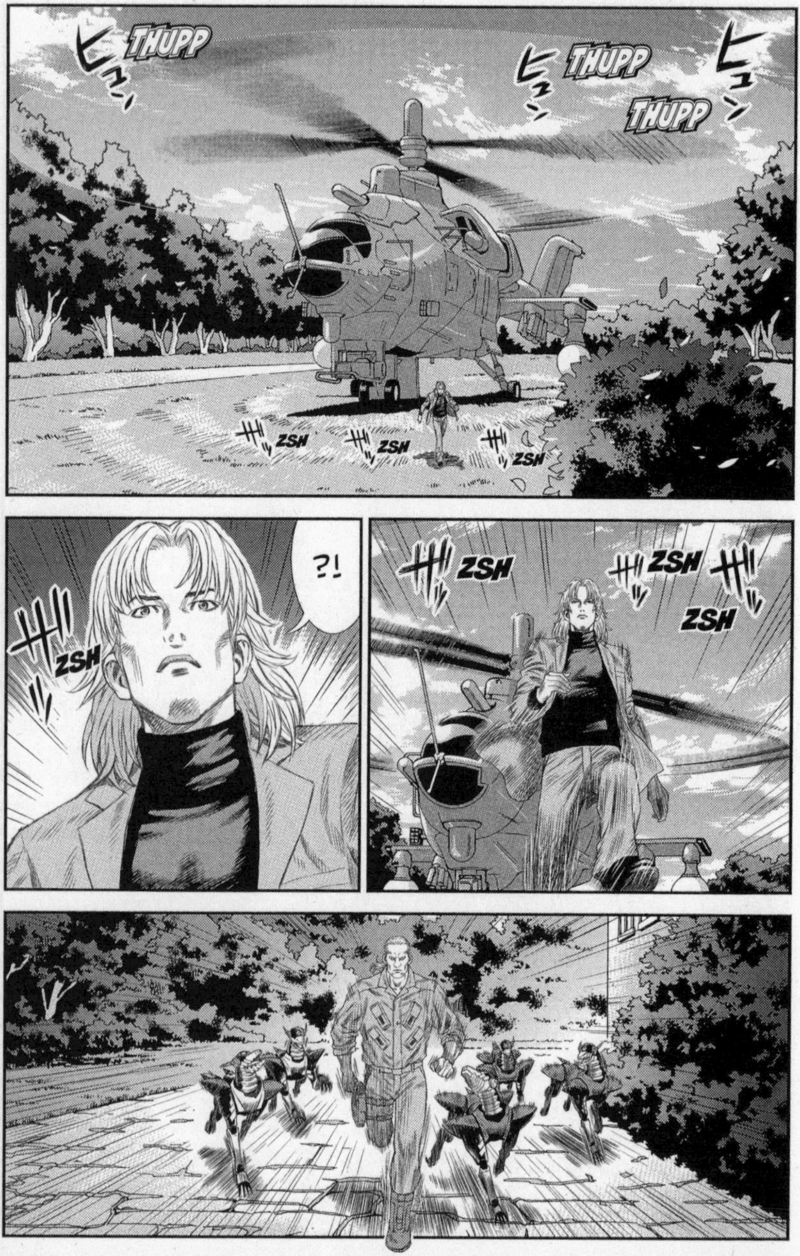

ヒュン
THUPP
THUPP
ヒュン
THUPP
ヒュン
THUPP
ザッ
ZSH
ザッ
ZSH
ザッ
ZSH
ザッ
ZSH
ザッ
ZSH
ZSH
?!
ザッ
ZSH

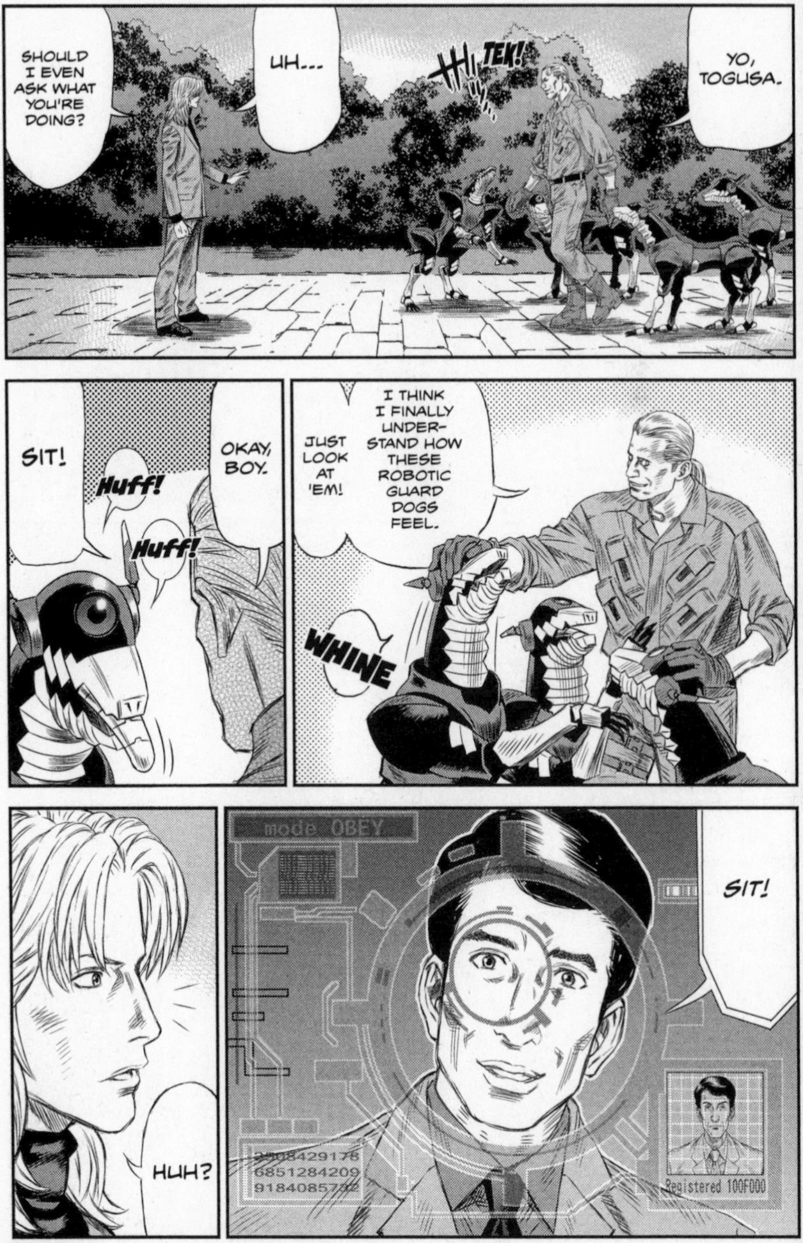
YO, TOGUSA.
TEK!
UH...
SHOULD I EVEN ASK WHAT YOU'RE DOING?
I THINK I FINALLY UNDER-STAND HOW THESE ROBOTIC GUARD DOGS FEEL.
JUST LOOK AT 'EM!
WHINE
OKAY, BOY.
Huff!
Huff!
SIT!
SIT!
mode OBEY
6851284209
Registered 100F000
HUH?

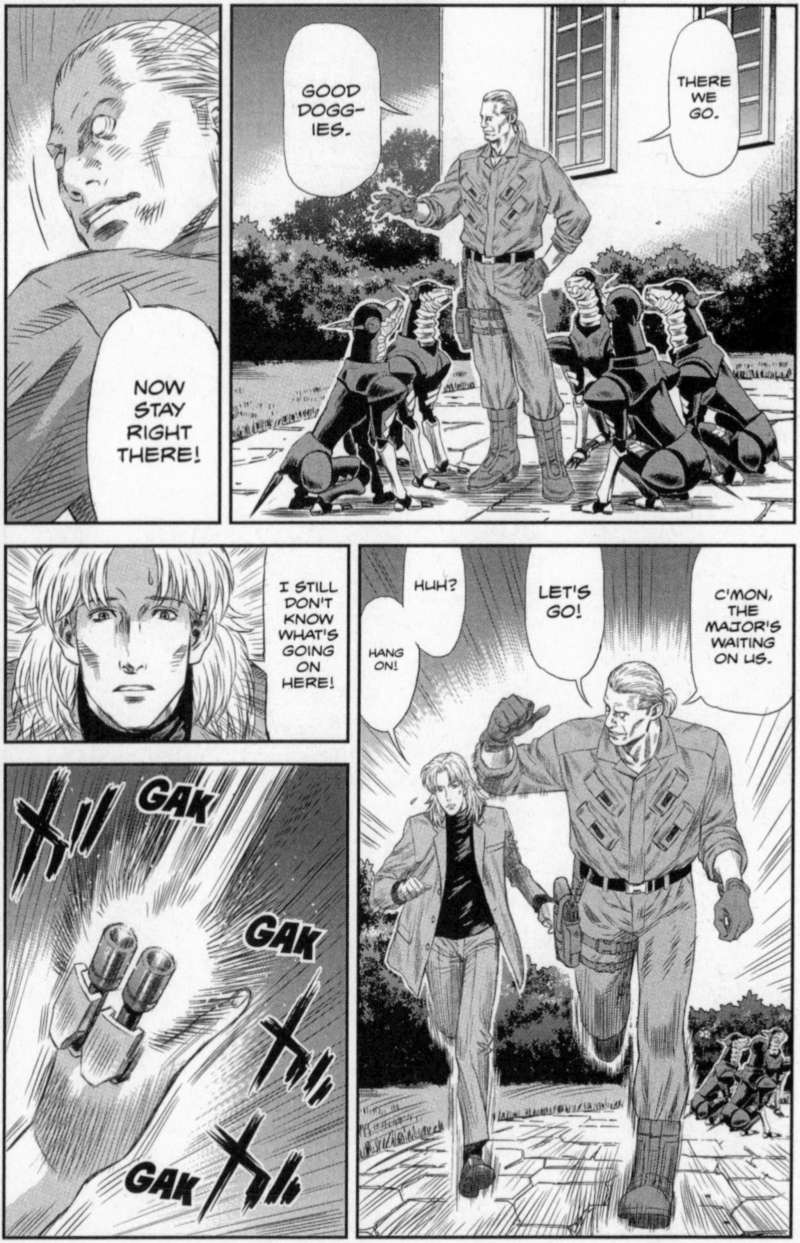
THERE WE GO.
GOOD DOGG-IES.
NOW STAY RIGHT THERE!
C'MON, THE MAJOR'S WAITING ON US.
LET'S GO!
HUH?
HANG ON!
I STILL DON'T KNOW WHAT'S GOING ON HERE!
GAK
GAK
GAK

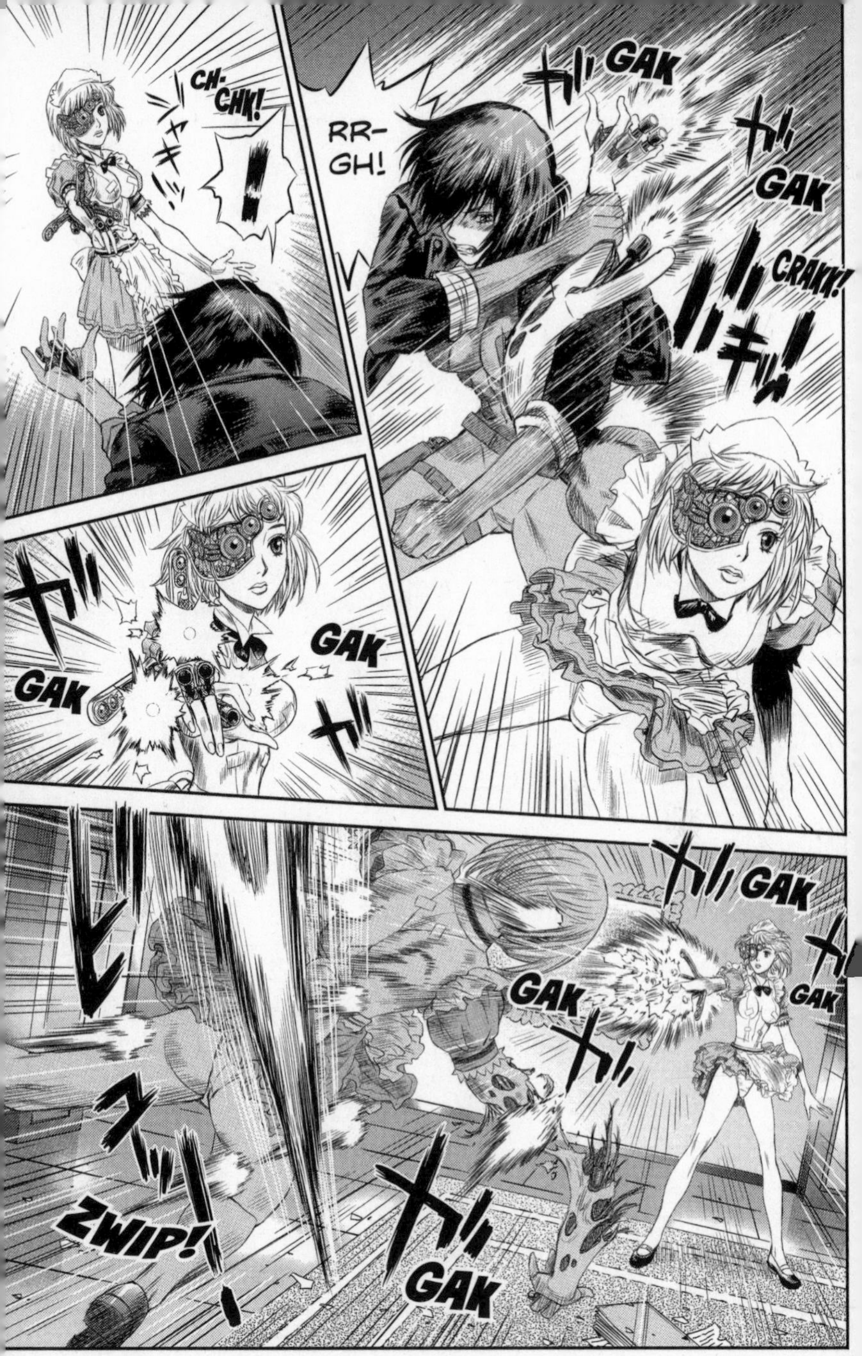
RR-GH!
GAK
GAK
CRAKK!
CH-CHK!
ジャキッ!!
GAK
GAK
GAK
GAK
GAK
ZWIP!
GAK

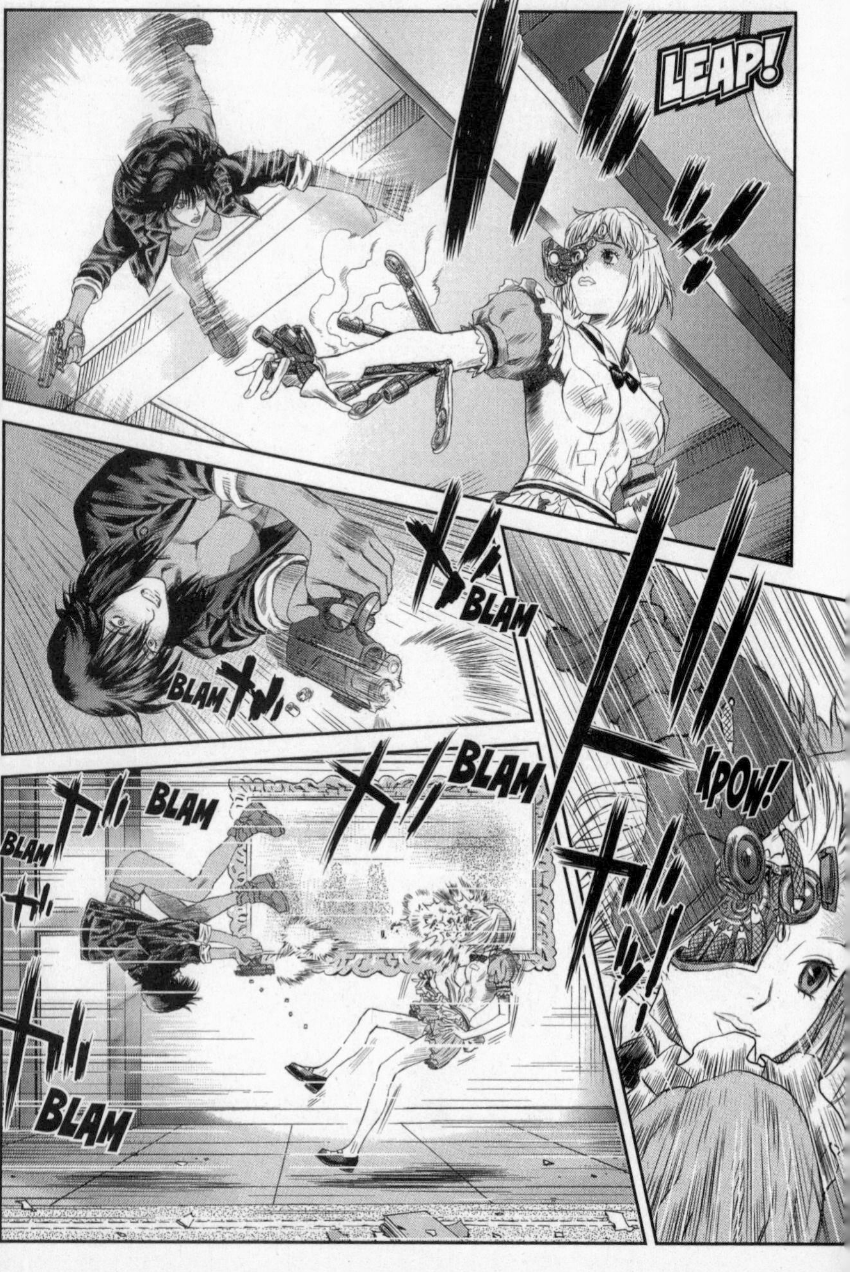
LEAP!
KPOW!
BLAM
BLAM
BLAM
BLAM
BLAM
BLAM

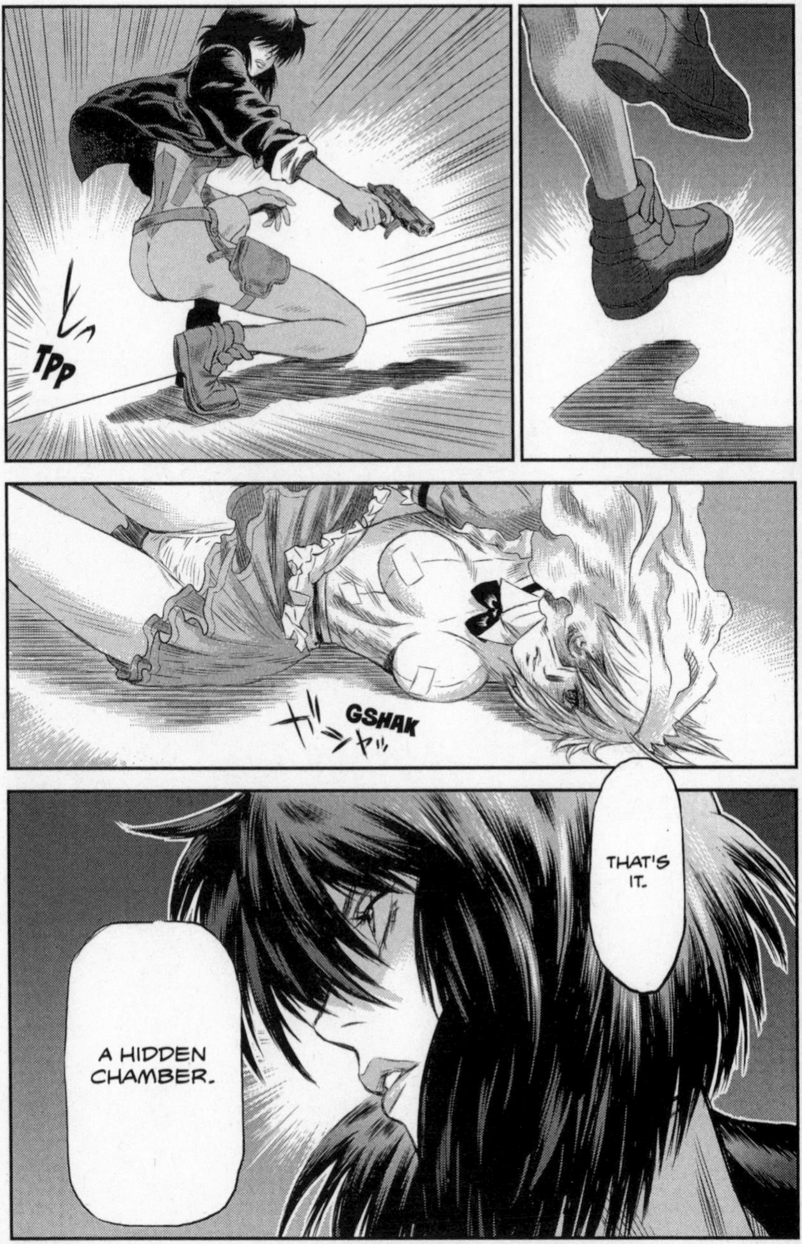
TPP
ガシャッ
GSHAK
THAT'S IT.
A HIDDEN CHAMBER.

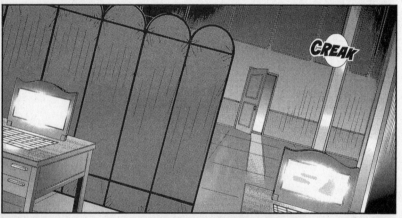

CREAK

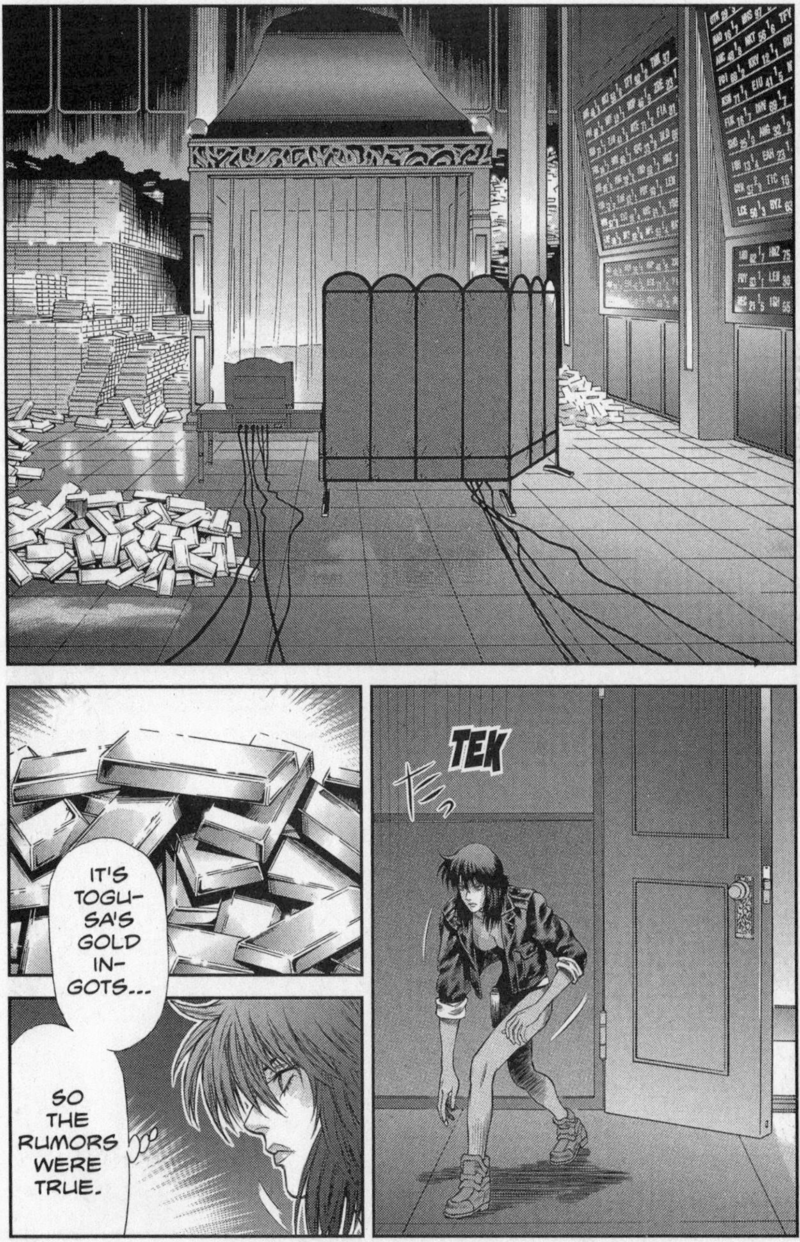
TEK
IT'S TOGUSA'S GOLD INGOTS...
SO THE RUMORS WERE TRUE.

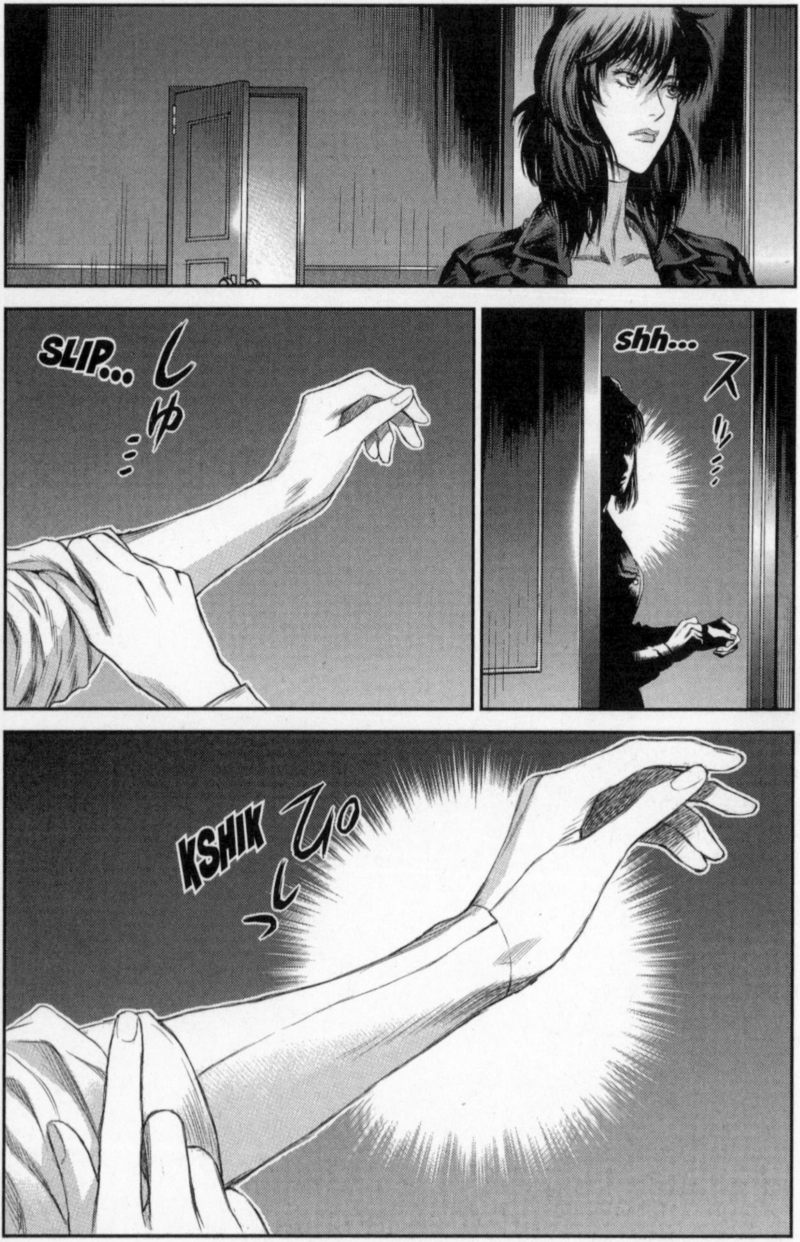
shh...
スッ…
SLIP...
しゅ…
KSHIK
ぴしっ

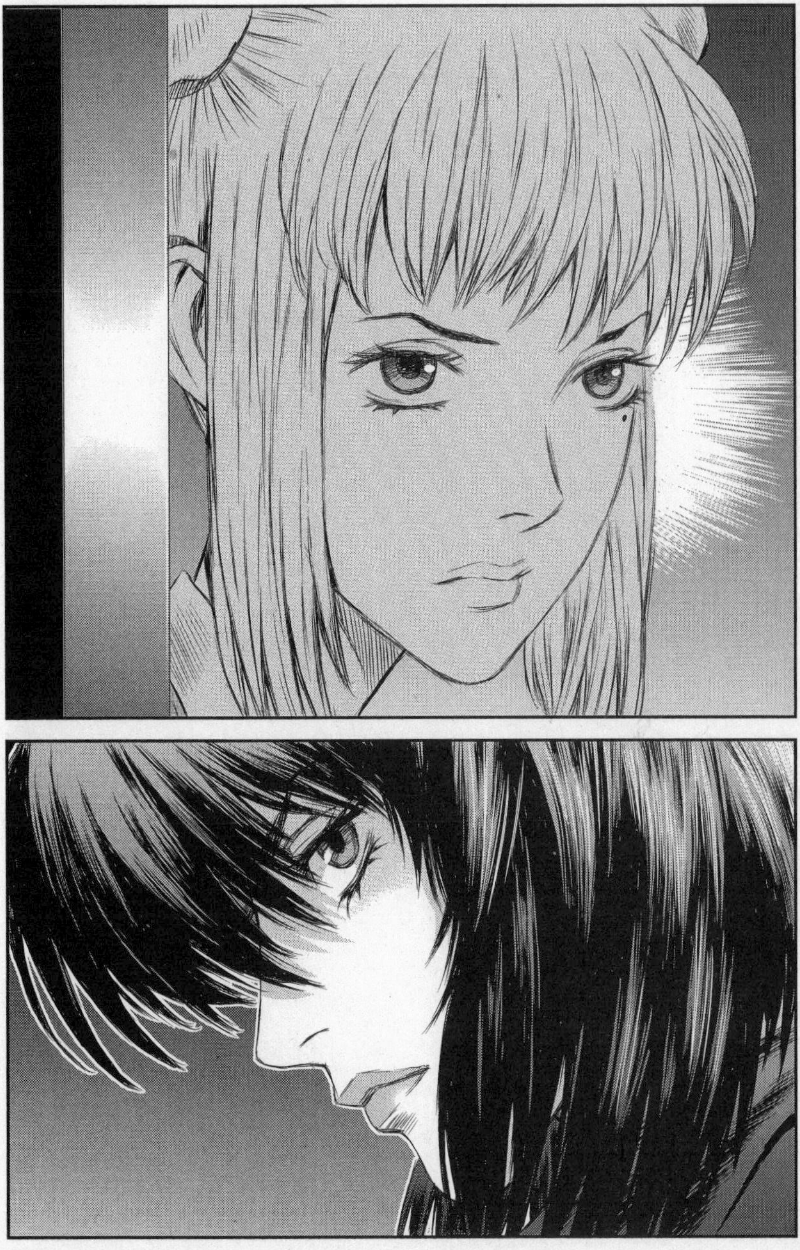

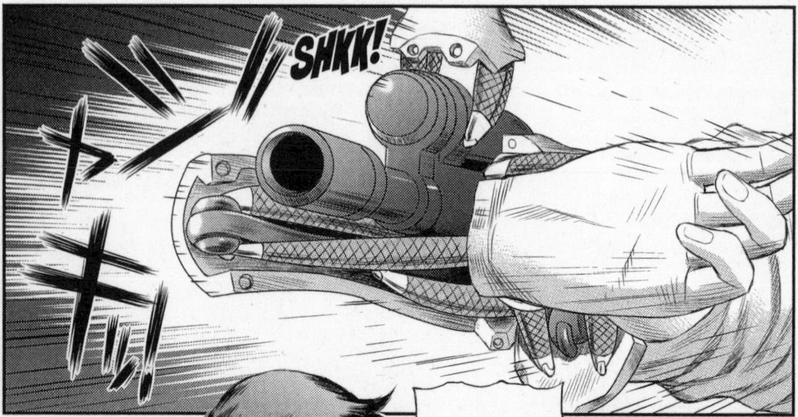
SHKK!

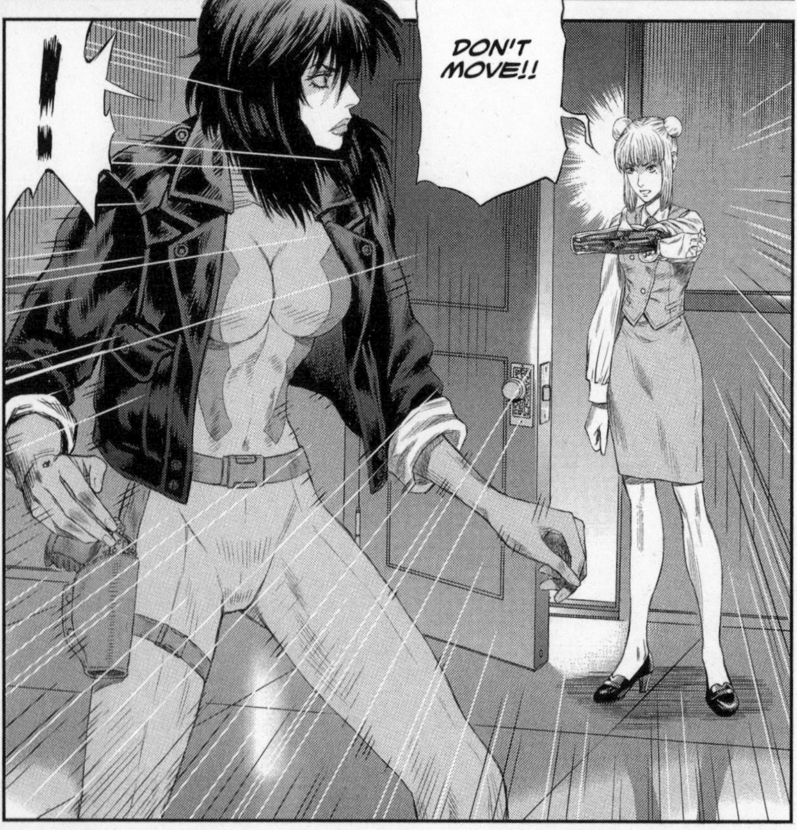
!!
DON'T MOVE!!

#028: END

#029: Sudden Battle

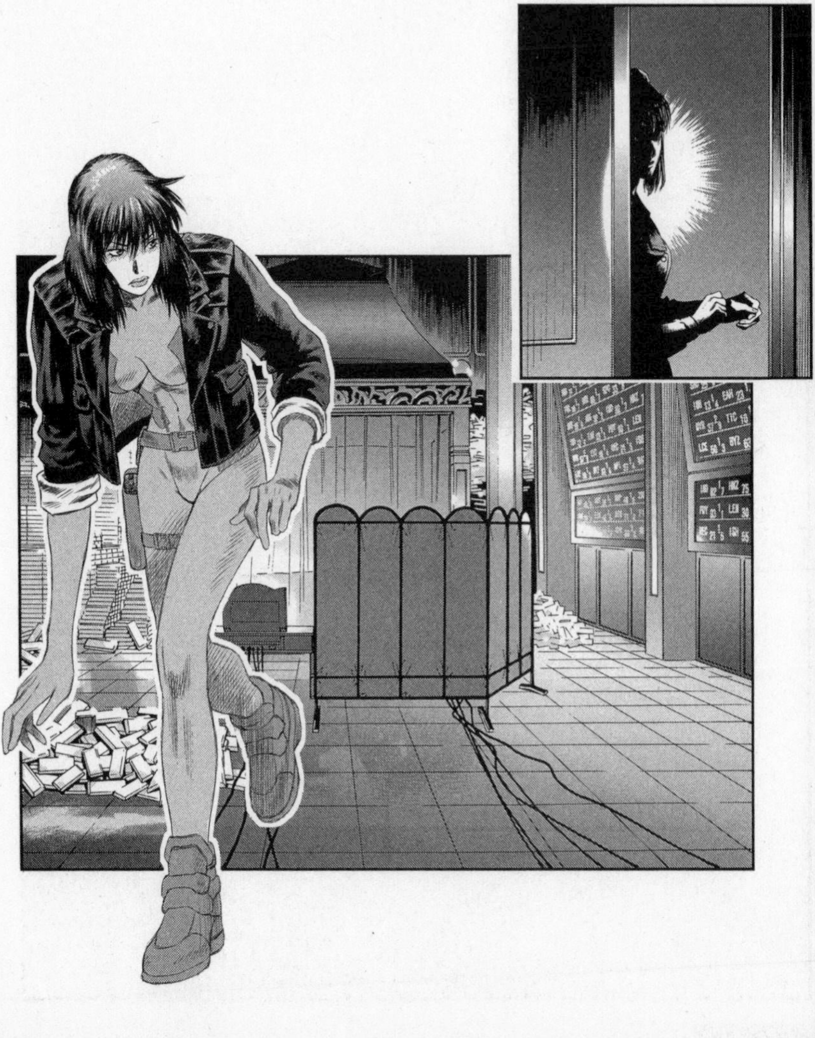

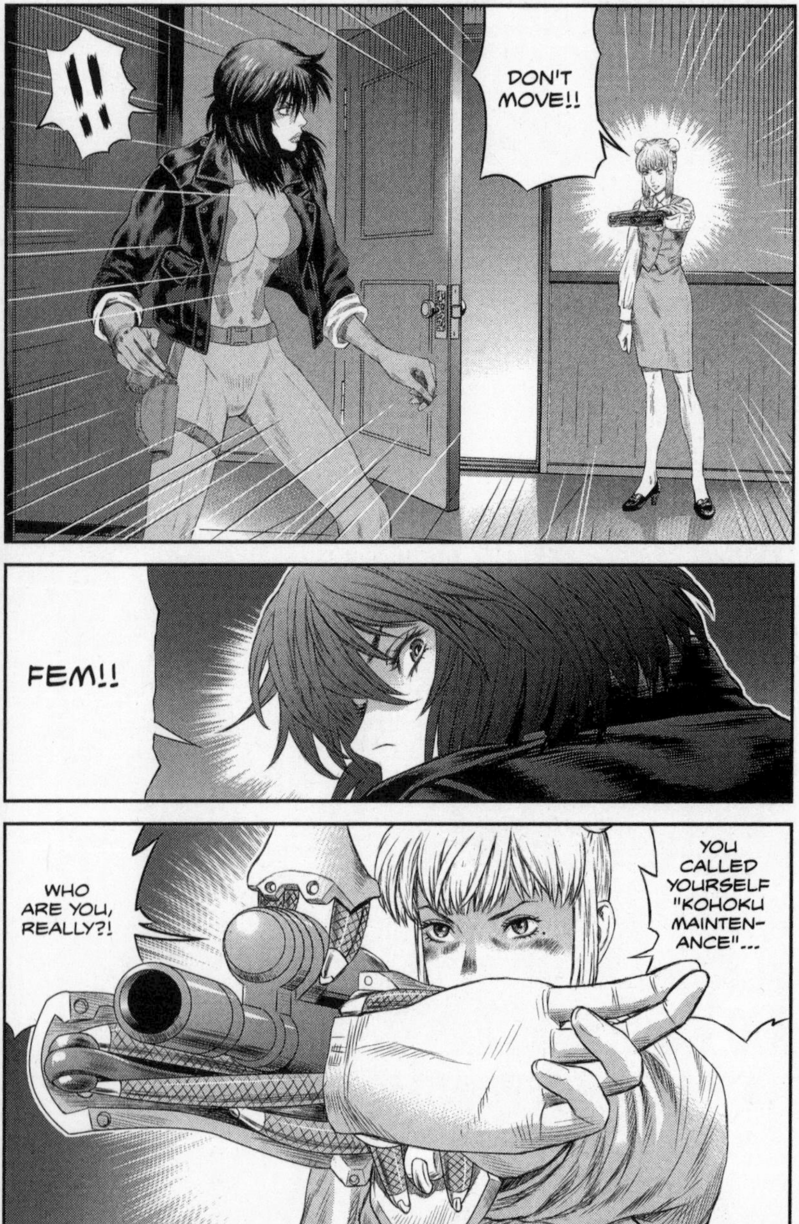
DON'T MOVE!!
!!
FEM!!
YOU CALLED YOURSELF "KOHOKU MAINTEN-ANCE"...
WHO ARE YOU, REALLY?!

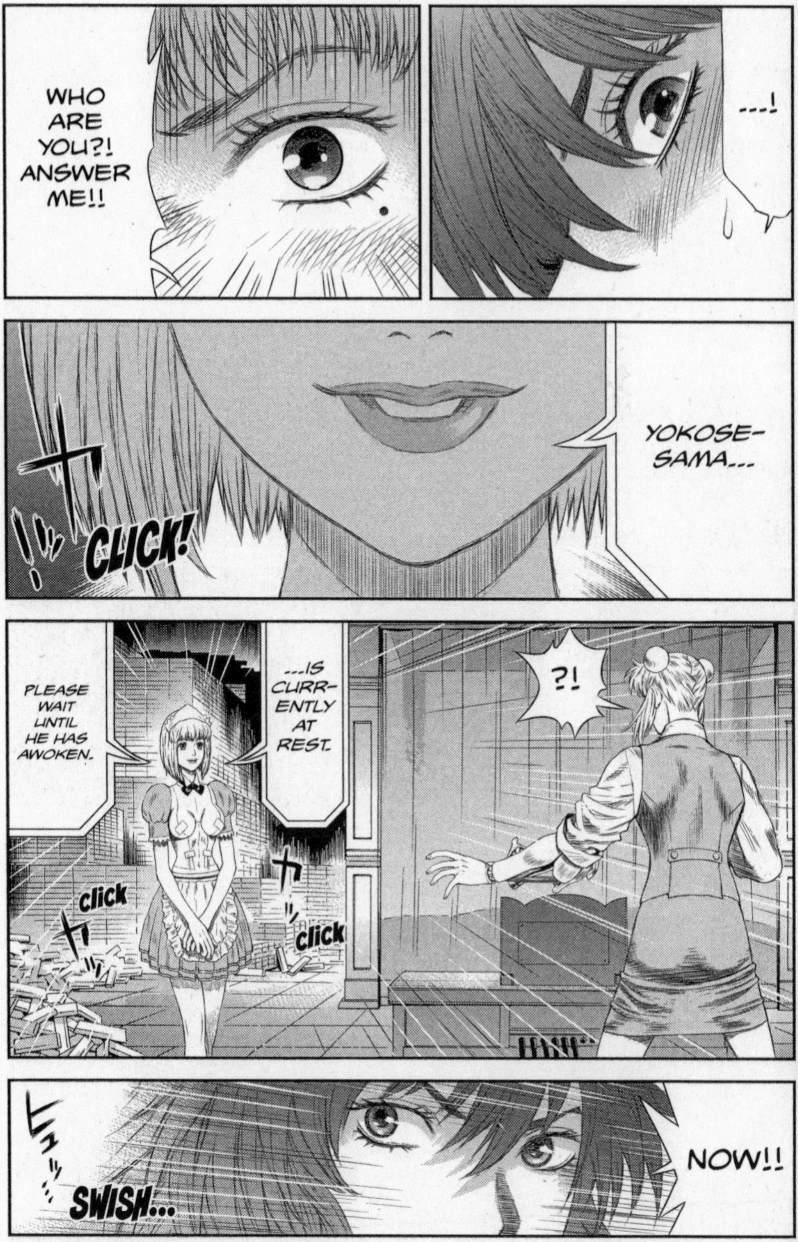
---!
WHO ARE YOU?! ANSWER ME!!
YOKOSE-SAMA...
CLICK!
?!
...IS CURR-ENTLY AT REST.
PLEASE WAIT UNTIL HE HAS AWOKEN.
click
click
NOW!!
SWISH...

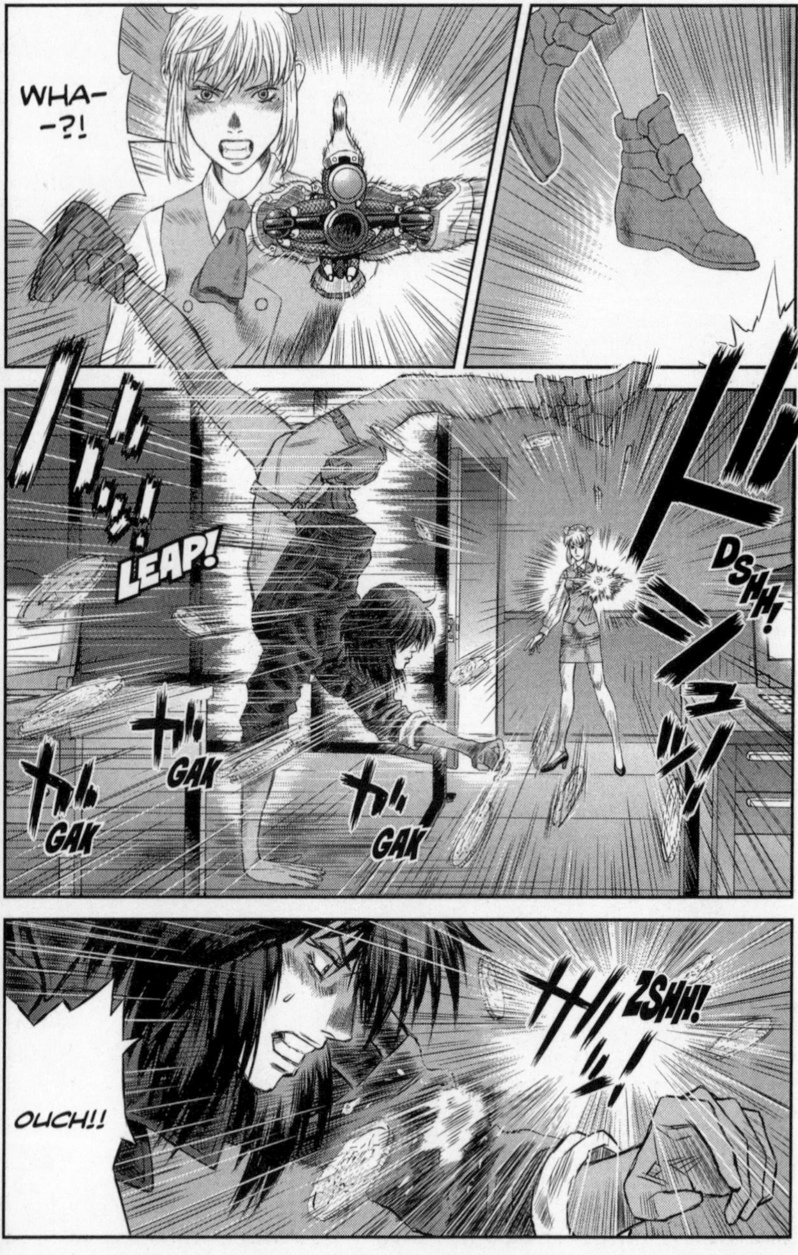
WHA--?!
DSHH!
LEAP!
GAK
GAK
GAK
ZSHH!
OUCH!!

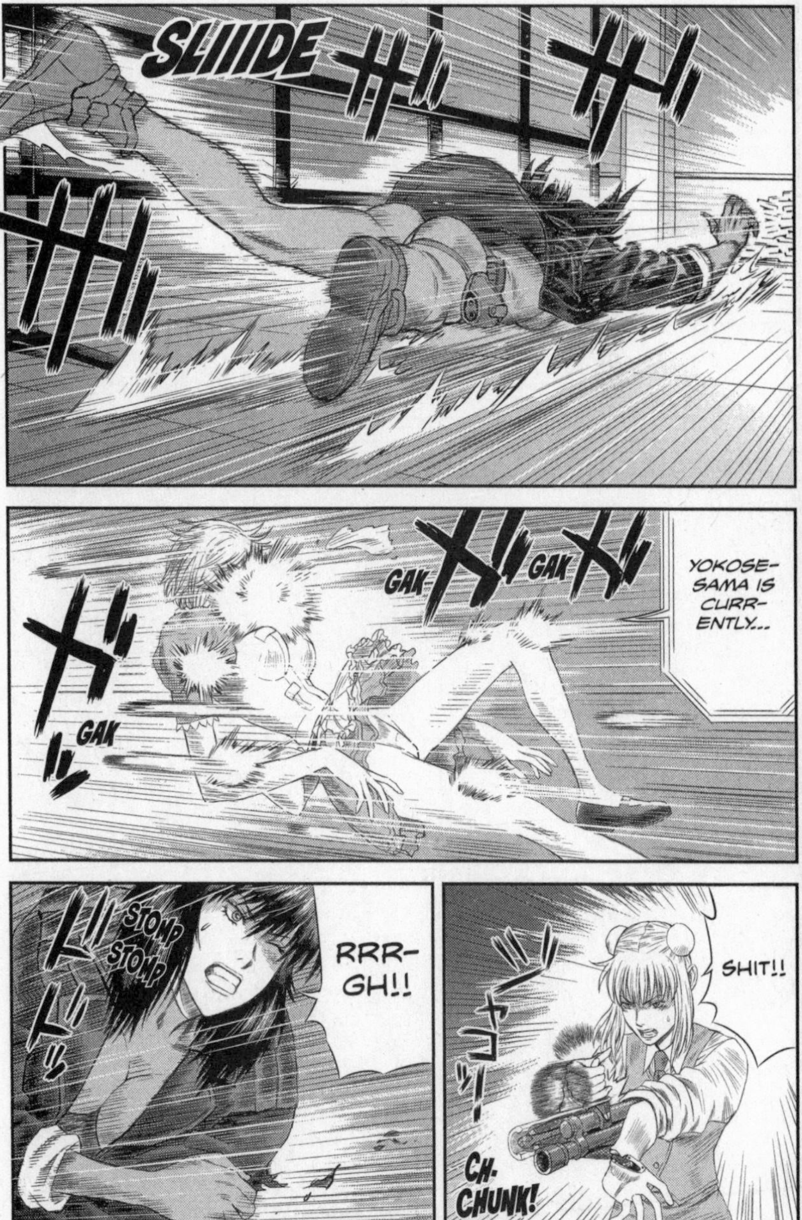
SLIIIDE
YOKOSE-SAMA IS CURR-ENTLY...
GAK
GAK
GAK
SHIT!!
CH-CHUNK!
RRR-GH!!
STOMP STOMP

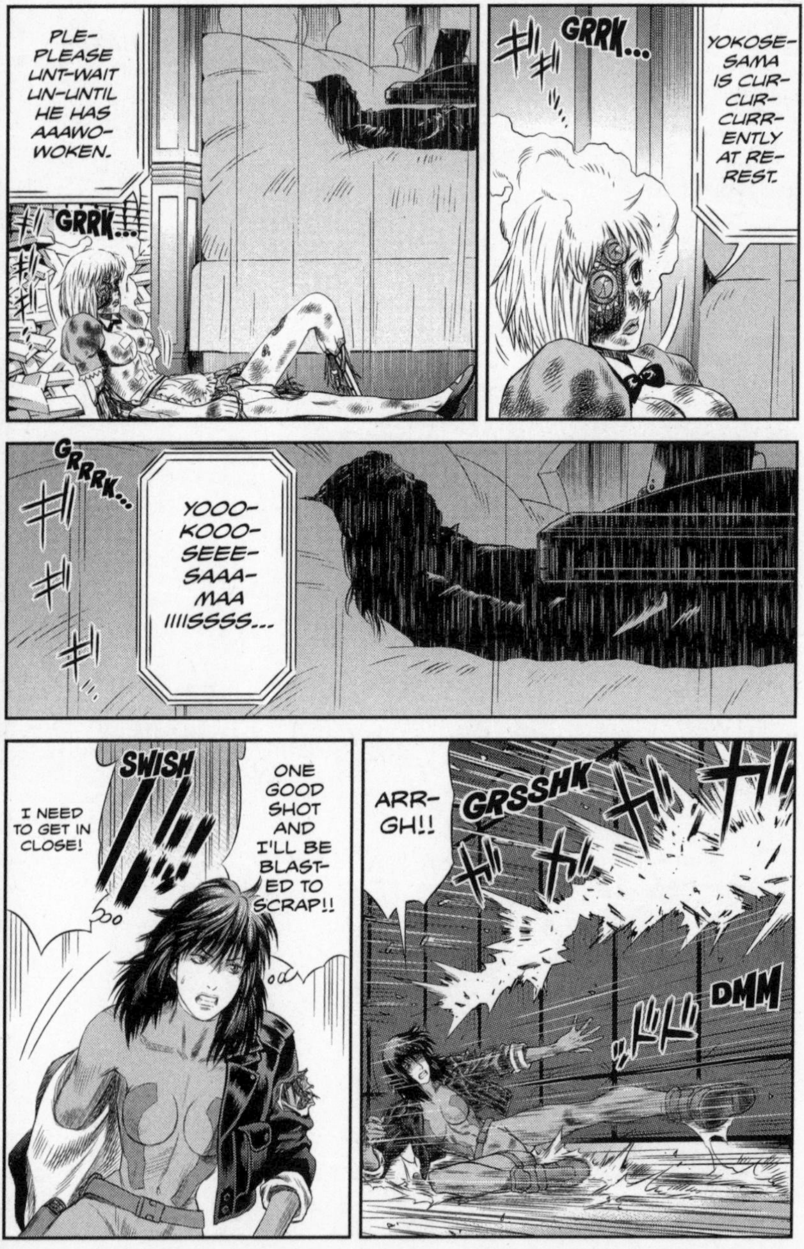
GRRK...
YOKOSE-SAMA IS CUR-CUR-CURR-ENTLY AT RE-REST.
PLE-PLEASE UNT-WAIT UN-UNTIL HE HAS AAAWO-WOKEN.
GRRK...!
GRRRK...
YOOO-KOOO-SEEE-SAAA-MAA IIIISSSS...
GRSSHK
ARR-GH!!
DMM
SWISH
ONE GOOD SHOT AND I'LL BE BLAST-ED TO SCRAP!!
I NEED TO GET IN CLOSE!

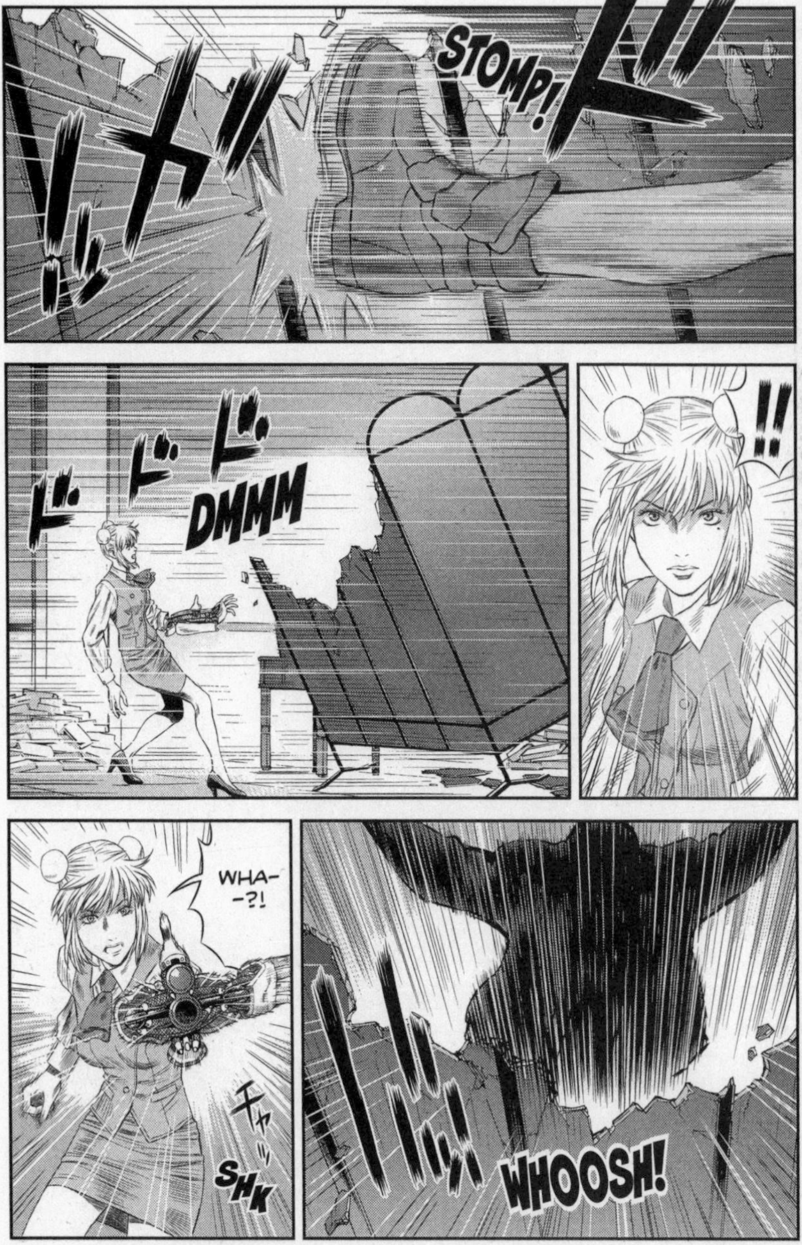
STOMP!
!!
DMMM
WHOOSH!
WHA-
-?!
SHK

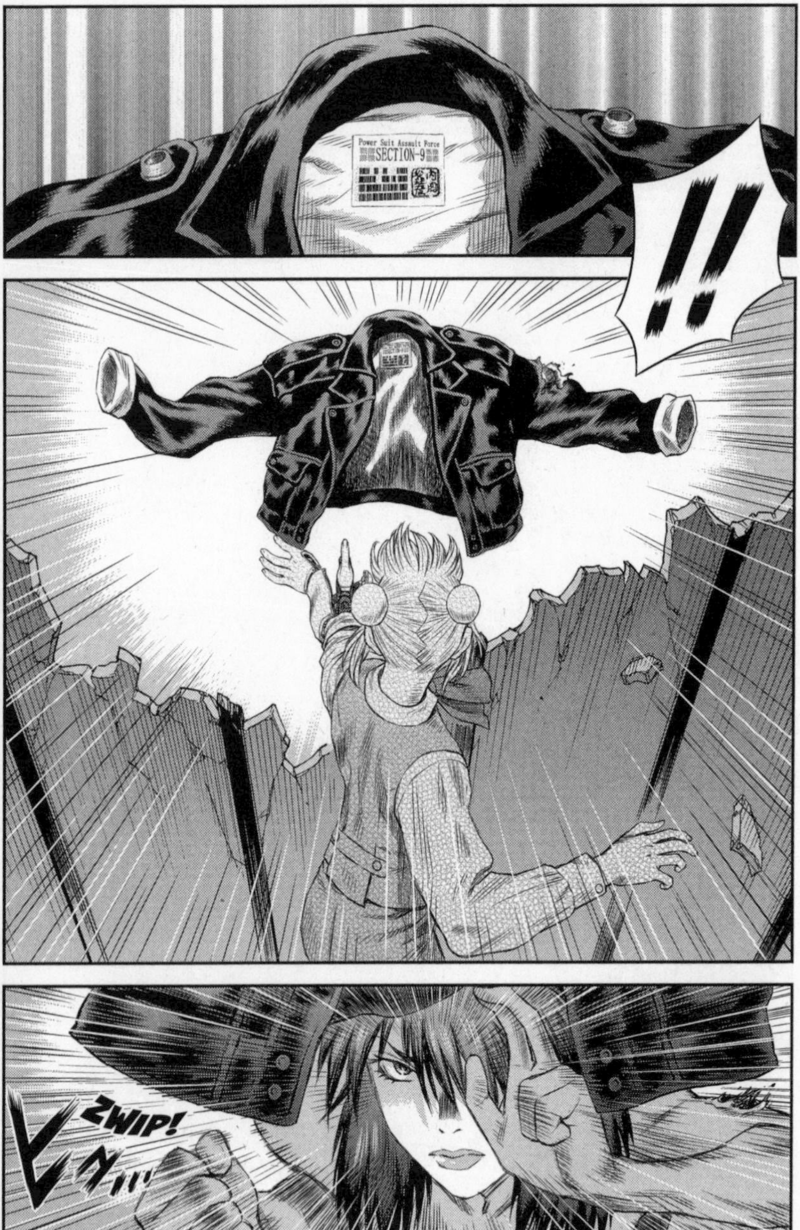
Power Suit Assault Force
SECTION-9
!!
ZWIP!

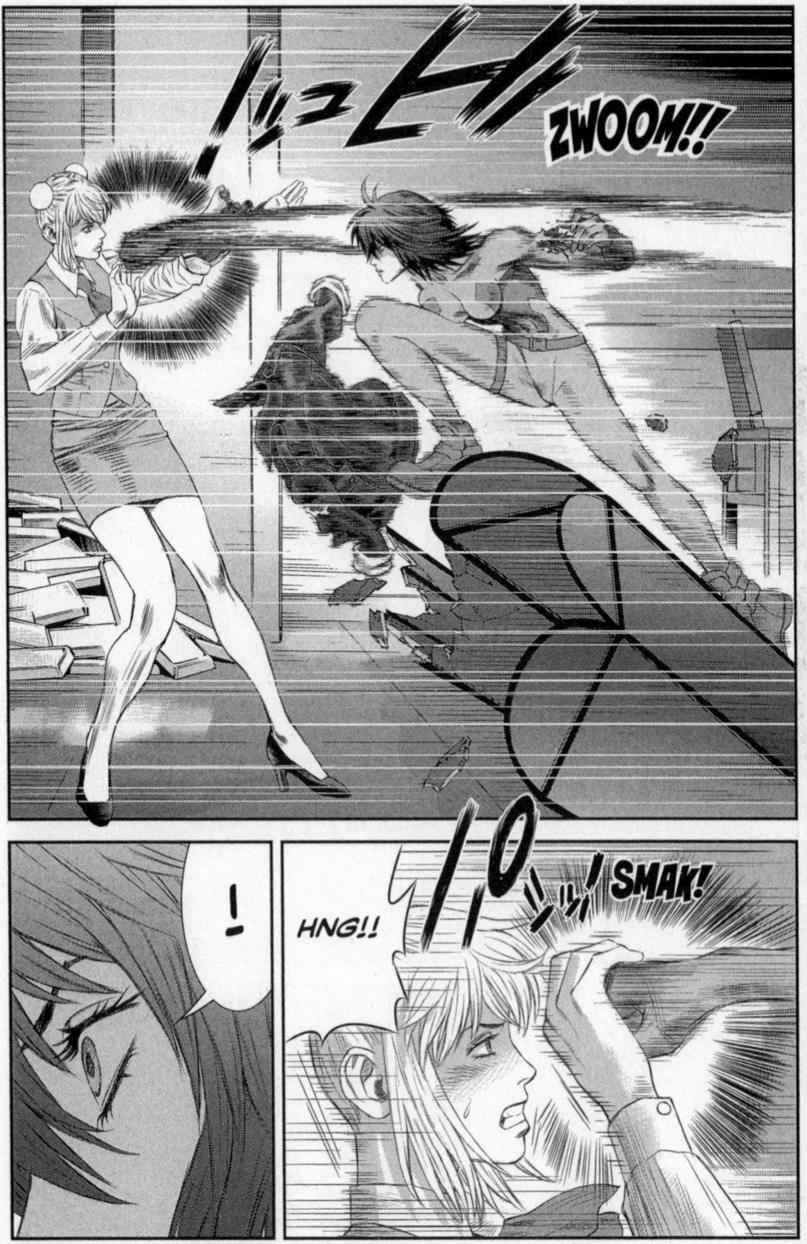
ZWOOM!!
SMAK!
HNG!!
!

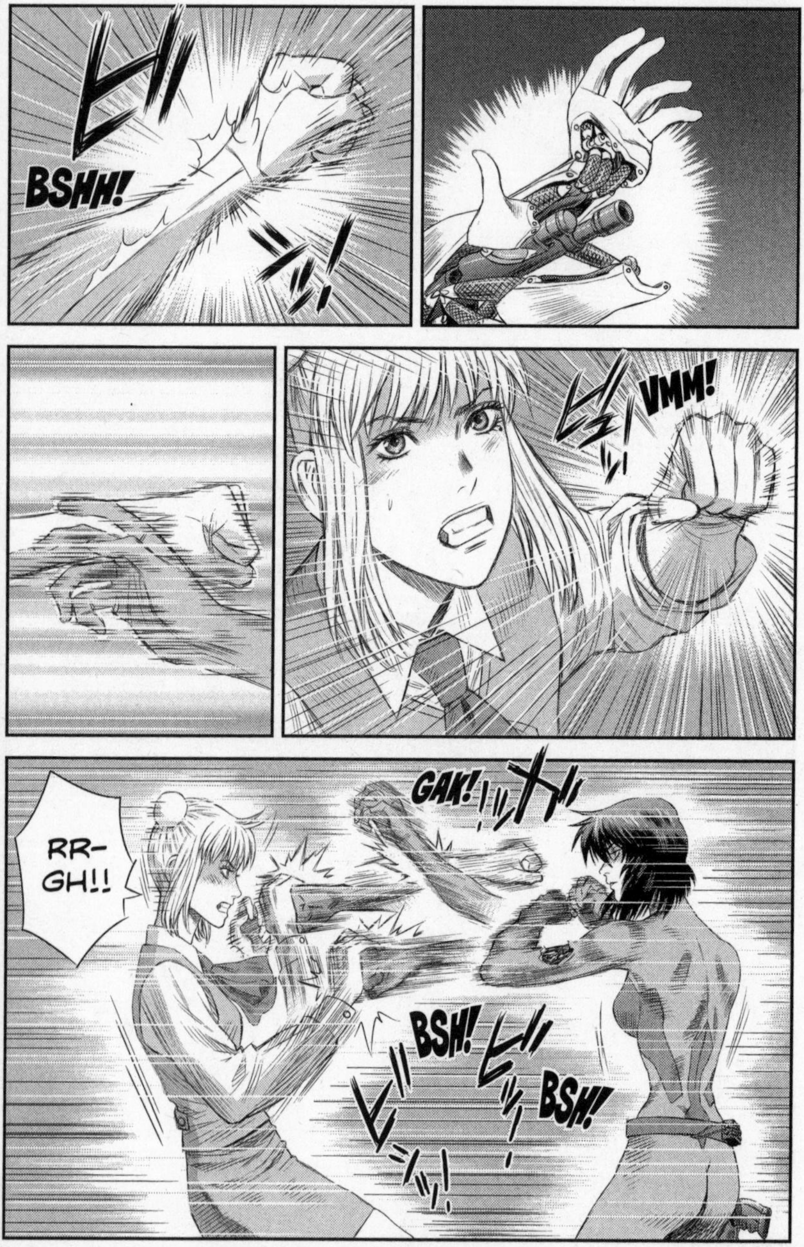

BSHH!
VMM!
GAK!
RR-GH!!
BSH!
BSH!

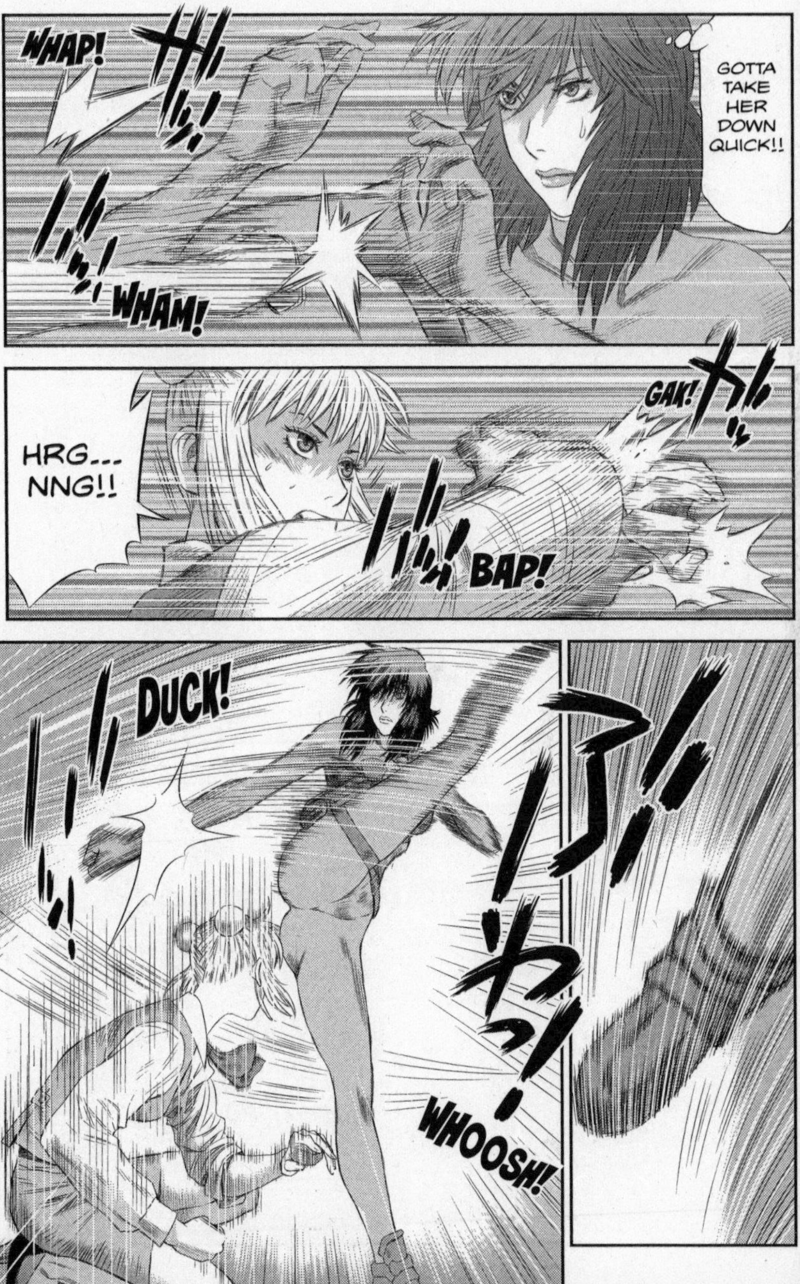
GOTTA TAKE HER DOWN QUICK!!
WHAP!
WHAM!
GAK!
HRG... NNG!!
BAP!
DUCK!
WHOOSH!

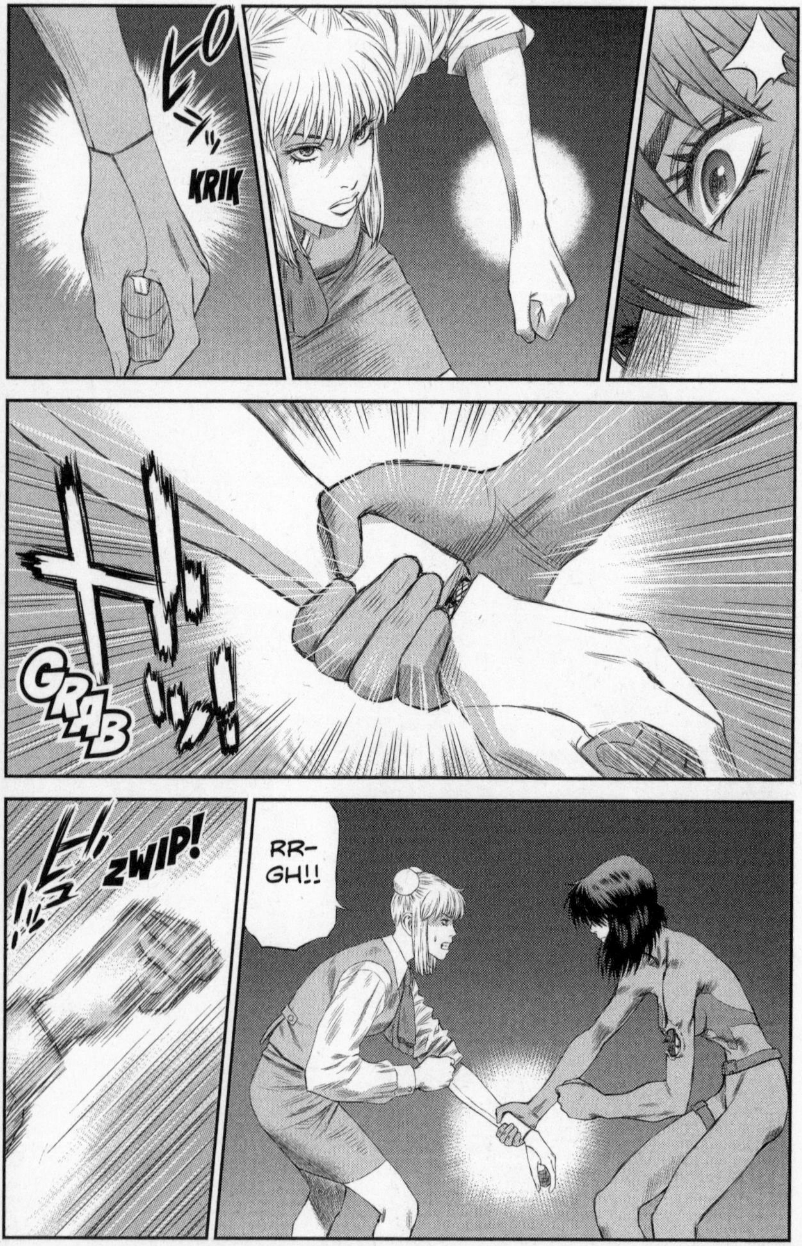
KRIK
GRAB
RR-GH!!
ZWIP!

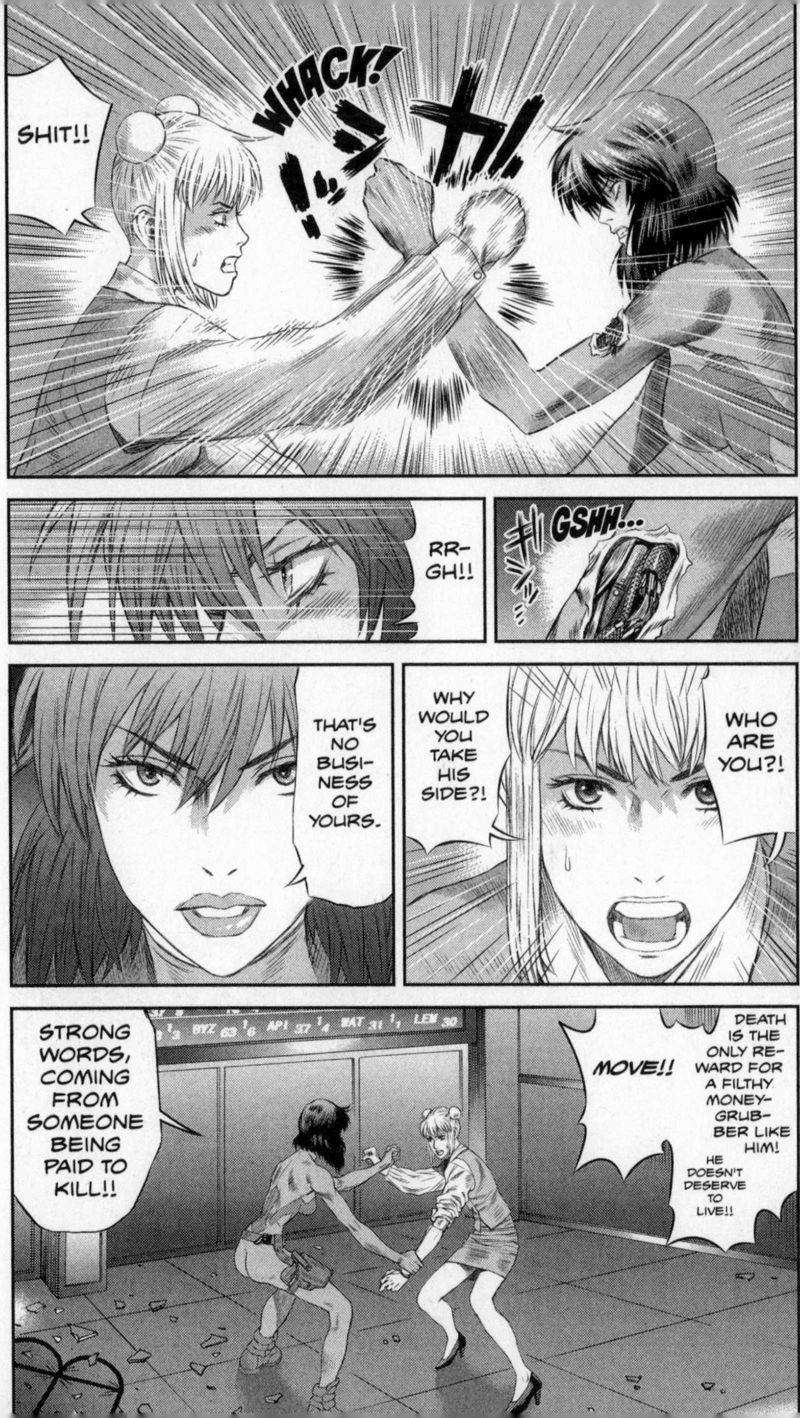
WHACK!
SHIT!!
GSHH...
RR-GH!!
WHO ARE YOU?!
WHY WOULD YOU TAKE HIS SIDE?!
THAT'S NO BUSINESS OF YOURS.
DEATH IS THE ONLY REWARD FOR A FILTHY MONEY-GRUBBER LIKE HIM!
MOVE!!
HE DOESN'T DESERVE TO LIVE!!
STRONG WORDS, COMING FROM SOMEONE BEING PAID TO KILL!!

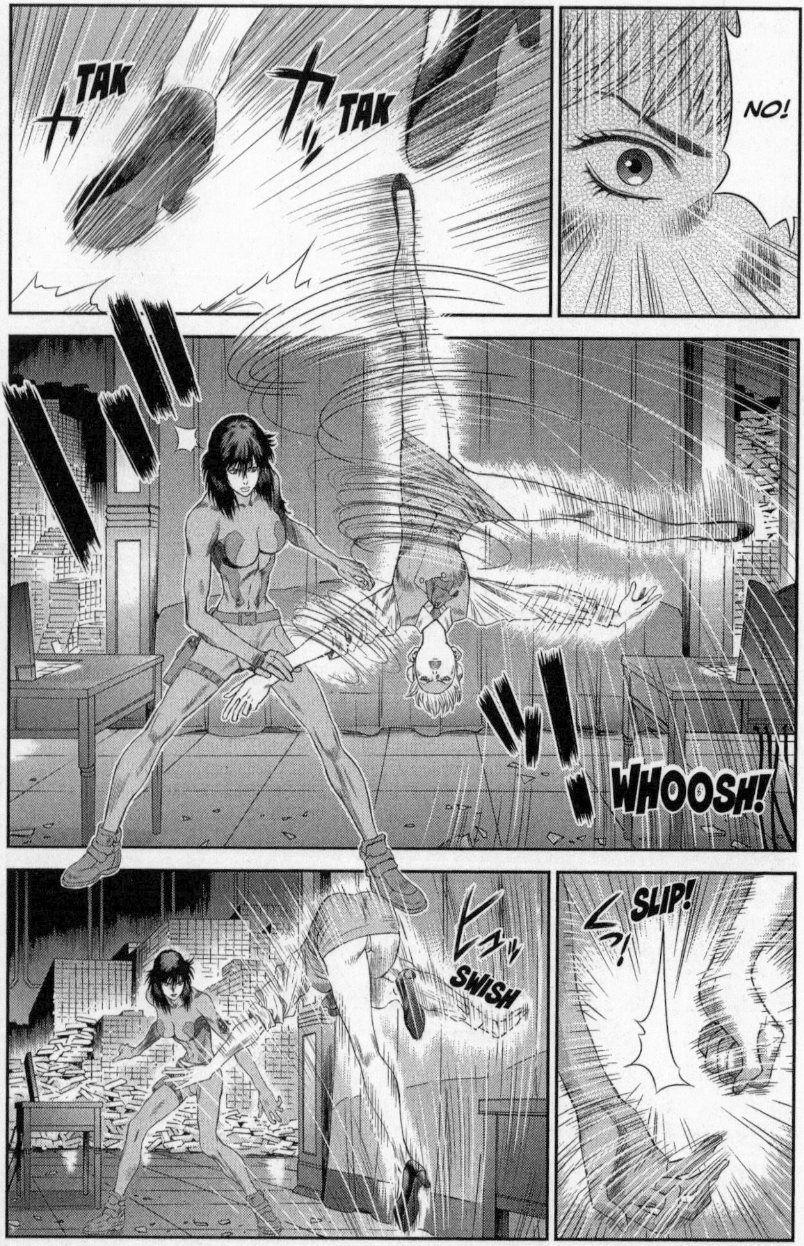
NO!
TAK
TAK
WHOOSH!
SLIP!
SWISH

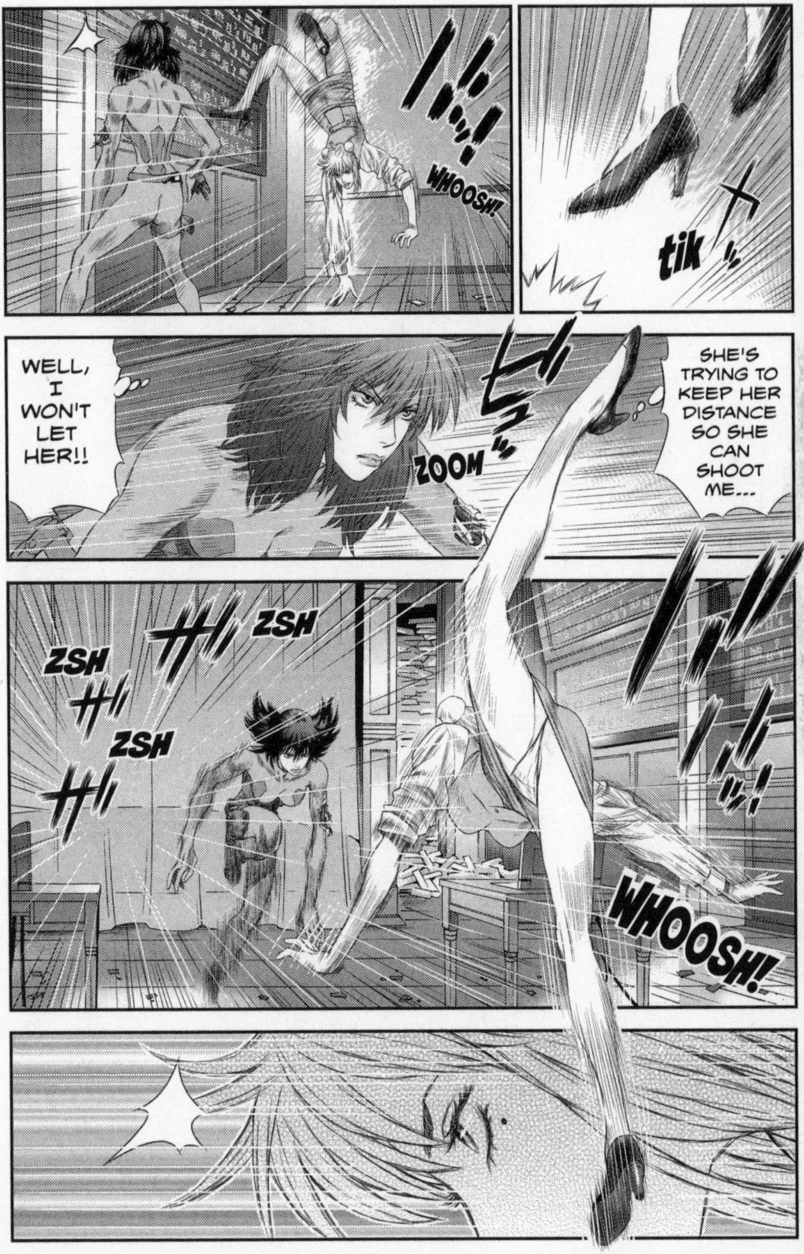
tik
WHOOSH!
SHE'S TRYING TO KEEP HER DISTANCE SO SHE CAN SHOOT ME...
WELL, I WON'T LET HER!!
ZOOM
WHOOSH!
ZSH
ZSH
ZSH

THUD!

HRRG... MMF!!

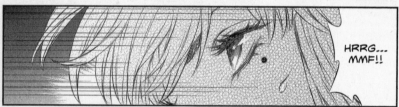

HUFF!

HUFF!

HUFF!

TAP

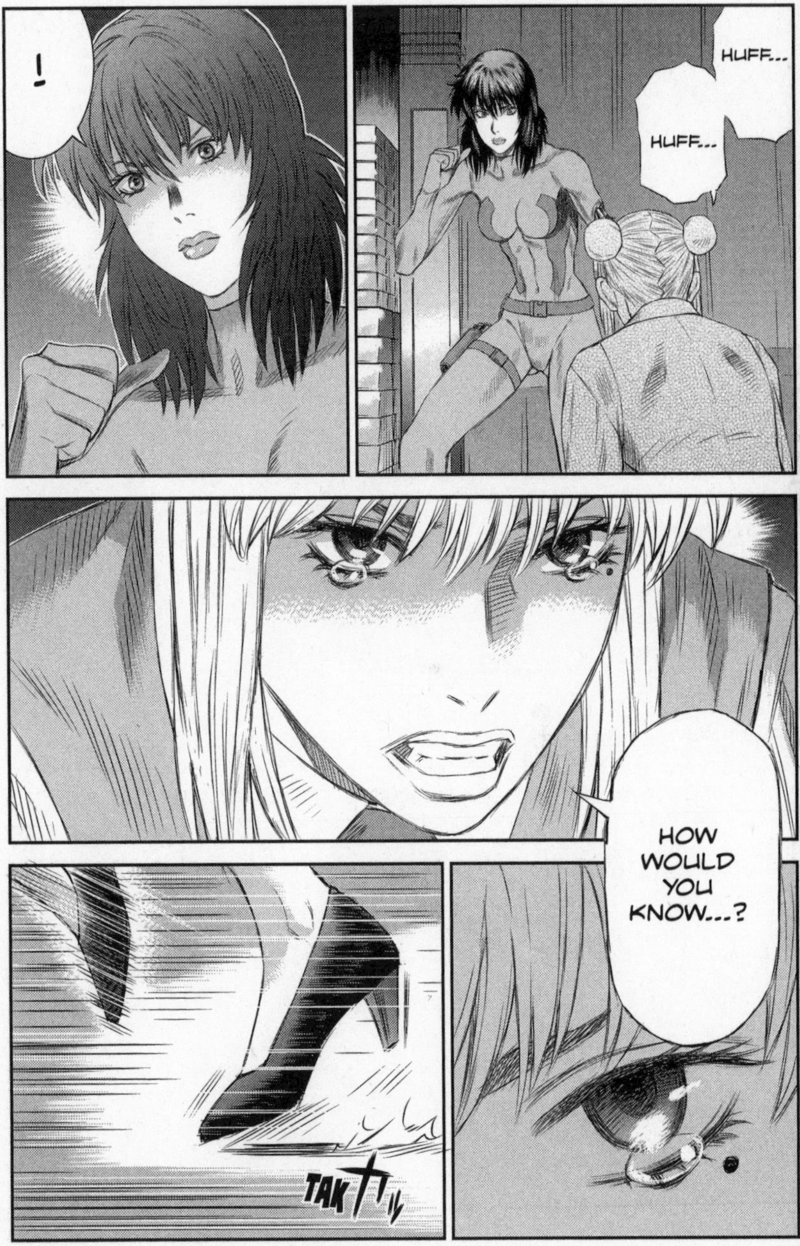
HUFF...
HUFF...
!
HOW WOULD YOU KNOW...?
TAK

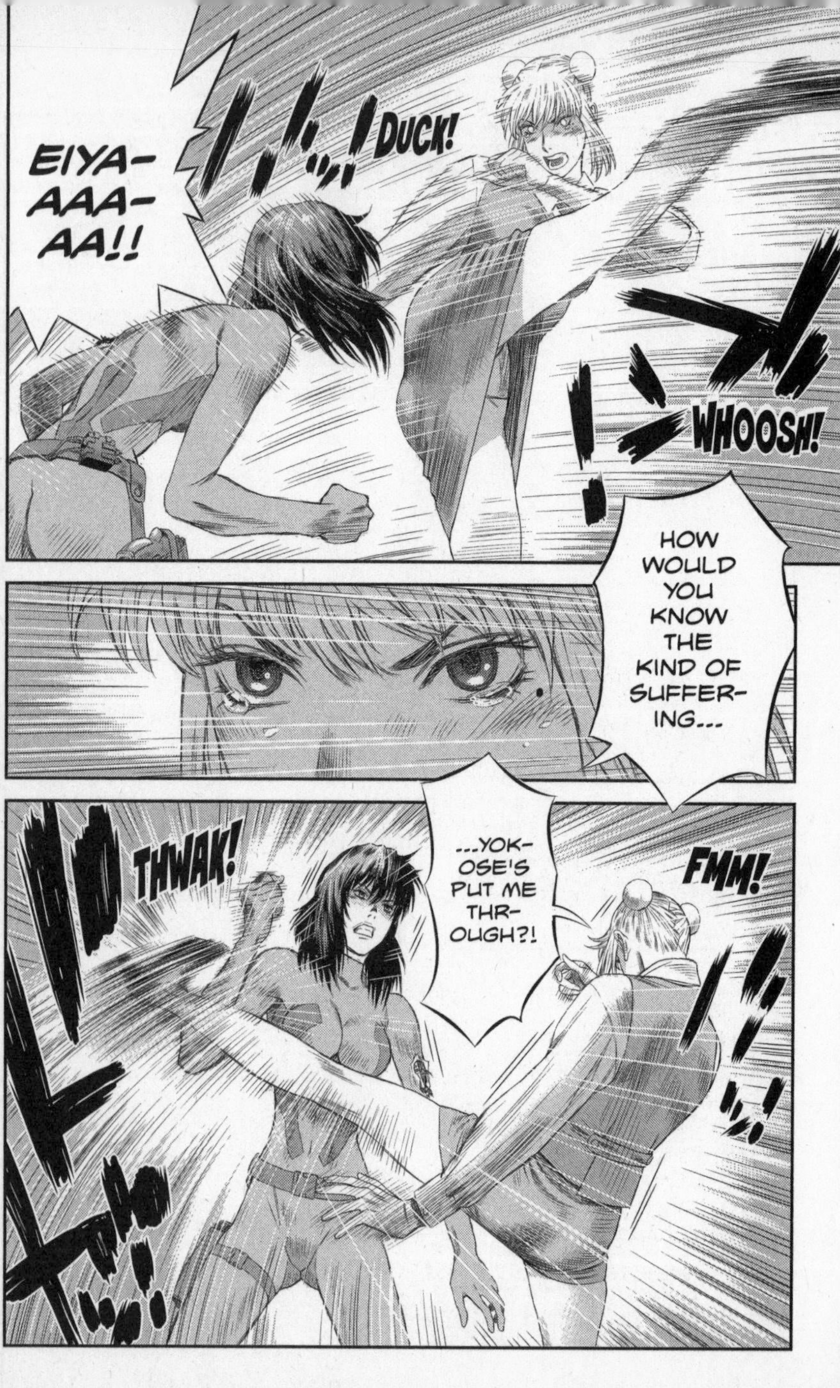
DUCK!
EIYA-AAA-AA!!
WHOOSH!
HOW WOULD YOU KNOW THE KIND OF SUFFER-ING...
FMM!
...YOK-OSE'S PUT ME THR-OUGH?!
THWAK!

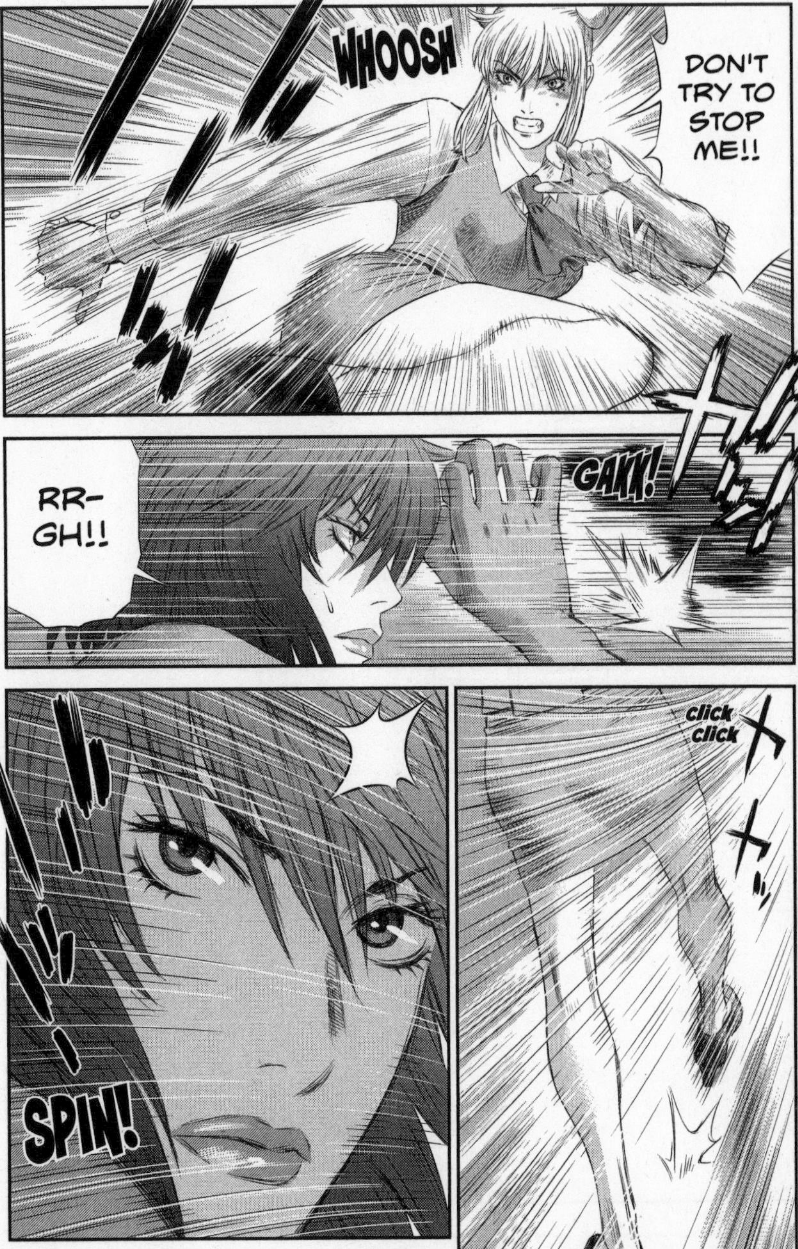
DON'T TRY TO STOP ME!!
WHOOSH
GAKK!
RR-GH!!
click click
SPIN!

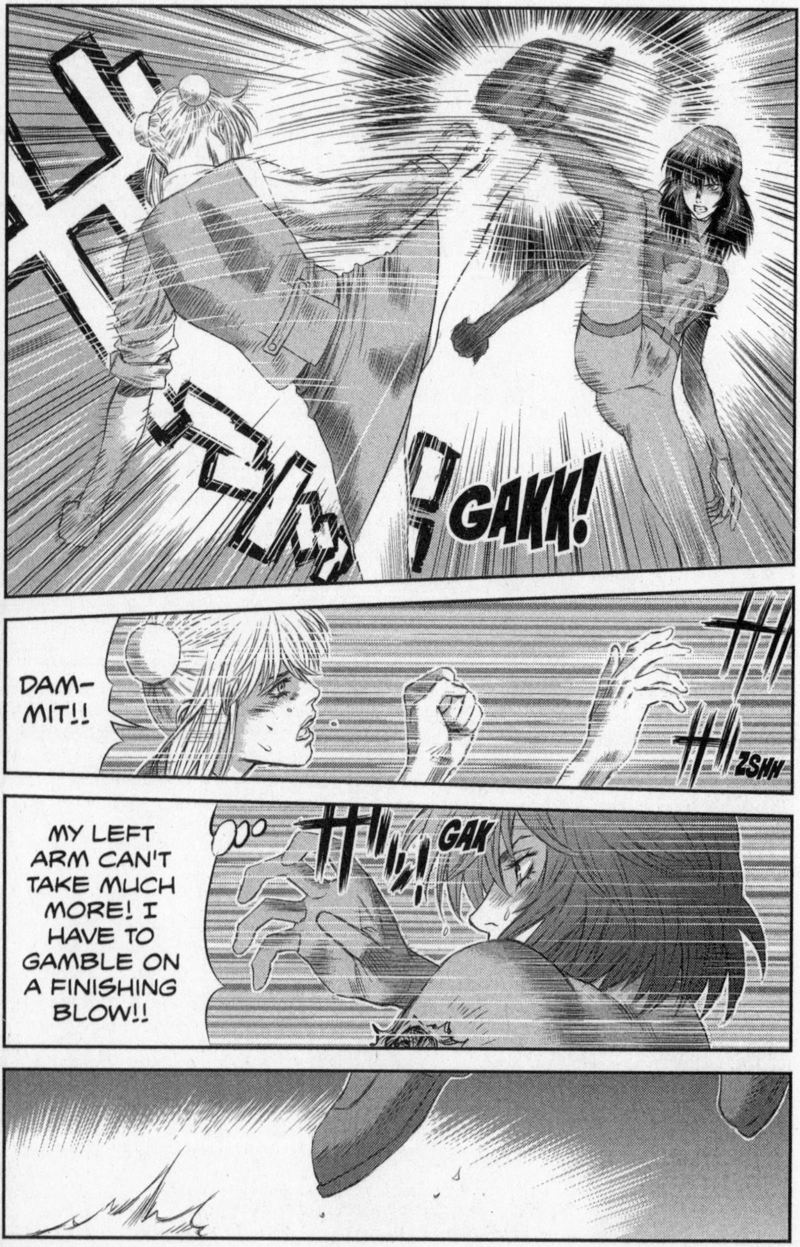
GAKK!
ZSHH
DAM-MIT!!
GAK
MY LEFT ARM CAN'T TAKE MUCH MORE! I HAVE TO GAMBLE ON A FINISHING BLOW!!

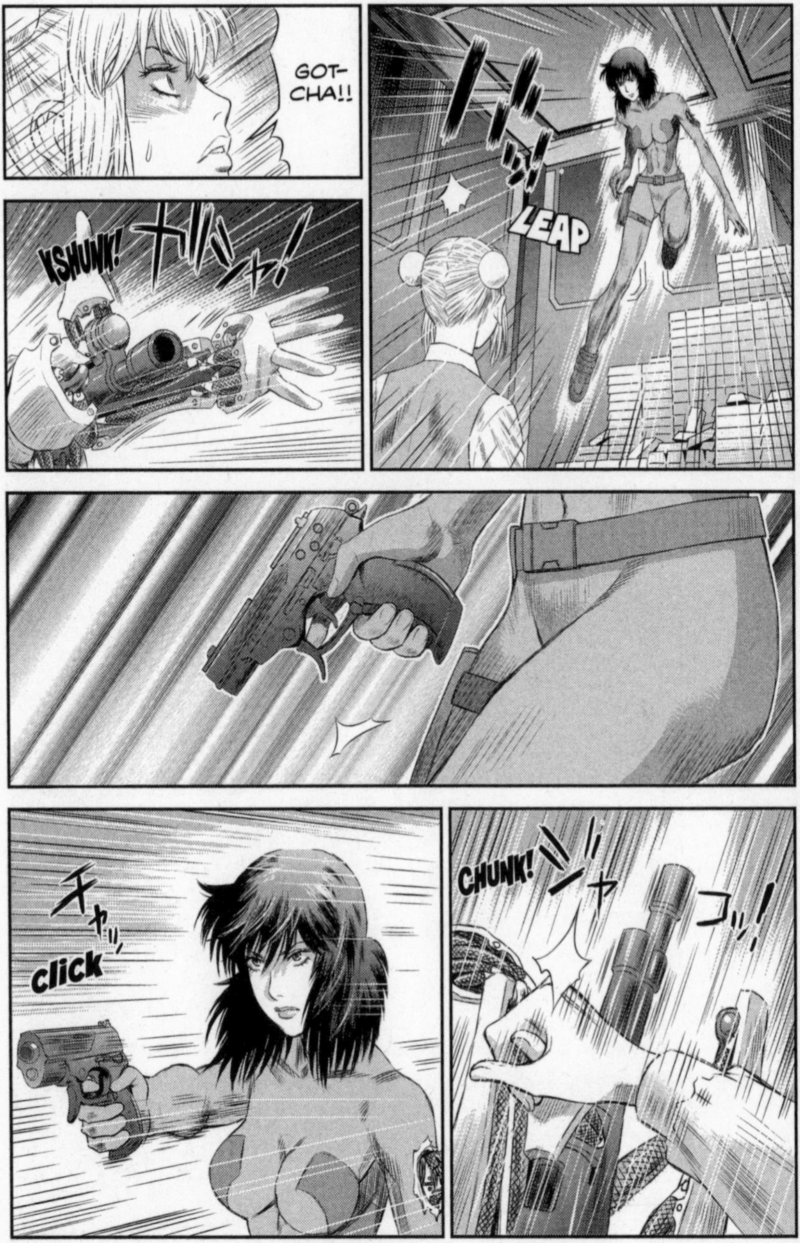
LEAP
GOT-CHA!!
KSHUNK!
CHUNK!
click

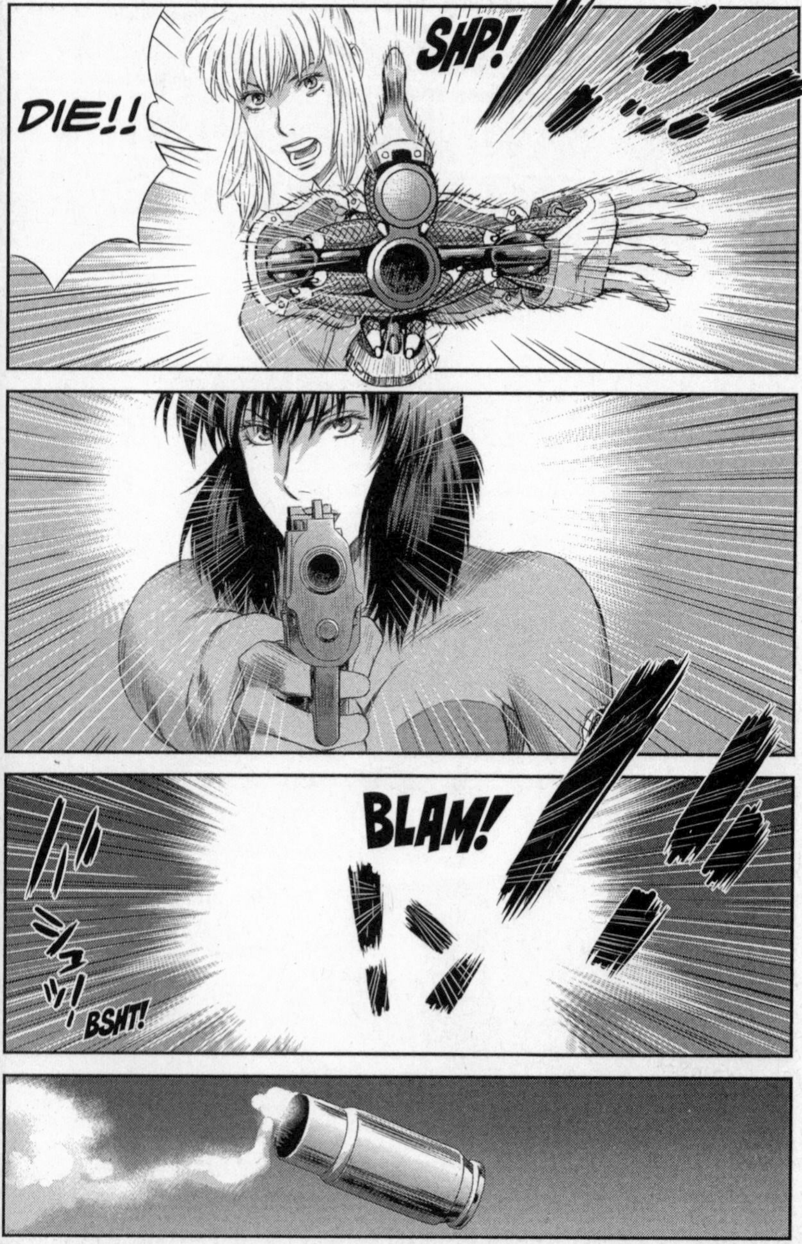
SHP!
DIE!!
BLAM!
シュッ!
BSHT!

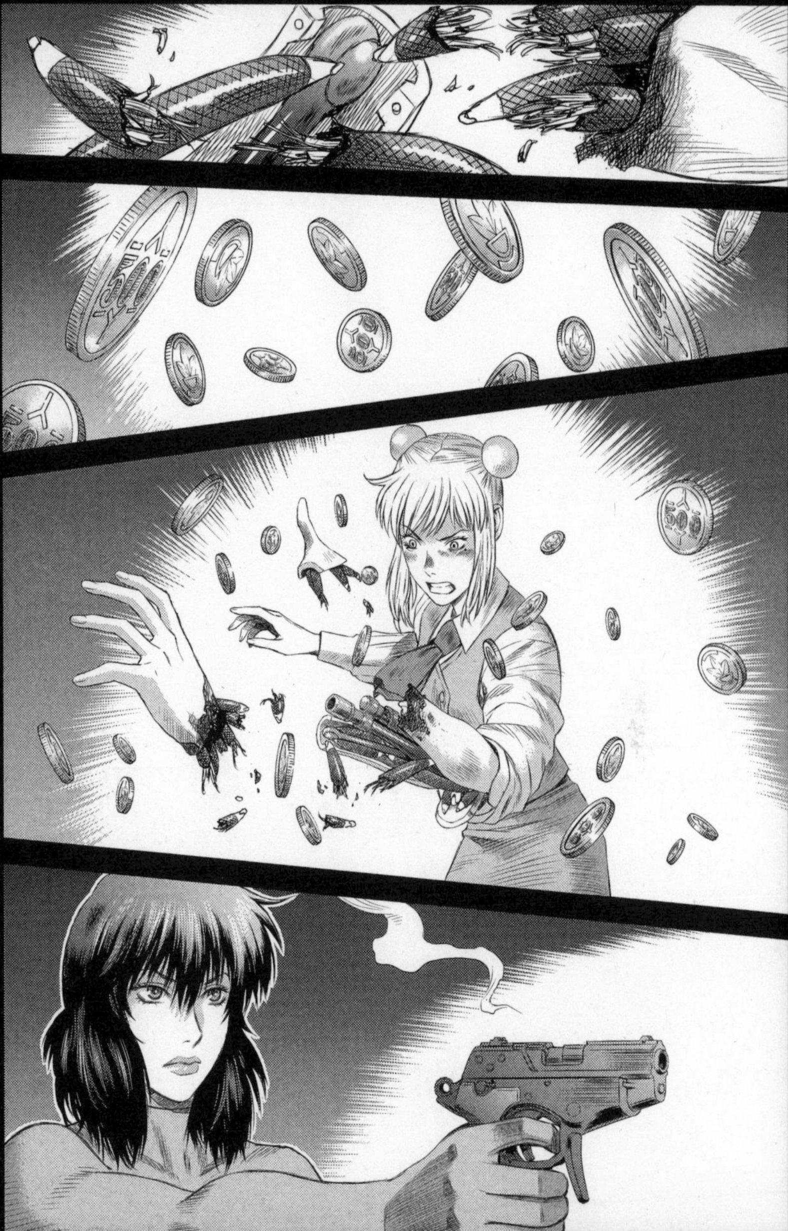

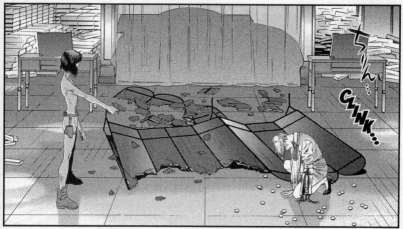

HN-
NG...

IT'S OVER.

GIVE YOUR-SELF UP.

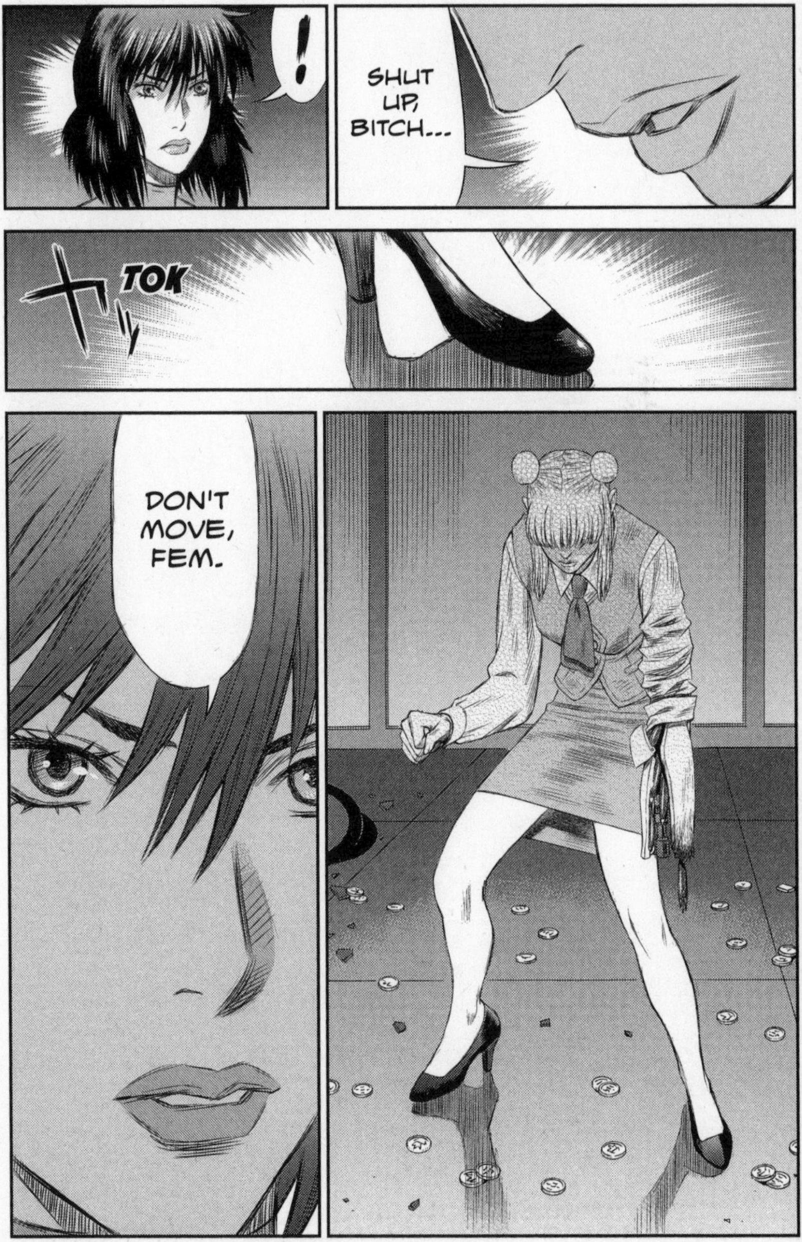
SHUT UP, BITCH...
!
TOK
DON'T MOVE, FEM.

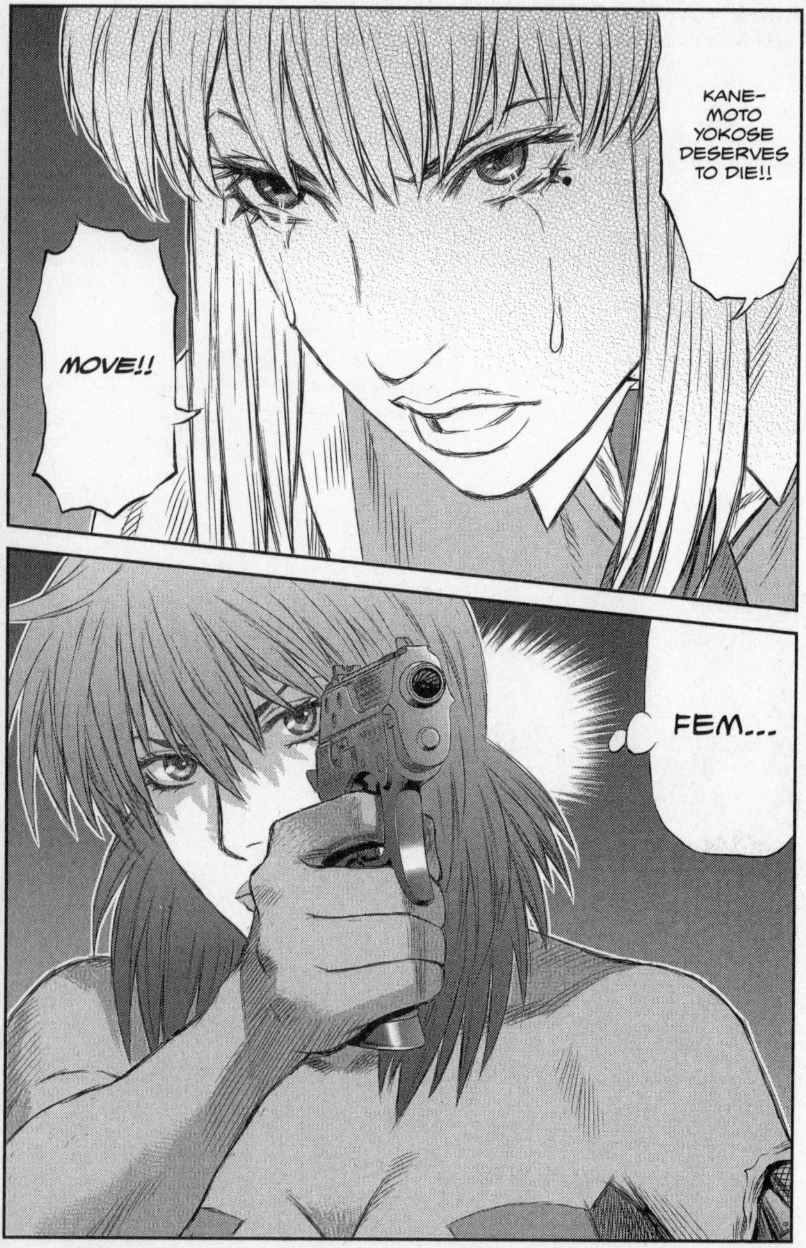
KANE-MOTO YOKOSE DESERVES TO DIE!!
MOVE!!
FEM...

#029: END

#030: The Tycoon and the Assassin

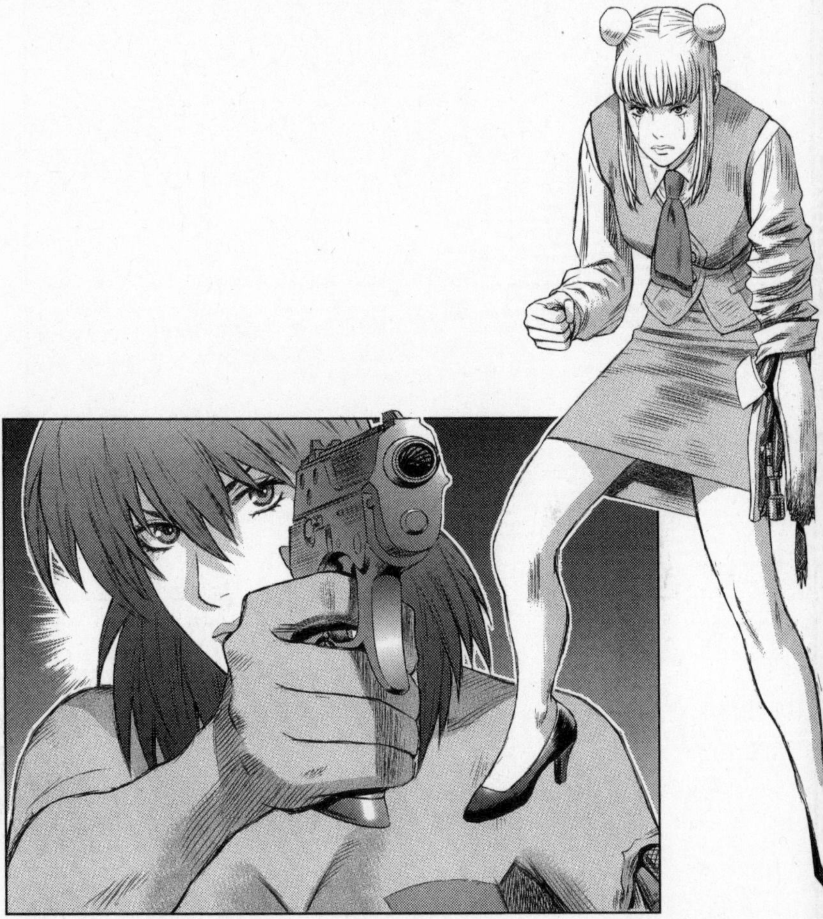

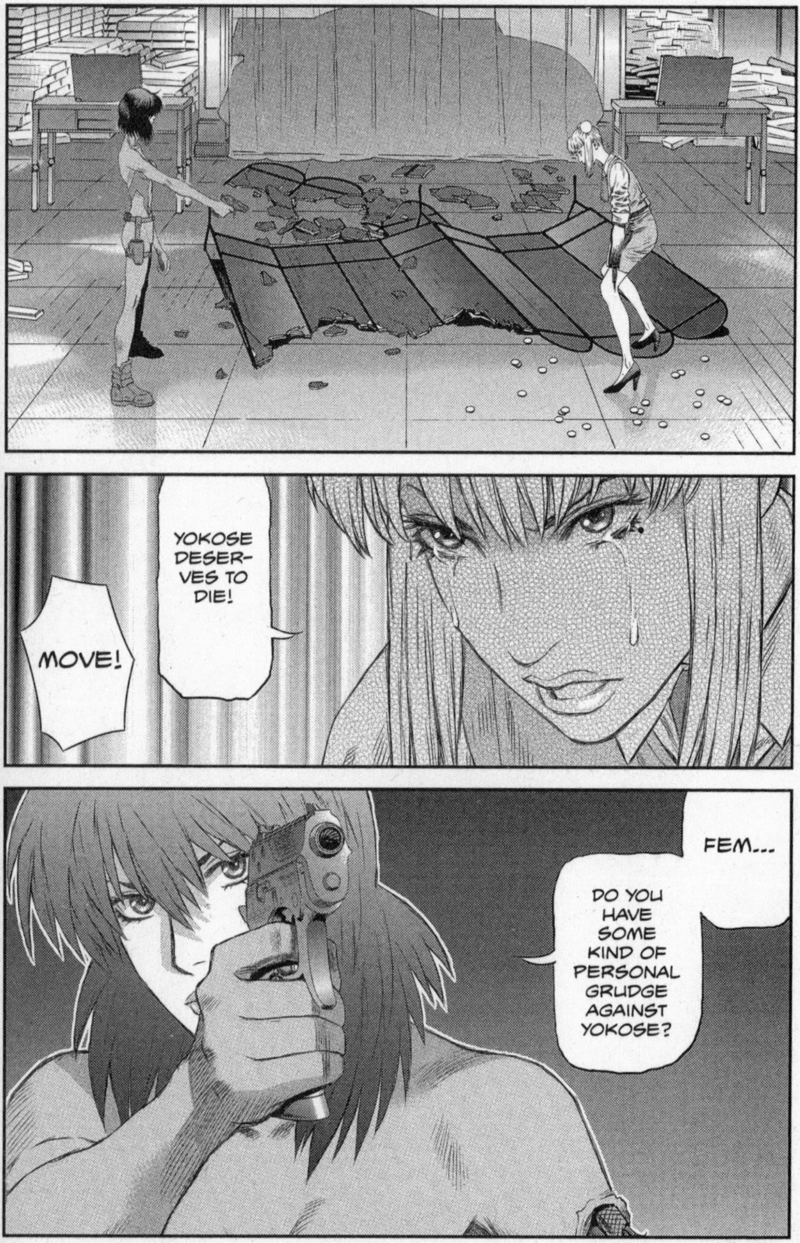
YOKOSE DESERVES TO DIE!
MOVE!
FEM...
DO YOU HAVE SOME KIND OF PERSONAL GRUDGE AGAINST YOKOSE?

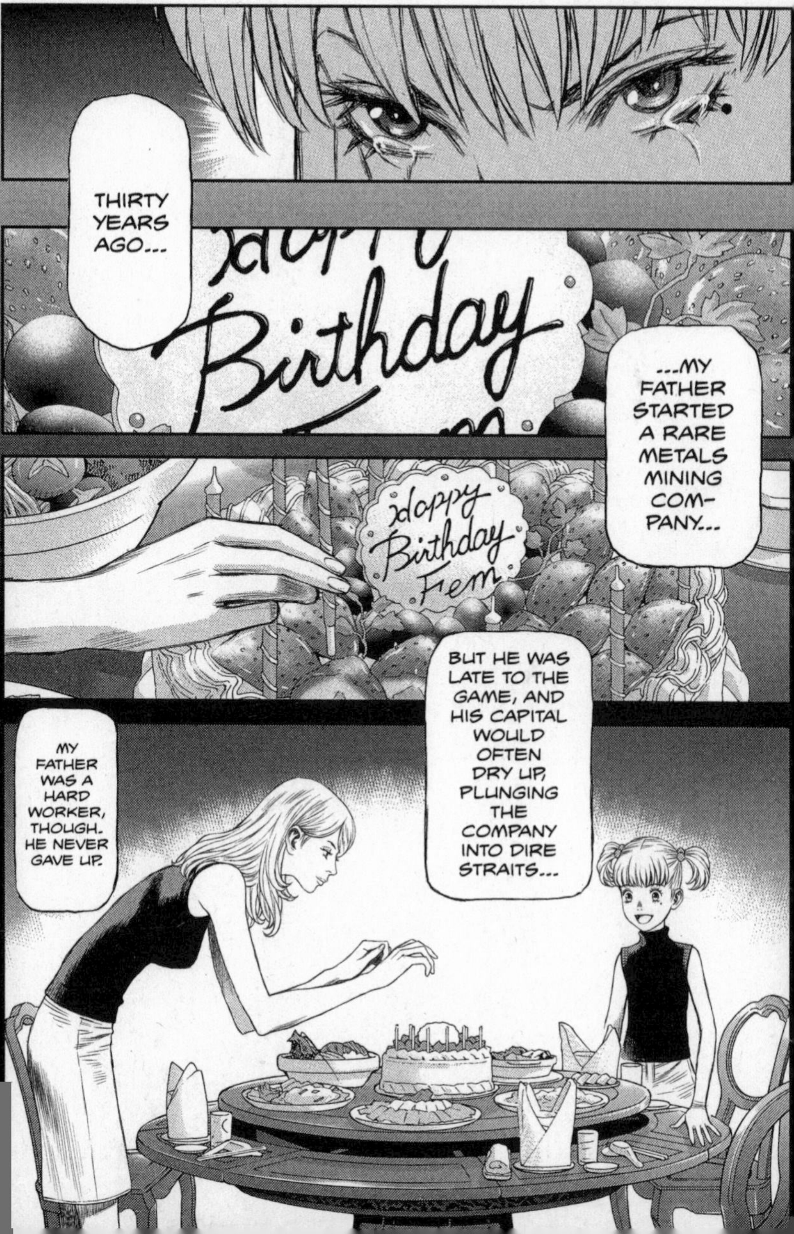
THIRTY YEARS AGO...
Birthday
...MY FATHER STARTED A RARE METALS MINING COM-PANY...
Happy Birthday Fem
BUT HE WAS LATE TO THE GAME, AND HIS CAPITAL WOULD OFTEN DRY UP, PLUNGING THE COMPANY INTO DIRE STRAITS...
MY FATHER WAS A HARD WORKER, THOUGH. HE NEVER GAVE UP.

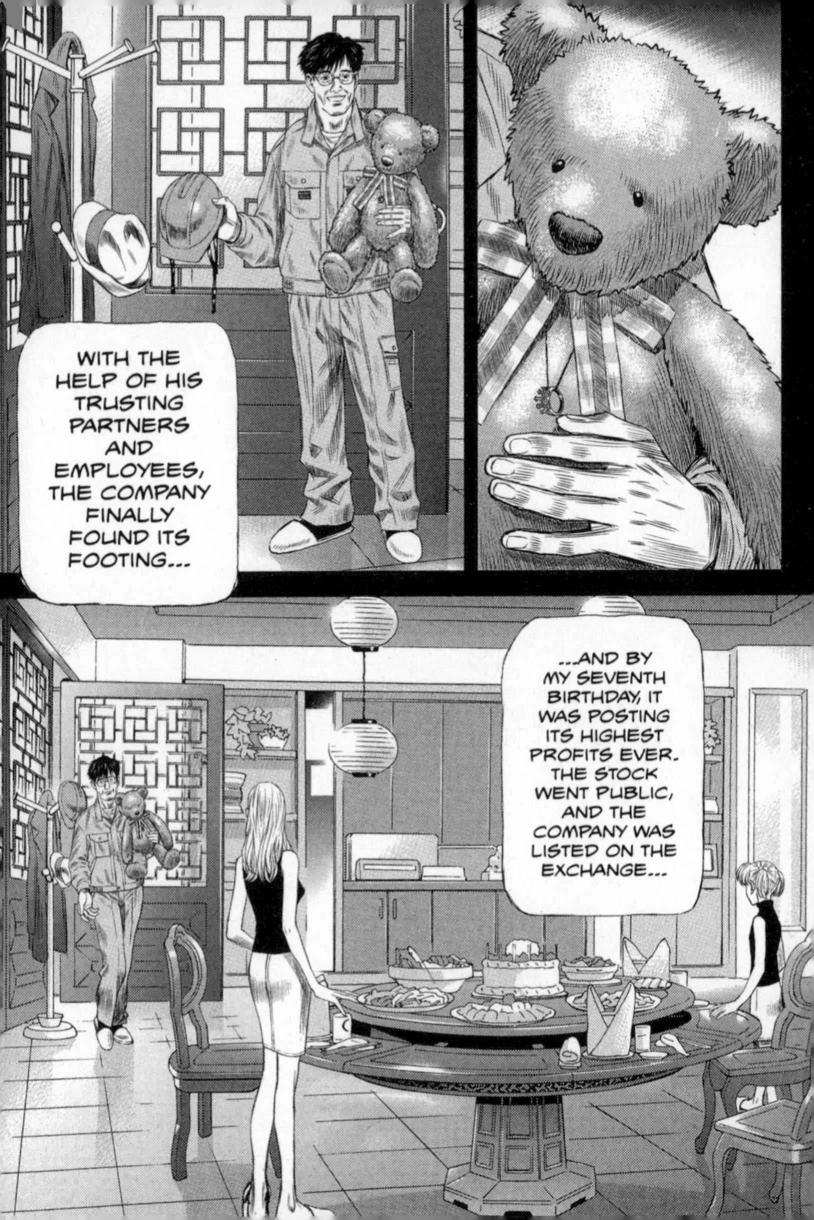
WITH THE HELP OF HIS TRUSTING PARTNERS AND EMPLOYEES, THE COMPANY FINALLY FOUND ITS FOOTING...
...AND BY MY SEVENTH BIRTHDAY, IT WAS POSTING ITS HIGHEST PROFITS EVER. THE STOCK WENT PUBLIC, AND THE COMPANY WAS LISTED ON THE EXCHANGE...

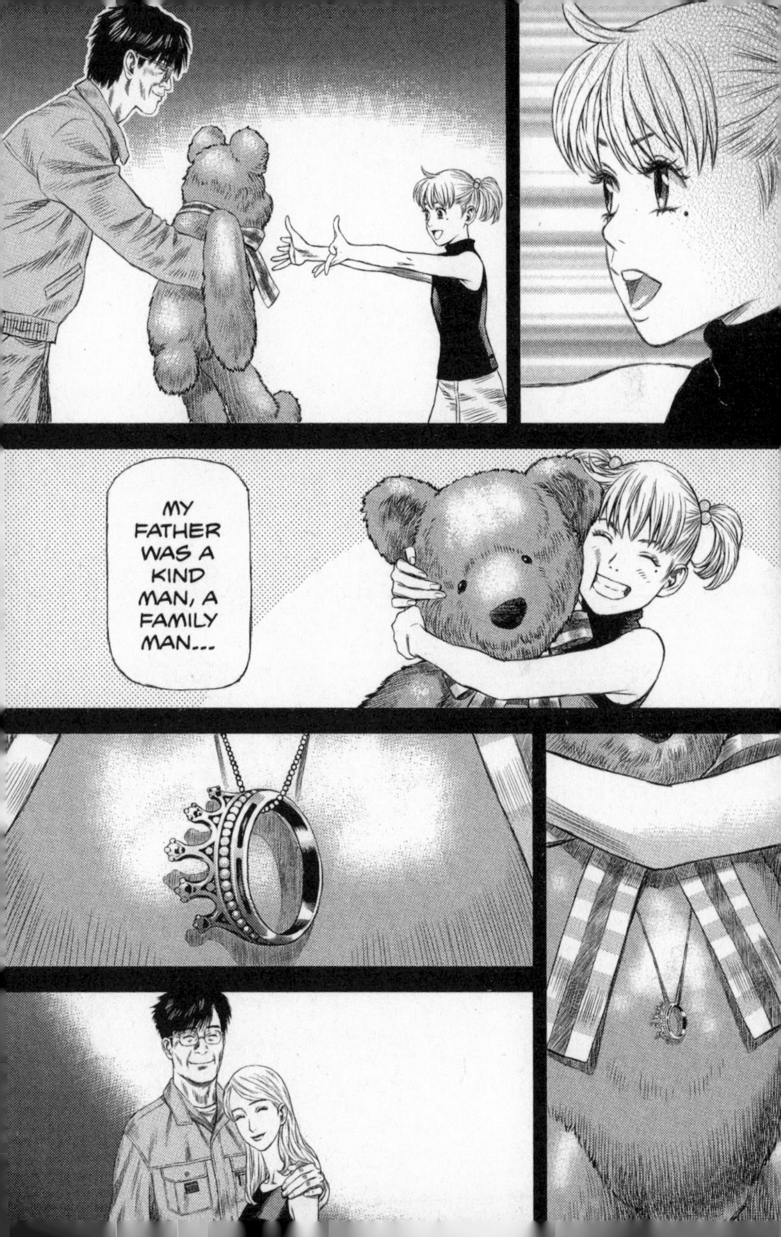
MY FATHER WAS A KIND MAN, A FAMILY MAN...

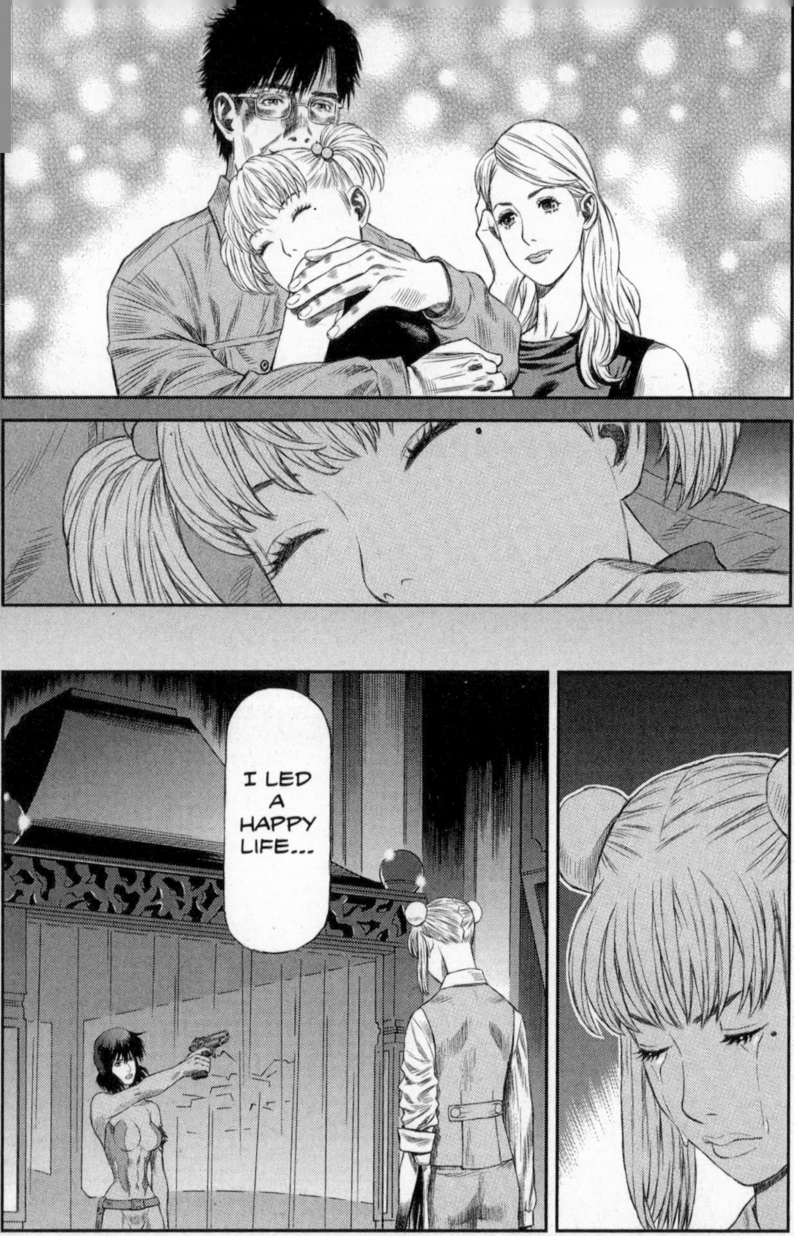
I LED A HAPPY LIFE...

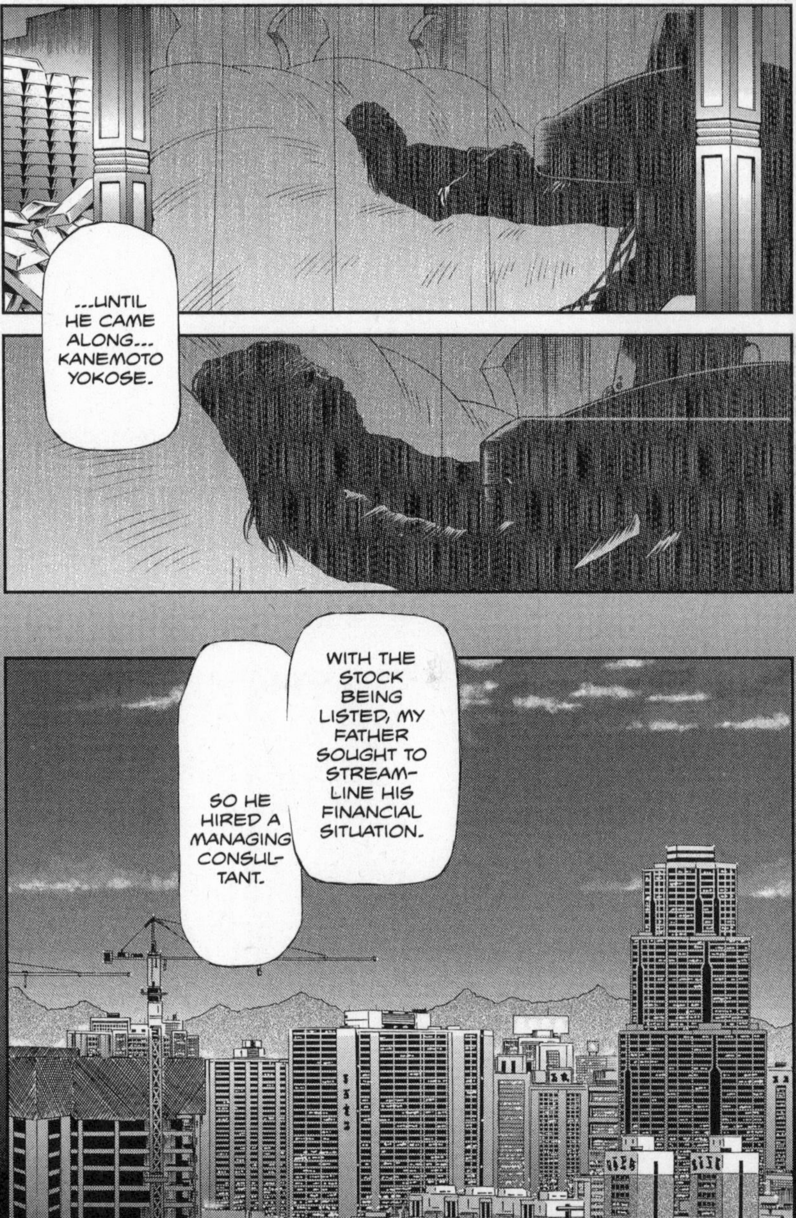
...UNTIL HE CAME ALONG... KANEMOTO YOKOSE.
WITH THE STOCK BEING LISTED, MY FATHER SOUGHT TO STREAM-LINE HIS FINANCIAL SITUATION.
SO HE HIRED A MANAGING CONSUL-TANT.

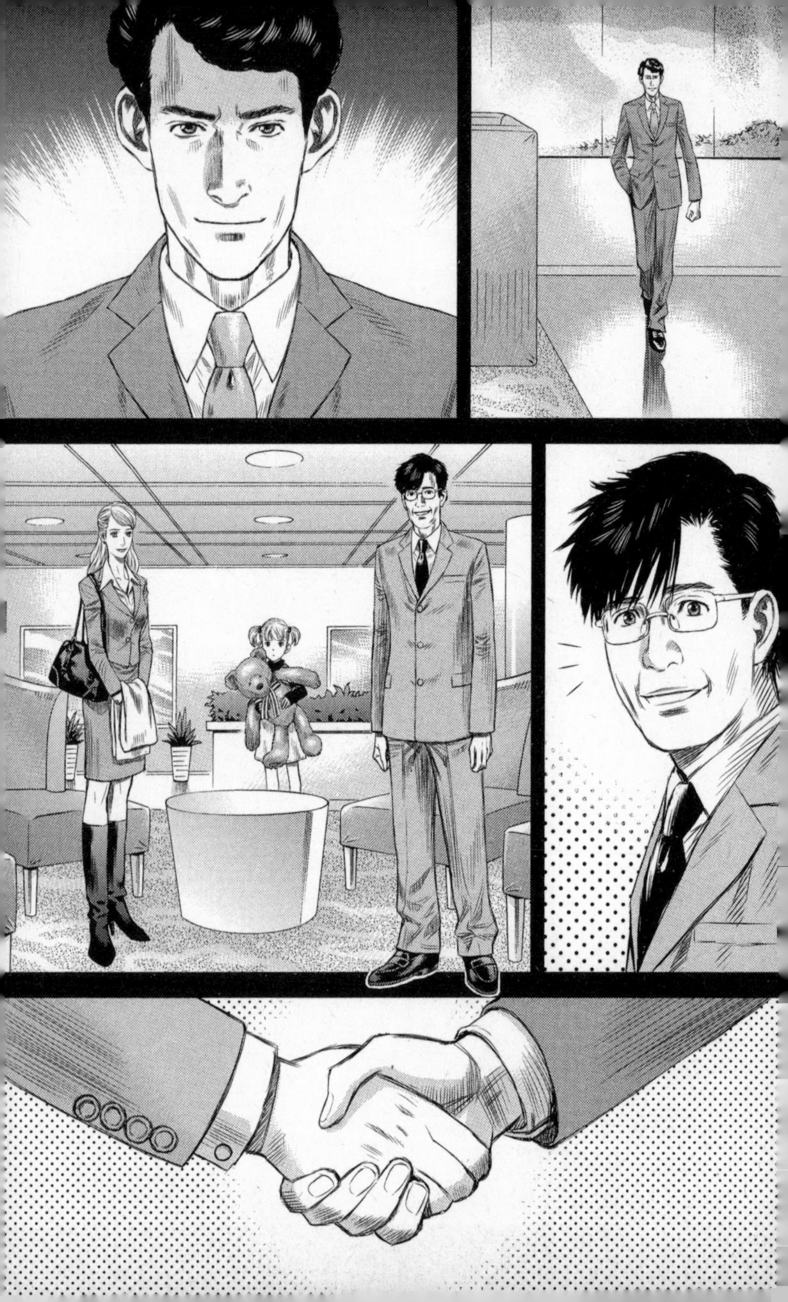

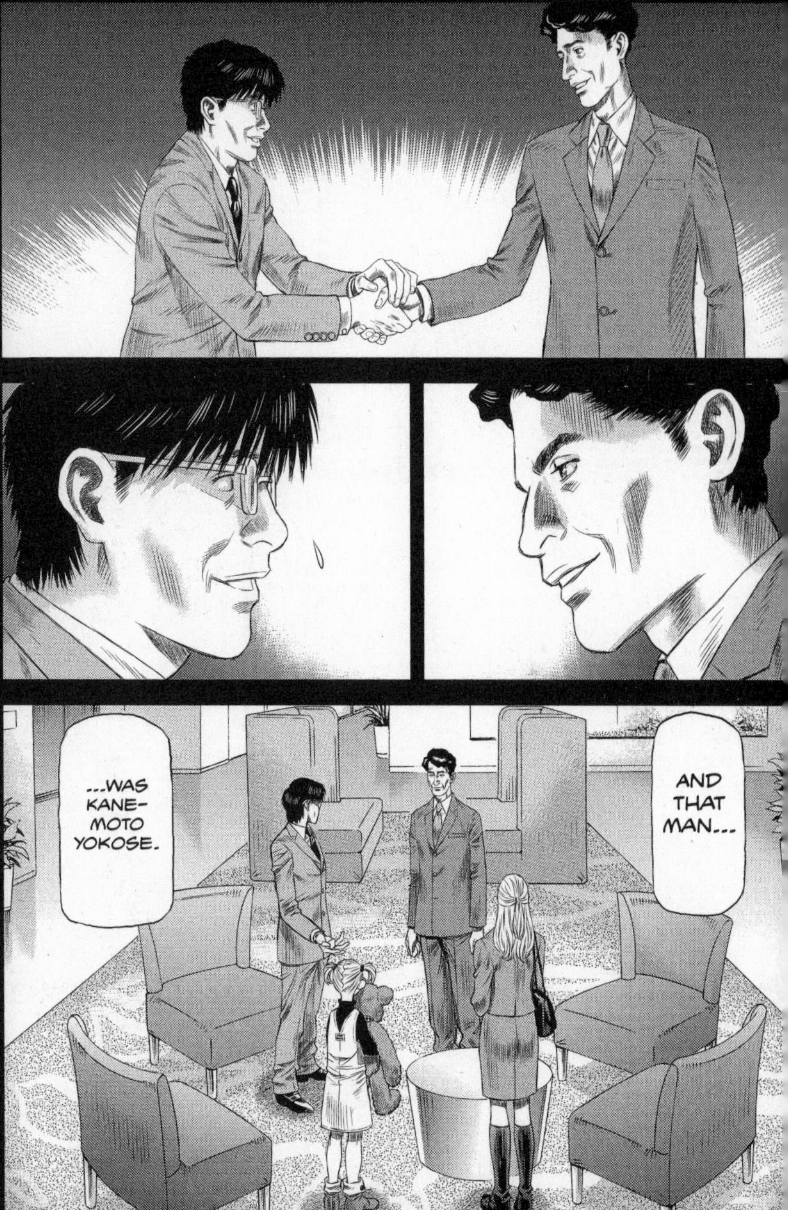
AND THAT MAN...
...WAS KANE-MOTO YOKOSE.

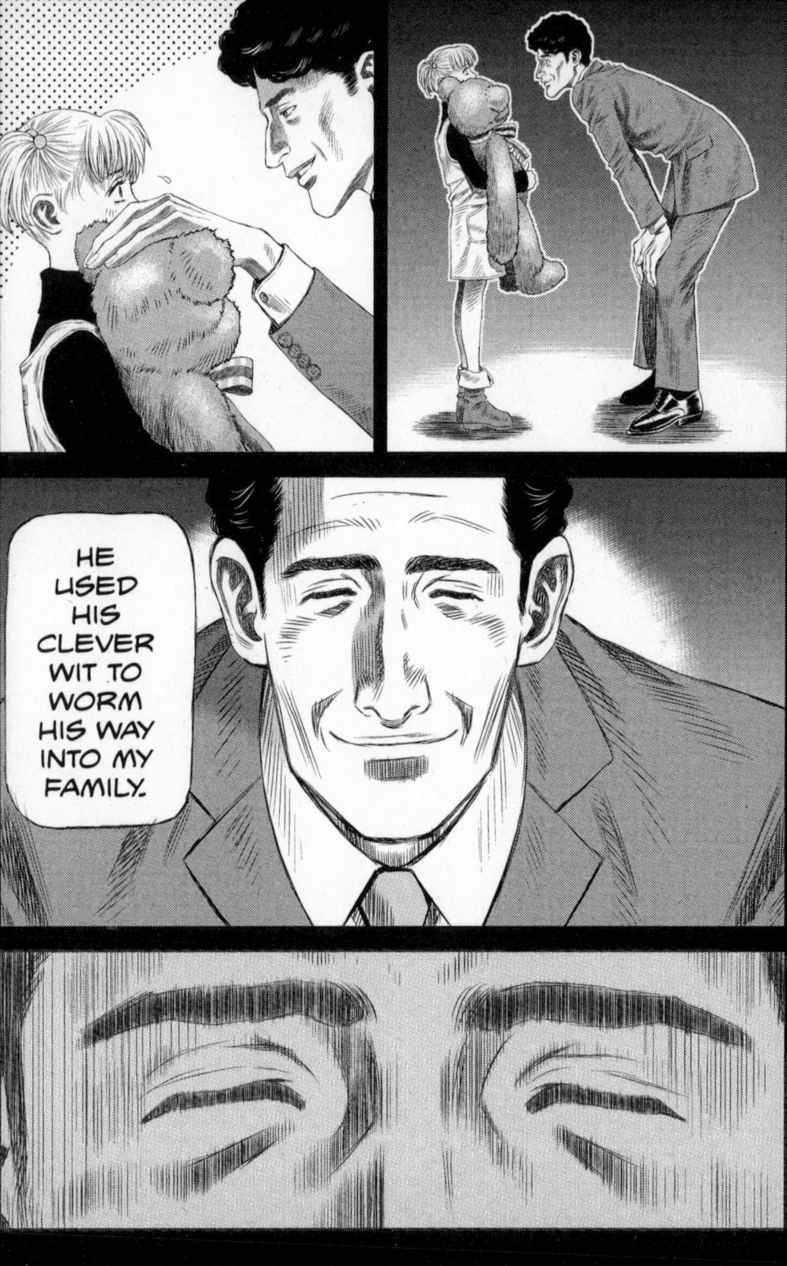
HE USED HIS CLEVER WIT TO WORM HIS WAY INTO MY FAMILY.

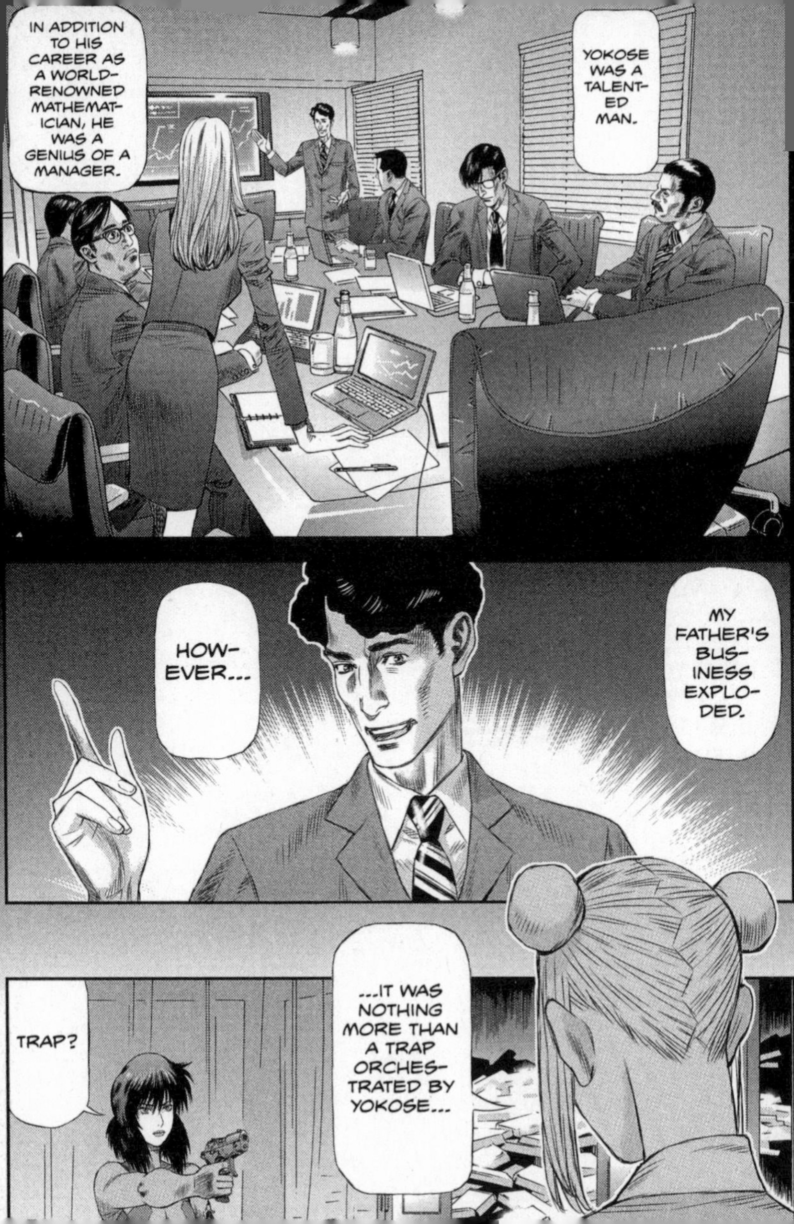
YOKOSE WAS A TALENTED MAN.
IN ADDITION TO HIS CAREER AS A WORLD-RENOWNED MATHEMATICIAN, HE WAS A GENIUS OF A MANAGER.
MY FATHER'S BUSINESS EXPLODED.
HOWEVER...
...IT WAS NOTHING MORE THAN A TRAP ORCHESTRATED BY YOKOSE...
TRAP?

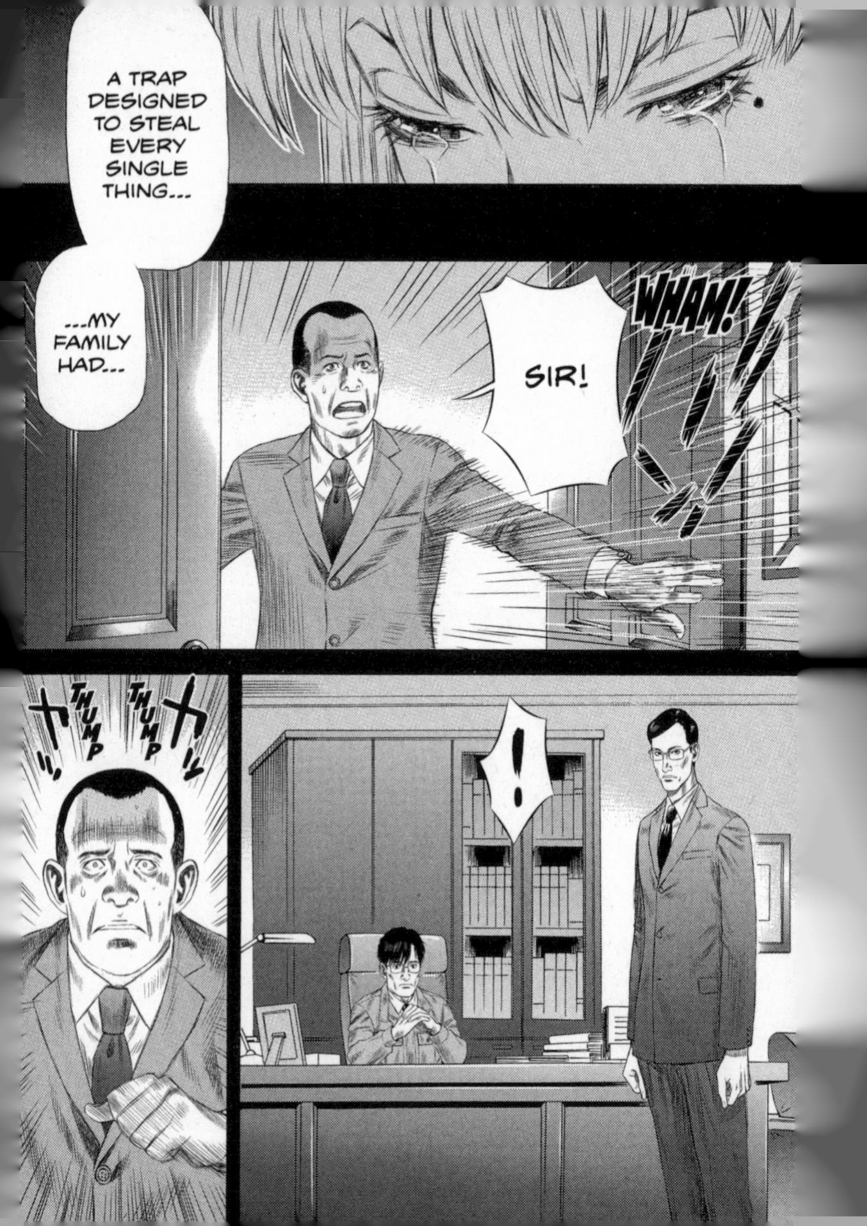
A TRAP DESIGNED TO STEAL EVERY SINGLE THING...
WHAM!
SIR!
...MY FAMILY HAD...
!
THUMP THUMP

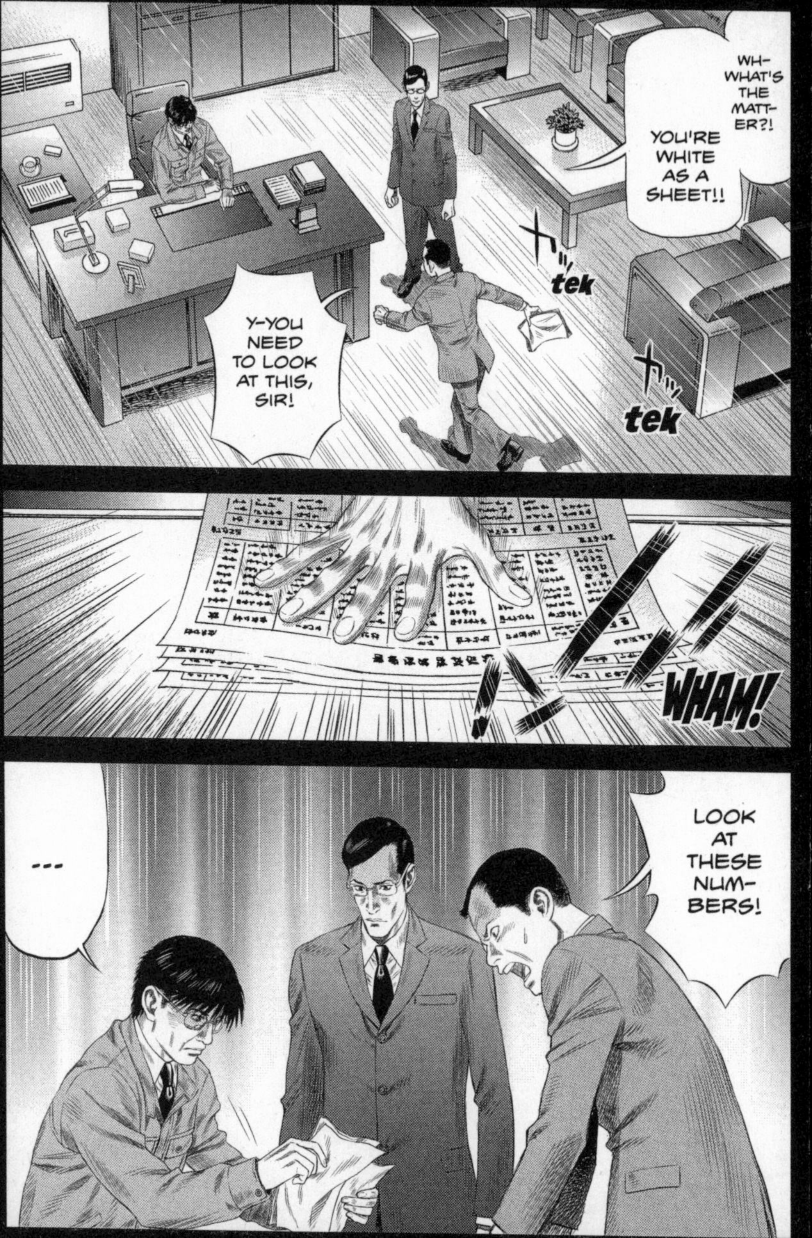
WH- WHAT'S THE MATT- ER?!
YOU'RE WHITE AS A SHEET!!
tek
tek
Y-YOU NEED TO LOOK AT THIS, SIR!
WHAM!
LOOK AT THESE NUM- BERS!
...

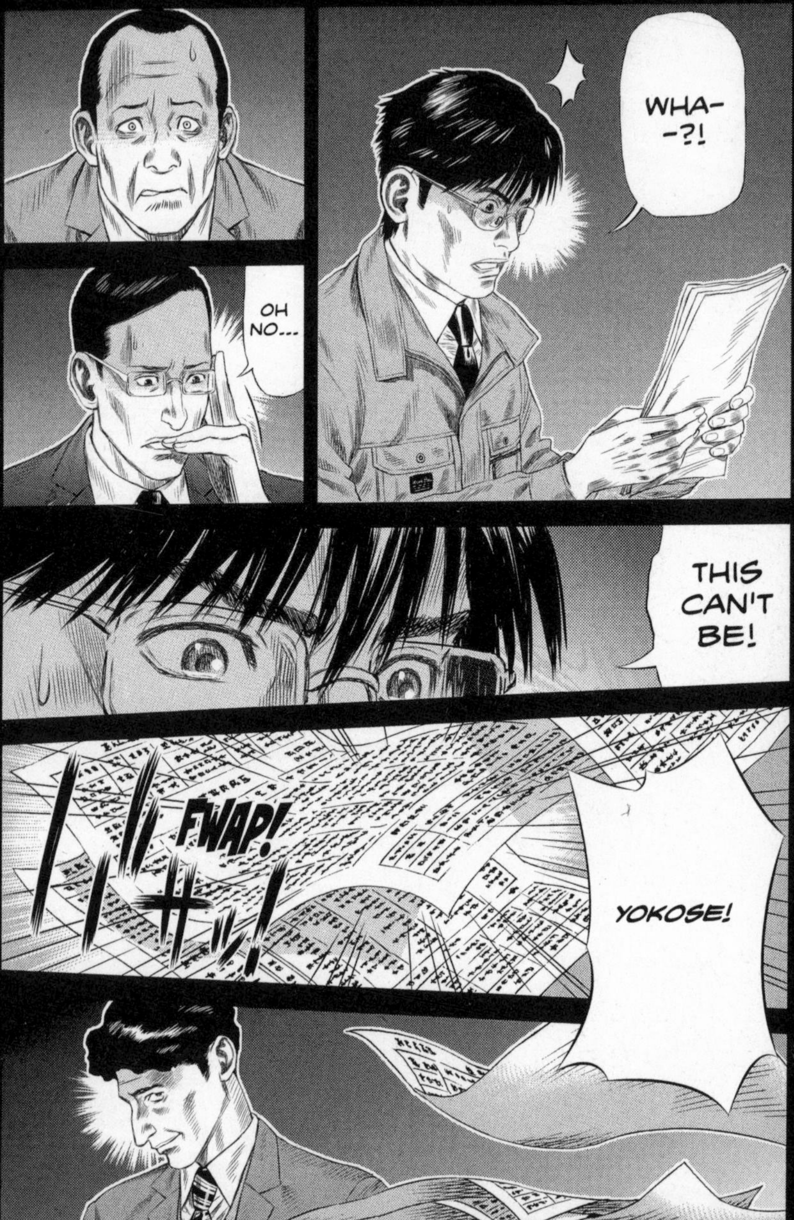
WHA--?!
OH NO...
THIS CAN'T BE!
FWAP!
YOKOSE!

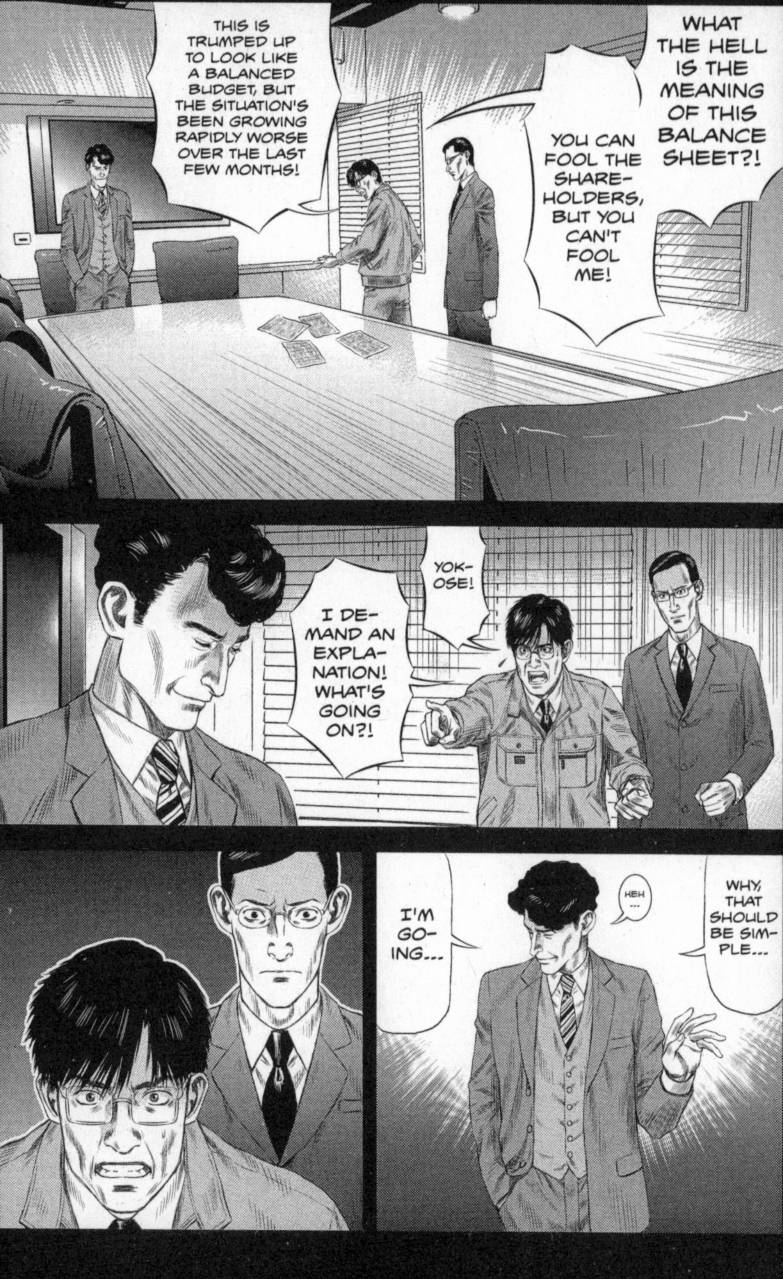
WHAT THE HELL IS THE MEANING OF THIS BALANCE SHEET?!
YOU CAN FOOL THE SHARE-HOLDERS, BUT YOU CAN'T FOOL ME!
THIS IS TRUMPED UP TO LOOK LIKE A BALANCED BUDGET, BUT THE SITUATION'S BEEN GROWING RAPIDLY WORSE OVER THE LAST FEW MONTHS!
YOK-OSE!
I DE-MAND AN EXPLA-NATION! WHAT'S GOING ON?!
WHY, THAT SHOULD BE SIM-PLE...
HEH...
I'M GO-ING...

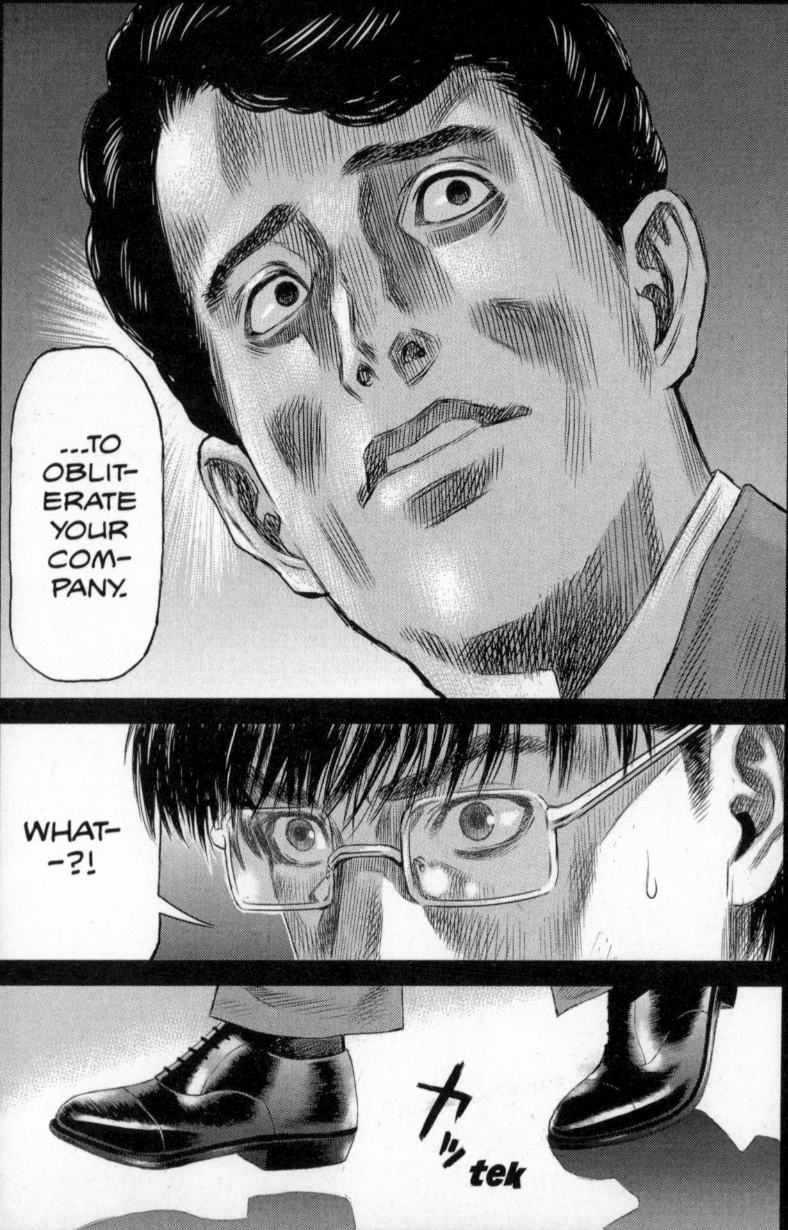
...TO OBLIT-ERATE YOUR COM-PANY.
WHAT--?!
tek

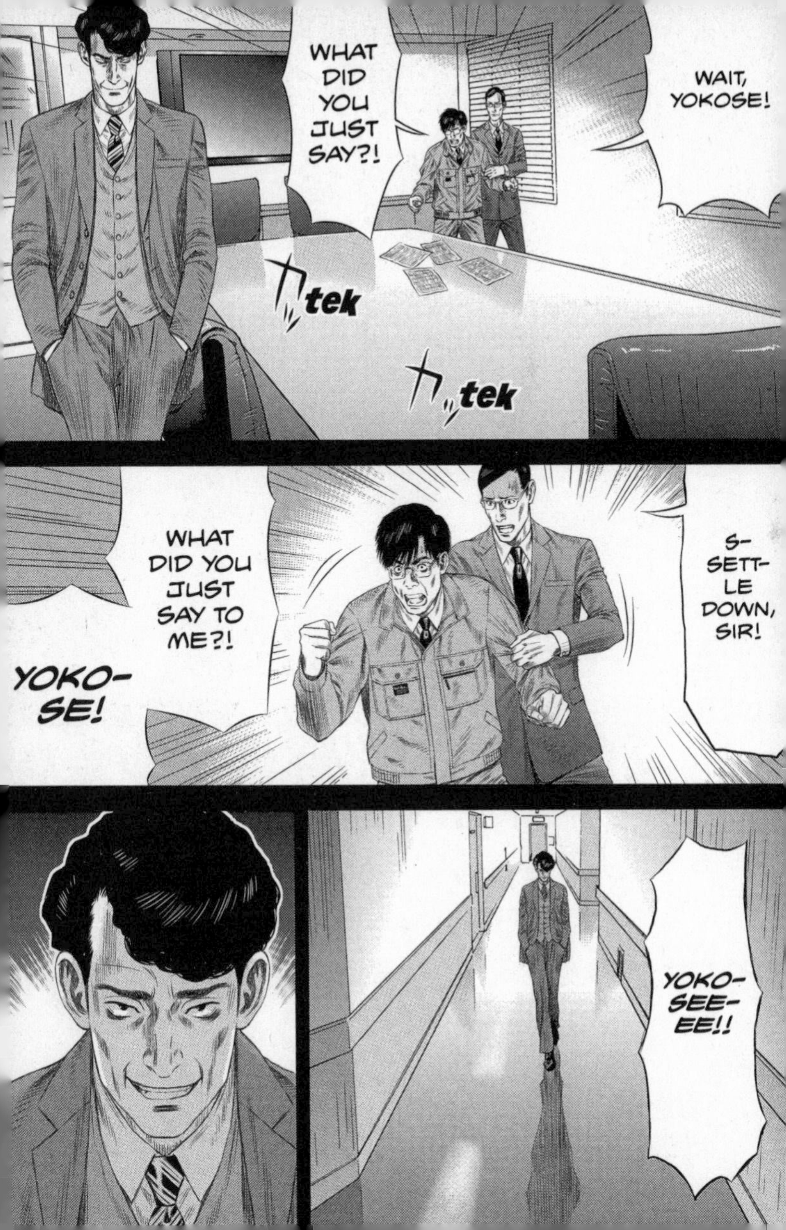
WAIT, YOKOSE!
WHAT DID YOU JUST SAY?!
tek
tek
S-SETT-LE DOWN, SIR!
WHAT DID YOU JUST SAY TO ME?!
YOKO-SE!
YOKO-SEEE-EE!!

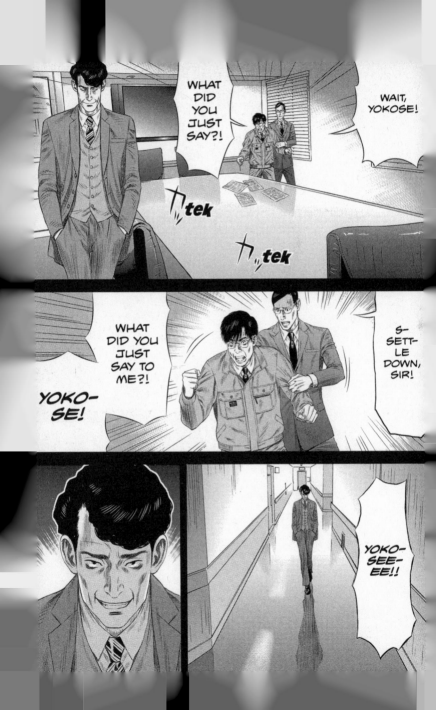

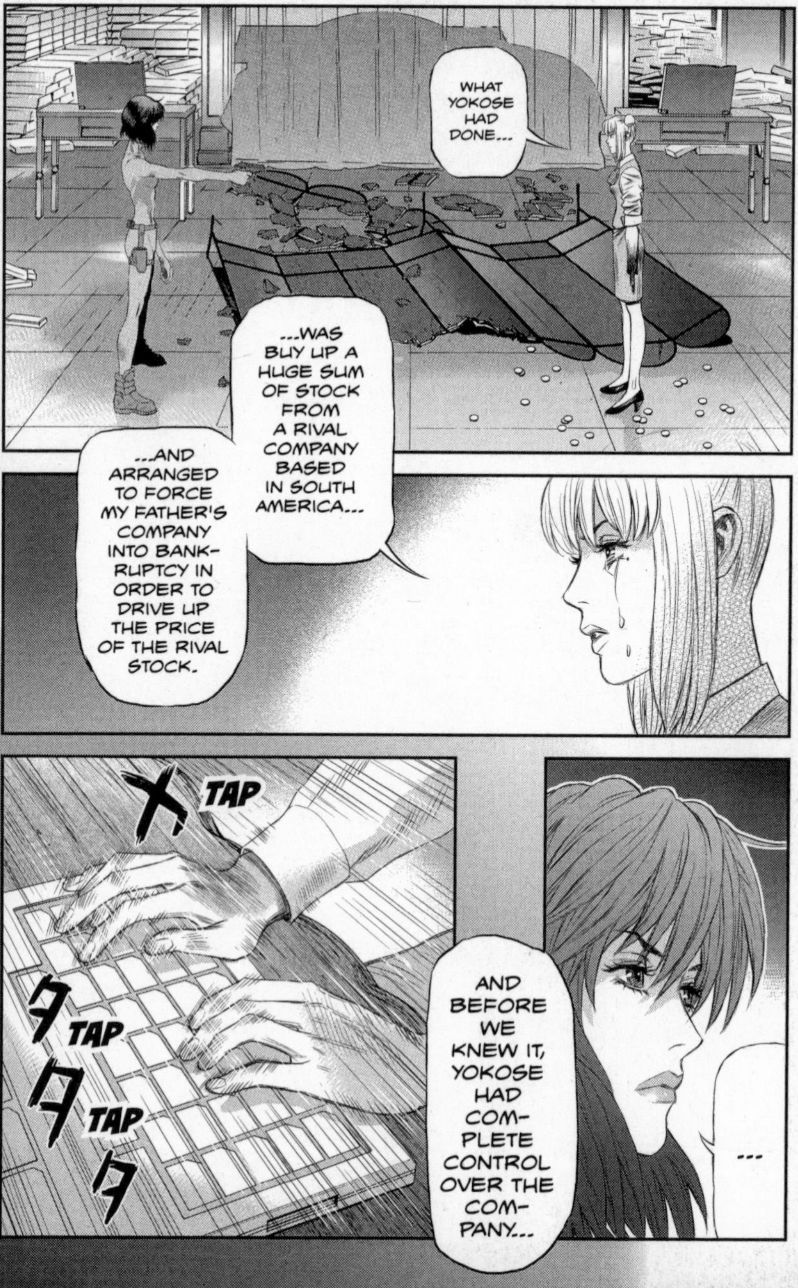
WHAT YOKOSE HAD DONE...
...WAS BUY UP A HUGE SUM OF STOCK FROM A RIVAL COMPANY BASED IN SOUTH AMERICA...
...AND ARRANGED TO FORCE MY FATHER'S COMPANY INTO BANK-RUPTCY IN ORDER TO DRIVE UP THE PRICE OF THE RIVAL STOCK.
AND BEFORE WE KNEW IT, YOKOSE HAD COM-PLETE CONTROL OVER THE COM-PANY...
...
タ
TAP
タ
TAP
タ
TAP
タ

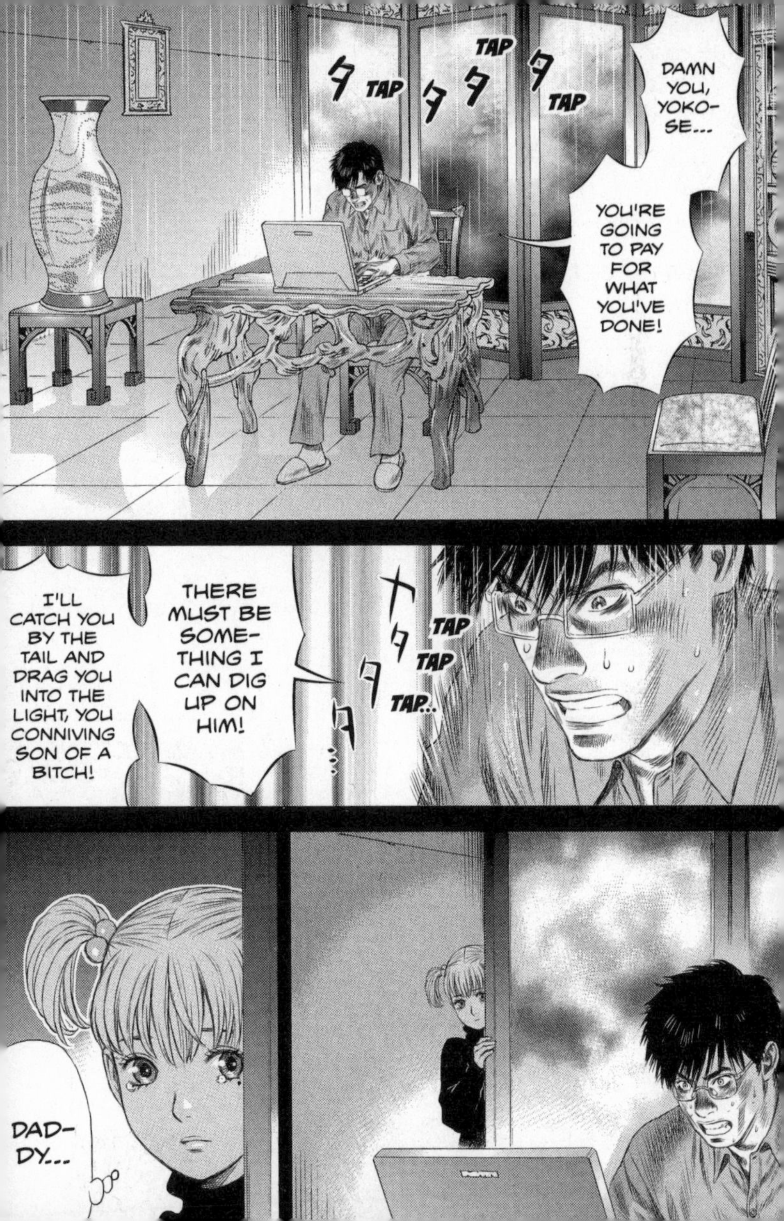
DAMN YOU, YOKO-SE...
YOU'RE GOING TO PAY FOR WHAT YOU'VE DONE!
タ TAP タ TAP タ TAP タ TAP
TAP TAP TAP...
THERE MUST BE SOME-THING I CAN DIG UP ON HIM!
I'LL CATCH YOU BY THE TAIL AND DRAG YOU INTO THE LIGHT, YOU CONNIVING SON OF A BITCH!
DAD-DY...

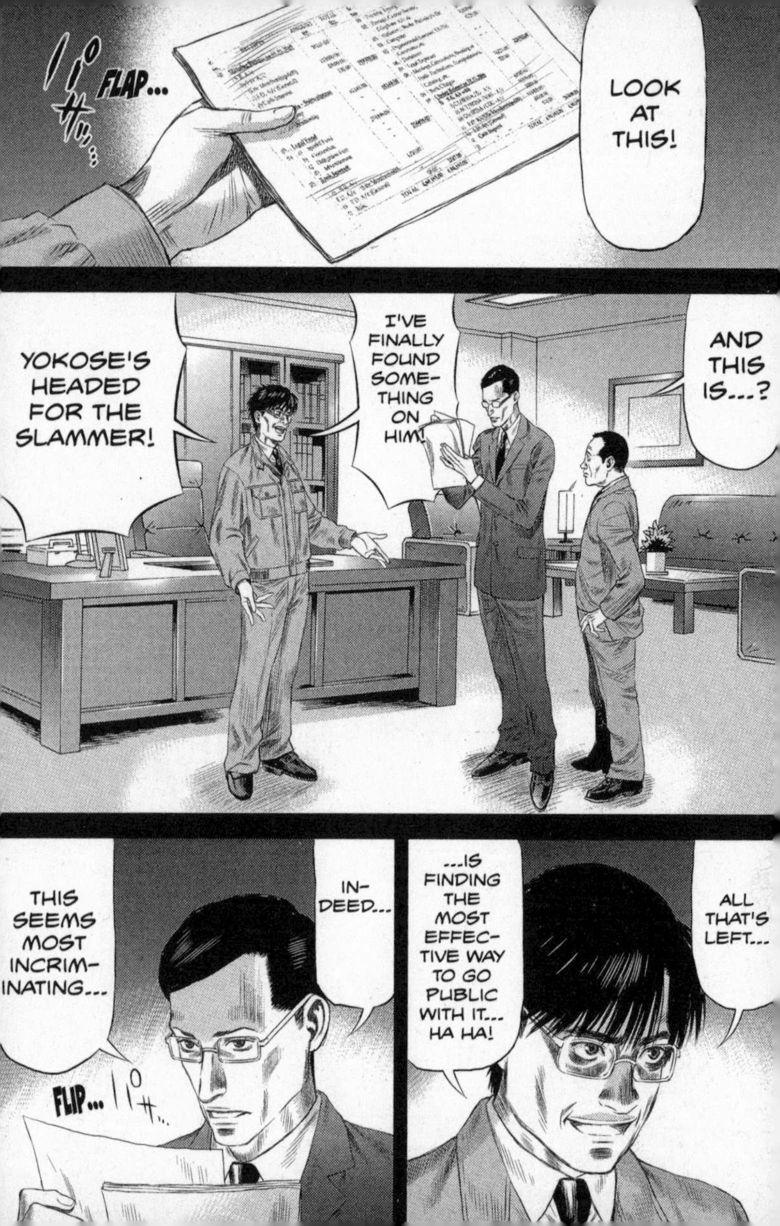
LOOK AT THIS!
FLAP...
AND THIS IS...?
I'VE FINALLY FOUND SOMETHING ON HIM!
YOKOSE'S HEADED FOR THE SLAMMER!
ALL THAT'S LEFT...
...IS FINDING THE MOST EFFECTIVE WAY TO GO PUBLIC WITH IT... HA HA!
INDEED...
THIS SEEMS MOST INCRIMINATING...
FLIP...

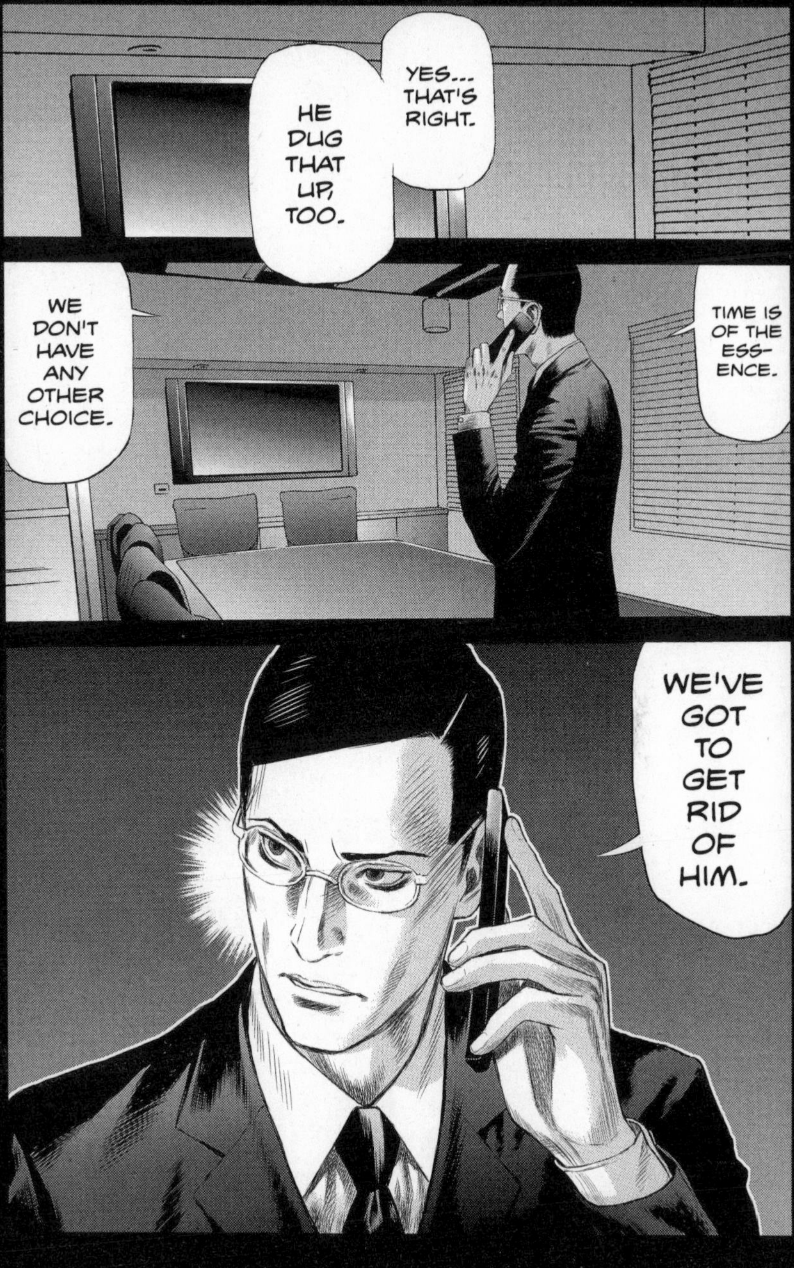
YES... THAT'S RIGHT.
HE DUG THAT UP, TOO.
TIME IS OF THE ESS-ENCE.
WE DON'T HAVE ANY OTHER CHOICE.
WE'VE GOT TO GET RID OF HIM.

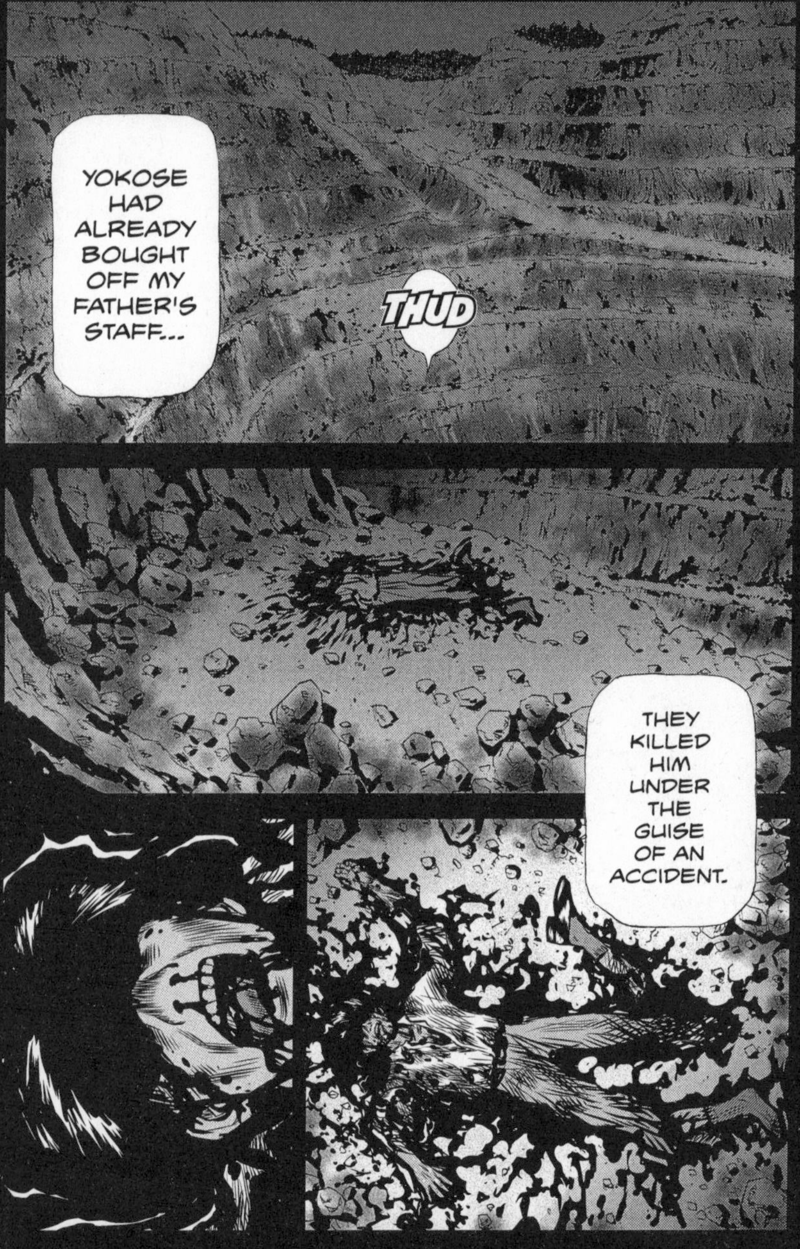
YOKOSE HAD ALREADY BOUGHT OFF MY FATHER'S STAFF...
THUD
THEY KILLED HIM UNDER THE GUISE OF AN ACCIDENT.

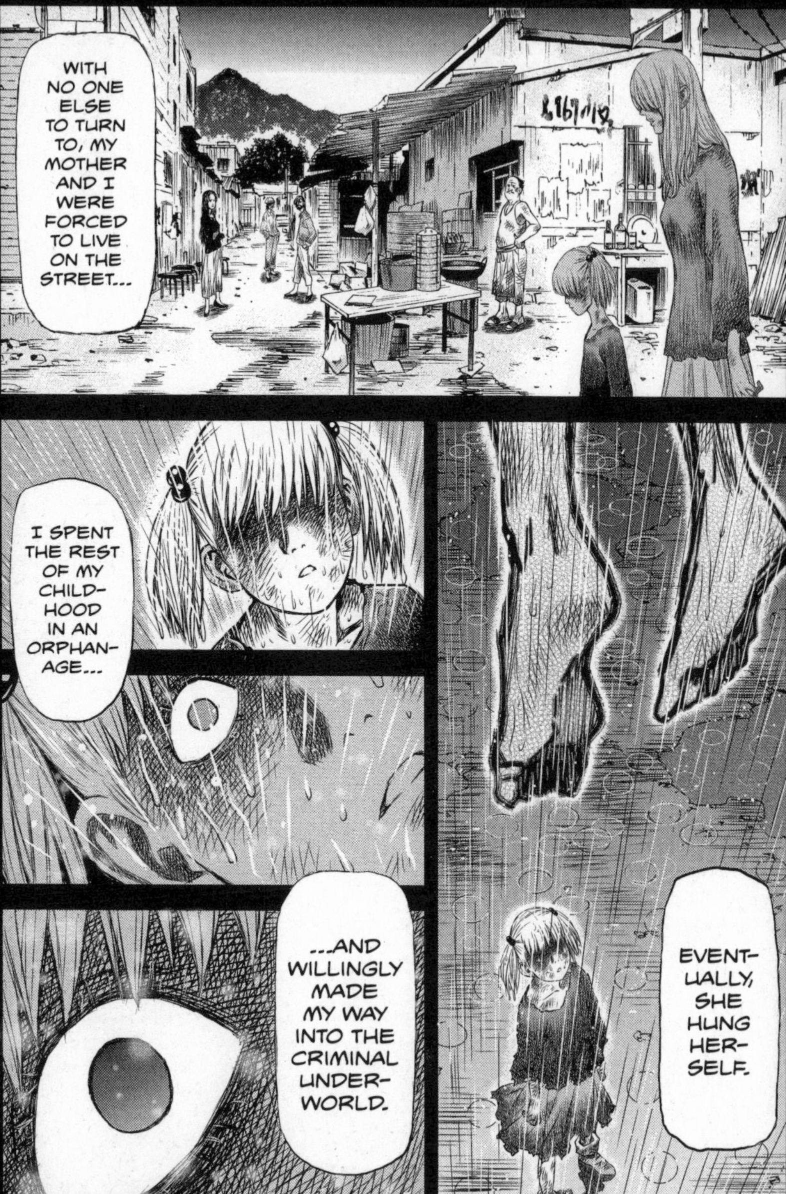
WITH NO ONE ELSE TO TURN TO, MY MOTHER AND I WERE FORCED TO LIVE ON THE STREET...
EVENTUALLY, SHE HUNG HERSELF.
I SPENT THE REST OF MY CHILDHOOD IN AN ORPHANAGE...
...AND WILLINGLY MADE MY WAY INTO THE CRIMINAL UNDERWORLD.

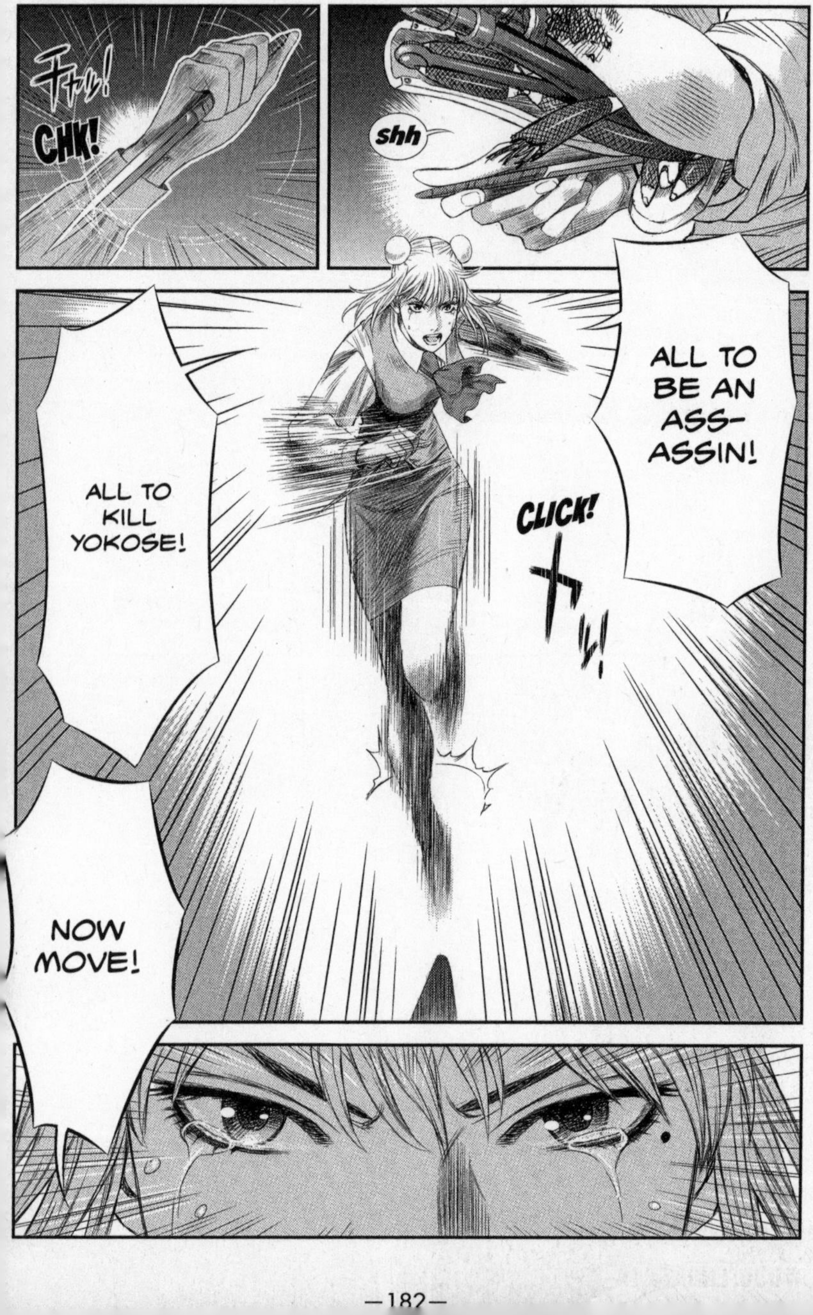
shh
チャッ!
CHK!
ALL TO BE AN ASS-ASSIN!
CLICK!
ヤッ!
ALL TO KILL YOKOSE!
NOW MOVE!

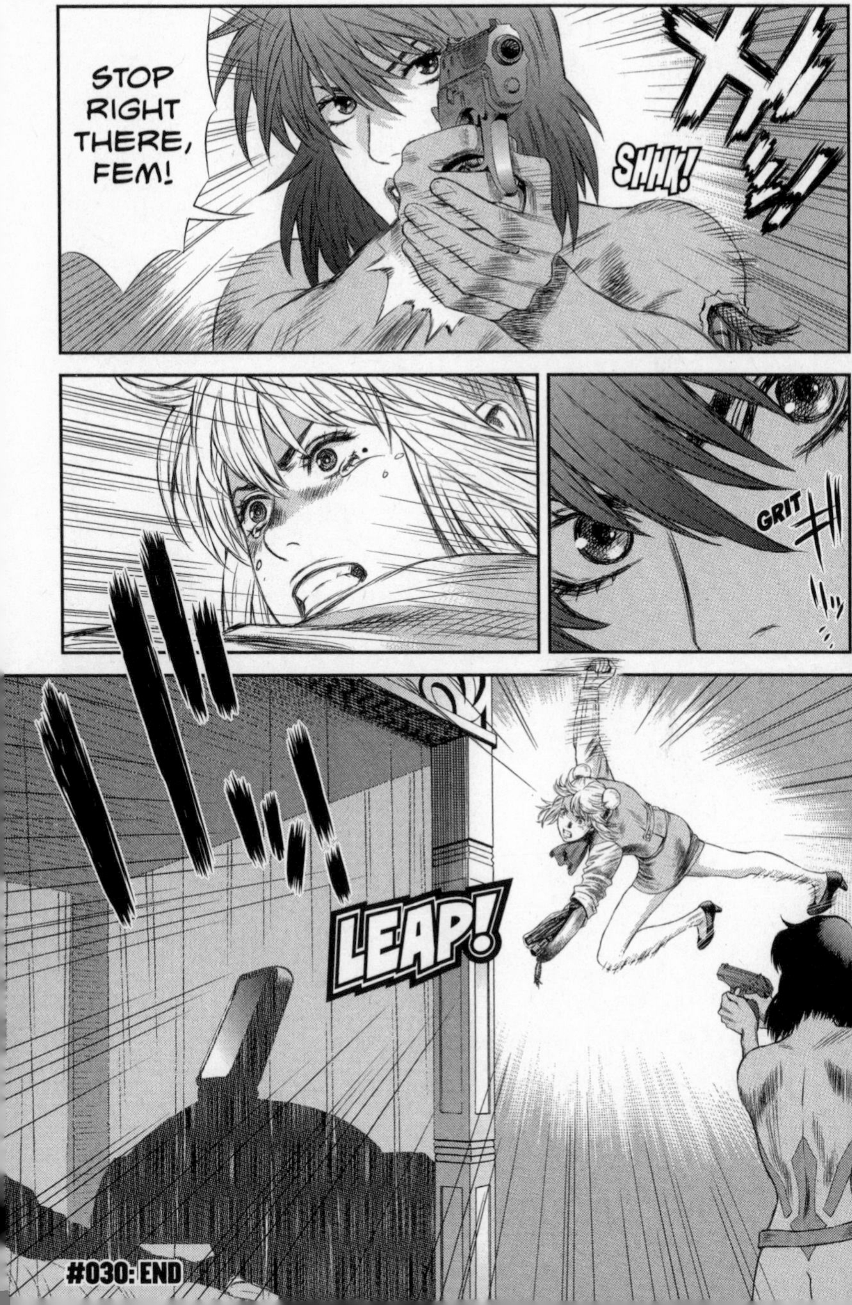
STOP RIGHT THERE, FEM!
SHHK!
GRIT
LEAP!

#030: END

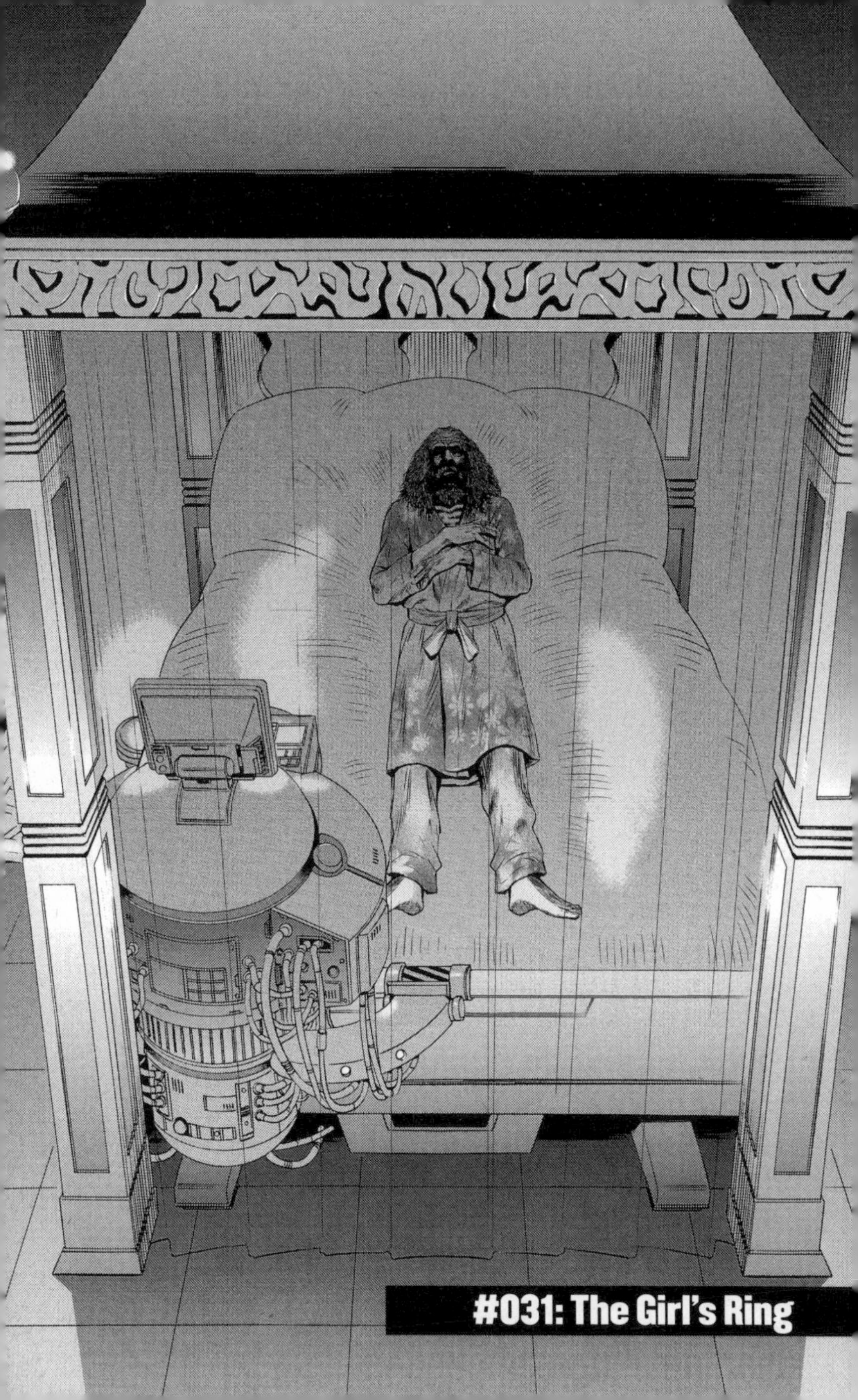

#031: The Girl's Ring

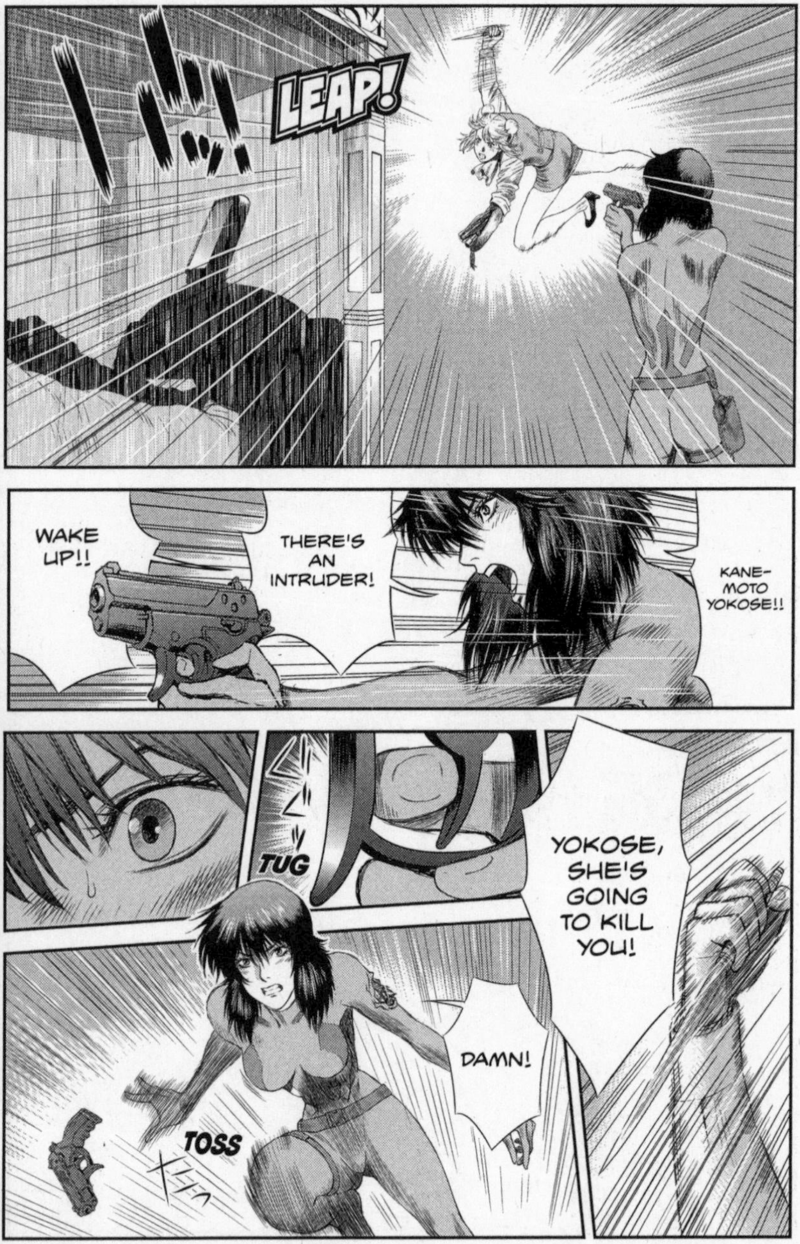
LEAP!
KANE-MOTO YOKOSE!!
THERE'S AN INTRUDER!
WAKE UP!!
YOKOSE, SHE'S GOING TO KILL YOU!
TUG
DAMN!
TOSS

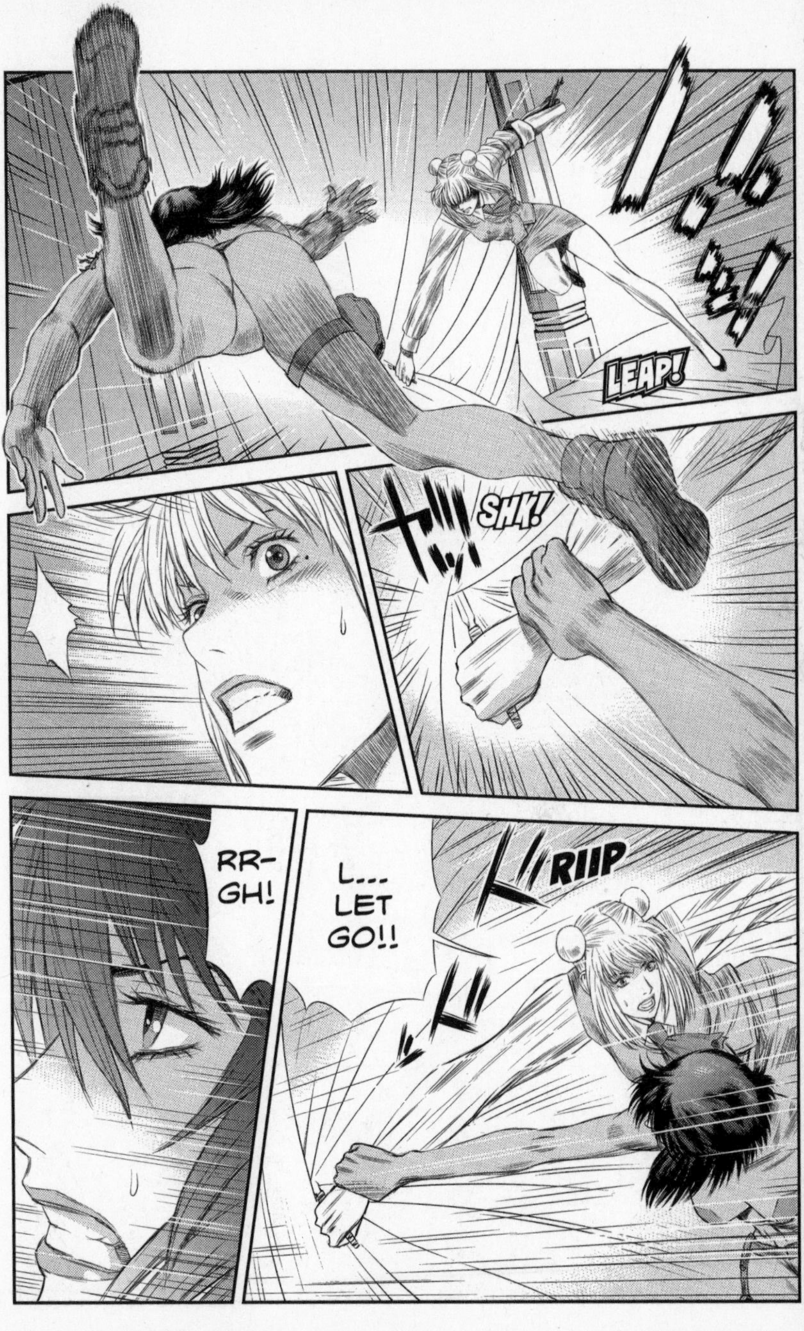
LEAP!
SHK!
RIIP
L... LET GO!!
RR-GH!

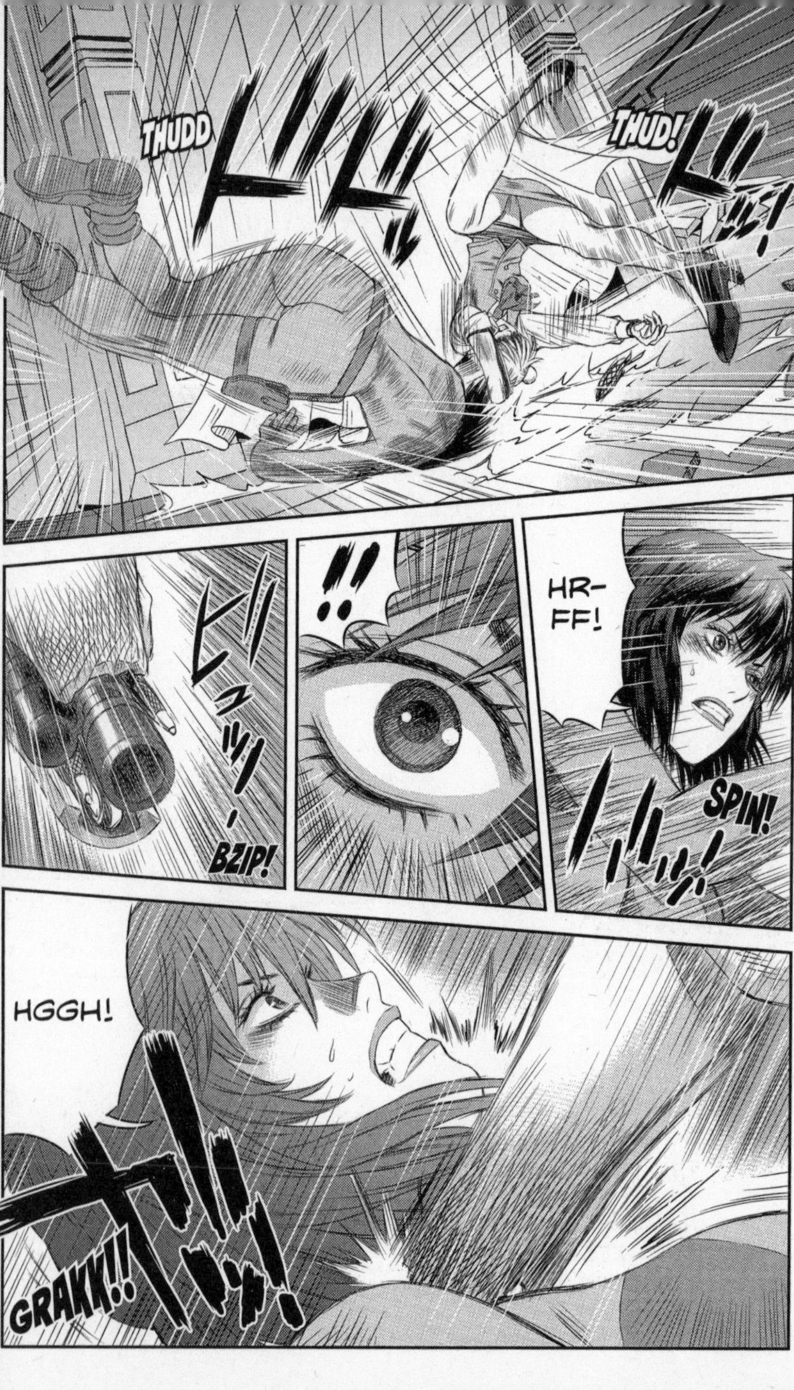
THUD!
THUDD
HR-FF!
SPIN!
BZIP!
HGGH!
GRAKK!!

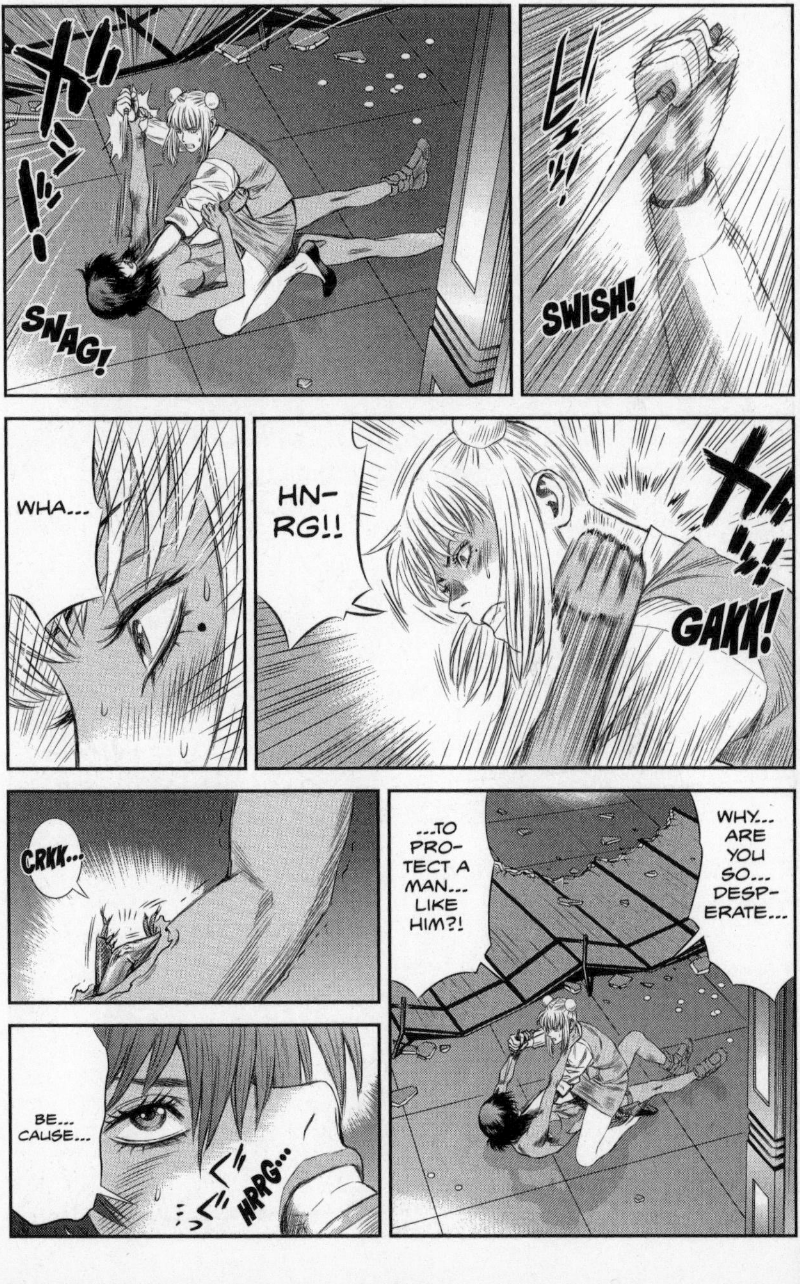
SWISH!
SNAG!
HN-RG!!
GAKK!
WHA...
WHY... ARE YOU SO... DESP-ERATE...
...TO PRO-TECT A MAN... LIKE HIM?!
CRKK...
BE... CAUSE...
HRRG...

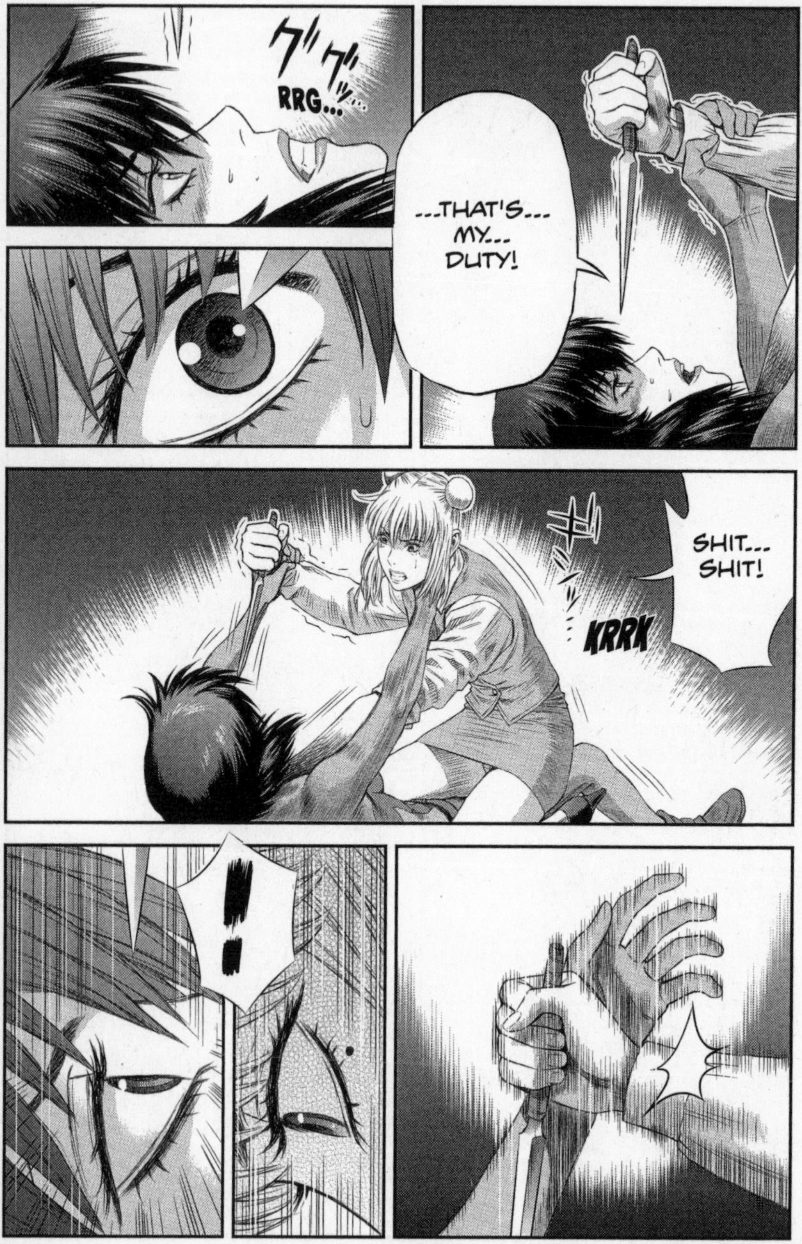
...THAT'S... MY... DUTY!
RRG...
KRRK
SHIT... SHIT!
!

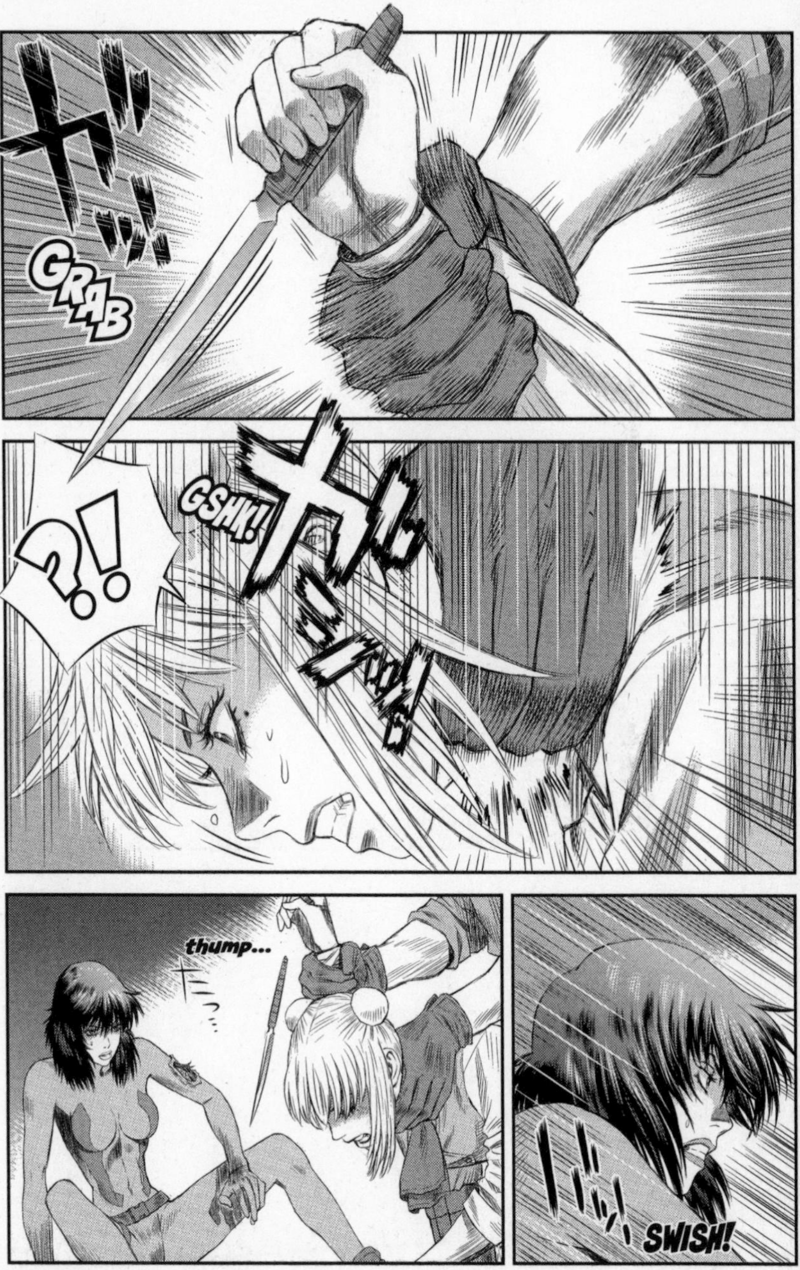
GRAB
?!
GSHK!
SWISH!
thump...

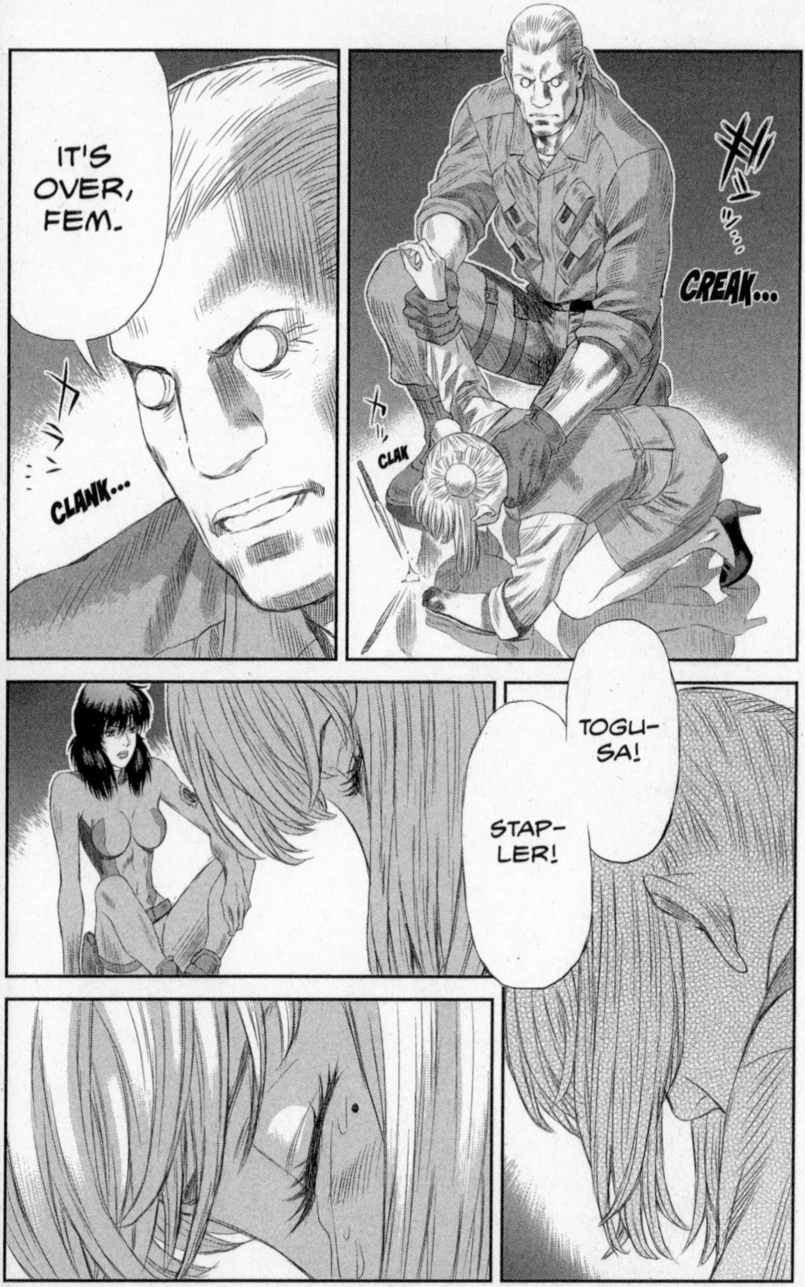
CREAK...
CLAK
IT'S OVER, FEM.
CLANK...
TOGU-SA!
STAP-LER!

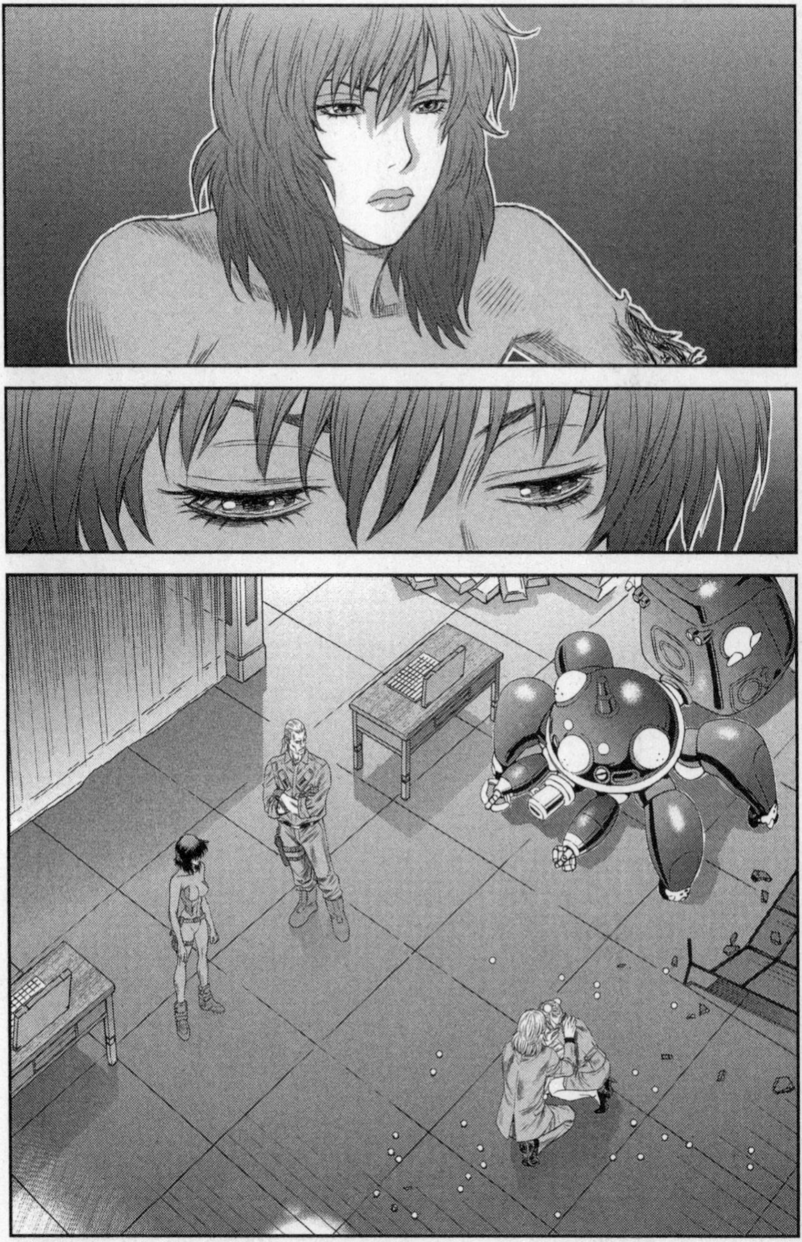

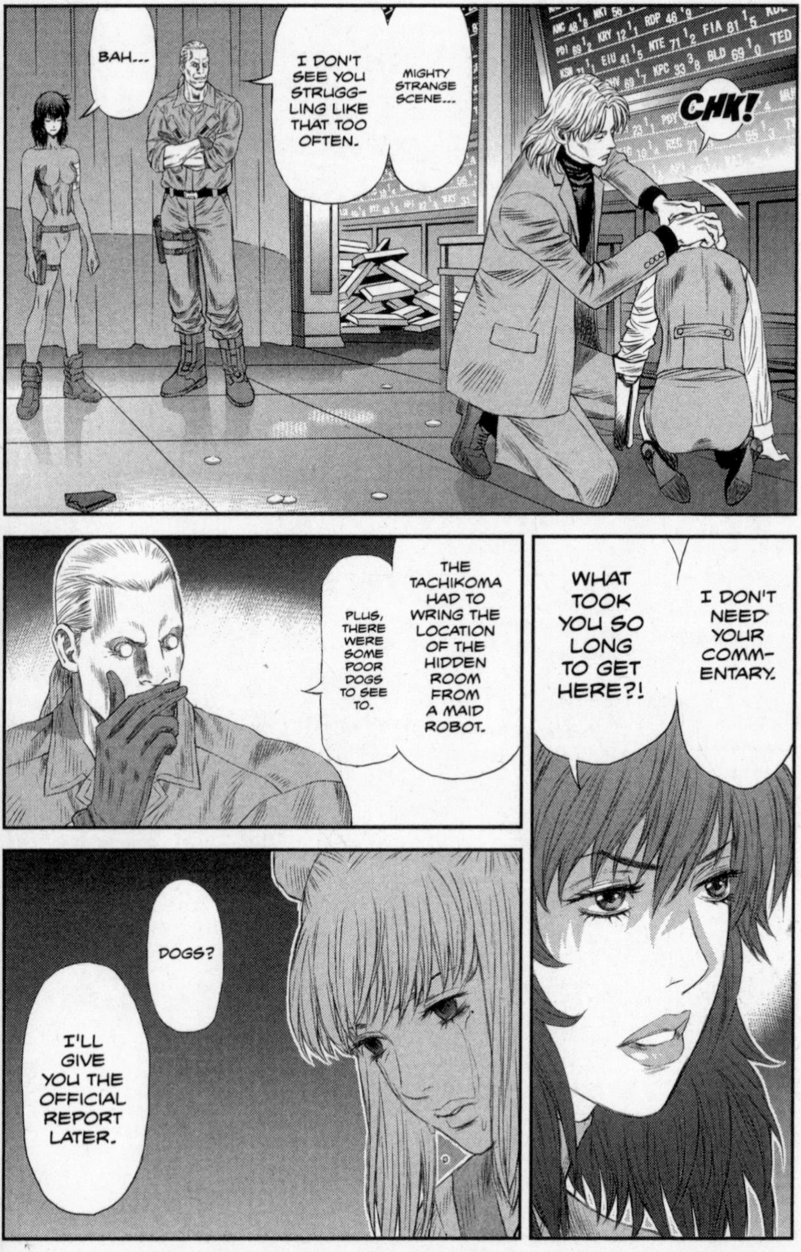
CHK!
MIGHTY STRANGE SCENE...
I DON'T SEE YOU STRUGGLING LIKE THAT TOO OFTEN.
BAH...
I DON'T NEED YOUR COMMENTARY.
WHAT TOOK YOU SO LONG TO GET HERE?!
THE TACHIKOMA HAD TO WRING THE LOCATION OF THE HIDDEN ROOM FROM A MAID ROBOT.
PLUS, THERE WERE SOME POOR DOGS TO SEE TO.
DOGS?
I'LL GIVE YOU THE OFFICIAL REPORT LATER.

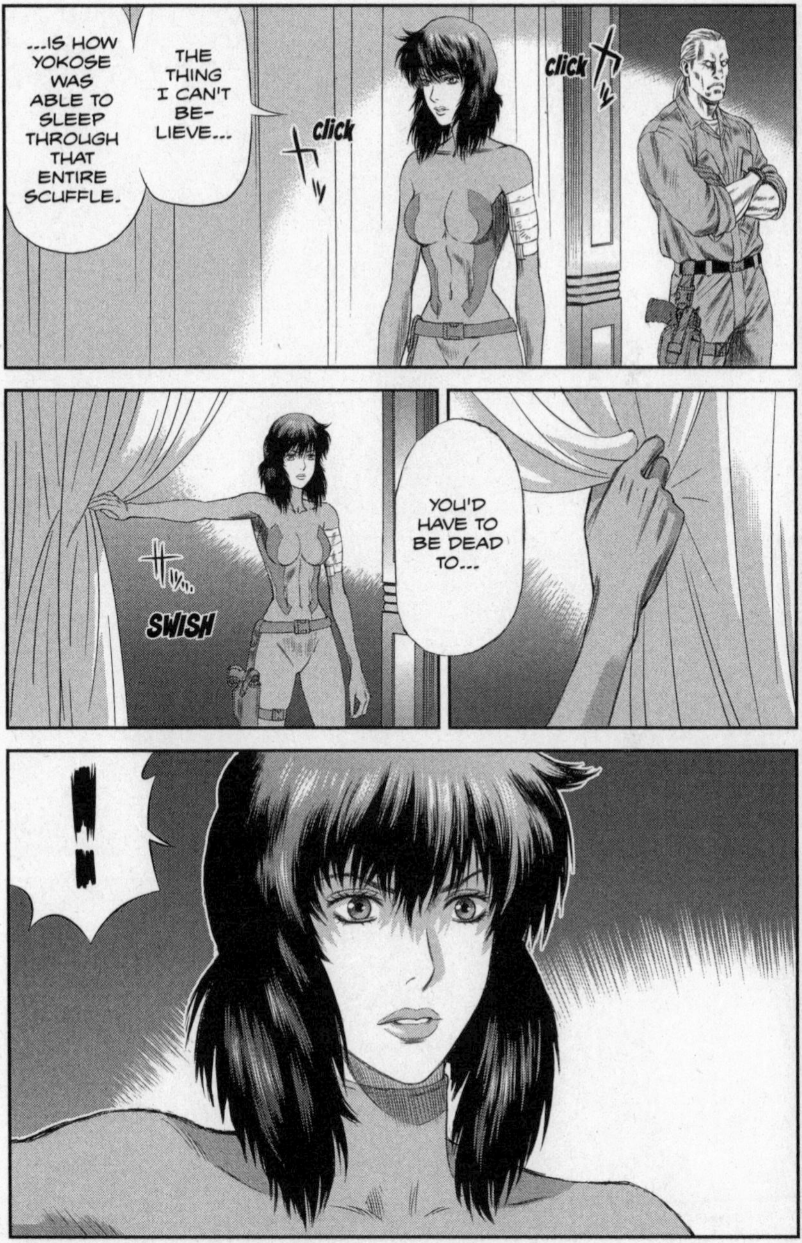
Click
THE THING I CAN'T BE- LIEVE...
...IS HOW YOKOSE WAS ABLE TO SLEEP THROUGH THAT ENTIRE SCUFFLE.
Click
YOU'D HAVE TO BE DEAD TO...
SWISH
!!

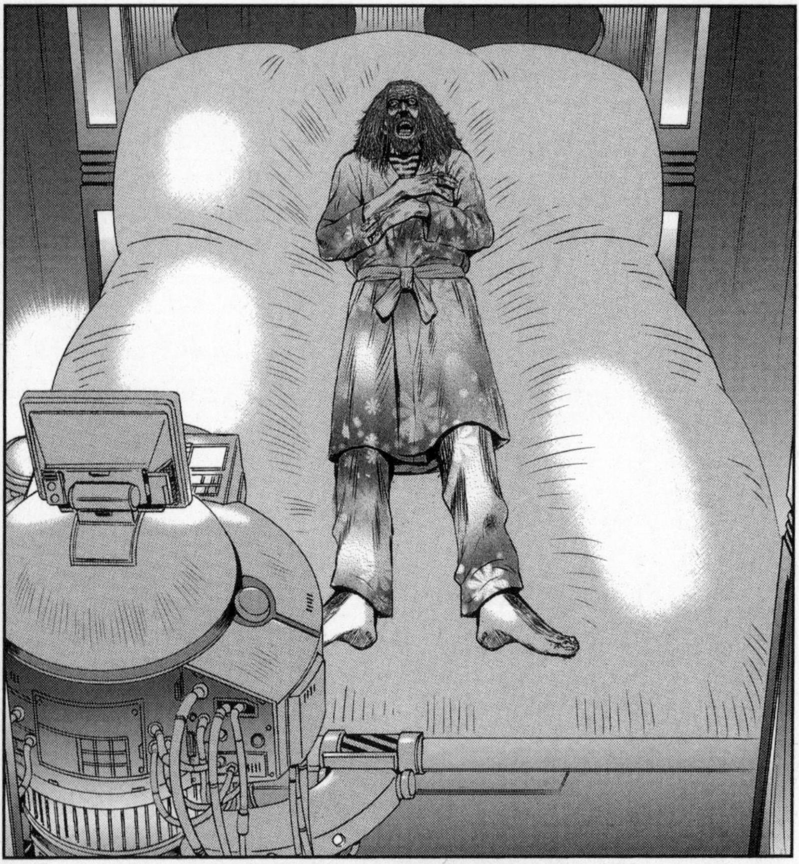
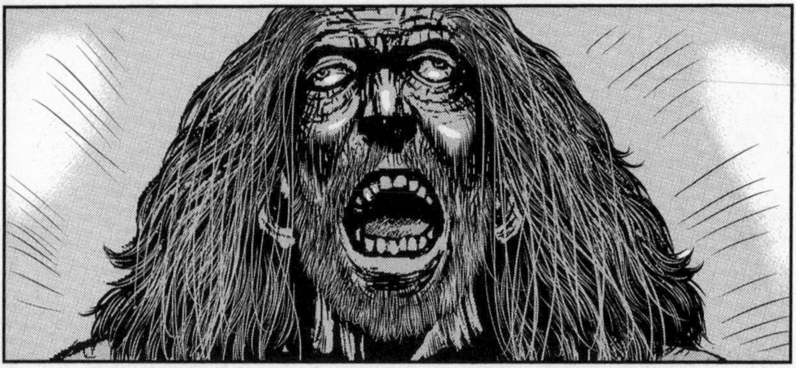

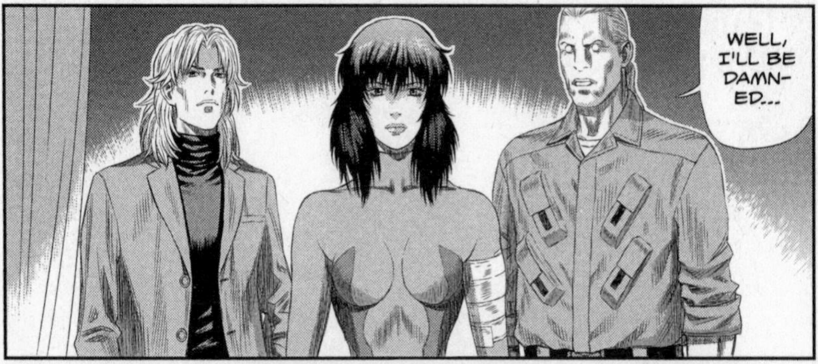
WELL, I'LL BE DAMNED...

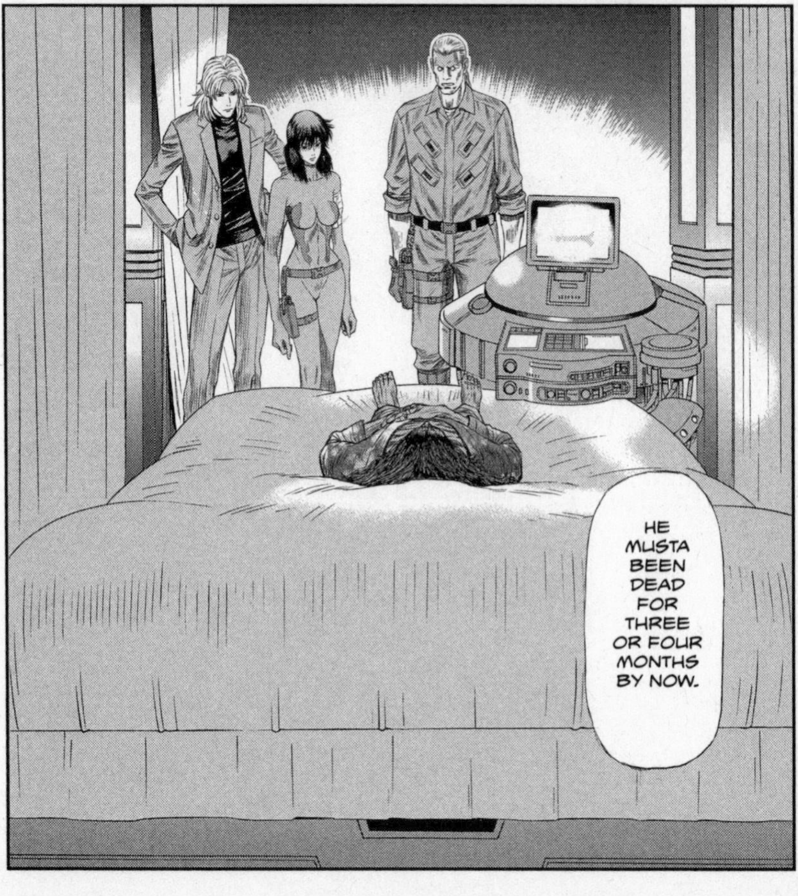
HE MUSTA BEEN DEAD FOR THREE OR FOUR MONTHS BY NOW.

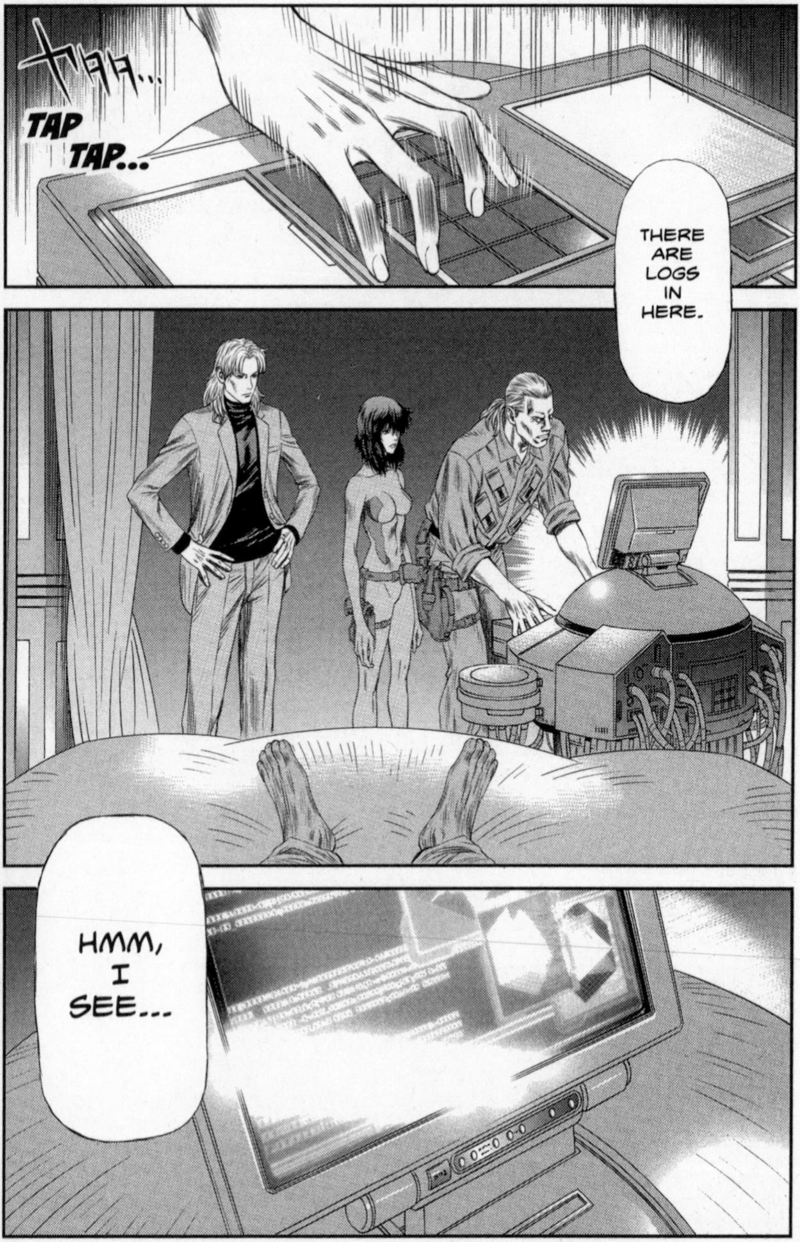
TAP TAP...
THERE ARE LOGS IN HERE.
HMM, I SEE...

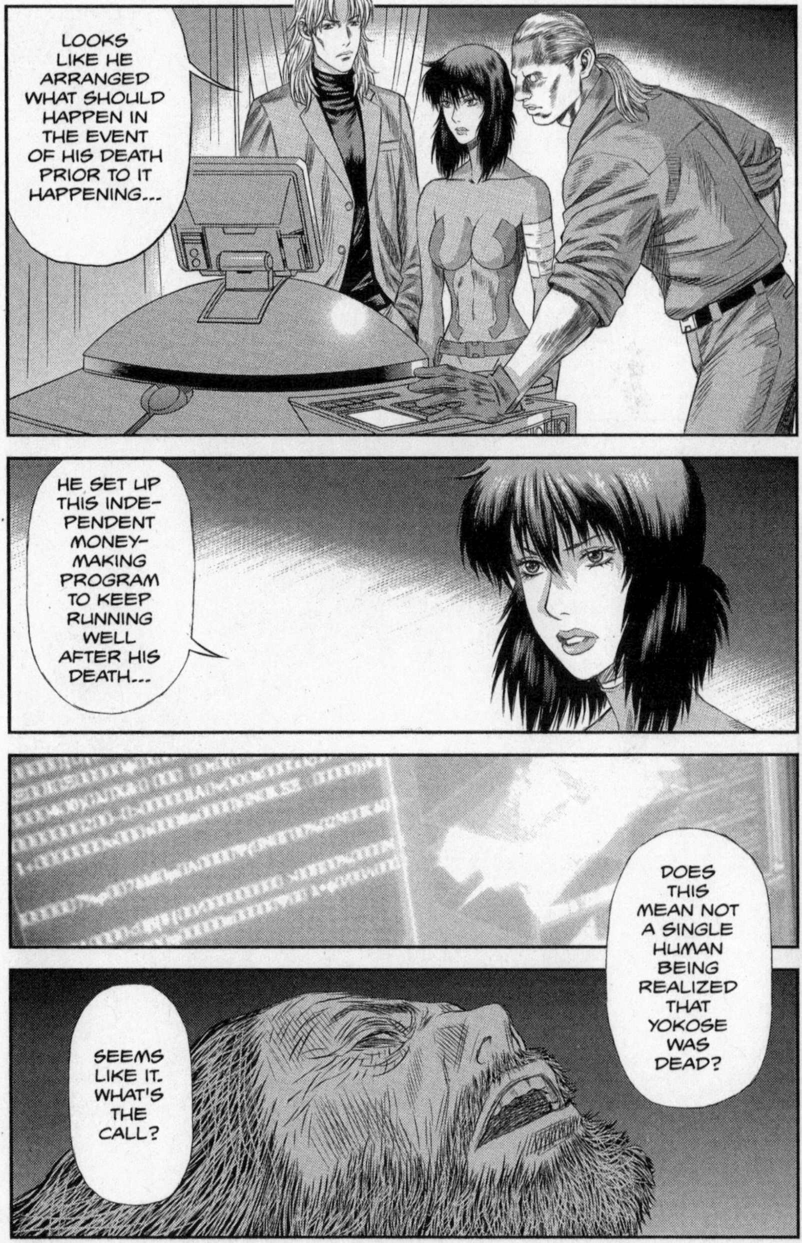
LOOKS LIKE HE ARRANGED WHAT SHOULD HAPPEN IN THE EVENT OF HIS DEATH PRIOR TO IT HAPPENING...
HE SET UP THIS INDEPENDENT MONEY-MAKING PROGRAM TO KEEP RUNNING WELL AFTER HIS DEATH...
DOES THIS MEAN NOT A SINGLE HUMAN BEING REALIZED THAT YOKOSE WAS DEAD?
SEEMS LIKE IT. WHAT'S THE CALL?

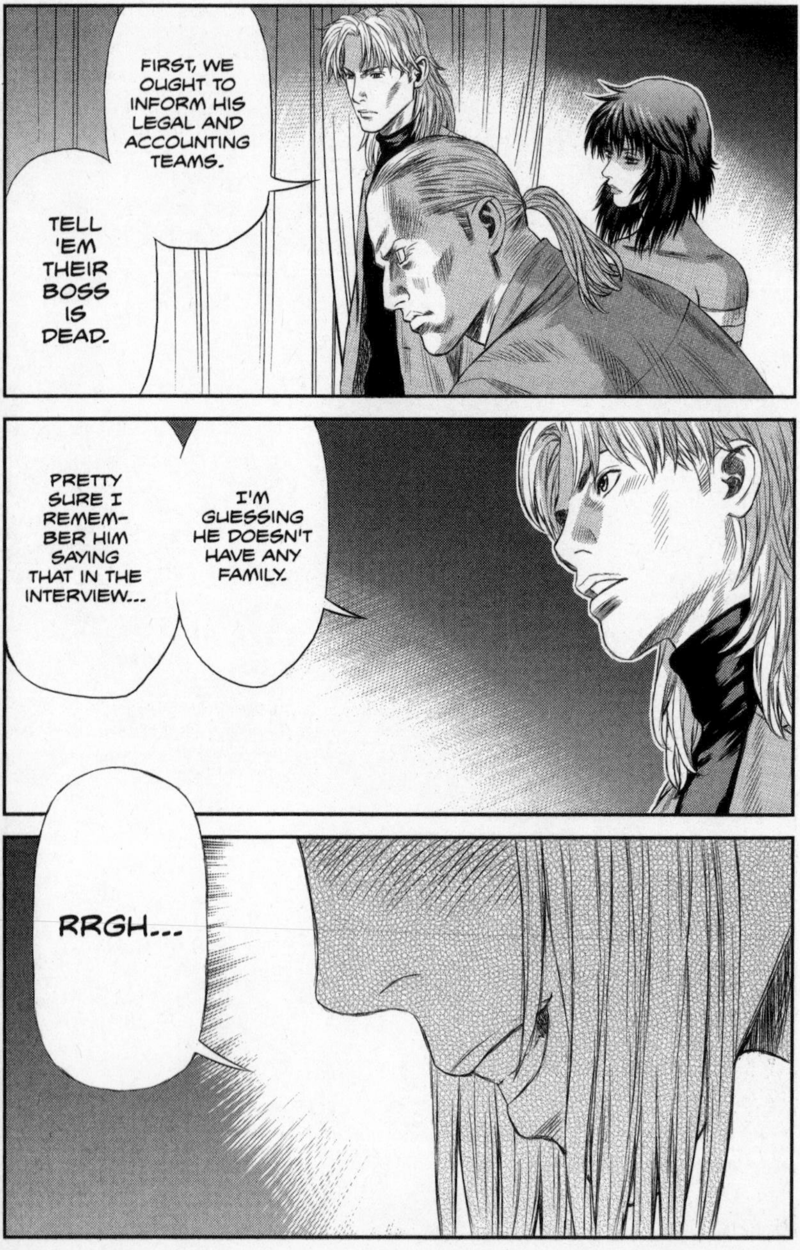
FIRST, WE OUGHT TO INFORM HIS LEGAL AND ACCOUNTING TEAMS.
TELL 'EM THEIR BOSS IS DEAD.
I'M GUESSING HE DOESN'T HAVE ANY FAMILY.
PRETTY SURE I REMEMBER HIM SAYING THAT IN THE INTERVIEW...
RRGH...

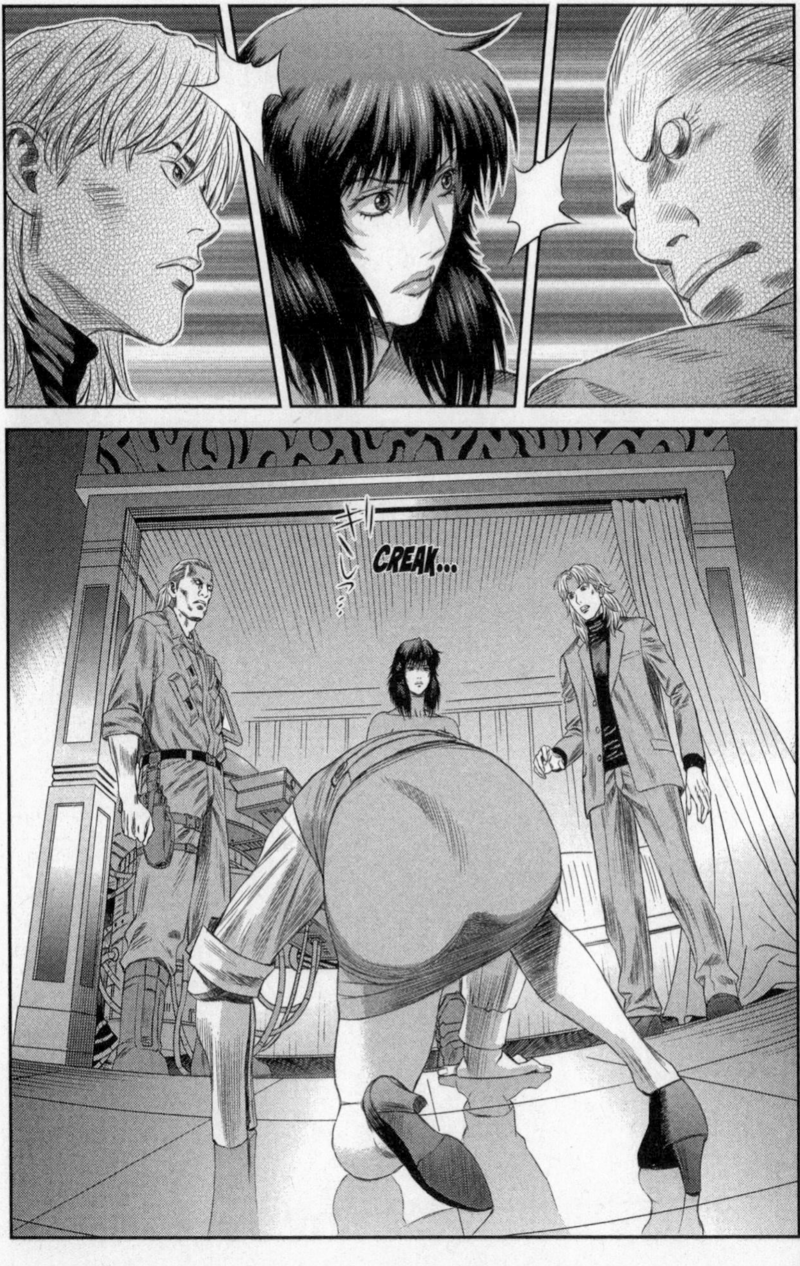
CREAK...

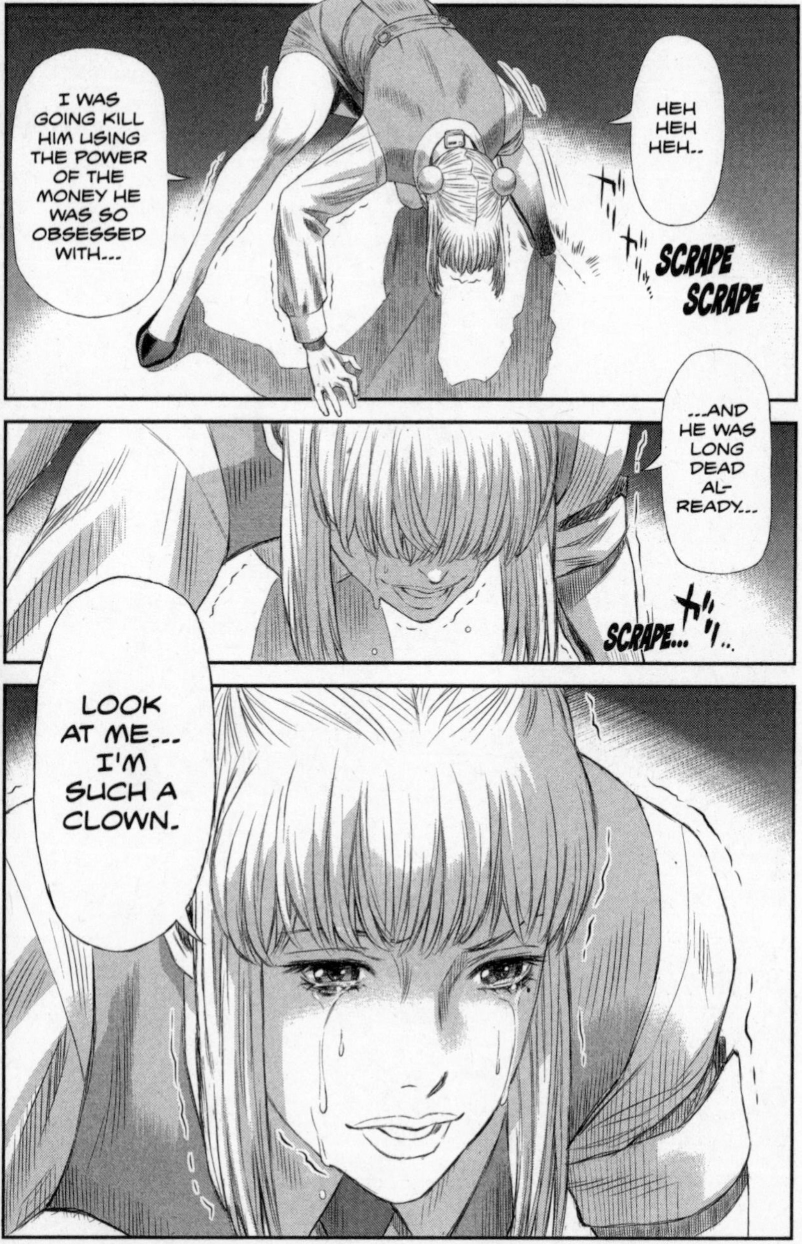
HEH HEH HEH...
SCRAPE SCRAPE
I WAS GOING KILL HIM USING THE POWER OF THE MONEY HE WAS SO OBSESSED WITH...
...AND HE WAS LONG DEAD AL-READY...
SCRAPE...
LOOK AT ME... I'M SUCH A CLOWN.

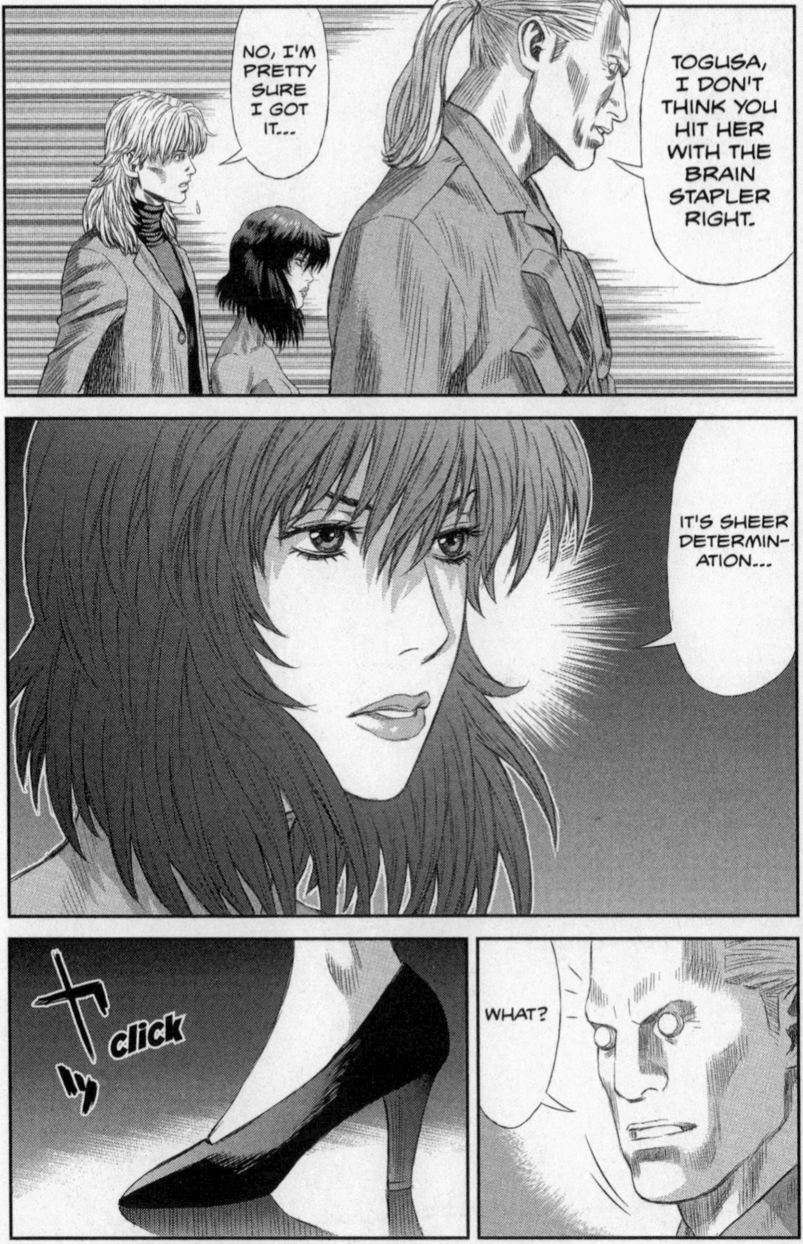
TOGUSA, I DON'T THINK YOU HIT HER WITH THE BRAIN STAPLER RIGHT.
NO, I'M PRETTY SURE I GOT IT...
IT'S SHEER DETERMINATION...
WHAT?
click

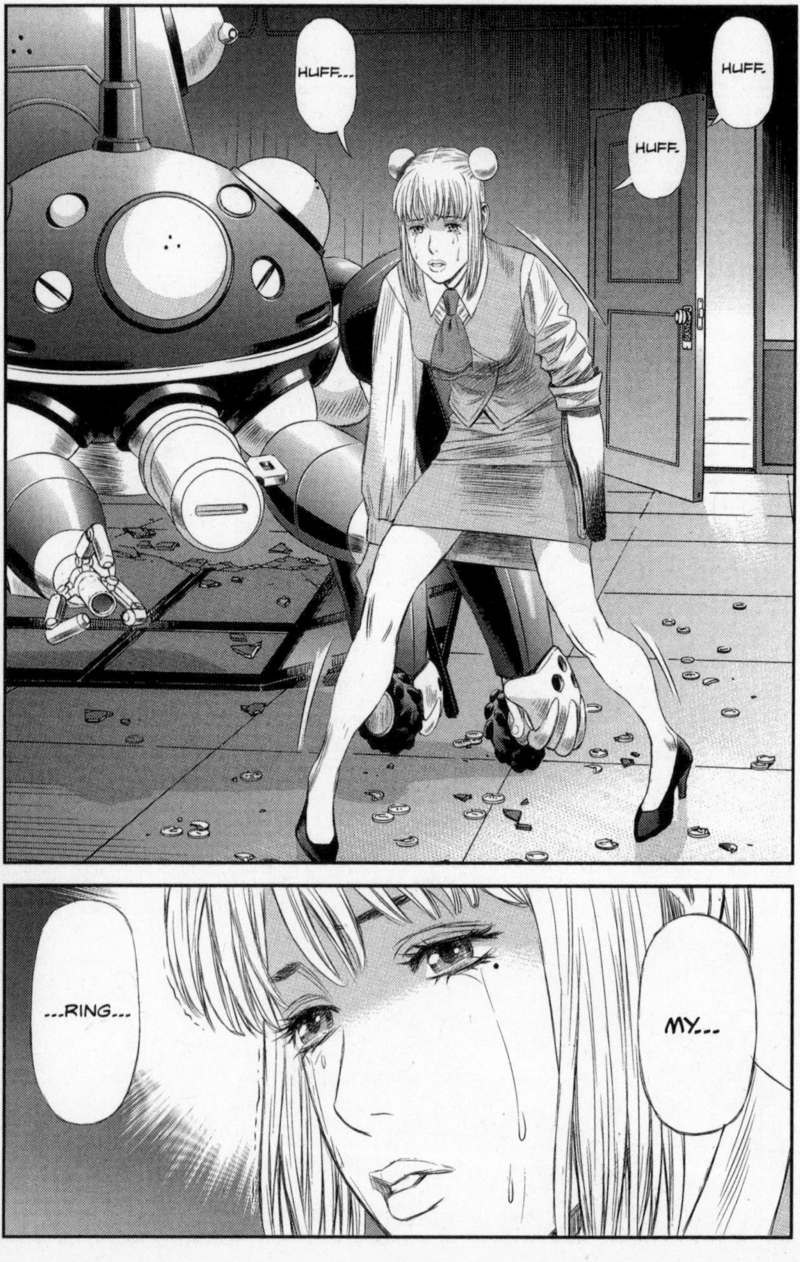
HUFF.
HUFF.
HUFF...
MY...
...RING...

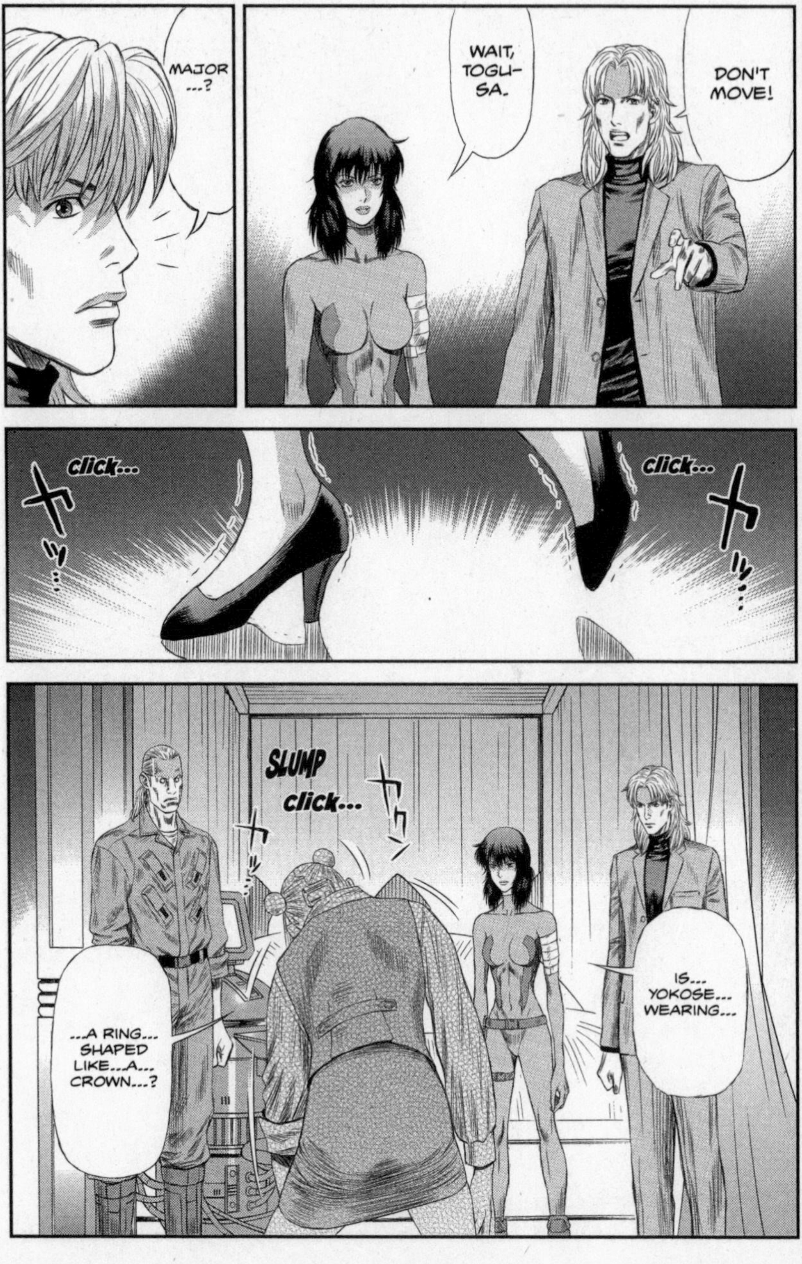

DON'T MOVE!
WAIT, TOGU-SA.
MAJOR ...?
click...
click...
SLUMP
click...
IS... YOKOSE... WEARING...
...A RING... SHAPED LIKE...A... CROWN...?

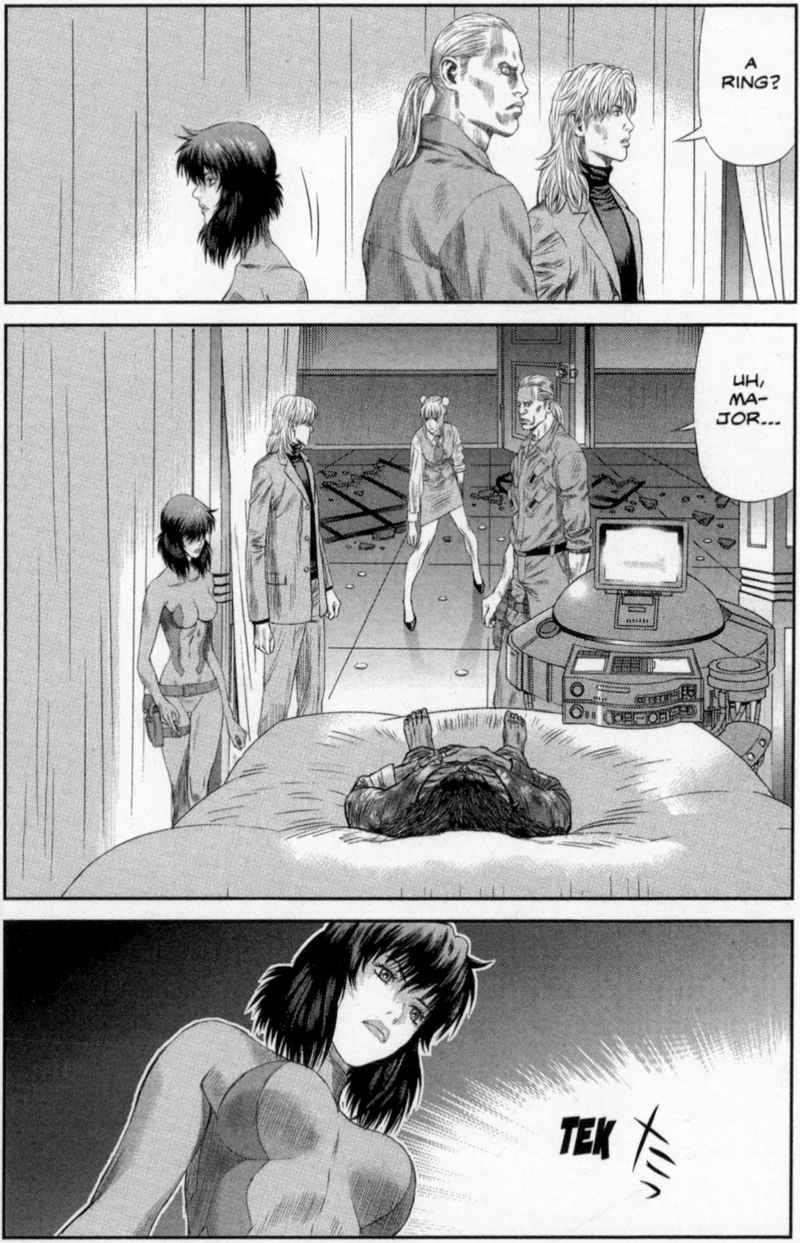
A RING?
UH, MA-JOR...
TEK

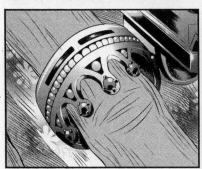

...THERE IT IS.

デン！ WHAM!

!

CRAK

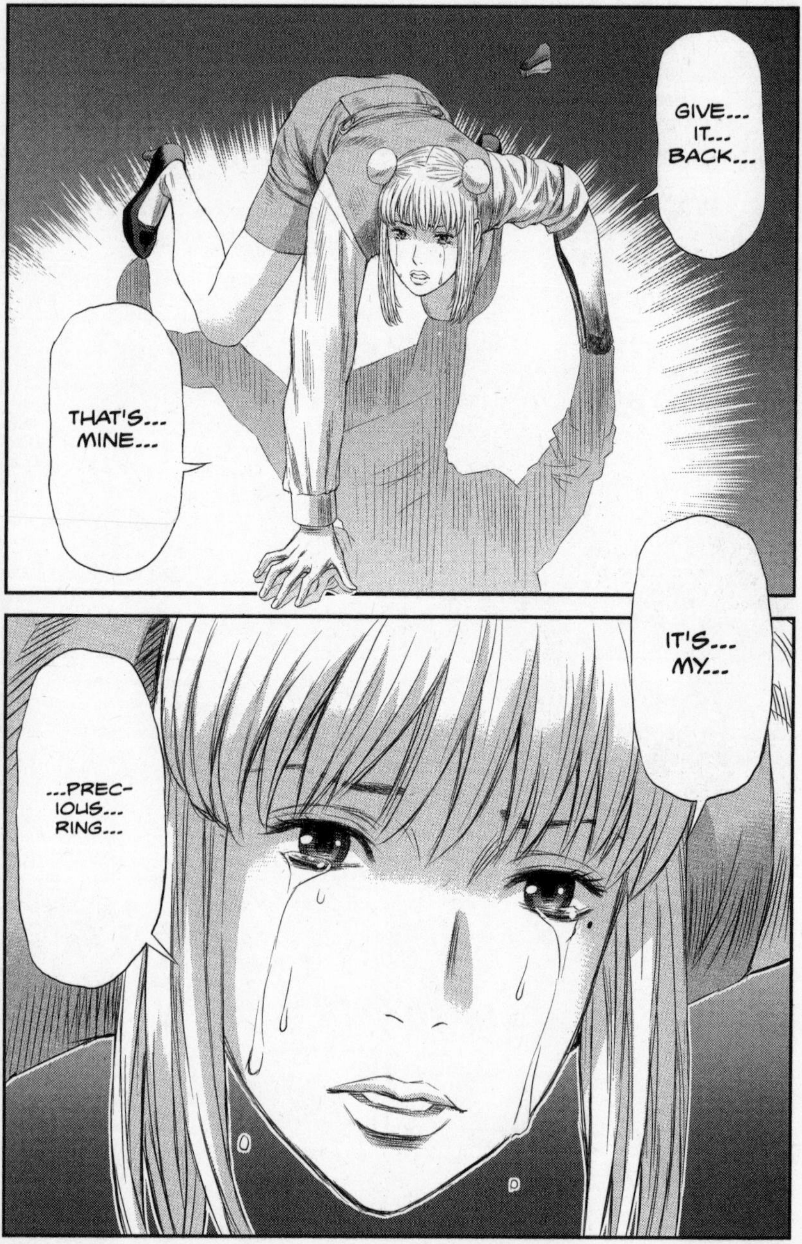
GIVE... IT... BACK...
THAT'S... MINE...
IT'S... MY...
...PREC-IOUS... RING...

ALL RIGHT.

EVERY-THING HERE HAS TO BE LEFT FOR FOREN-SICS...

WE CAN'T.

I SAID, IT'S ALL RIGHT.

MAJOR!

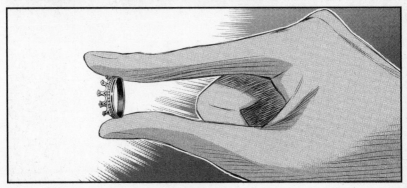

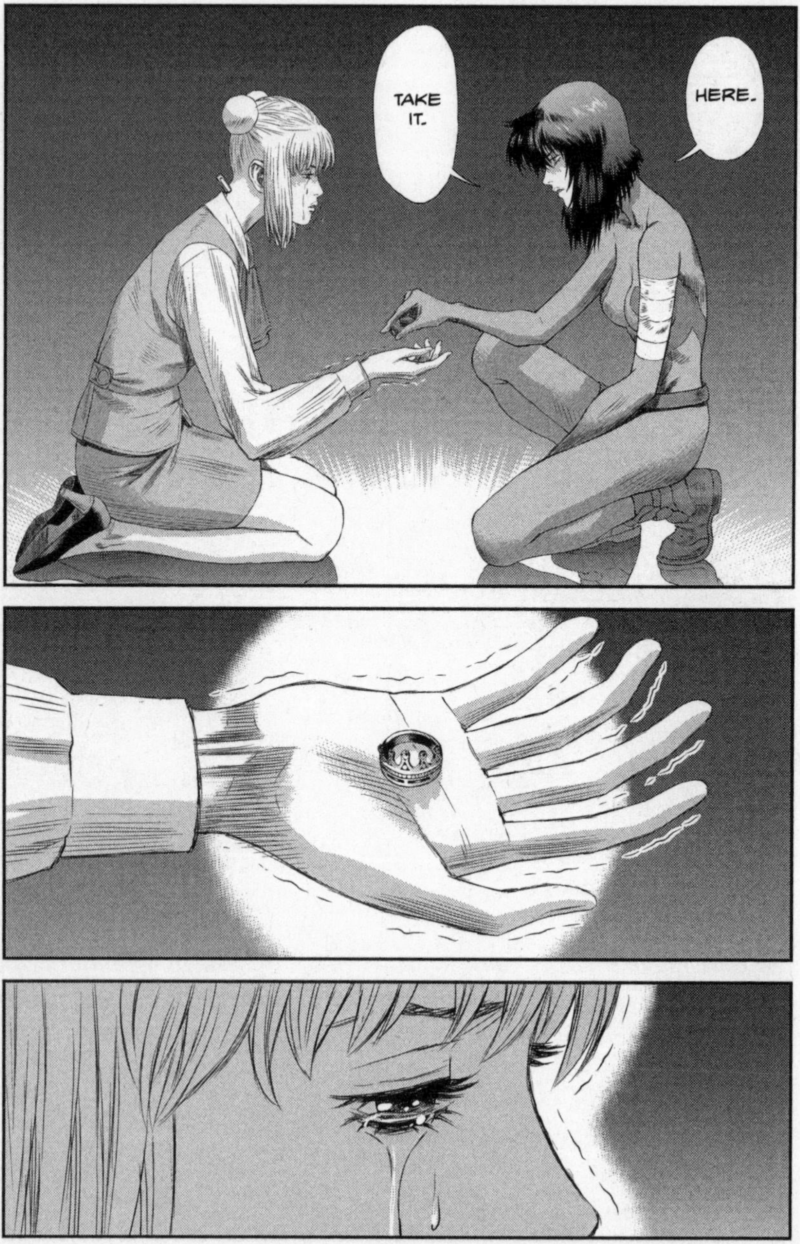
HERE.
TAKE IT.

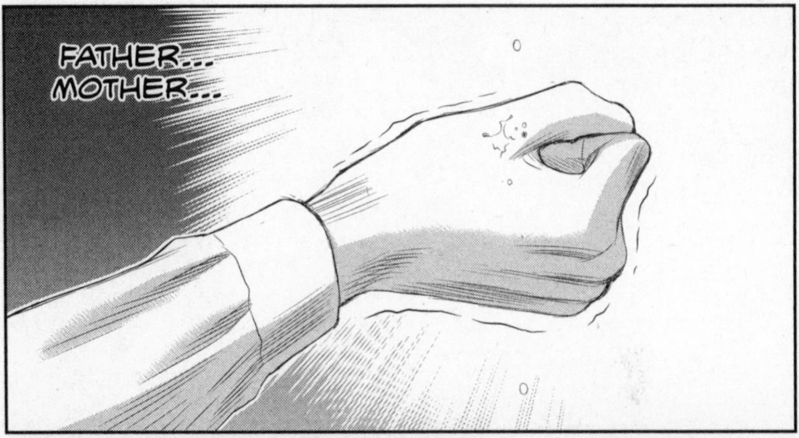
FATHER...
MOTHER...

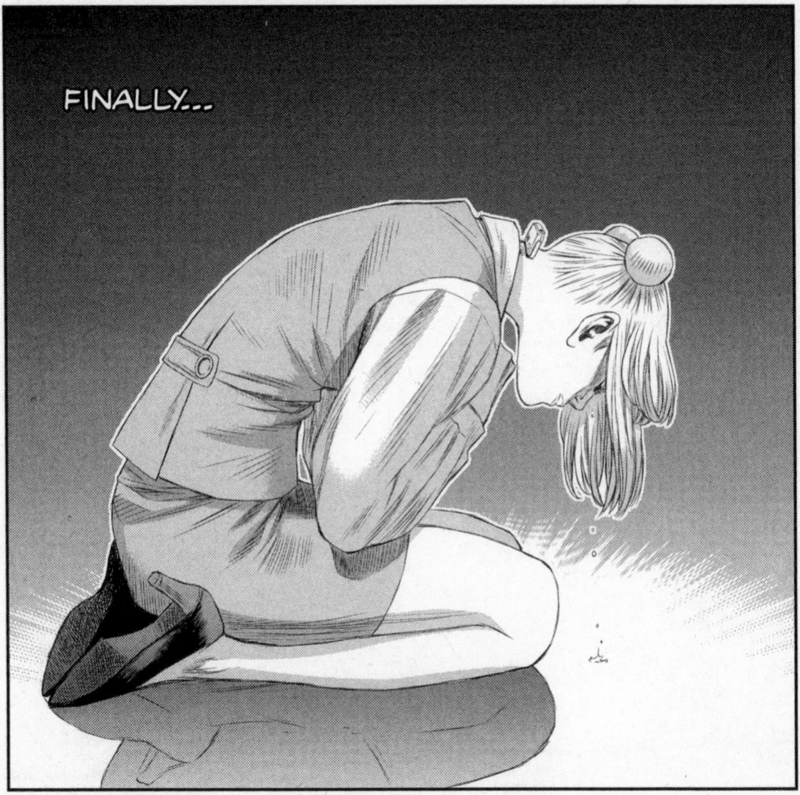
FINALLY...

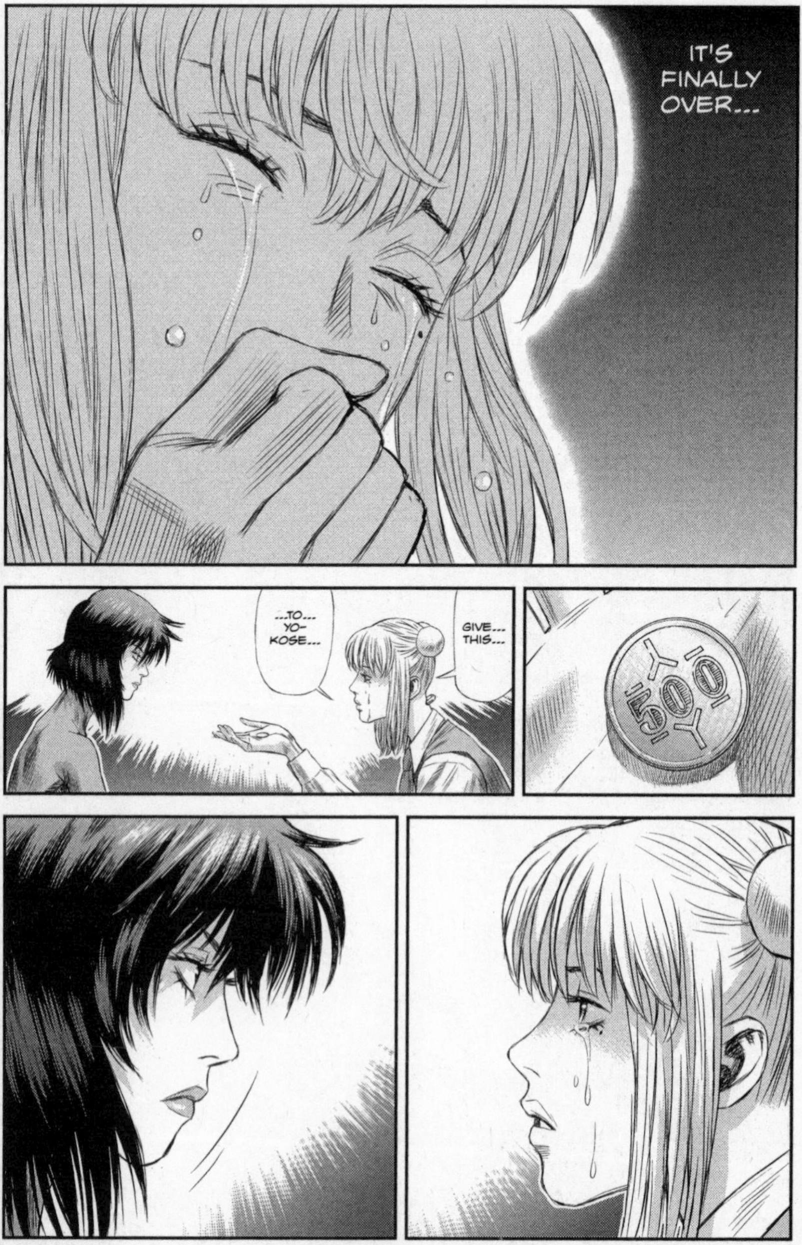
IT'S FINALLY OVER...
GIVE... THIS...
...TO... YO-KOSE...

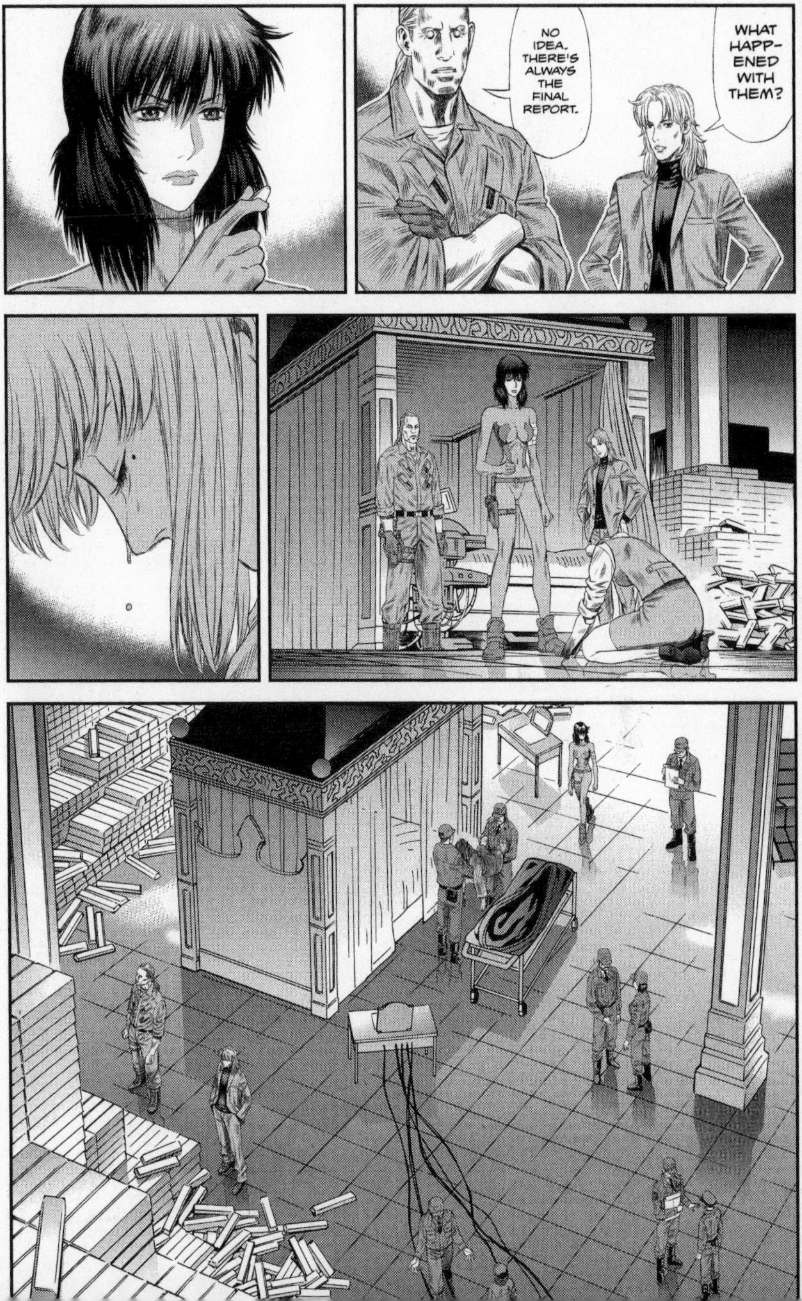
WHAT HAPP-ENED WITH THEM?
NO IDEA. THERE'S ALWAYS THE FINAL REPORT.

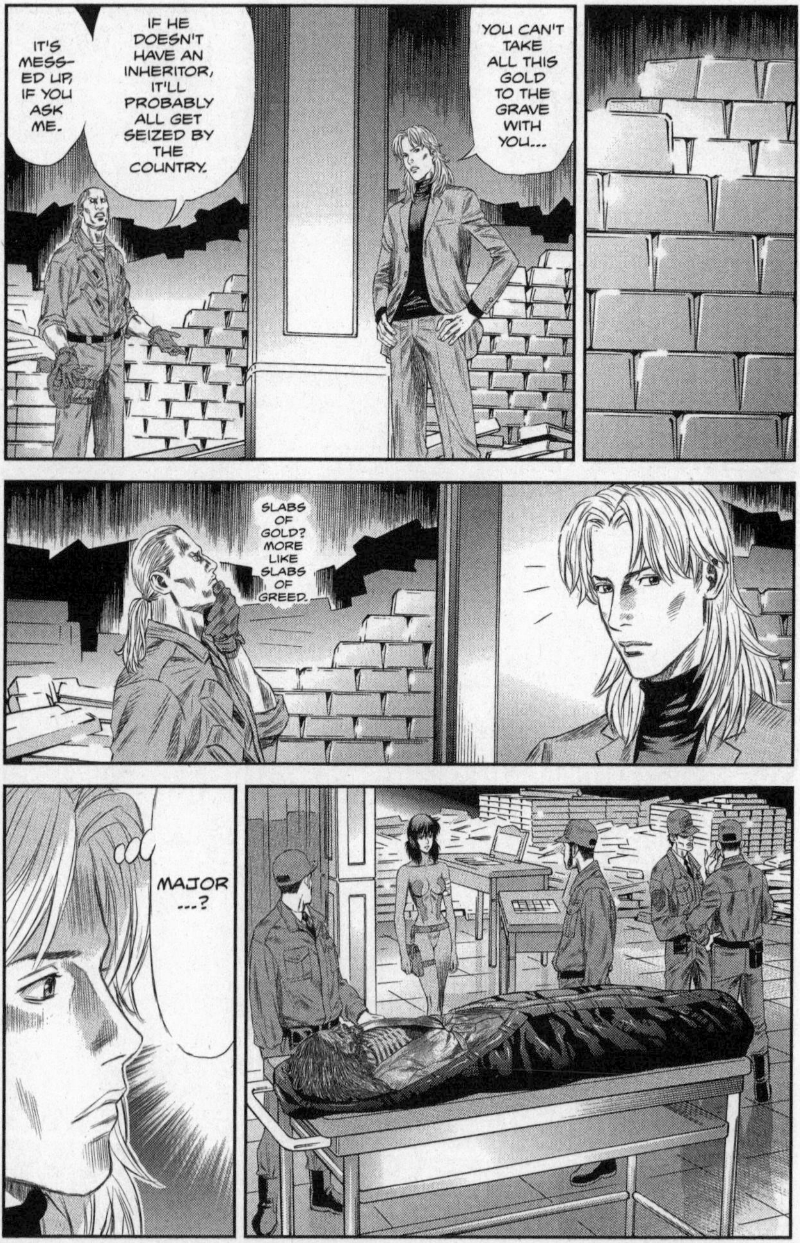
YOU CAN'T TAKE ALL THIS GOLD TO THE GRAVE WITH YOU...
IF HE DOESN'T HAVE AN INHERITOR, IT'LL PROBABLY ALL GET SEIZED BY THE COUNTRY.
IT'S MESS-ED UP, IF YOU ASK ME.
SLABS OF GOLD? MORE LIKE SLABS OF GREED.
MAJOR ...?

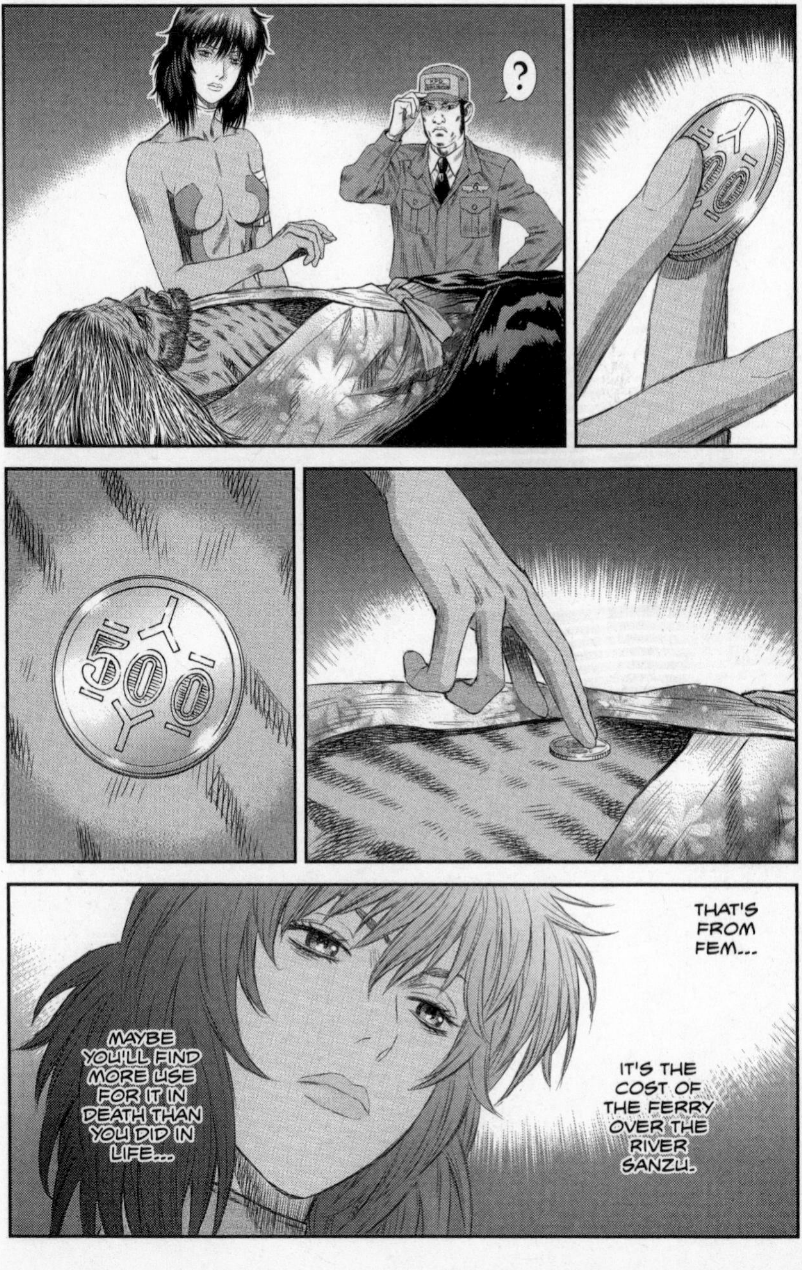
?
THAT'S FROM FEM...
IT'S THE COST OF THE FERRY OVER THE RIVER SANZU.
MAYBE YOU'LL FIND MORE USE FOR IT IN DEATH THAN YOU DID IN LIFE...

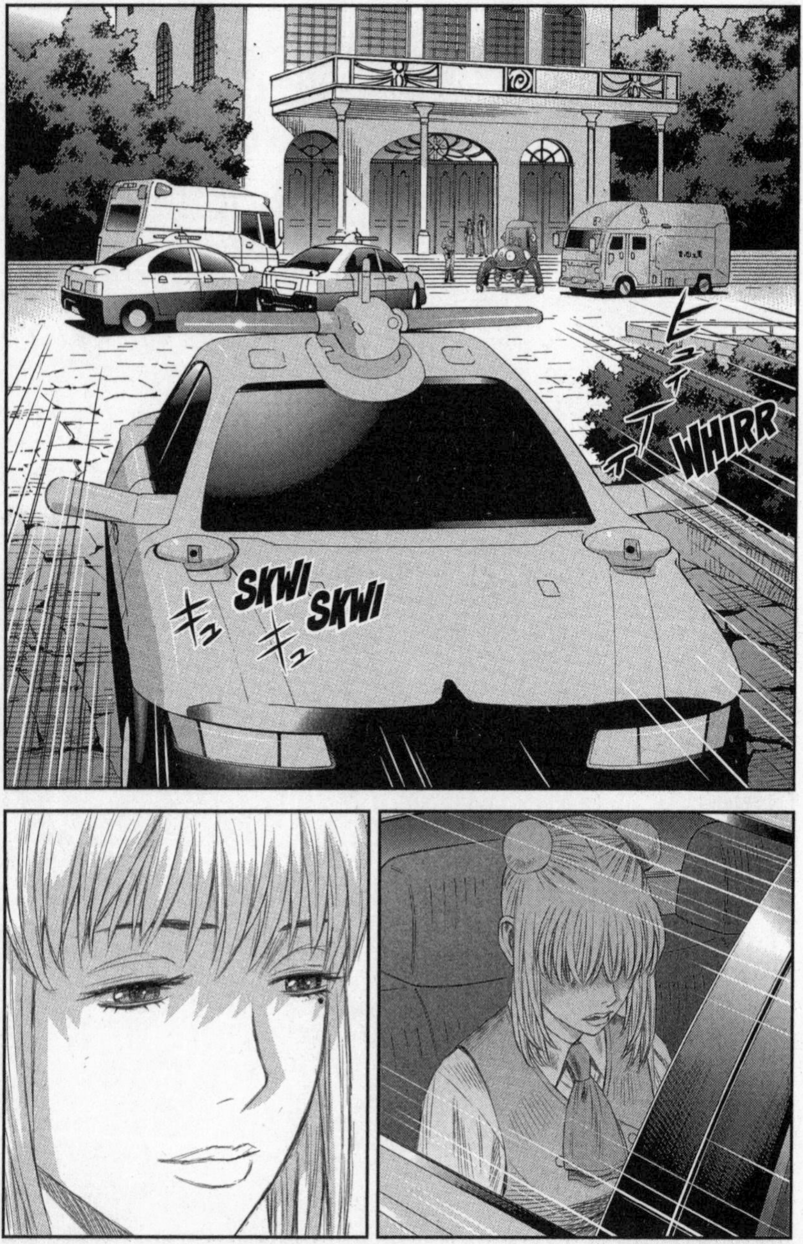
ヒュイイイ
WHIRR
SKWI
SKWI
キュ
キュ

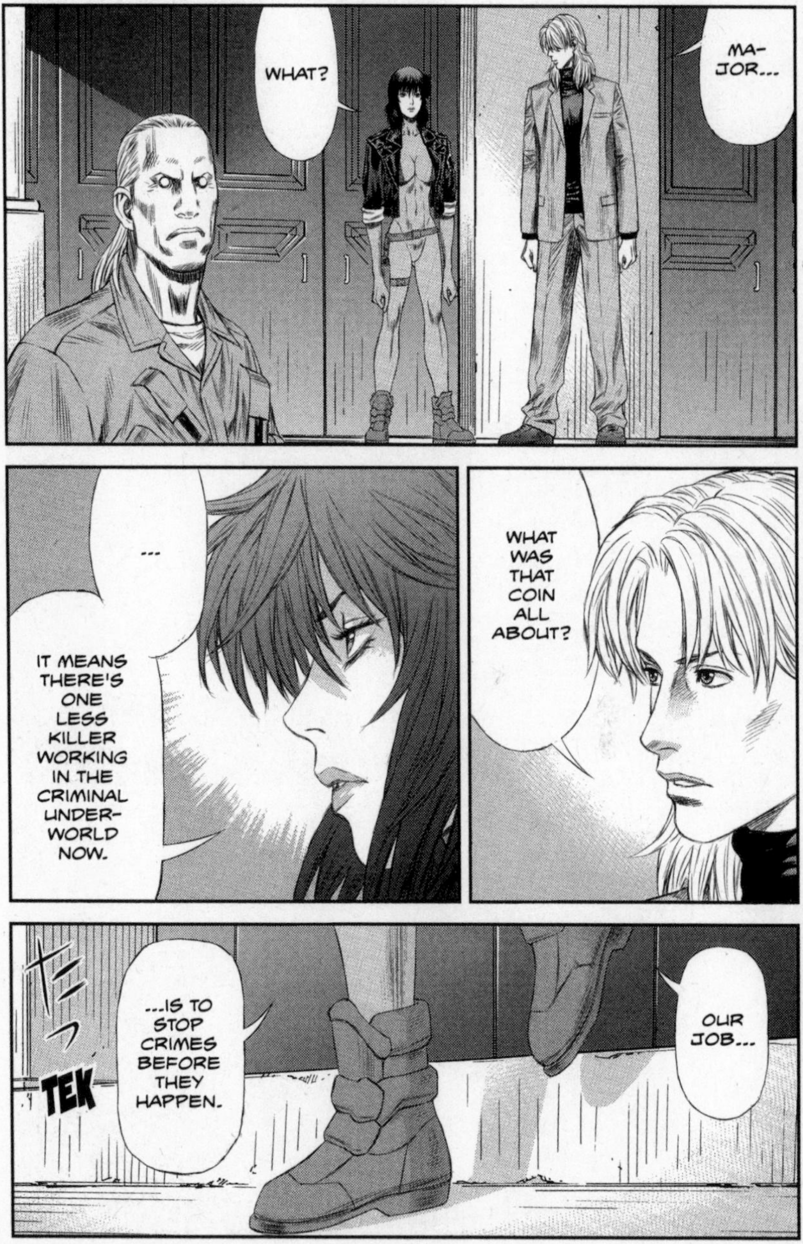
MA-JOR...
WHAT?
WHAT WAS THAT COIN ALL ABOUT?
...
IT MEANS THERE'S ONE LESS KILLER WORKING IN THE CRIMINAL UNDER-WORLD NOW.
OUR JOB...
...IS TO STOP CRIMES BEFORE THEY HAPPEN.
TEK

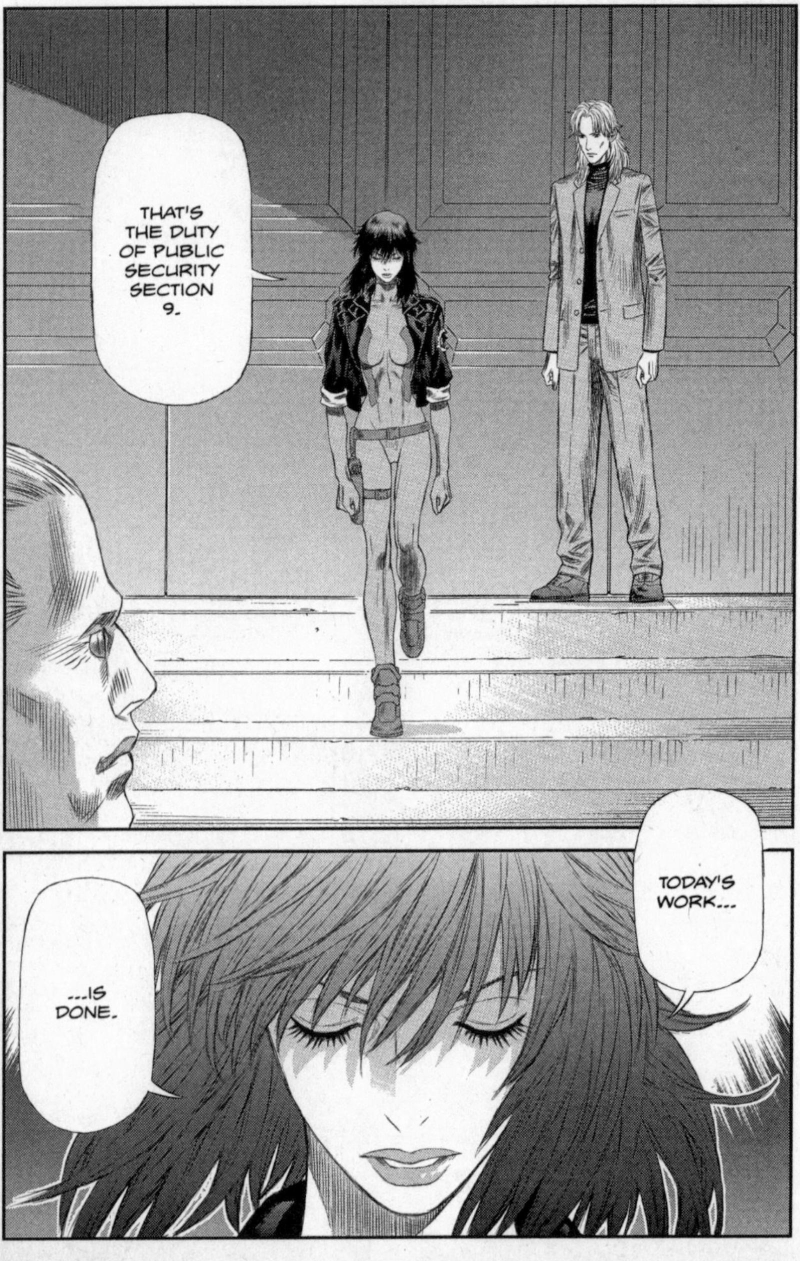
THAT'S THE DUTY OF PUBLIC SECURITY SECTION 9.
TODAY'S WORK...
...IS DONE.

#031: END

#032: Ghost of Capitalism

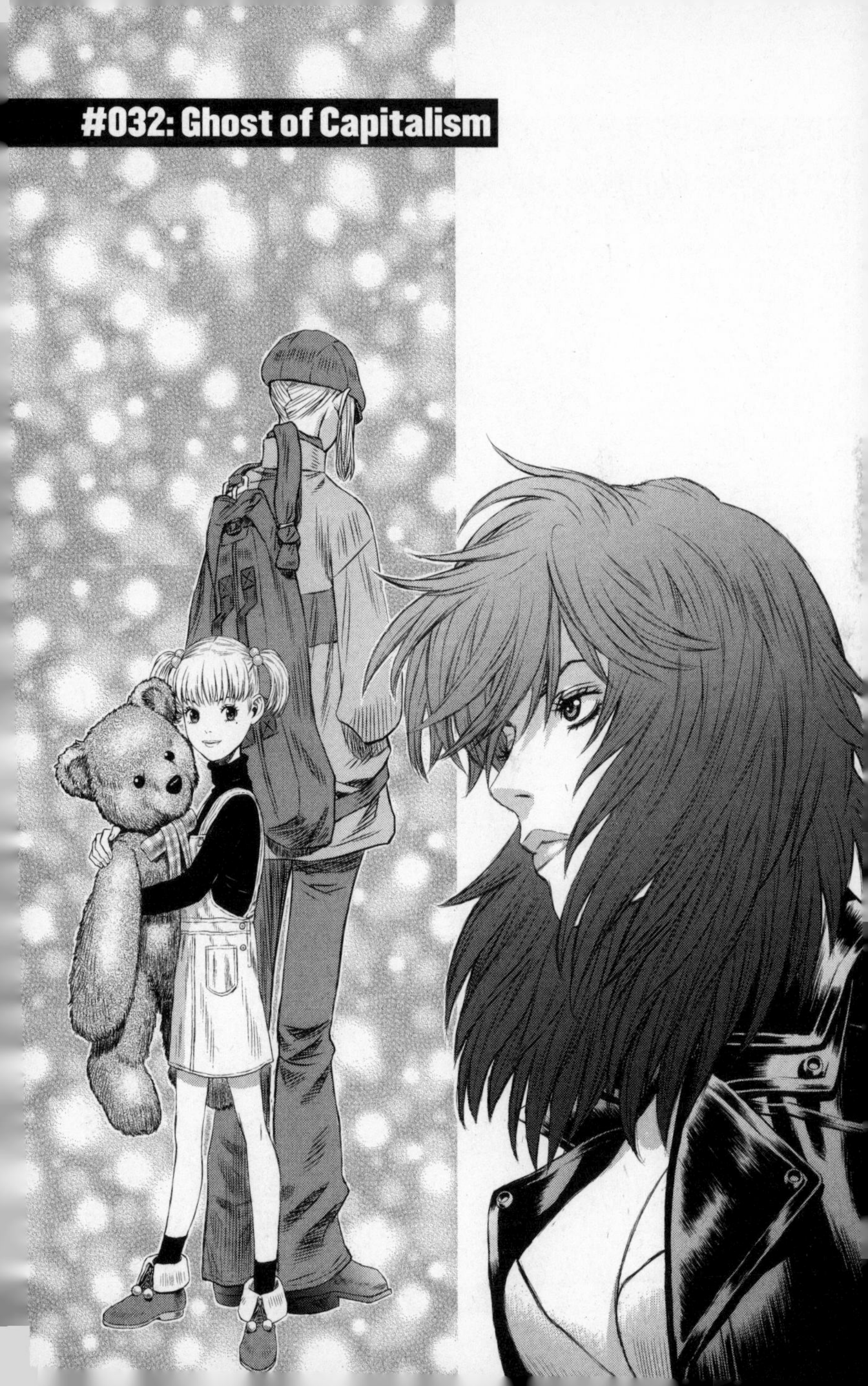

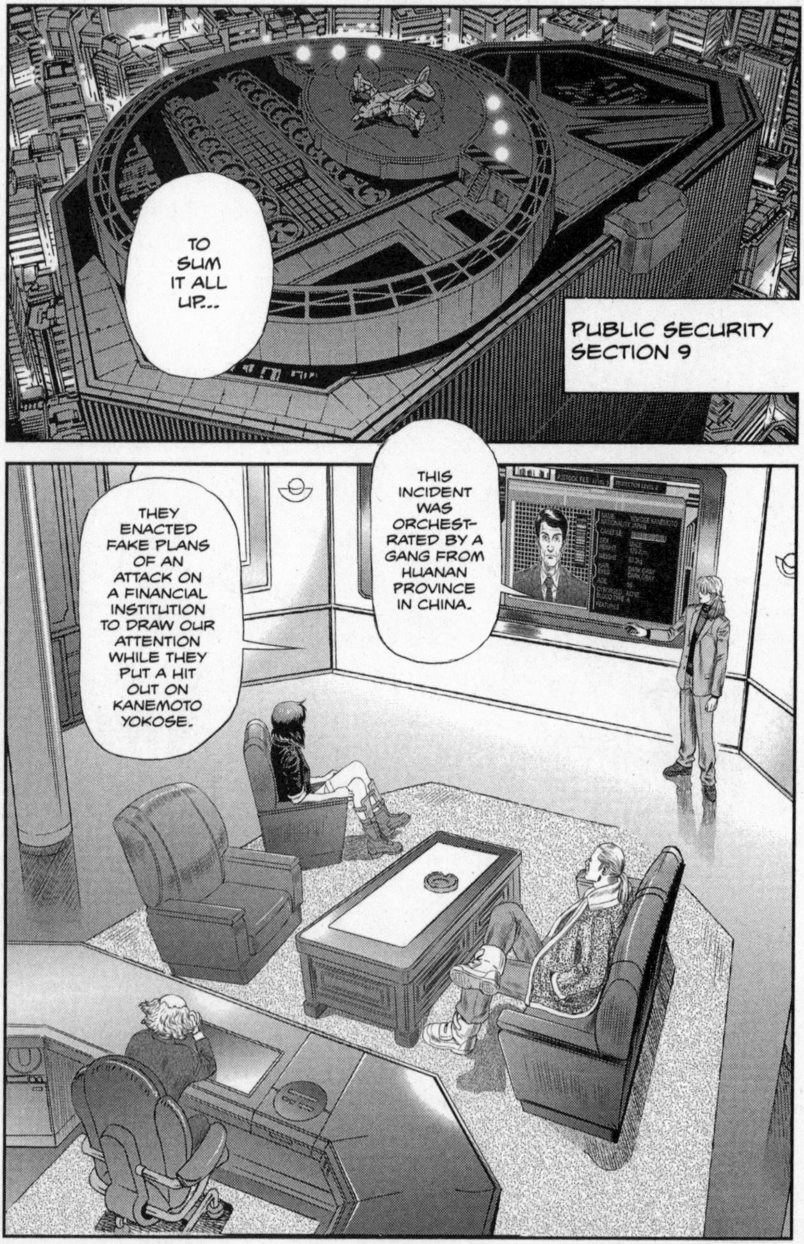
PUBLIC SECURITY SECTION 9
TO SUM IT ALL UP...
THIS INCIDENT WAS ORCHESTRATED BY A GANG FROM HUANAN PROVINCE IN CHINA.
THEY ENACTED FAKE PLANS OF AN ATTACK ON A FINANCIAL INSTITUTION TO DRAW OUR ATTENTION WHILE THEY PUT A HIT OUT ON KANEMOTO YOKOSE.

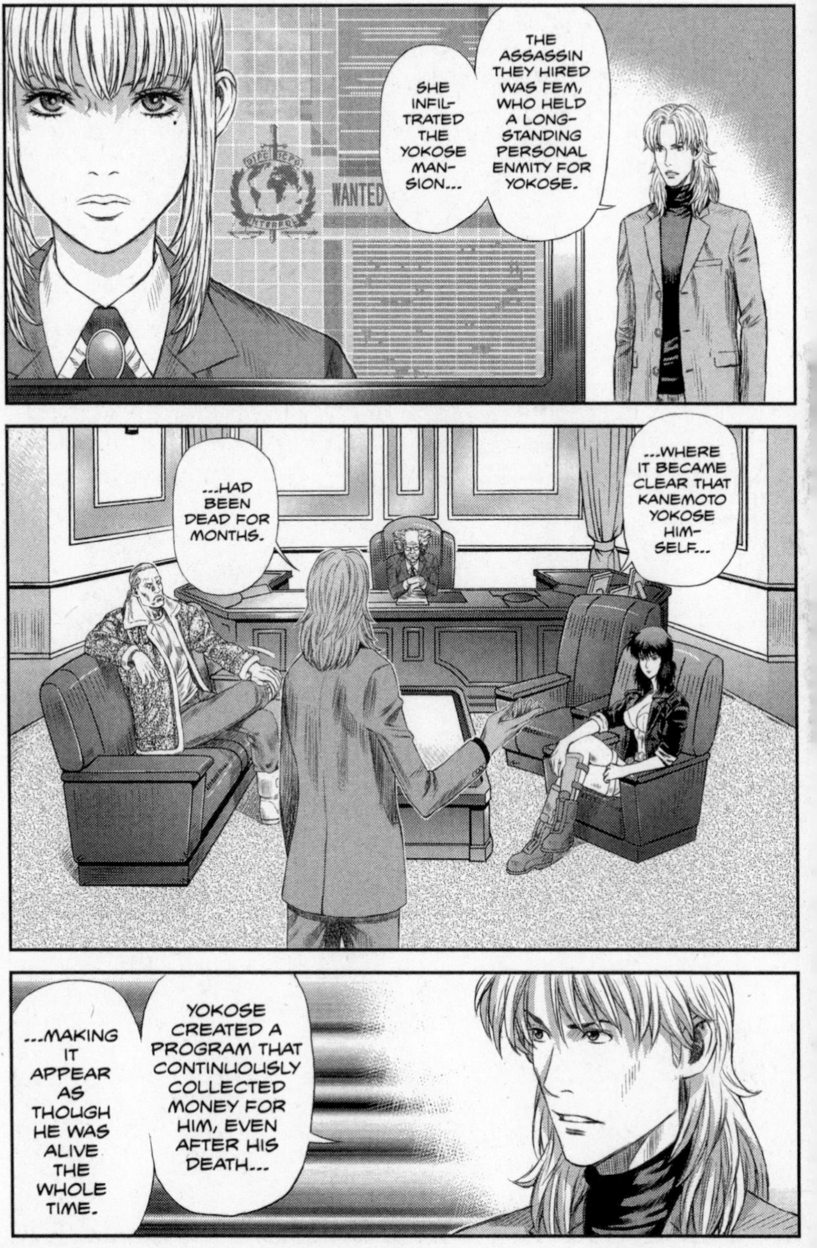
THE ASSASSIN THEY HIRED WAS FEM, WHO HELD A LONG-STANDING PERSONAL ENMITY FOR YOKOSE.
SHE INFILTRATED THE YOKOSE MANSION...
WANTED
...WHERE IT BECAME CLEAR THAT KANEMOTO YOKOSE HIMSELF...
...HAD BEEN DEAD FOR MONTHS.
YOKOSE CREATED A PROGRAM THAT CONTINUOUSLY COLLECTED MONEY FOR HIM, EVEN AFTER HIS DEATH...
...MAKING IT APPEAR AS THOUGH HE WAS ALIVE THE WHOLE TIME.

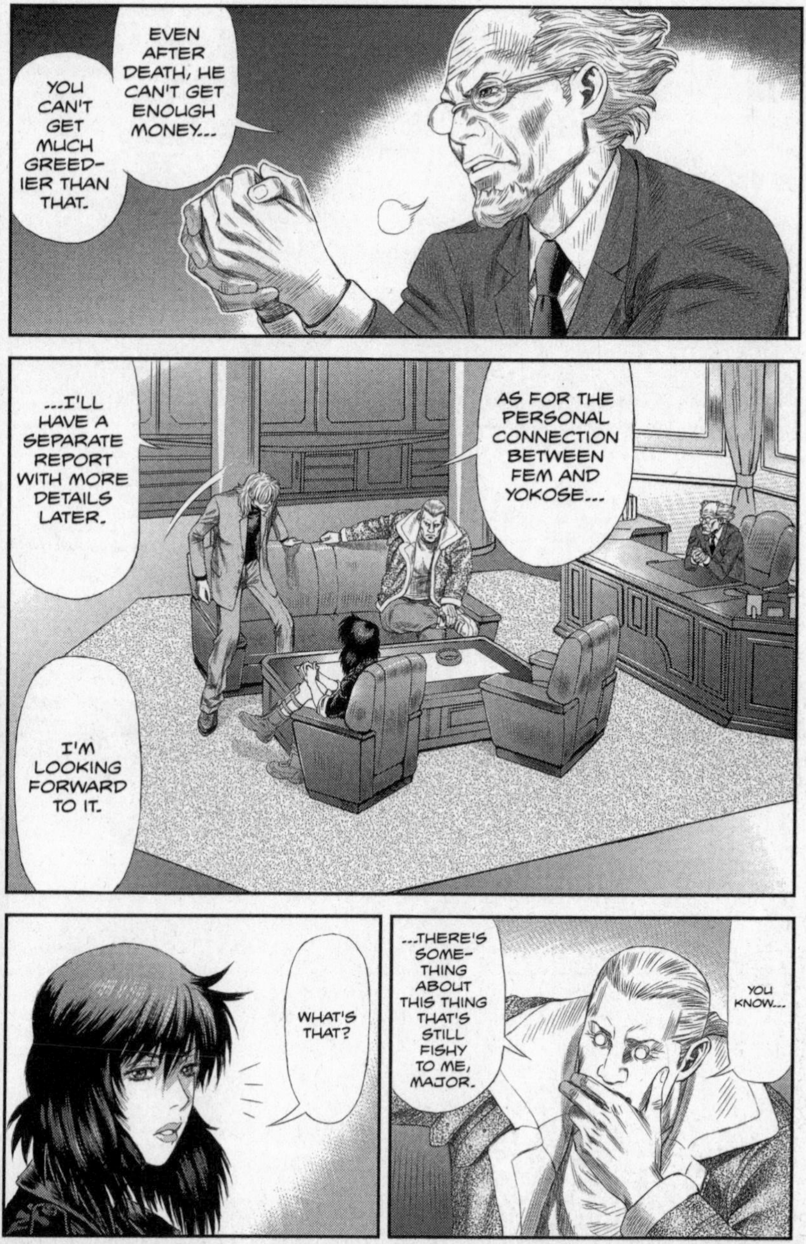
EVEN AFTER DEATH, HE CAN'T GET ENOUGH MONEY...
YOU CAN'T GET MUCH GREEDIER THAN THAT.
AS FOR THE PERSONAL CONNECTION BETWEEN FEM AND YOKOSE...
...I'LL HAVE A SEPARATE REPORT WITH MORE DETAILS LATER.
I'M LOOKING FORWARD TO IT.
YOU KNOW...
...THERE'S SOME-THING ABOUT THIS THING THAT'S STILL FISHY TO ME, MAJOR.
WHAT'S THAT?

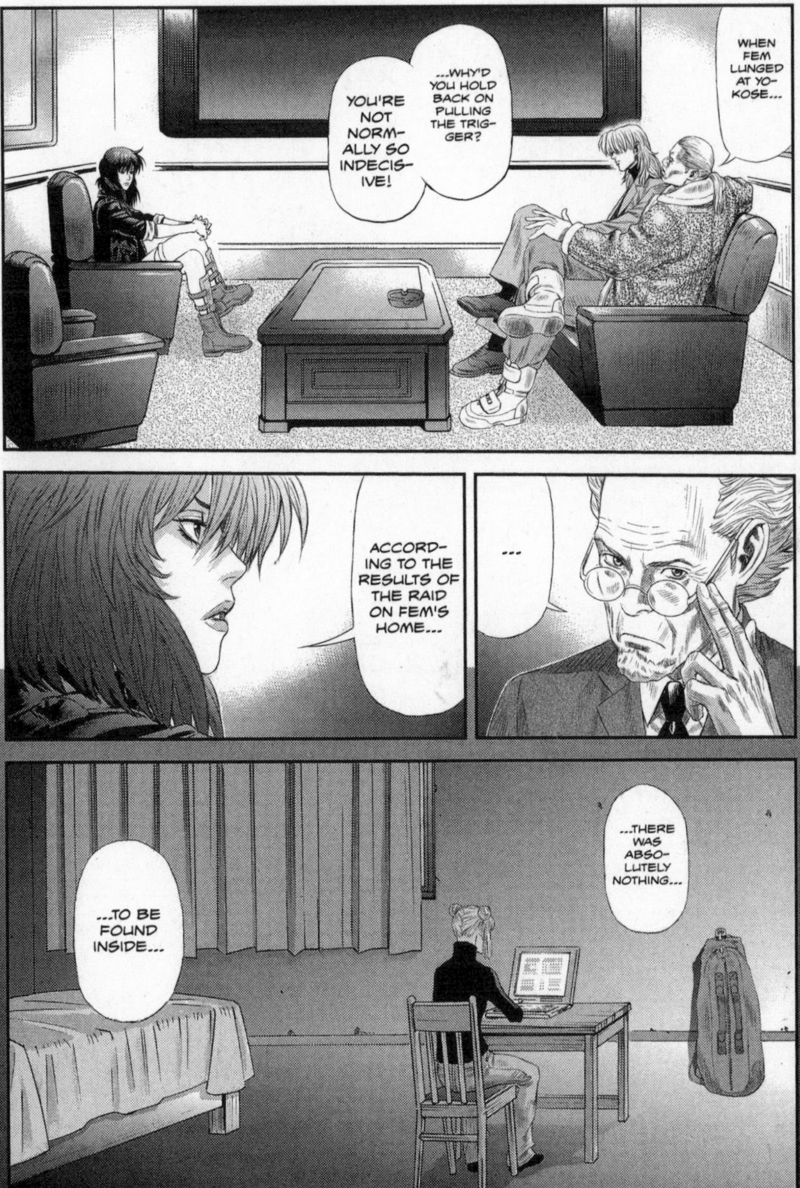
WHEN FEM LUNGED AT YO-KOSE...
...WHY'D YOU HOLD BACK ON PULLING THE TRIG-GER?
YOU'RE NOT NORM-ALLY SO INDECIS-IVE!
...
ACCORD-ING TO THE RESULTS OF THE RAID ON FEM'S HOME...
...THERE WAS ABSO-LUTELY NOTHING...
...TO BE FOUND INSIDE...

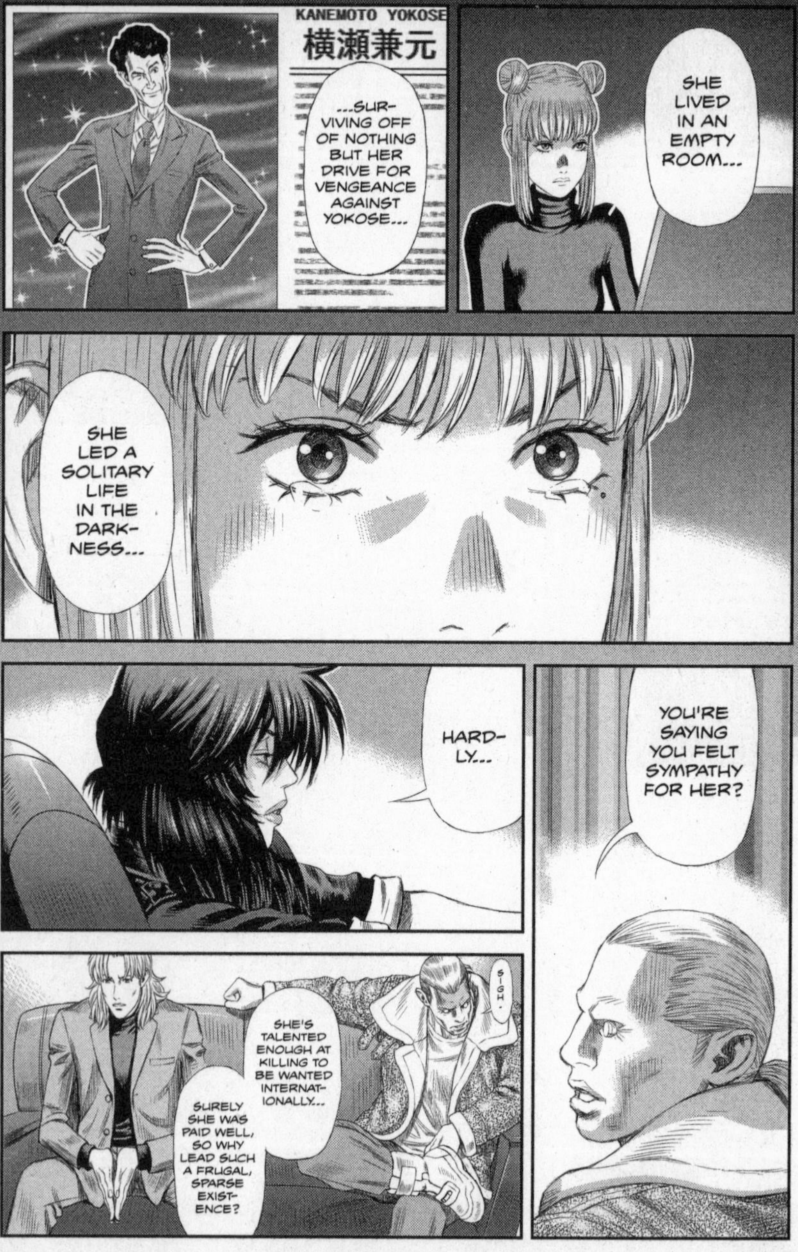
SHE LIVED IN AN EMPTY ROOM...
KANEMOTO YOKOSE
横瀬兼元
...SURVIVING OFF OF NOTHING BUT HER DRIVE FOR VENGEANCE AGAINST YOKOSE...
SHE LED A SOLITARY LIFE IN THE DARKNESS...
YOU'RE SAYING YOU FELT SYMPATHY FOR HER?
HARDLY...
SIGH.
SHE'S TALENTED ENOUGH AT KILLING TO BE WANTED INTERNATIONALLY...
SURELY SHE WAS PAID WELL, SO WHY LEAD SUCH A FRUGAL, SPARSE EXISTENCE?

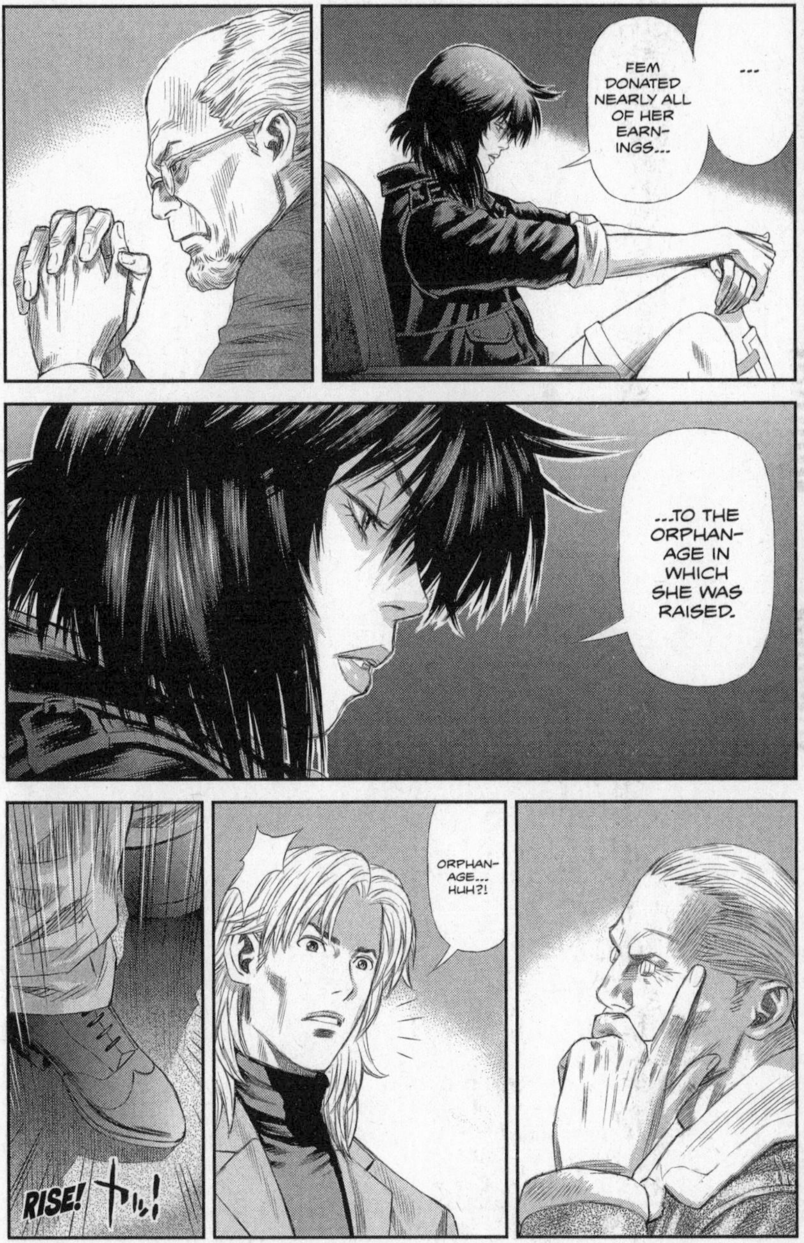
...
FEM DONATED NEARLY ALL OF HER EARN-INGS...
...TO THE ORPHAN-AGE IN WHICH SHE WAS RAISED.
ORPHAN-AGE... HUH?!
RISE! トッ!

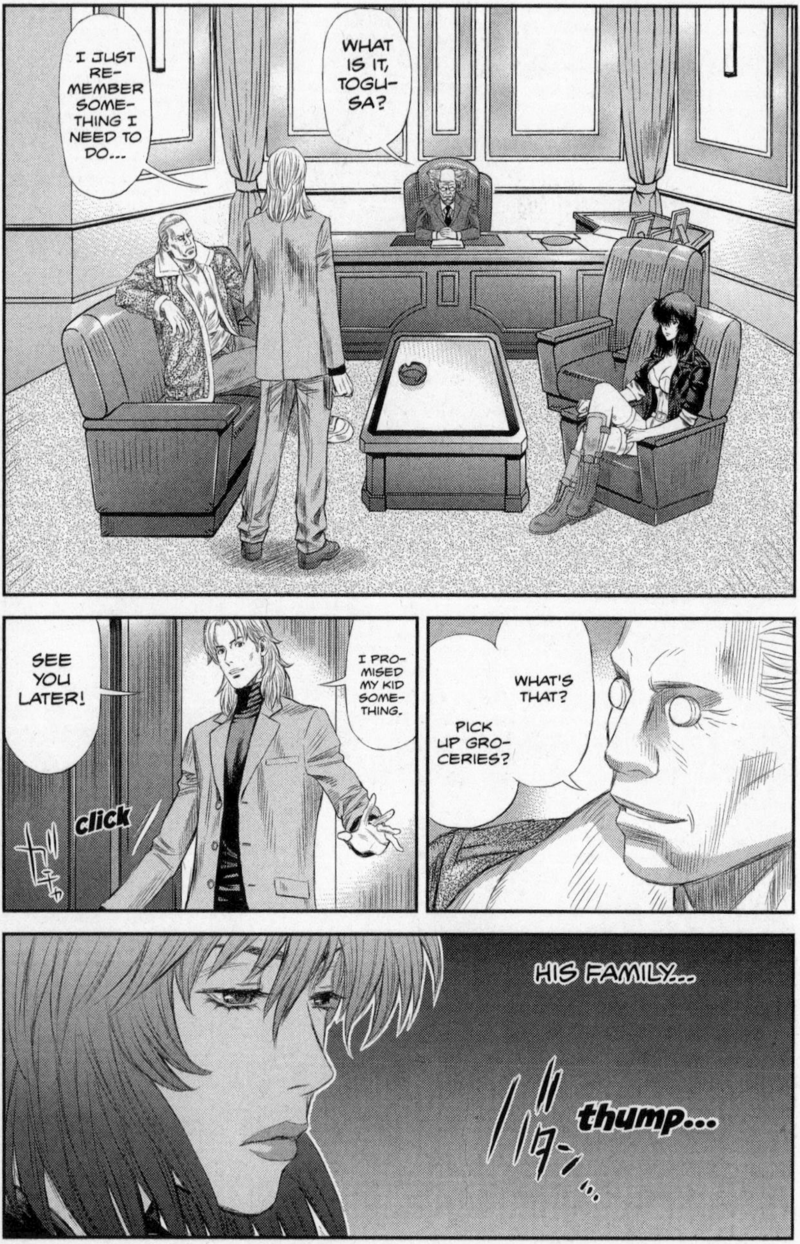
WHAT IS IT, TOGU-SA?
I JUST RE-MEMBER SOME-THING I NEED TO DO...
WHAT'S THAT?
PICK UP GRO-CERIES?
I PRO-MISED MY KID SOME-THING.
SEE YOU LATER!
click
HIS FAMILY...
thump...

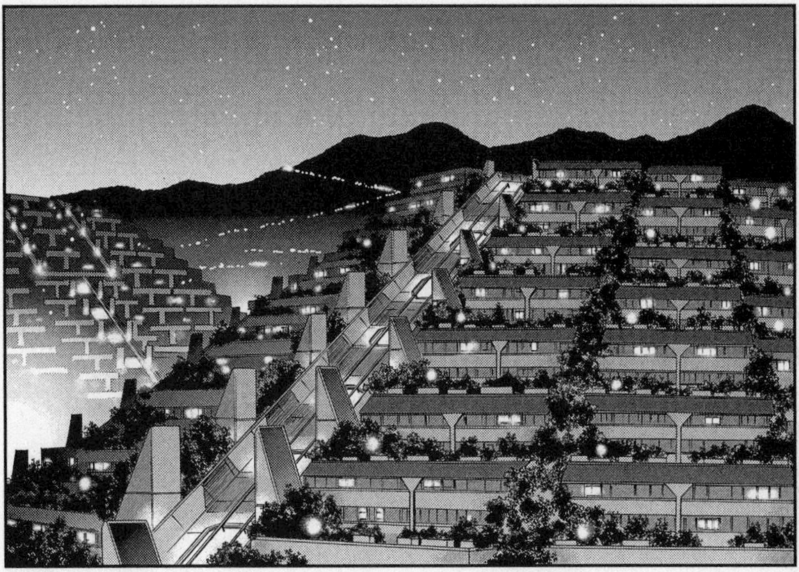

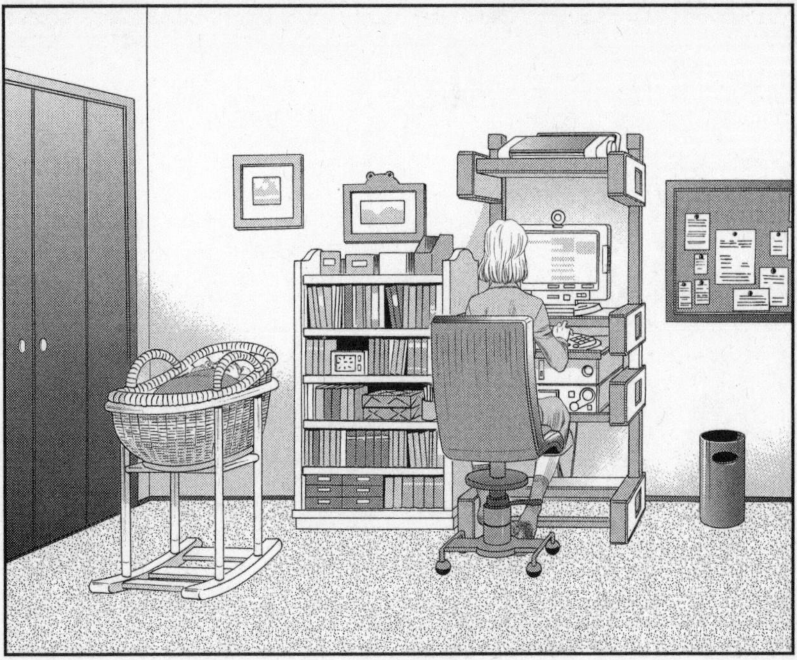

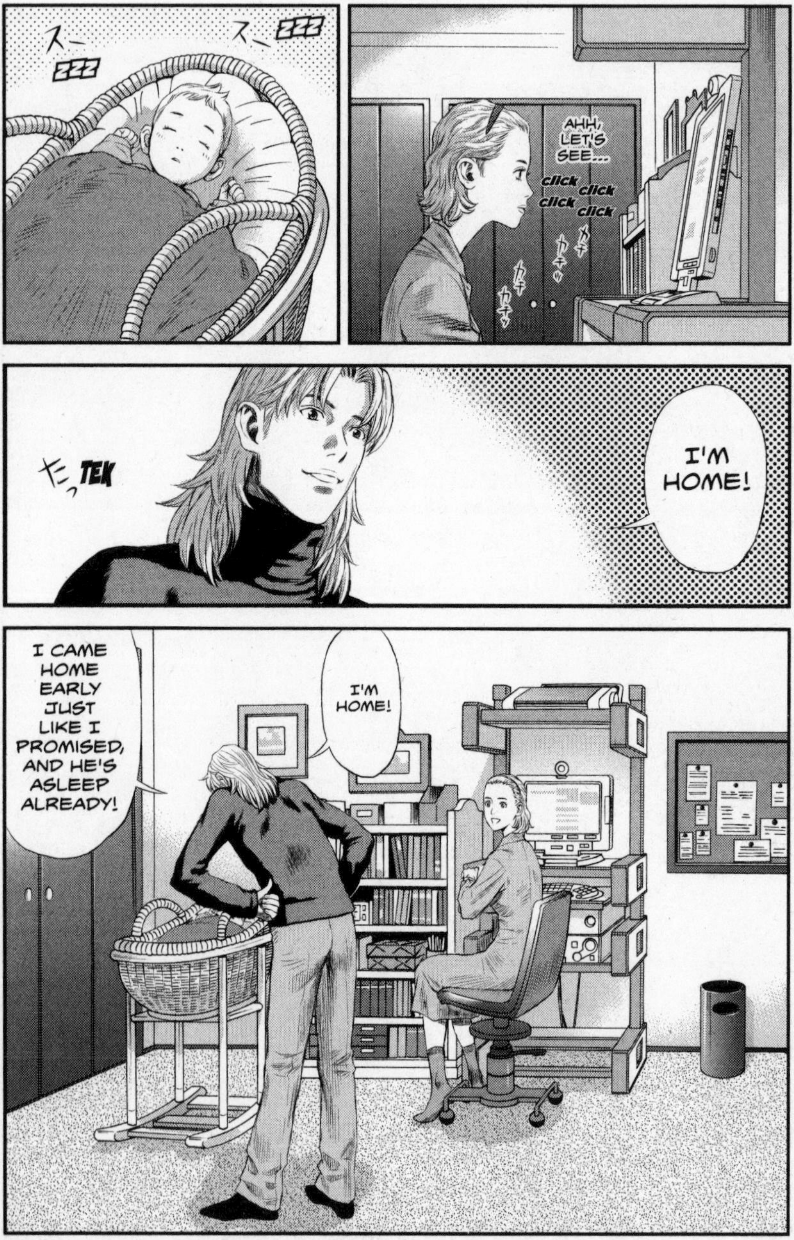
AHH, LET'S SEE...
click click click click
ZZZ
ZZZ
I'M HOME!
TEK
I'M HOME!
I CAME HOME EARLY JUST LIKE I PROMISED, AND HE'S ASLEEP ALREADY!

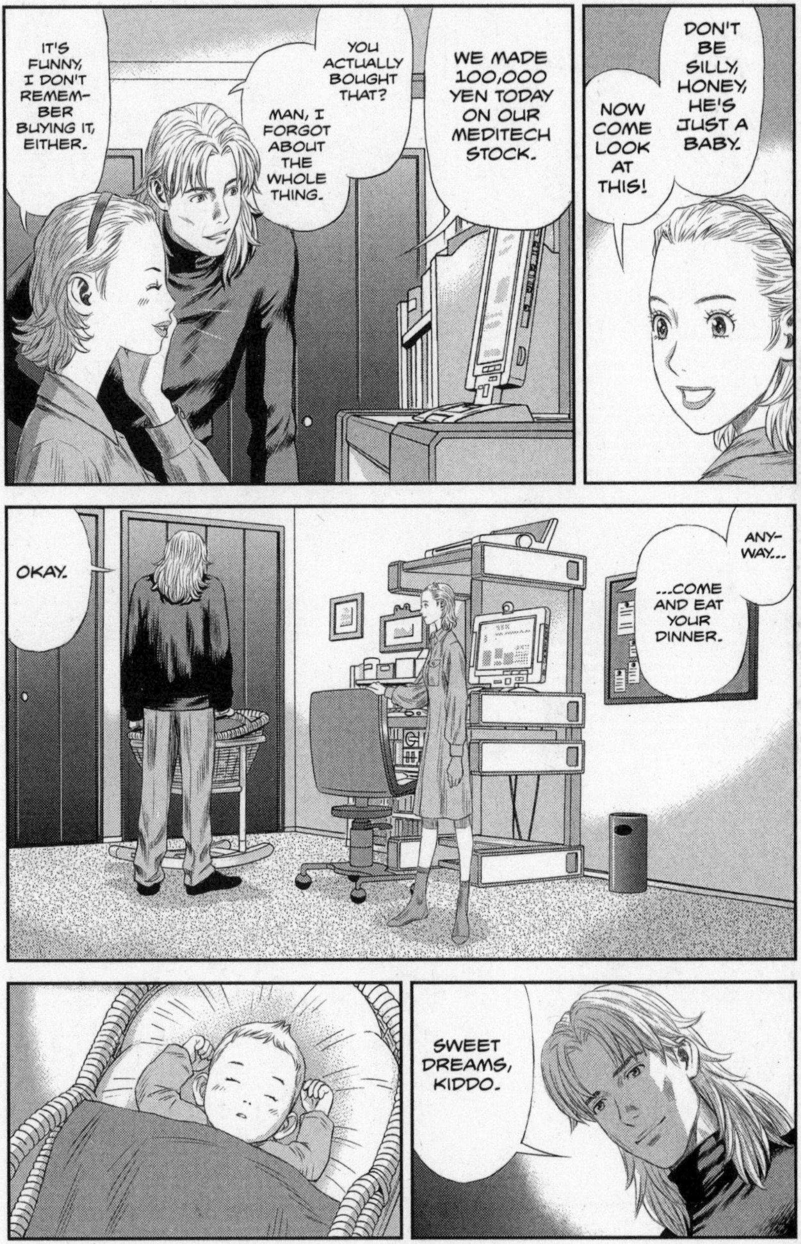
DON'T BE SILLY, HONEY, HE'S JUST A BABY.
NOW COME LOOK AT THIS!
WE MADE 100,000 YEN TODAY ON OUR MEDITECH STOCK.
YOU ACTUALLY BOUGHT THAT?
MAN, I FORGOT ABOUT THE WHOLE THING.
IT'S FUNNY, I DON'T REMEMBER BUYING IT, EITHER.
ANYWAY...
...COME AND EAT YOUR DINNER.
OKAY.
SWEET DREAMS, KIDDO.

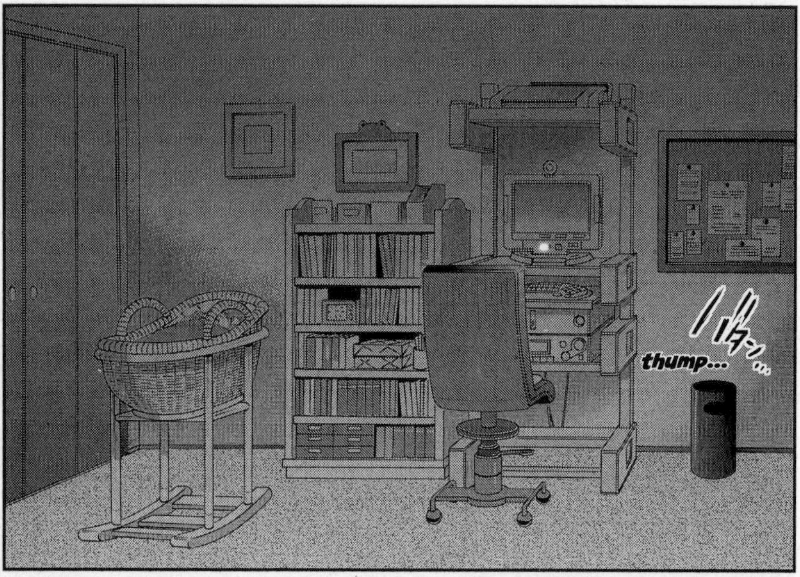
thump...
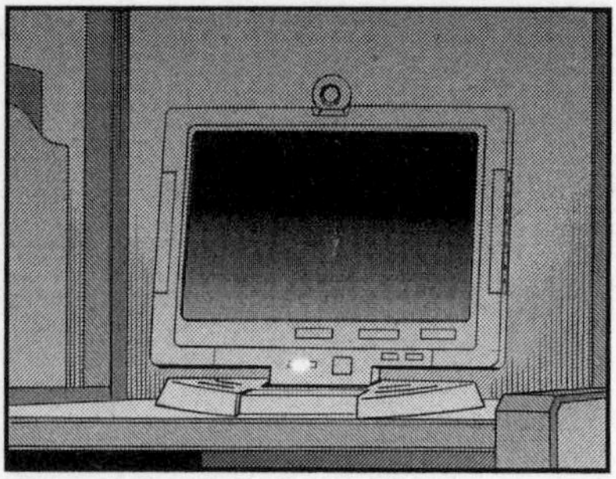
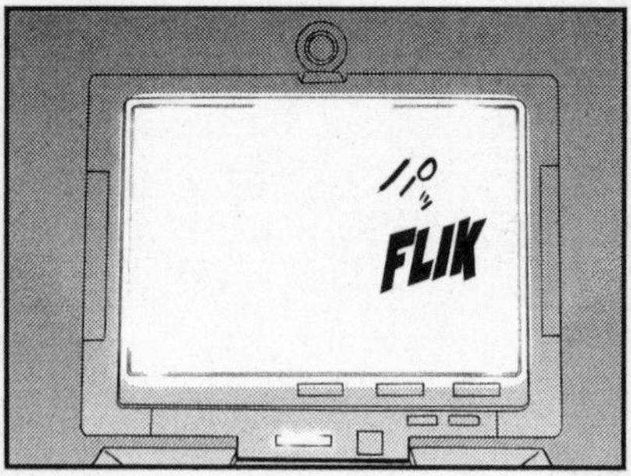
FLIK
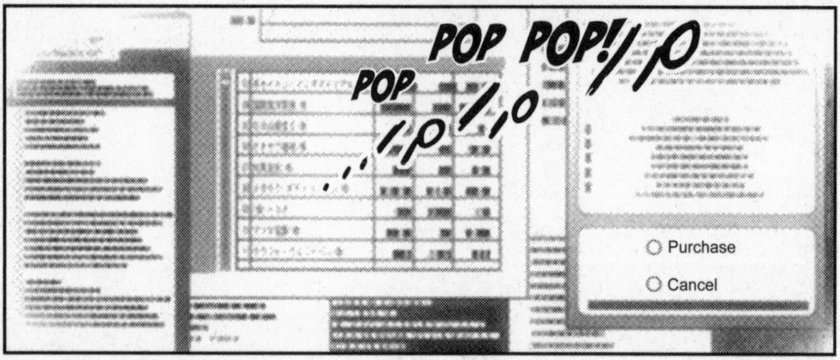
POP
POP POP!
Purchase
Cancel

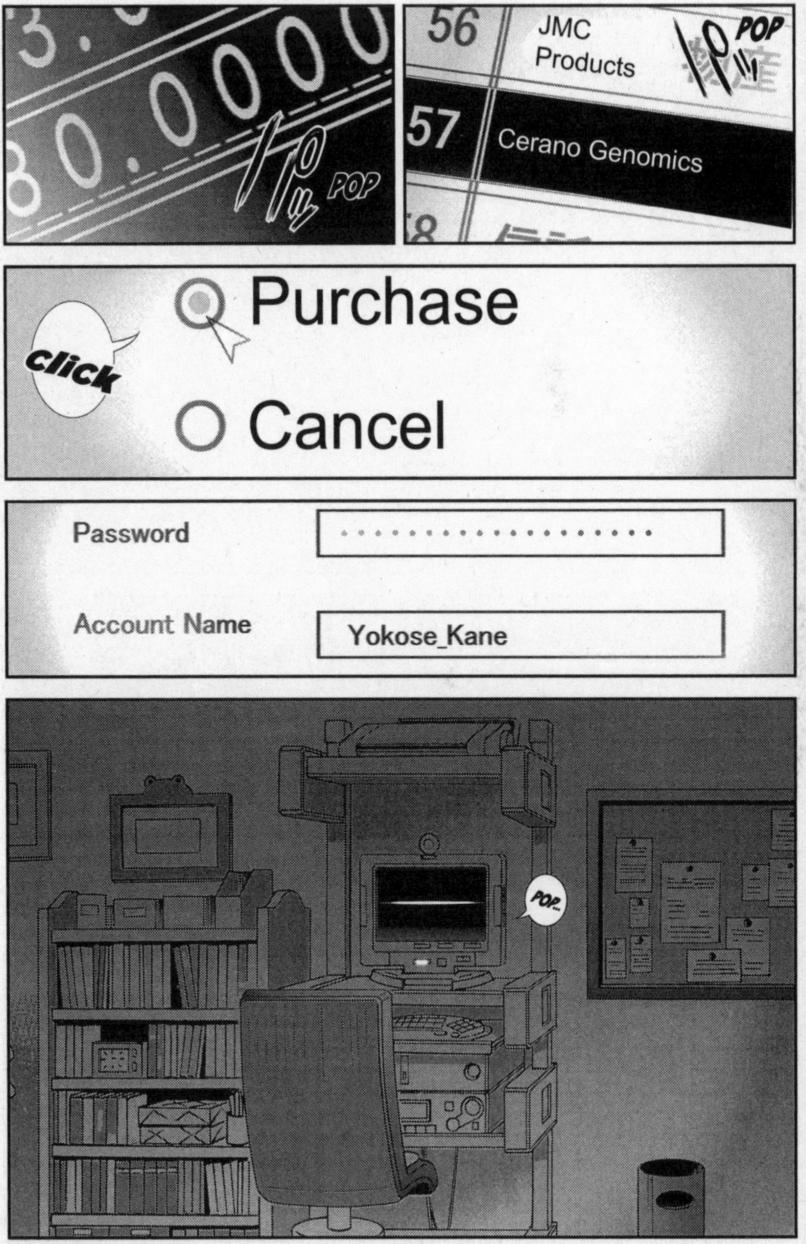
56
JMC Products
POP
57
Cerano Genomics
POP
Purchase
Cancel
click
Password
Account Name
Yokose_Kane
POP...

#032: END

EPISODE

Next Volume Preview

Dive into an enormous abandoned facility shrouded in mystery!!

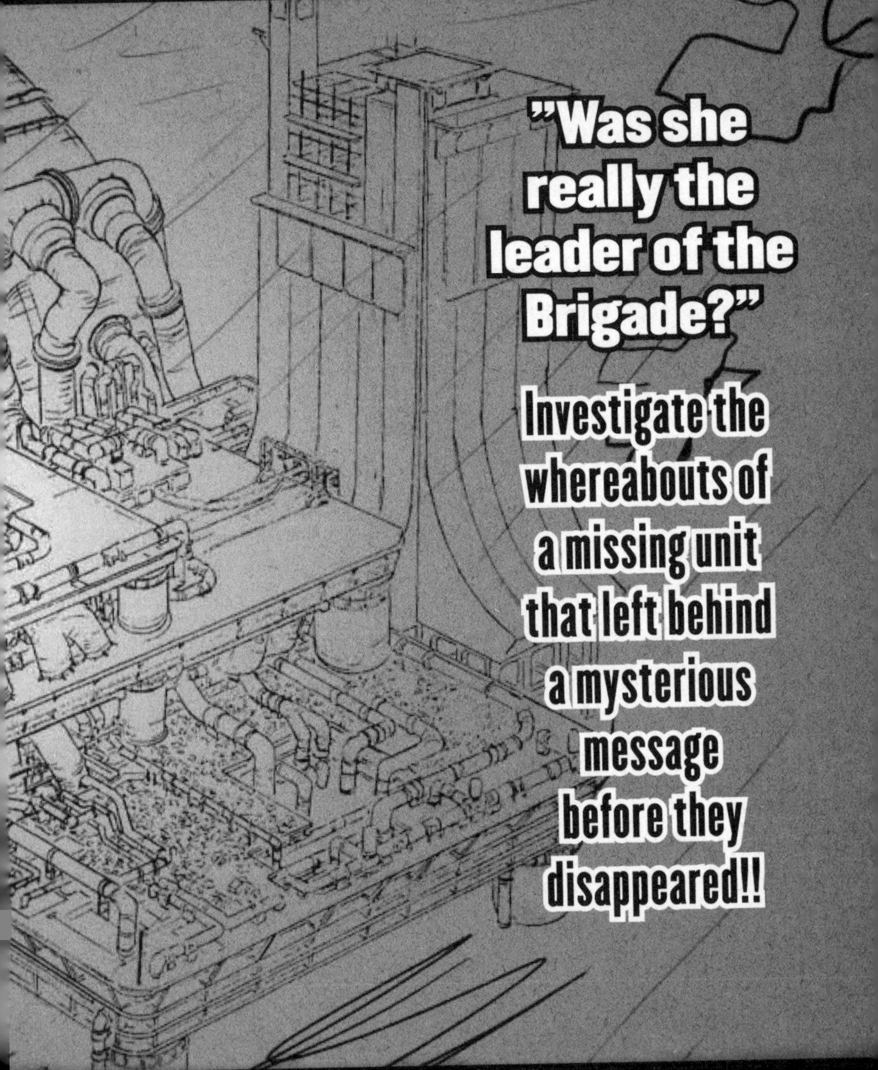
"Was she really the leader of the Brigade?"
Investigate the whereabouts of a missing unit that left behind a mysterious message before they disappeared!!

nplex Volume 5 coming soon!!

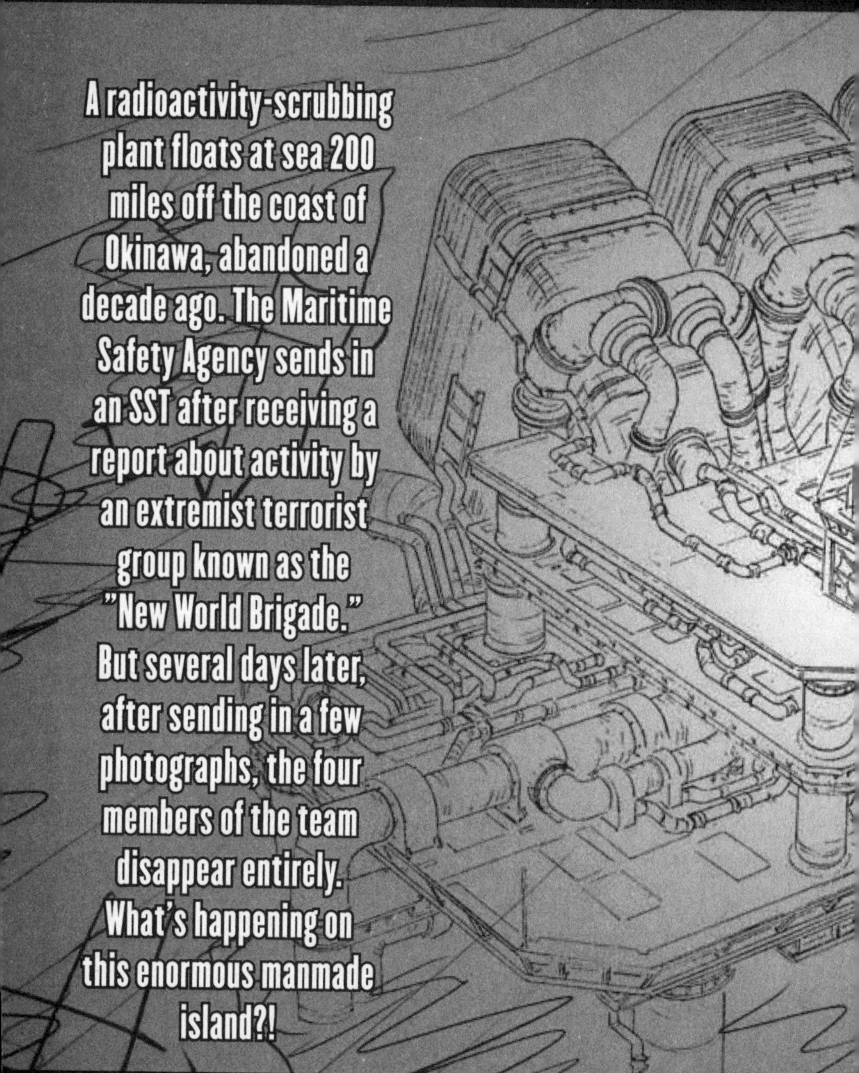

A radioactivity-scrubbing plant floats at sea 200 miles off the coast of Okinawa, abandoned a decade ago. The Maritime Safety Agency sends in an SST after receiving a report about activity by an extremist terrorist group known as the "New World Brigade." But several days later, after sending in a few photographs, the four members of the team disappear entirely. What's happening on this enormous manmade island?!

Ghost in the Shell: Stand Alone

GHOST IN THE SHELL
STAND ALONE COMPLEX
Tachikomatic Days

Plot:
Yoshiki
Sakurai
Art:
Masayuki
Yamamoto

EXTRA 001

Thoughts on Meat and Potatoes

THERE ARE FOUR BOOKS OUT, STARRING NOTHING BUT US!!

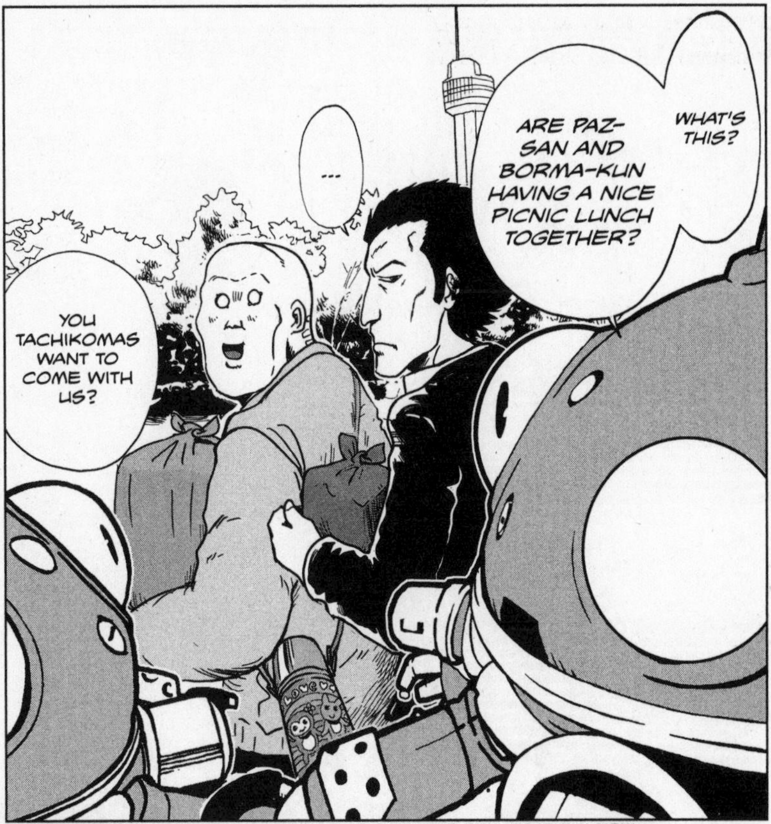
WHAT'S THIS?
ARE PAZ-SAN AND BORMA-KUN HAVING A NICE PICNIC LUNCH TOGETHER?
...
YOU TACHIKOMAS WANT TO COME WITH US?

* ORIGINALLY PRINTED IN VOLUME 4 OF GITS:SAC TACHIKOMATIC DAYS, ONLY AVAILABLE IN JAPAN.

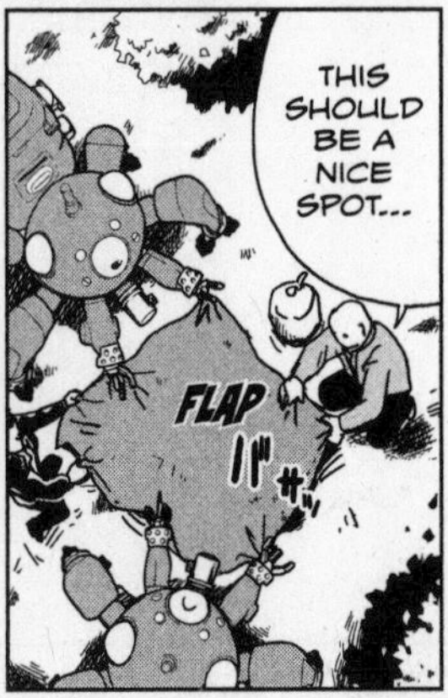
THIS SHOULD BE A NICE SPOT...
FLAP

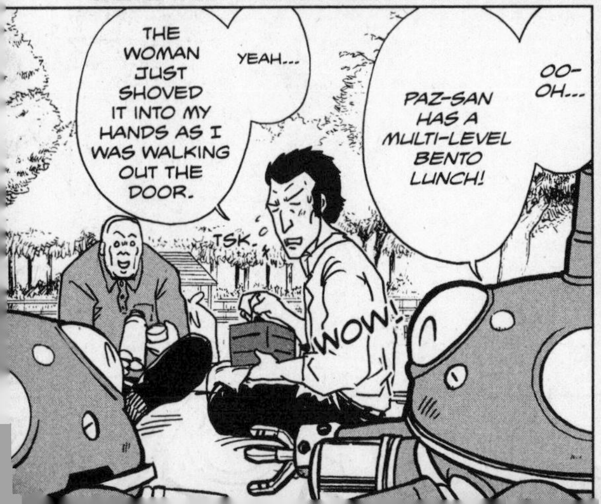
OO-OH...
PAZ-SAN HAS A MULTI-LEVEL BENTO LUNCH!
YEAH...
THE WOMAN JUST SHOVED IT INTO MY HANDS AS I WAS WALKING OUT THE DOOR.
TSK.
WOW!

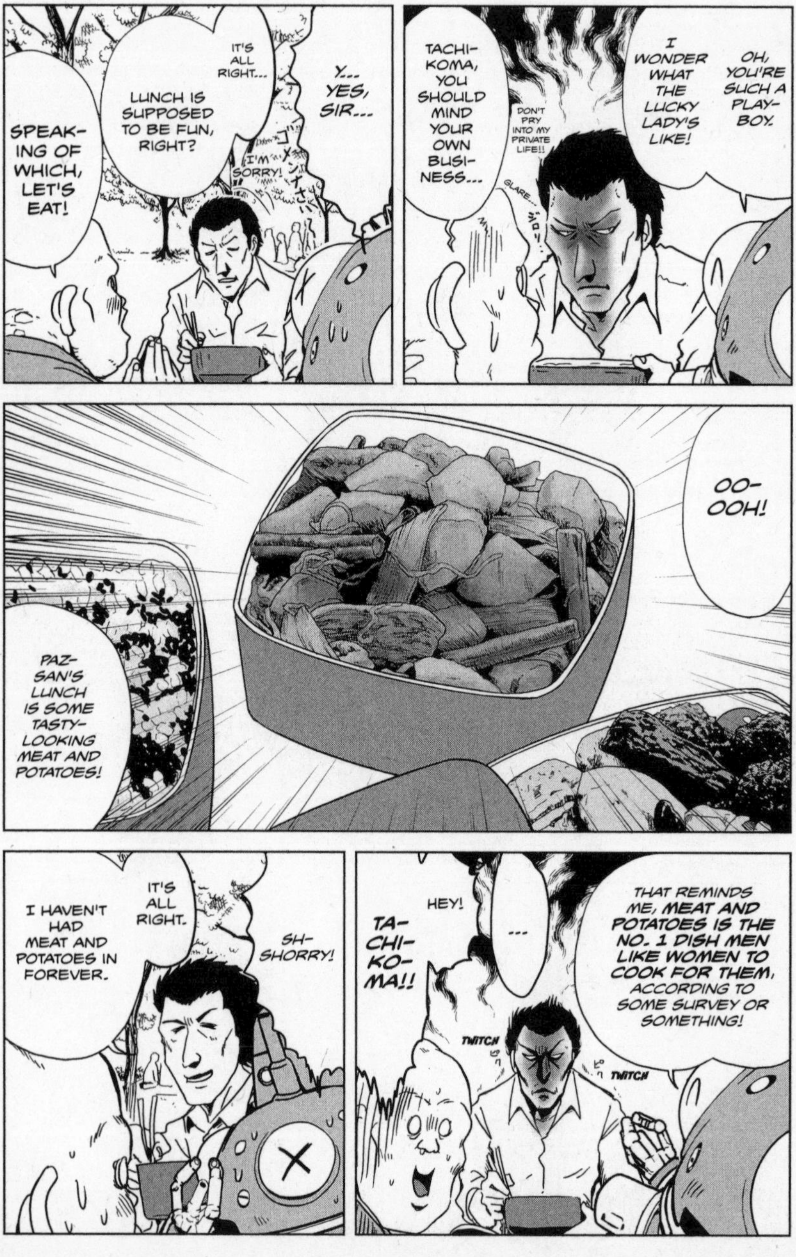
OH, YOU'RE SUCH A PLAYBOY.
I WONDER WHAT THE LUCKY LADY'S LIKE!
TACHIKOMA, YOU SHOULD MIND YOUR OWN BUSINESS...
DON'T PRY INTO MY PRIVATE LIFE!!
GLARE...
Y... YES, SIR...
I'M SORRY!
IT'S ALL RIGHT...
LUNCH IS SUPPOSED TO BE FUN, RIGHT?
SPEAKING OF WHICH, LET'S EAT!
OO-OOH!
PAZ-SAN'S LUNCH IS SOME TASTY-LOOKING MEAT AND POTATOES!
THAT REMINDS ME, MEAT AND POTATOES IS THE NO. 1 DISH MEN LIKE WOMEN TO COOK FOR THEM, ACCORDING TO SOME SURVEY OR SOMETHING!
...
HEY!
TACHIKOMA!!
TWITCH
TWITCH
SH-SHORRY!
IT'S ALL RIGHT.
I HAVEN'T HAD MEAT AND POTATOES IN FOREVER.

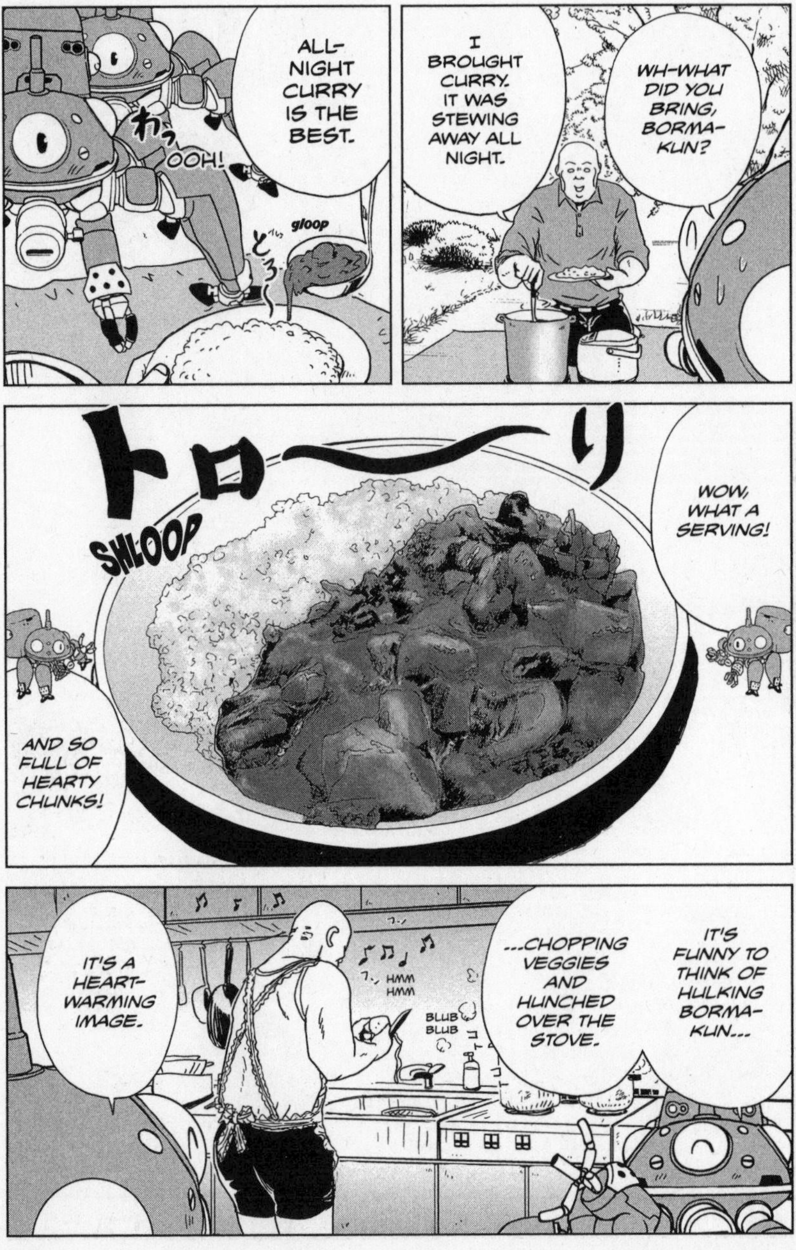
WH-WHAT DID YOU BRING, BORMA-KUN?
I BROUGHT CURRY. IT WAS STEWING AWAY ALL NIGHT.
ALL-NIGHT CURRY IS THE BEST.
わっ
OOH!
gloop
トロ～～リ
SHLOOP
WOW, WHAT A SERVING!
AND SO FULL OF HEARTY CHUNKS!
IT'S FUNNY TO THINK OF HULKING BORMA-KUN...
...CHOPPING VEGGIES AND HUNCHED OVER THE STOVE.
HMM HMM
BLUB BLUB
IT'S A HEART-WARMING IMAGE.

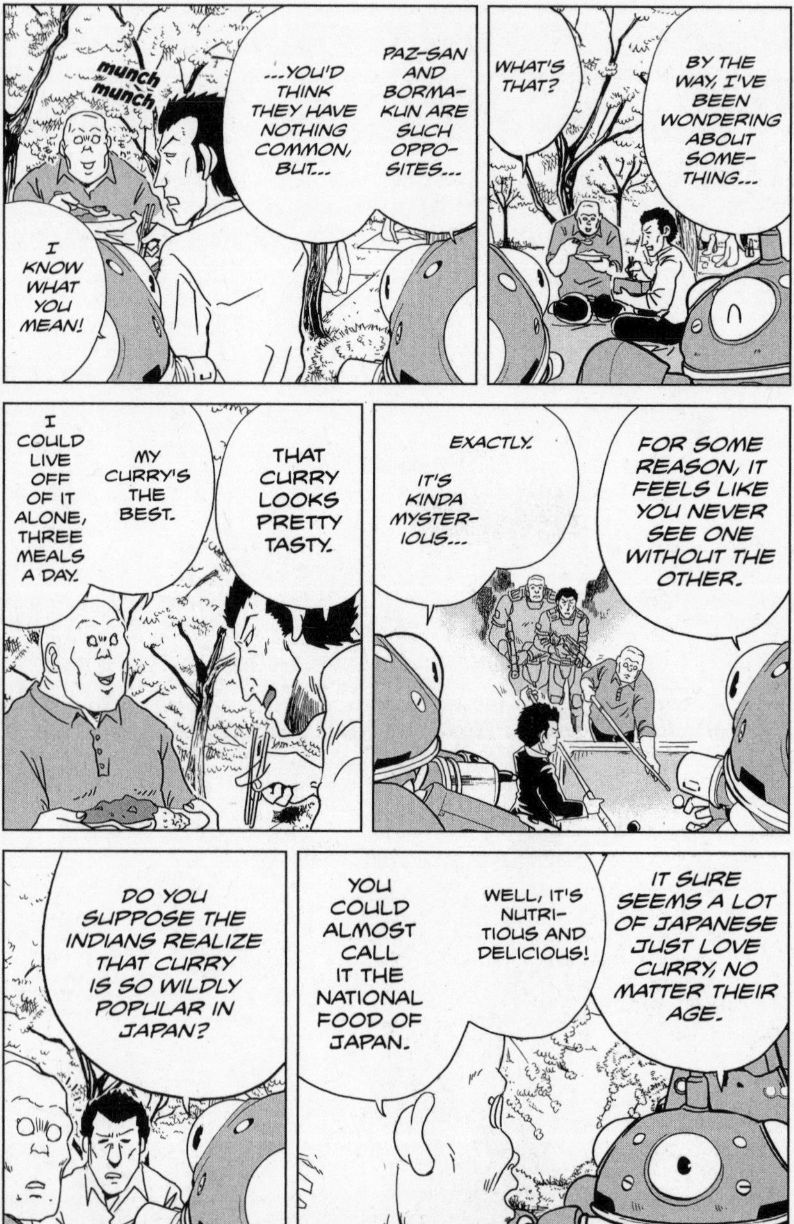
BY THE WAY, I'VE BEEN WONDERING ABOUT SOMETHING...
WHAT'S THAT?
PAZ-SAN AND BORMA-KUN ARE SUCH OPPOSITES...
...YOU'D THINK THEY HAVE NOTHING COMMON, BUT...
munch munch
I KNOW WHAT YOU MEAN!
FOR SOME REASON, IT FEELS LIKE YOU NEVER SEE ONE WITHOUT THE OTHER.
EXACTLY.
IT'S KINDA MYSTERIOUS...
THAT CURRY LOOKS PRETTY TASTY.
MY CURRY'S THE BEST.
I COULD LIVE OFF OF IT ALONE, THREE MEALS A DAY.
IT SURE SEEMS A LOT OF JAPANESE JUST LOVE CURRY, NO MATTER THEIR AGE.
WELL, IT'S NUTRITIOUS AND DELICIOUS!
YOU COULD ALMOST CALL IT THE NATIONAL FOOD OF JAPAN.
DO YOU SUPPOSE THE INDIANS REALIZE THAT CURRY IS SO WILDLY POPULAR IN JAPAN?

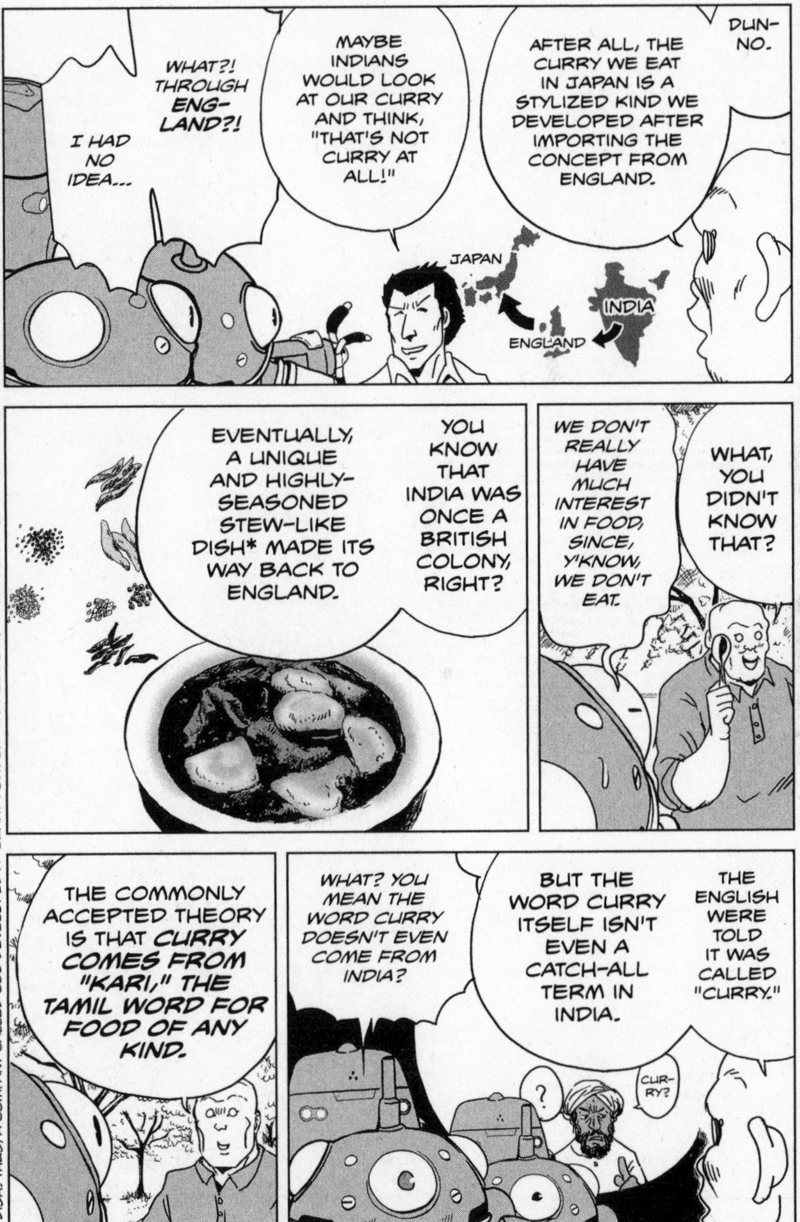
DUN-NO.
AFTER ALL, THE CURRY WE EAT IN JAPAN IS A STYLIZED KIND WE DEVELOPED AFTER IMPORTING THE CONCEPT FROM ENGLAND.
MAYBE INDIANS WOULD LOOK AT OUR CURRY AND THINK, "THAT'S NOT CURRY AT ALL!"
JAPAN
INDIA
ENGLAND
WHAT?! THROUGH ENG-LAND?!
I HAD NO IDEA...
WHAT, YOU DIDN'T KNOW THAT?
WE DON'T REALLY HAVE MUCH INTEREST IN FOOD, SINCE, Y'KNOW, WE DON'T EAT.
YOU KNOW THAT INDIA WAS ONCE A BRITISH COLONY, RIGHT?
EVENTUALLY, A UNIQUE AND HIGHLY-SEASONED STEW-LIKE DISH* MADE ITS WAY BACK TO ENGLAND.
THE ENGLISH WERE TOLD IT WAS CALLED "CURRY."
BUT THE WORD CURRY ITSELF ISN'T EVEN A CATCH-ALL TERM IN INDIA.
WHAT? YOU MEAN THE WORD CURRY DOESN'T EVEN COME FROM INDIA?
CUR-RY?
?
THE COMMONLY ACCEPTED THEORY IS THAT CURRY COMES FROM "KARI," THE TAMIL WORD FOR FOOD OF ANY KIND.

*INDIAN CURRY WAS FIRST INTRODUCED TO ENGLAND IN THE 19TH CENTURY, BUT IT WAS DIFFICULT FOR THE ENGLISH TO COMBINE THE VARIETY OF SPICES NECESSARY FOR THE DISH. THUS, A COMPANY CALLED C&B DEVELOPED A "CURRY POWDER" THAT COMBINED ALL THE SEASONINGS, MAKING CURRY A VIABLE HOME DISH FOR ENGLISH KITCHENS.

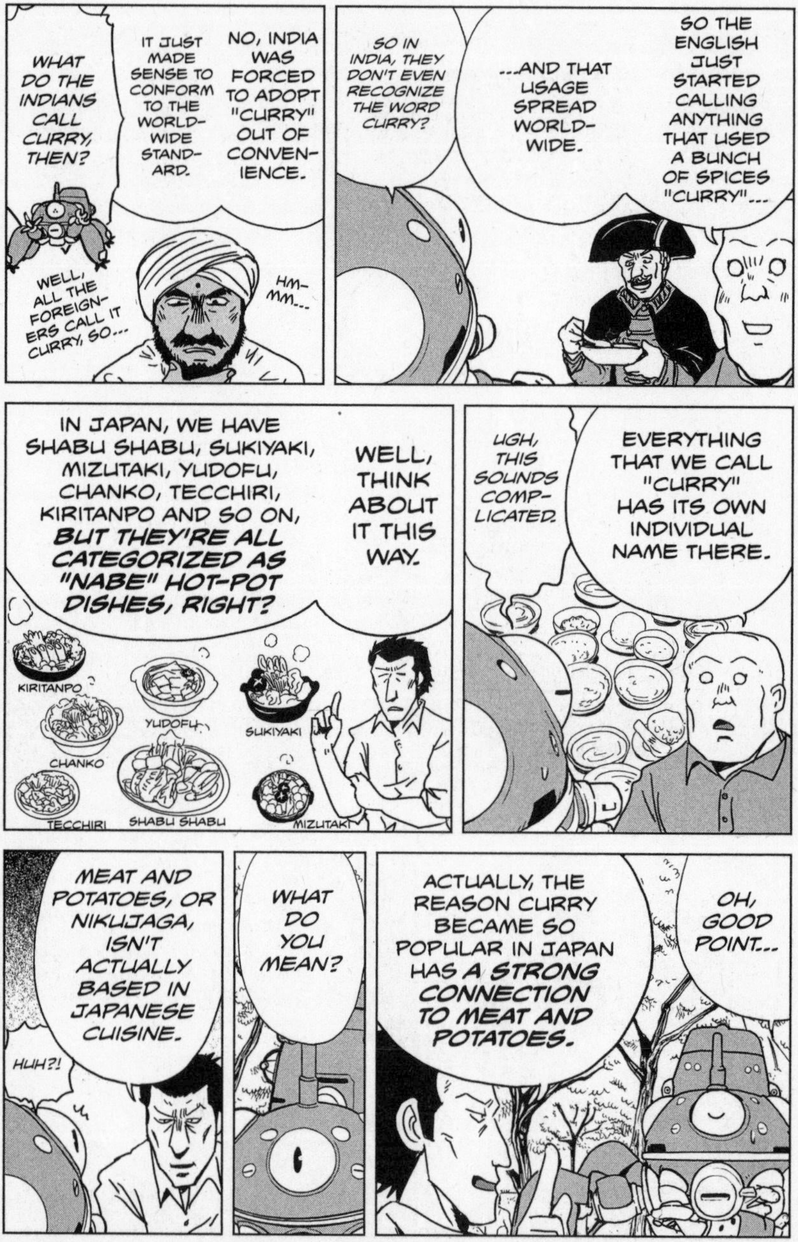
SO THE ENGLISH JUST STARTED CALLING ANYTHING THAT USED A BUNCH OF SPICES "CURRY"...
...AND THAT USAGE SPREAD WORLD-WIDE.
SO IN INDIA, THEY DON'T EVEN RECOGNIZE THE WORD CURRY?
NO, INDIA WAS FORCED TO ADOPT "CURRY" OUT OF CONVEN-IENCE.
IT JUST MADE SENSE TO CONFORM TO THE WORLD-WIDE STAND-ARD.
WHAT DO THE INDIANS CALL CURRY, THEN?
HM-MM...
WELL, ALL THE FOREIGN-ERS CALL IT CURRY, SO...
EVERYTHING THAT WE CALL "CURRY" HAS ITS OWN INDIVIDUAL NAME THERE.
UGH, THIS SOUNDS COMP-LICATED.
WELL, THINK ABOUT IT THIS WAY.
IN JAPAN, WE HAVE SHABU SHABU, SUKIYAKI, MIZUTAKI, YUDOFU, CHANKO, TECCHIRI, KIRITANPO AND SO ON, BUT THEY'RE ALL CATEGORIZED AS "NABE" HOT-POT DISHES, RIGHT?
KIRITANPO
YUDOFU
SUKIYAKI
CHANKO
TECCHIRI
SHABU SHABU
MIZUTAKI
OH, GOOD POINT...
ACTUALLY, THE REASON CURRY BECAME SO POPULAR IN JAPAN HAS A STRONG CONNECTION TO MEAT AND POTATOES.
WHAT DO YOU MEAN?
MEAT AND POTATOES, OR NIKUJAGA, ISN'T ACTUALLY BASED IN JAPANESE CUISINE.
HUH?!

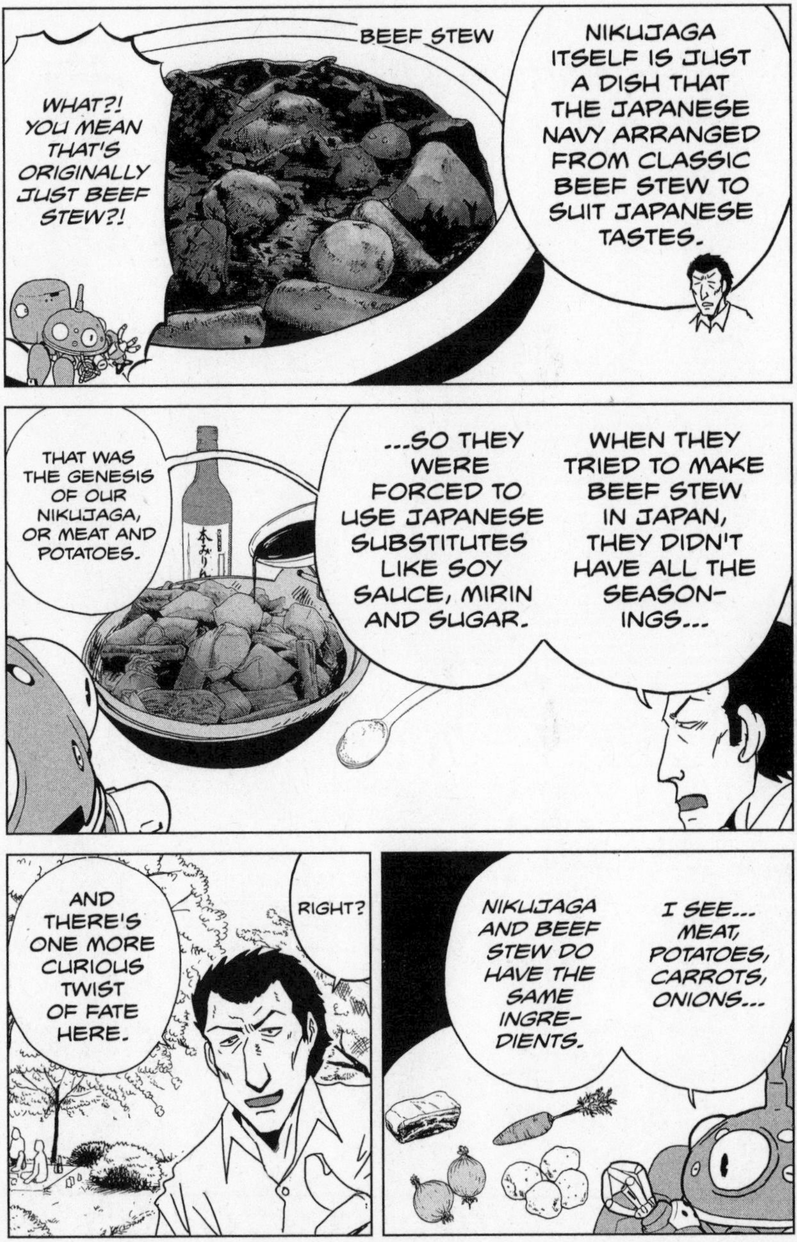
NIKUJAGA ITSELF IS JUST A DISH THAT THE JAPANESE NAVY ARRANGED FROM CLASSIC BEEF STEW TO SUIT JAPANESE TASTES.
BEEF STEW
WHAT?! YOU MEAN THAT'S ORIGINALLY JUST BEEF STEW?!
WHEN THEY TRIED TO MAKE BEEF STEW IN JAPAN, THEY DIDN'T HAVE ALL THE SEASON-INGS...
...SO THEY WERE FORCED TO USE JAPANESE SUBSTITUTES LIKE SOY SAUCE, MIRIN AND SUGAR.
THAT WAS THE GENESIS OF OUR NIKUJAGA, OR MEAT AND POTATOES.
I SEE... MEAT, POTATOES, CARROTS, ONIONS...
NIKUJAGA AND BEEF STEW DO HAVE THE SAME INGRE-DIENTS.
RIGHT?
AND THERE'S ONE MORE CURIOUS TWIST OF FATE HERE.

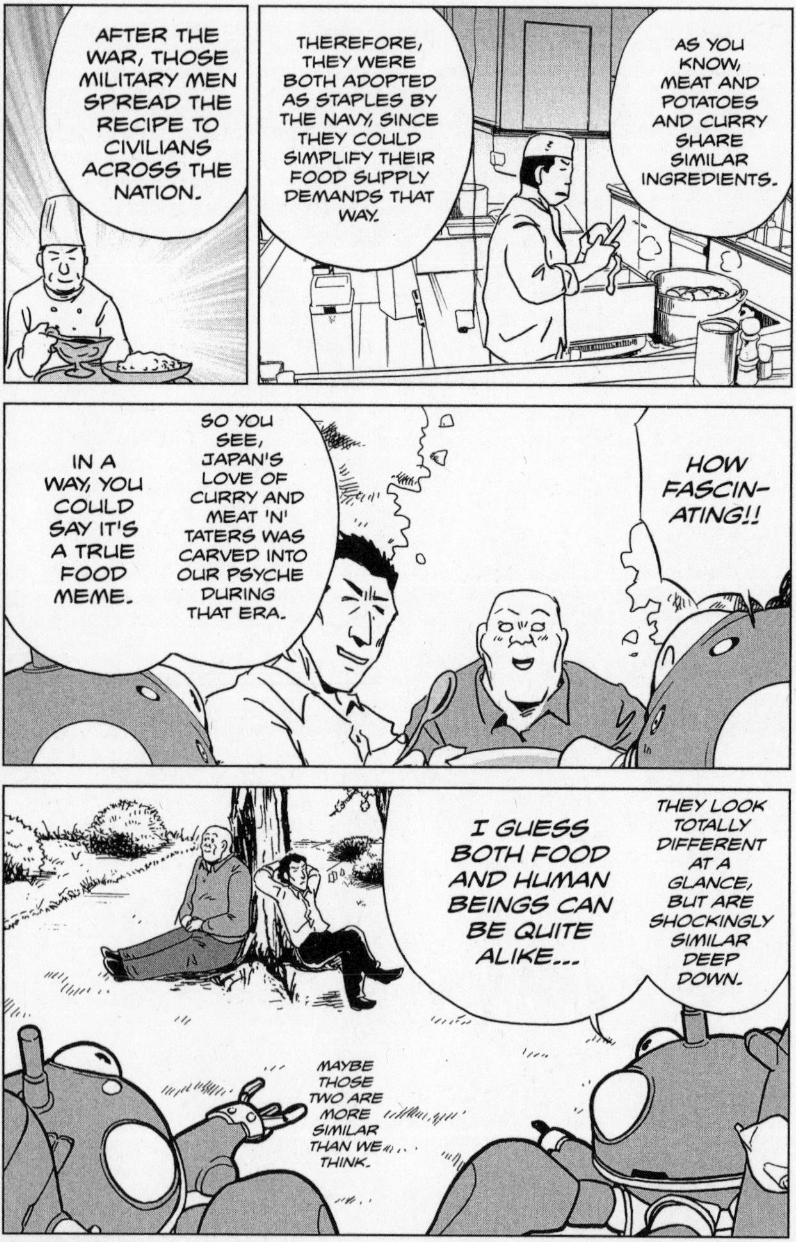
AS YOU KNOW, MEAT AND POTATOES AND CURRY SHARE SIMILAR INGREDIENTS.
THEREFORE, THEY WERE BOTH ADOPTED AS STAPLES BY THE NAVY, SINCE THEY COULD SIMPLIFY THEIR FOOD SUPPLY DEMANDS THAT WAY.
AFTER THE WAR, THOSE MILITARY MEN SPREAD THE RECIPE TO CIVILIANS ACROSS THE NATION.
HOW FASCIN-ATING!!
SO YOU SEE, JAPAN'S LOVE OF CURRY AND MEAT 'N' TATERS WAS CARVED INTO OUR PSYCHE DURING THAT ERA.
IN A WAY, YOU COULD SAY IT'S A TRUE FOOD MEME.
THEY LOOK TOTALLY DIFFERENT AT A GLANCE, BUT ARE SHOCKINGLY SIMILAR DEEP DOWN.
I GUESS BOTH FOOD AND HUMAN BEINGS CAN BE QUITE ALIKE...
MAYBE THOSE TWO ARE MORE SIMILAR THAN WE THINK.

Extra 001: End

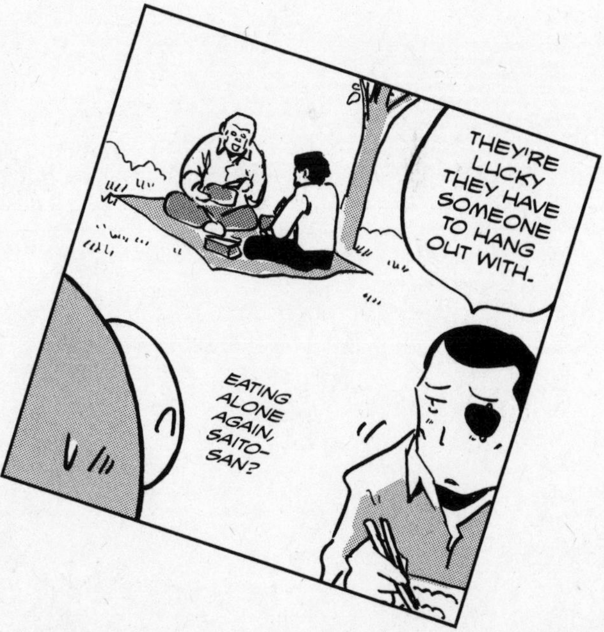
THEY'RE LUCKY THEY HAVE SOMEONE TO HANG OUT WITH.
EATING ALONE AGAIN, SAITO-SAN?

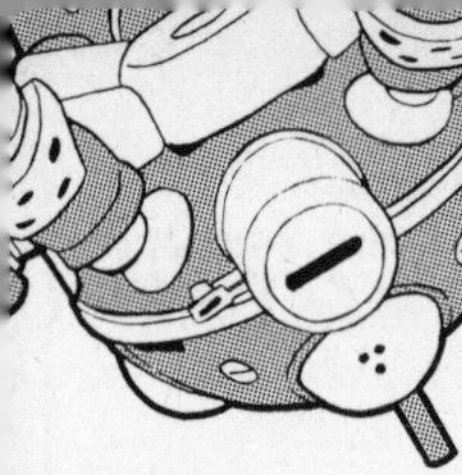

Bonus Manga (2)

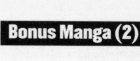

EXTRA 002

Thoughts on Characterization

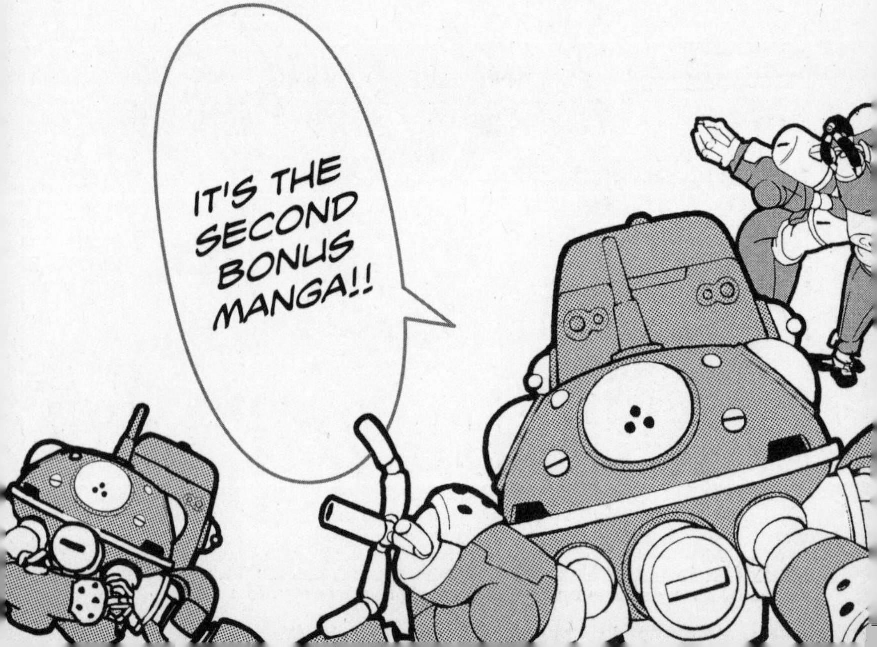
IT'S THE SECOND BONUS MANGA!!

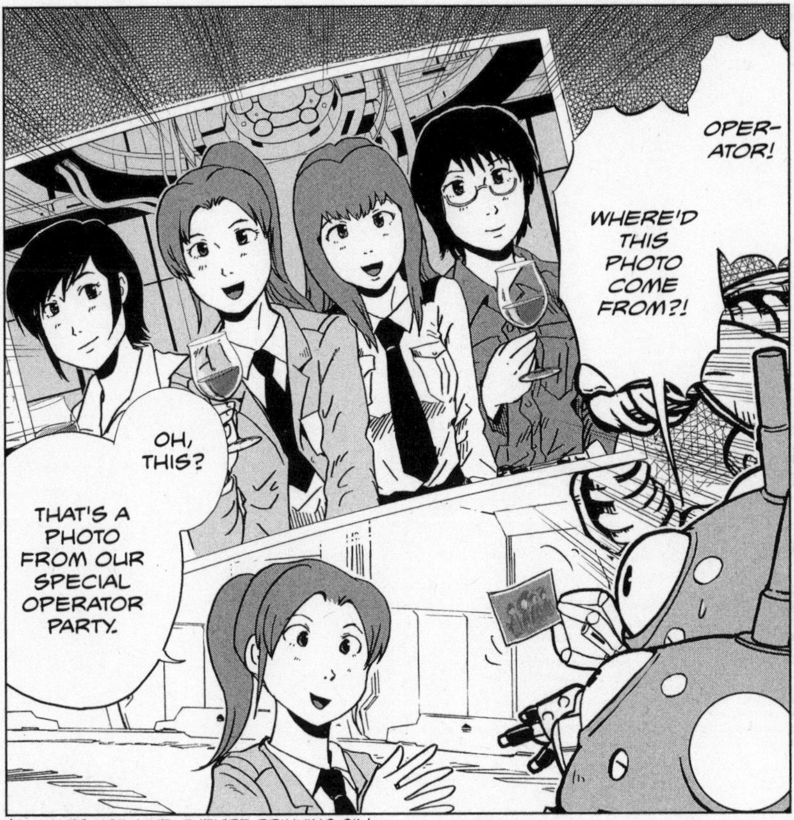
OPERATOR!
WHERE'D THIS PHOTO COME FROM?!
OH, THIS?
THAT'S A PHOTO FROM OUR SPECIAL OPERATOR PARTY.

*1: THAT'S NOT WINE; THEY'RE DRINKING OIL!

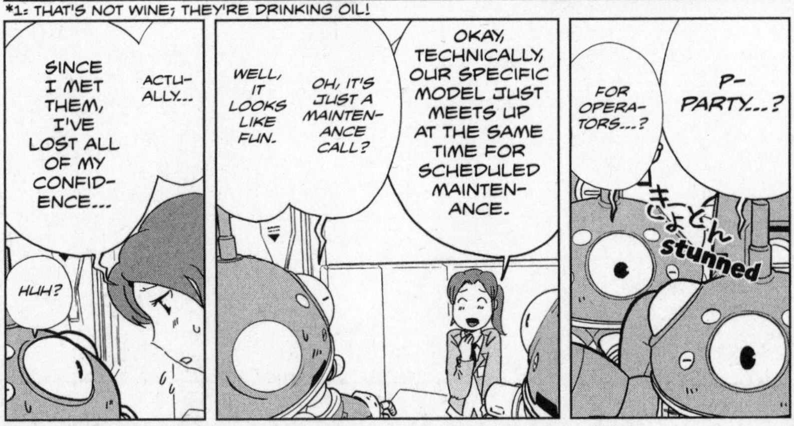
P-PARTY...?
FOR OPERATORS...?
きょとん
stunned
OKAY, TECHNICALLY, OUR SPECIFIC MODEL JUST MEETS UP AT THE SAME TIME FOR SCHEDULED MAINTENANCE.
OH, IT'S JUST A MAINTENANCE CALL?
WELL, IT LOOKS LIKE FUN.
ACTUALLY...
SINCE I MET THEM, I'VE LOST ALL OF MY CONFIDENCE...
HUH?

* ORIGINALLY PRINTED IN MONTHLY YOUNG MAGAZINE, DECEMBER 2011 ISSUE.

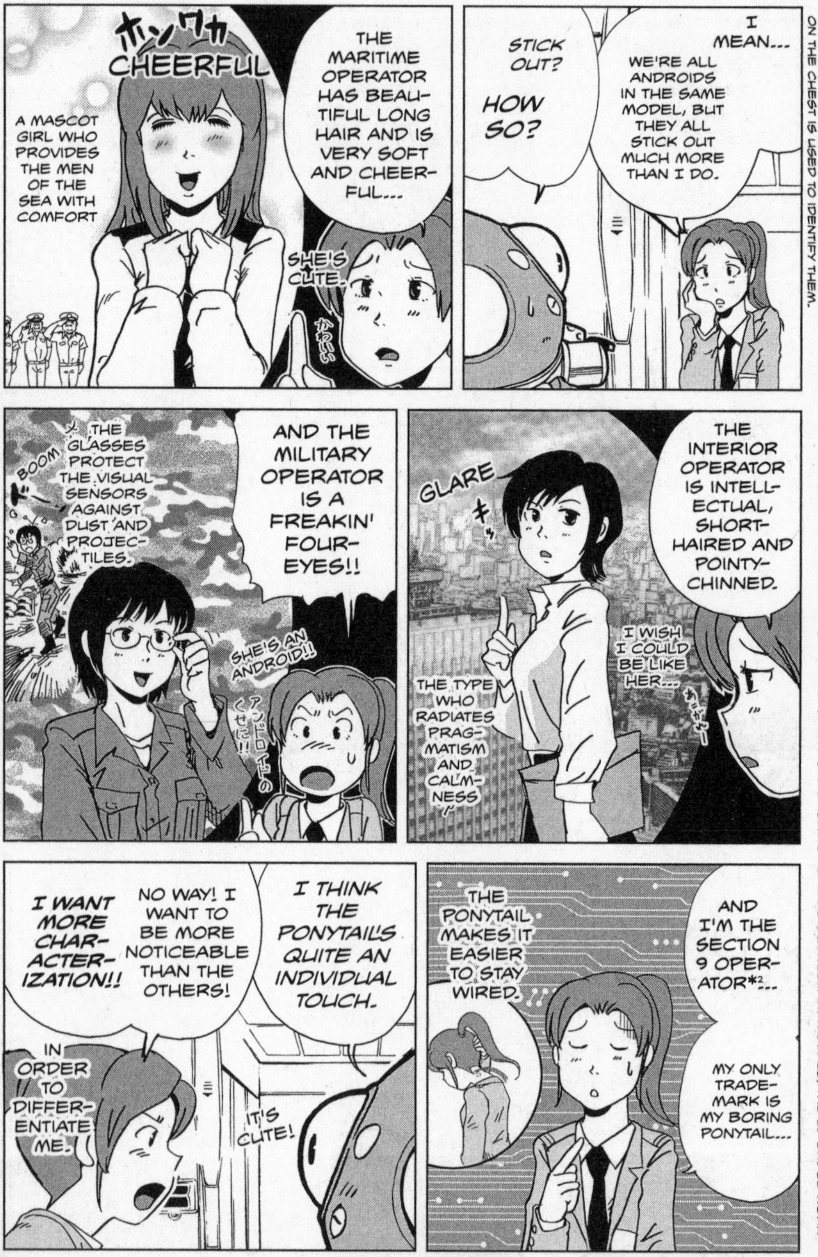
I MEAN...
WE'RE ALL ANDROIDS IN THE SAME MODEL, BUT THEY ALL STICK OUT MUCH MORE THAN I DO.
STICK OUT?
HOW SO?
THE MARITIME OPERATOR HAS BEAUTIFUL LONG HAIR AND IS VERY SOFT AND CHEERFUL...
ホンワカ CHEERFUL
A MASCOT GIRL WHO PROVIDES THE MEN OF THE SEA WITH COMFORT
SHE'S CUTE.
かわいい
THE INTERIOR OPERATOR IS INTELLECTUAL, SHORT-HAIRED AND POINTY-CHINNED.
GLARE
I WISH I COULD BE LIKE HER...
THE TYPE WHO RADIATES PRAGMATISM AND CALMNESS
AND THE MILITARY OPERATOR IS A FREAKIN' FOUR-EYES!!
THE GLASSES PROTECT THE VISUAL SENSORS AGAINST DUST AND PROJECTILES.
BOOM
SHE'S AN ANDROID!!
アンドロイドのくせに!!
AND I'M THE SECTION 9 OPERATOR*2...
THE PONYTAIL MAKES IT EASIER TO STAY WIRED.
MY ONLY TRADEMARK IS MY BORING PONYTAIL...
I THINK THE PONYTAIL'S QUITE AN INDIVIDUAL TOUCH.
NO WAY! I WANT TO BE MORE NOTICEABLE THAN THE OTHERS!
I WANT MORE CHARACTERIZATION!!
IN ORDER TO DIFFERENTIATE ME.
IT'S CUTE!

*2: THE SECTION 9 ANDROIDS, NICKNAMED "OPEKO," UNDERTAKE NOT JUST CONTROL ROOM OPERATIONS, BUT TEA PREPARATION, OFFICE WORK, AND SUPPORT AND BACKUP FOR MEMBERS IN THE FIELD. THEY OFTEN DRIVE VEHICLES AND TILT-ROTORS AS WELL. BECAUSE THERE IS NO DISTINGUISHING FEATURE BETWEEN INDIVIDUALS, THE ID BADGE WORN ON THE CHEST IS USED TO IDENTIFY THEM.

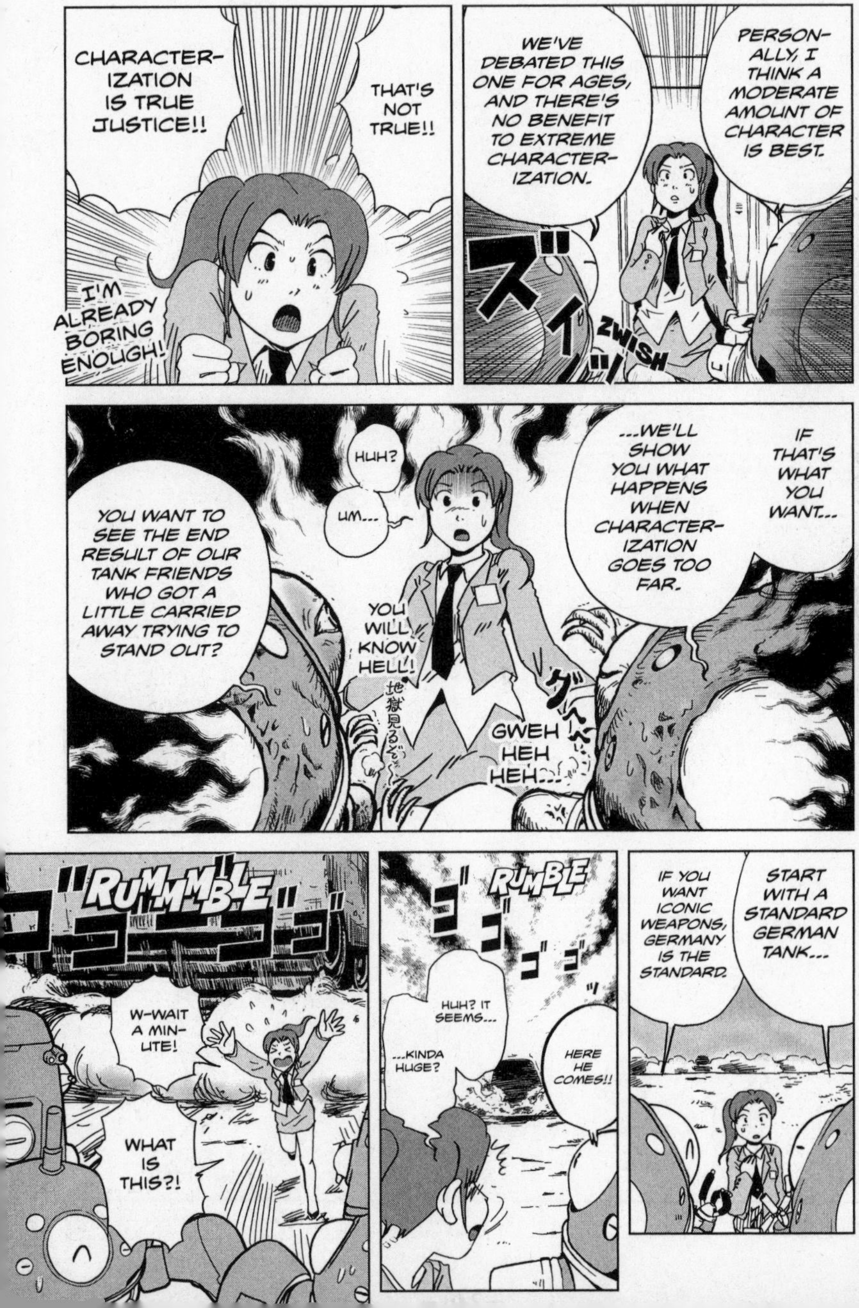
PERSONALLY, I THINK A MODERATE AMOUNT OF CHARACTER IS BEST.
WE'VE DEBATED THIS ONE FOR AGES, AND THERE'S NO BENEFIT TO EXTREME CHARACTERIZATION.
ズイッ
ZWISH
THAT'S NOT TRUE!!
CHARACTERIZATION IS TRUE JUSTICE!!
I'M ALREADY BORING ENOUGH!
IF THAT'S WHAT YOU WANT...
...WE'LL SHOW YOU WHAT HAPPENS WHEN CHARACTERIZATION GOES TOO FAR.
HUH?
UM...
YOU WANT TO SEE THE END RESULT OF OUR TANK FRIENDS WHO GOT A LITTLE CARRIED AWAY TRYING TO STAND OUT?
YOU WILL KNOW HELL!
地獄見るぞ~
ゲヘヘ
GWEH HEH HEH...
START WITH A STANDARD GERMAN TANK...
IF YOU WANT ICONIC WEAPONS, GERMANY IS THE STANDARD.
RUMBLE
ゴゴゴゴ
HUH? IT SEEMS...
...KINDA HUGE?
HERE HE COMES!!
RUMMMBLE
ゴゴゴゴ
W-WAIT A MINUTE!
WHAT IS THIS?!

*3: OFFICIALLY, THE LANDKREUZER P.1000 RATTE.
*4: TIGER I, OFFICIALLY, THE PANZERKAMPFWAGEN VS AUSF. E (SD KFZ 181). 8.45 M LONG, 6.316 M FRAME, 3.705 M WIDTH, 3 M HEIGHT, 57 TONS.

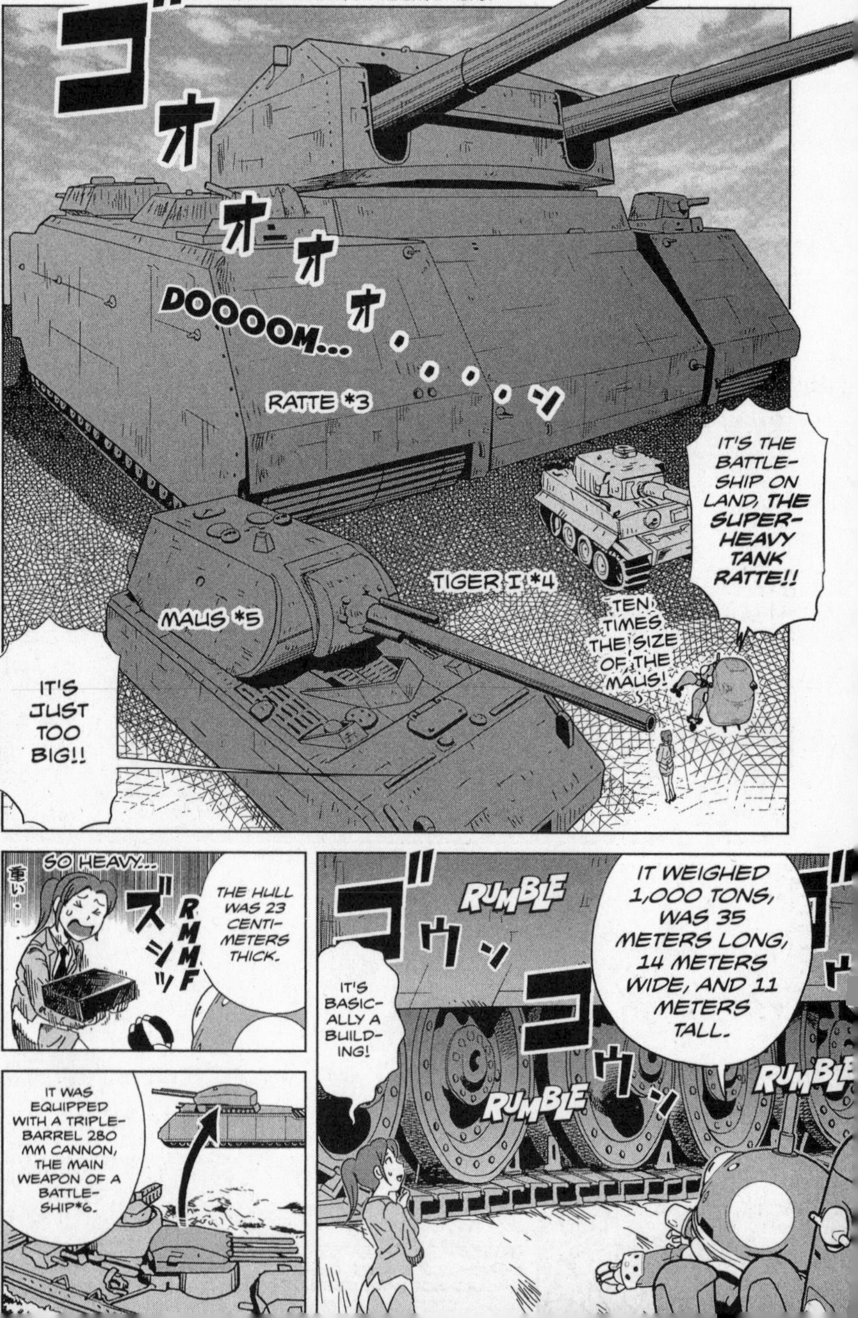
ゴォォォォ・・・・ッ
DOOOOOM...
RATTE *3
IT'S THE BATTLESHIP ON LAND, THE SUPER-HEAVY TANK RATTE!!
TIGER I *4
TEN TIMES THE SIZE OF THE MAUS!
MAUS *5
IT'S JUST TOO BIG!!
ゴゥン
RUMBLE
IT WEIGHED 1,000 TONS, WAS 35 METERS LONG, 14 METERS WIDE, AND 11 METERS TALL.
IT'S BASICALLY A BUILDING!
ゴゥン
RUMBLE
RUMBLE
SO HEAVY...
重い・・・
ズシッ
RMMF
THE HULL WAS 23 CENTIMETERS THICK.
IT WAS EQUIPPED WITH A TRIPLE-BARREL 280 MM CANNON, THE MAIN WEAPON OF A BATTLESHIP*6.

*5: MAUS, OFFICIALLY TITLED THE PORSCHE TYPE 205. DESIGNED BY FERDINAND PORSCHE. WEIGHED 188 TONS. POWERED BY THE 1080-HP MB509 V12 GASOLINE ENGINE. MAIN ARMAMENT, 128 MM KWK 44 GUN L/55. 240 MM ARMOR AT ITS THICKEST.
*6: THE RATTE WAS PLANNED TO FEATURE A DOUBLE-BARREL ADAPTATION OF THE 280 MM CANNONS USED ON BATTLECRUISERS LIKE THE SCHARNHORST.

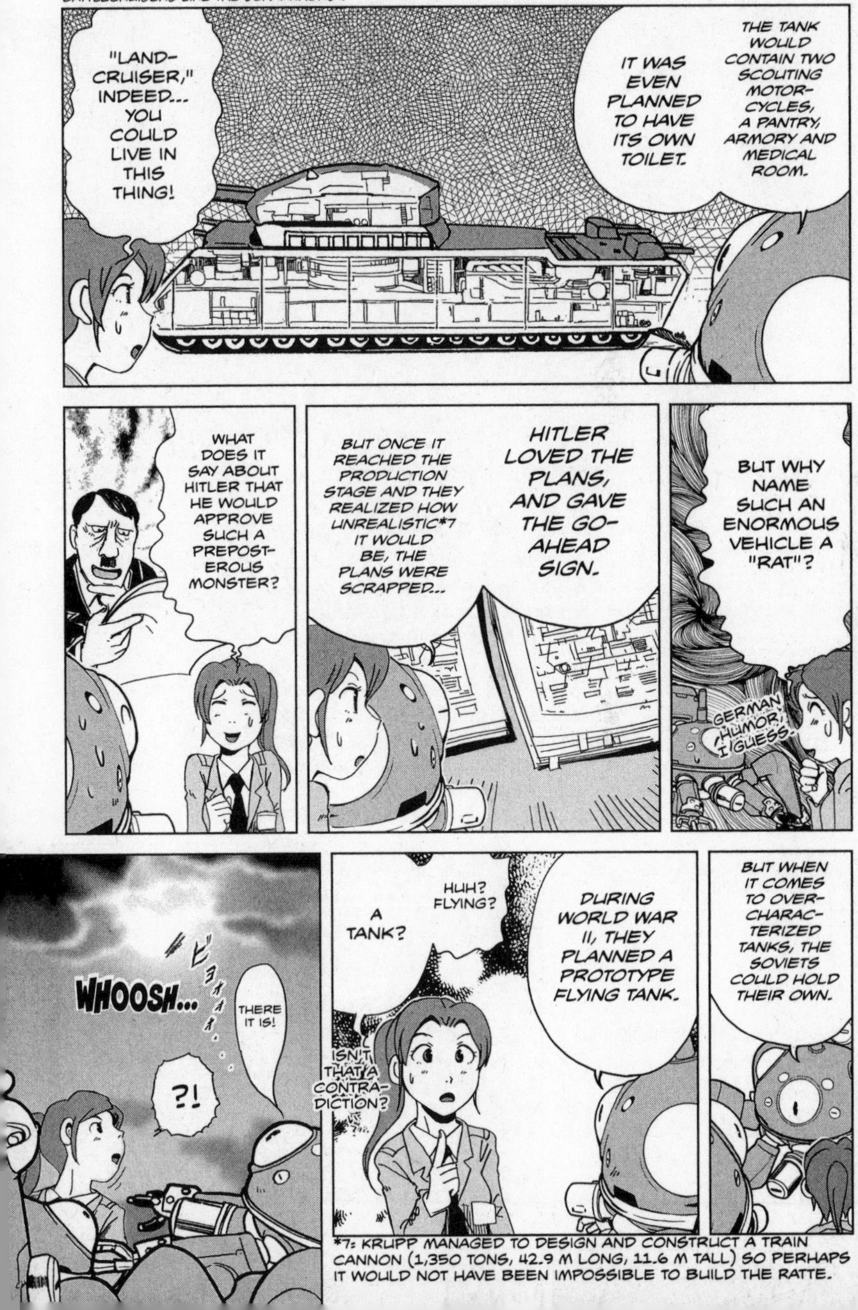
THE TANK WOULD CONTAIN TWO SCOUTING MOTOR-CYCLES, A PANTRY, ARMORY AND MEDICAL ROOM.
IT WAS EVEN PLANNED TO HAVE ITS OWN TOILET.
"LAND-CRUISER," INDEED... YOU COULD LIVE IN THIS THING!
BUT WHY NAME SUCH AN ENORMOUS VEHICLE A "RAT"?
GERMAN HUMOR, I GUESS.
HITLER LOVED THE PLANS, AND GAVE THE GO-AHEAD SIGN.
BUT ONCE IT REACHED THE PRODUCTION STAGE AND THEY REALIZED HOW UNREALISTIC*7 IT WOULD BE, THE PLANS WERE SCRAPPED...
WHAT DOES IT SAY ABOUT HITLER THAT HE WOULD APPROVE SUCH A PREPOST-EROUS MONSTER?
BUT WHEN IT COMES TO OVER-CHARAC-TERIZED TANKS, THE SOVIETS COULD HOLD THEIR OWN.
DURING WORLD WAR II, THEY PLANNED A PROTOTYPE FLYING TANK.
HUH? FLYING?
A TANK?
ISN'T THAT A CONTRA-DICTION?
THERE IT IS!
WHOOSH...
?!

*7: KRUPP MANAGED TO DESIGN AND CONSTRUCT A TRAIN CANNON (1,350 TONS, 42.9 M LONG, 11.6 M TALL) SO PERHAPS IT WOULD NOT HAVE BEEN IMPOSSIBLE TO BUILD THE RATTE.

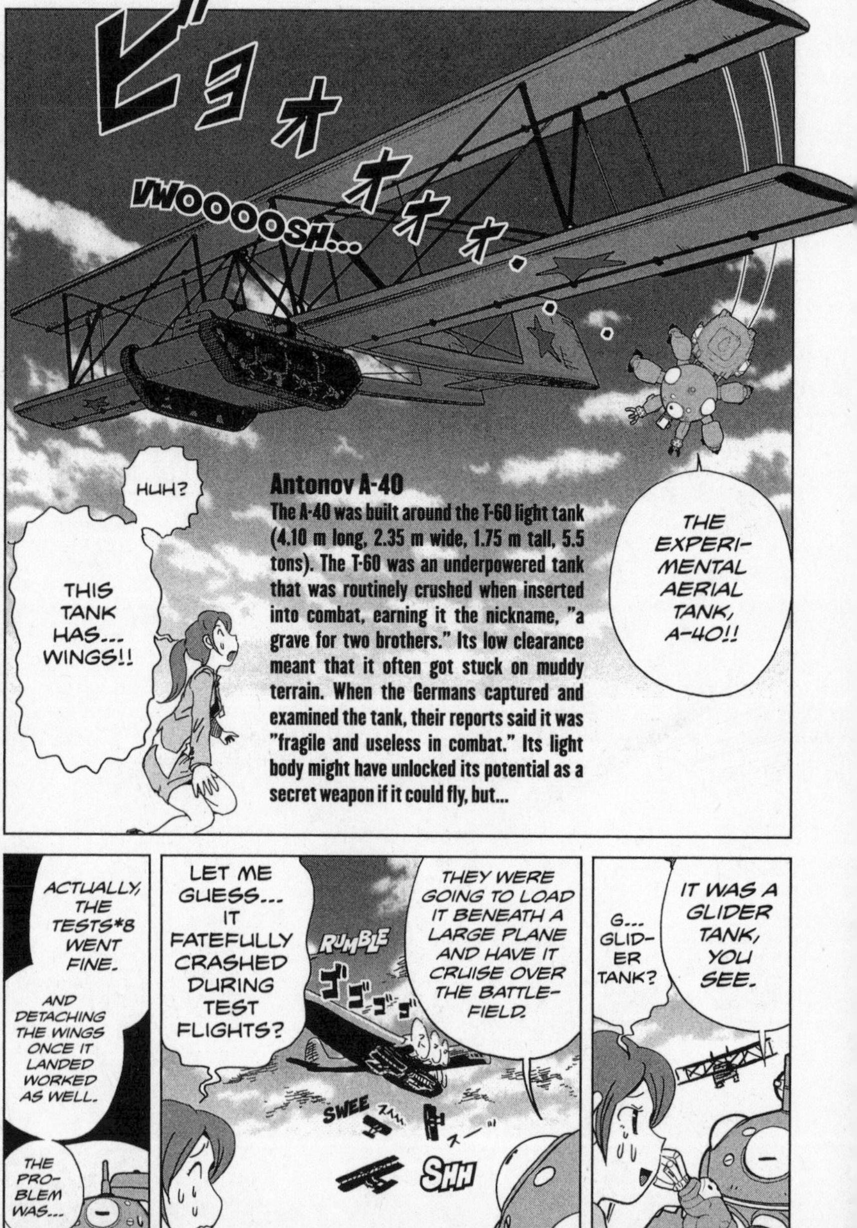
ビョオオオオ・・・
VWOOOOOSH...
THE EXPERIMENTAL AERIAL TANK, A-40!!
HUH?
THIS TANK HAS... WINGS!!
Antonov A-40
The A-40 was built around the T-60 light tank (4.10 m long, 2.35 m wide, 1.75 m tall, 5.5 tons). The T-60 was an underpowered tank that was routinely crushed when inserted into combat, earning it the nickname, "a grave for two brothers." Its low clearance meant that it often got stuck on muddy terrain. When the Germans captured and examined the tank, their reports said it was "fragile and useless in combat." Its light body might have unlocked its potential as a secret weapon if it could fly, but...
IT WAS A GLIDER TANK, YOU SEE.
G... GLIDER TANK?
THEY WERE GOING TO LOAD IT BENEATH A LARGE PLANE AND HAVE IT CRUISE OVER THE BATTLEFIELD.
RUMBLE
ゴゴゴゴ
LET ME GUESS... IT FATEFULLY CRASHED DURING TEST FLIGHTS?
SWEE
スィー
スーッ
SHH
ACTUALLY, THE TESTS*8 WENT FINE.
AND DETACHING THE WINGS ONCE IT LANDED WORKED AS WELL.
THE PROBLEM WAS...

*8: THE WEIGHT OF THE A-40 CAUSED THE BOMBER CARRYING IT TO OVERHEAT, BUT ONCE IT WAS CUT LOOSE TO GLIDE, THE FLIGHT ITSELF WAS REASONABLY STABLE. THE TANK TREADS WERE RUNNING AS IT LANDED TO CUSHION THE SHOCK.

*9: IF THE SOVIETS HAD EVER COMPLETED THE SUPER-SIZED KALININ K-7, THE ANTONOV A-40 MIGHT HAVE COME TO FRUITION. IN THE LATTER STAGES OF WWII, THE BRITISH SUCCESSFULLY COMBINED THE MK. VII TETRARCH AND HAMILCAR GLIDERS TO MAKE A FLYING TANK. THE COMBINATION WAS FAMOUSLY UTILIZED IN THE BATTLE OF NORMANDY.

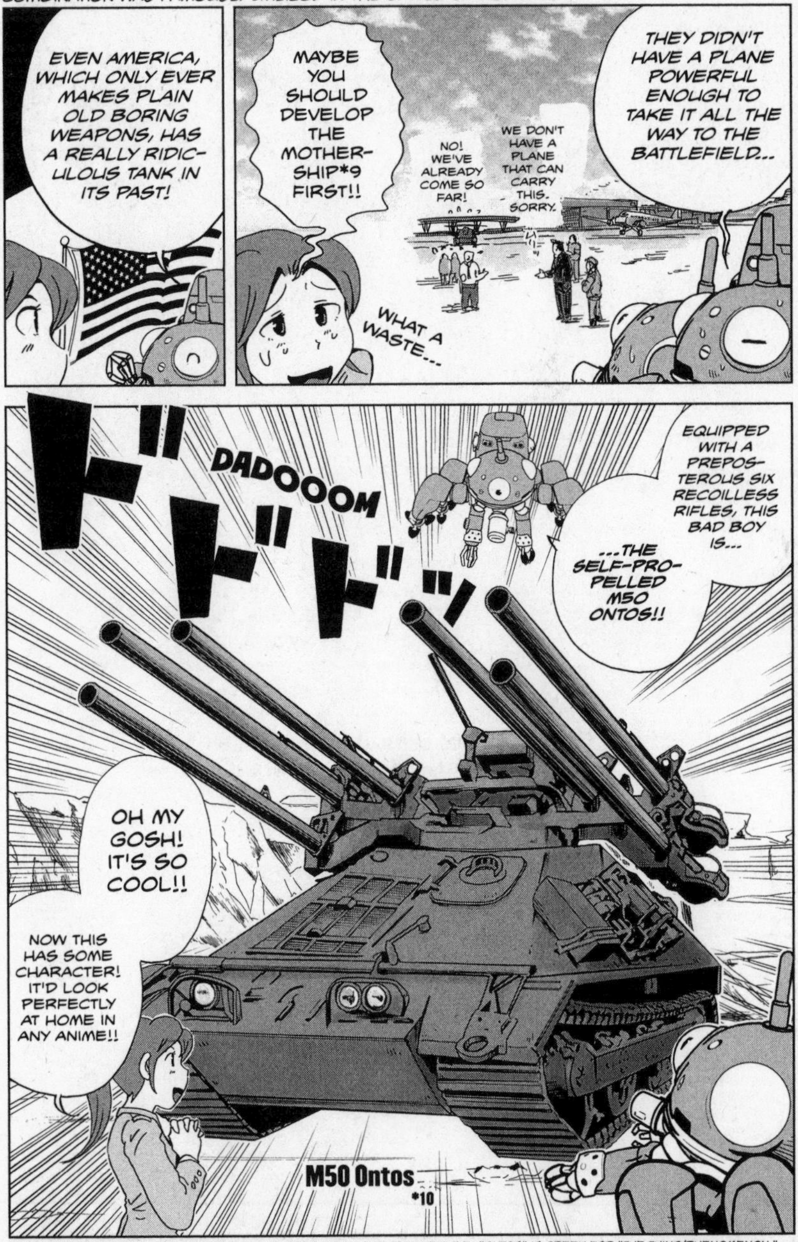
THEY DIDN'T HAVE A PLANE POWERFUL ENOUGH TO TAKE IT ALL THE WAY TO THE BATTLEFIELD...
WE DON'T HAVE A PLANE THAT CAN CARRY THIS. SORRY.
NO! WE'VE ALREADY COME SO FAR!
MAYBE YOU SHOULD DEVELOP THE MOTHER-SHIP*9 FIRST!!
WHAT A WASTE...
EVEN AMERICA, WHICH ONLY EVER MAKES PLAIN OLD BORING WEAPONS, HAS A REALLY RIDIC-ULOUS TANK IN ITS PAST!
EQUIPPED WITH A PREPOS-TEROUS SIX RECOILLESS RIFLES, THIS BAD BOY IS...
...THE SELF-PRO-PELLED M50 ONTOS!!
DADOOOM
OH MY GOSH! IT'S SO COOL!!
NOW THIS HAS SOME CHARACTER! IT'D LOOK PERFECTLY AT HOME IN ANY ANIME!!
M50 Ontos *10

*10: THE M50 ONTOS WAS DEVELOPED IN THE 1950S AS AN ANTI-TANK VEHICLE. "ONTOS" IS GREEK FOR "THE THING/PHENOMENON." IT MOUNTED SIX M40 106 MM RECOILLESS RIFLES. A RECOILLESS RIFLE PROPELS THE BLAST FORCE FROM FIRING OUT OF A NOZZLE IN THE REAR TO CUT DOWN ON THE RECOIL. BECAUSE THERE IS MUCH LESS SHOCK THAN A TRADITIONAL CANNON, LARGE-SCALE WEAPONS CAN BE LOADED ON MUCH LIGHTER VEHICLES, PROVIDING A POWERFUL YET MOBILE TOOL FOR COUNTERING ENEMY TANKS. 3.83 M LONG, 2.598 M WIDE, 2.121 M TALL, 8.641 TONS, CREW OF THREE.

*11: PLUS, THE CREW HAD TO EXIT THE INTERIOR AND PERFORM THE RELOAD MANUALLY. WITH THE DEVELOPMENT OF GUIDED ANTI-TANK MISSILES AND ANTI-TANK HELICOPTERS, THIS CLASS OF VEHICLE IS NOW ESSENTIALLY OBSOLETE.

*12: JUST AFTER THE M50 ONTOS WAS CREATED, ANTI-TANK MISSILES BECAME COMMON, RENDERING IT MOSTLY USELESS. HOWEVER, BECAUSE ITS SMALL AND LIGHT BODY WAS MOBILE, IT WAS USED FOR INFANTRY SUPPORT IN THE JUNGLE TERRAIN OF VIETNAM. IT WAS STILL A HEADACHE, HOWEVER, DUE TO THE RELOAD AND SUPPLY ISSUES.

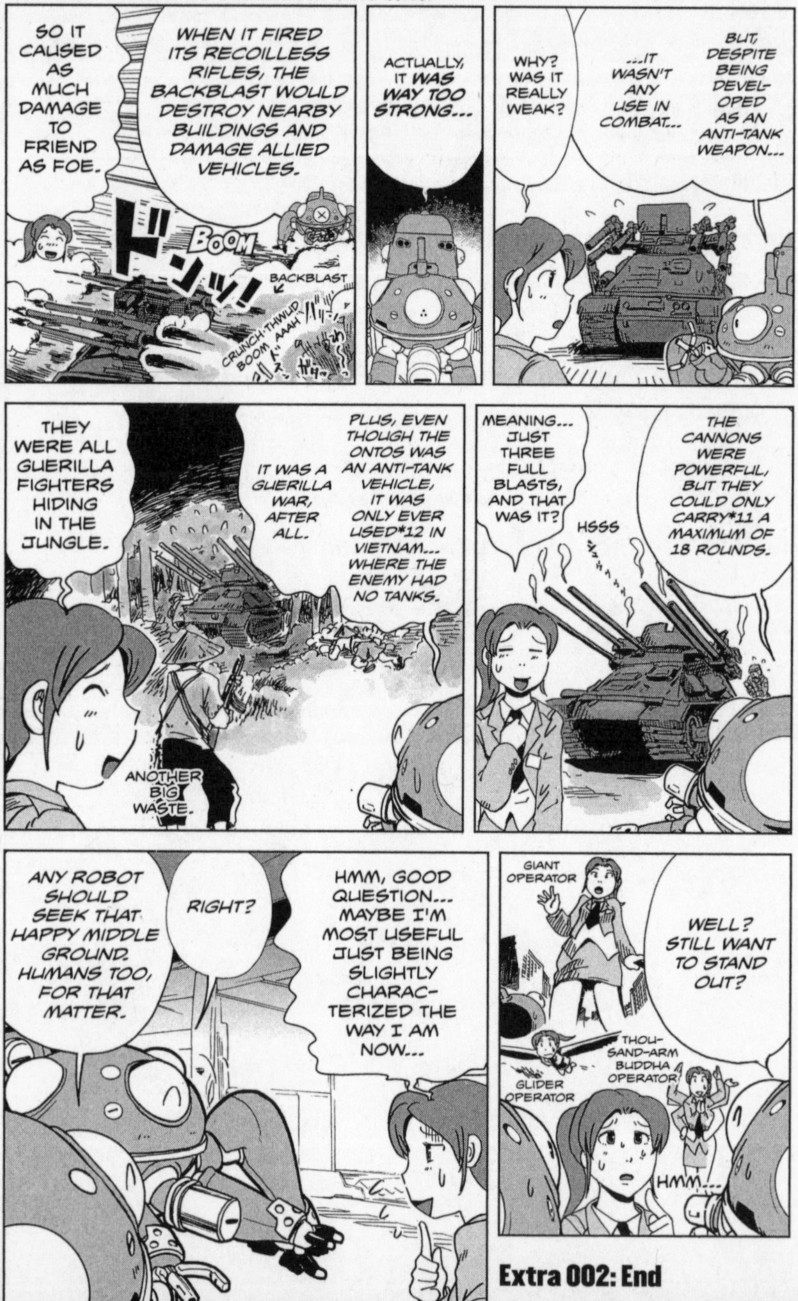
BUT, DESPITE BEING DEVELOPED AS AN ANTI-TANK WEAPON...
...IT WASN'T ANY USE IN COMBAT...
WHY? WAS IT REALLY WEAK?
ACTUALLY, IT WAS WAY TOO STRONG...
WHEN IT FIRED ITS RECOILLESS RIFLES, THE BACKBLAST WOULD DESTROY NEARBY BUILDINGS AND DAMAGE ALLIED VEHICLES.
BOOM
BACKBLAST
SO IT CAUSED AS MUCH DAMAGE TO FRIEND AS FOE.
CRUNCH THWUD BOOM AAAH
THE CANNONS WERE POWERFUL, BUT THEY COULD ONLY CARRY*11 A MAXIMUM OF 18 ROUNDS.
MEANING... JUST THREE FULL BLASTS, AND THAT WAS IT?
HSSS
PLUS, EVEN THOUGH THE ONTOS WAS AN ANTI-TANK VEHICLE, IT WAS ONLY EVER USED*12 IN VIETNAM... WHERE THE ENEMY HAD NO TANKS.
IT WAS A GUERILLA WAR, AFTER ALL.
THEY WERE ALL GUERILLA FIGHTERS HIDING IN THE JUNGLE.
ANOTHER BIG WASTE.
GIANT OPERATOR
WELL? STILL WANT TO STAND OUT?
THOU-SAND-ARM BUDDHA OPERATOR
GLIDER OPERATOR
HMM...
HMM, GOOD QUESTION... MAYBE I'M MOST USEFUL JUST BEING SLIGHTLY CHARAC-TERIZED THE WAY I AM NOW...
RIGHT?
ANY ROBOT SHOULD SEEK THAT HAPPY MIDDLE GROUND. HUMANS TOO, FOR THAT MATTER.

Extra 002: End

Ghost In the Shell: Stand Alone Complex: Episode 4: **¥€$** *is a work of fiction. Names, characters, places, and incidents are the products of the author's imagination or are used fictitiously. Any resemblance to actual events, locales, or persons, living or dead, is entirely coincidental.*

A Kodansha Comics Trade Paperback Original.

Published in the United States by Kodansha Comics, an imprint of Kodansha USA Publishing, LLC, New York.

Publication rights for this English edition arranged through Kodansha Ltd., Tokyo.

First published in Japan in 2012 by Kodansha Ltd., Tokyo.

ISBN 978-1-61262-095-4

Printed in the United States of America.

www.kodanshacomics.com

9 8 7 6 5 4 3 2 1

Translator: Stephen Paul
Lettering: Paige Pumphrey

GHOST IN THE SHELL
STAND ALONE COMPLEX
EPISODE YES